Winner of the
Jules and Frances Landry Award
for 2012

THE RICHMOND THEATER FIRE

EARLY AMERICA'S FIRST GREAT DISASTER

MEREDITH HENNE BAKER

UPDATED EDITION

FOREWORD BY RACHEL BEANLAND

LOUISIANA STATE UNIVERSITY PRESS BATON ROUGE

Published by Louisiana State University Press
lsupress.org

Louisiana Paperback Edition, 2022

DESIGNER: *Mandy McDonald Scallan*
TYPEFACE: *Whitman*

Cover illustration: "The burning of the Theatre in Richmond, Virginia, on the
night of the 26th, December 1811." Aquatint published February 25, 1812, by
Benjamin Tanner of Philadelphia. Courtesy of the Library of Virginia, Richmond,
Virginia.

Library of Congress Cataloging-in-Publication Data
Names: Baker, Meredith Henne, 1979, author.
Title: The Richmond Theater fire : early America's first great disaster /
    Meredith Henne Baker.
Other titles: Early America's first great disaster
Description: Updated edition. | Baton Rouge : Louisiana State University
    Press, 2022.
Identifiers: LCCN 2021047229 (print) | LCCN 2021047230 (ebook) | ISBN
    978-0-8071-4374-2 (cloth) | ISBN 978-0-8071-4375-9 (pdf) | ISBN
    978-0-8071-4376-6 (epub) | ISBN 978-0-8071-7708-2 (paperback)
Subjects: LCSH: Richmond Theater (Richmond, Va.)—Fire, 1811. |
    Fires—Virginia—Richmond. | Theaters—Accidents—Virginia—Richmond. |
    Richmond Theater (Richmond, Va.)—History. | Richmond
    (Va.)—History—19th century.
Classification: LCC F234.R557 B35 2022 (print) | LCC F234.R557 (ebook) |
    DDC 975.5/45103—dc23
LC record available at https://lccn.loc.gov/2021047229
LC ebook record available at https://lccn.loc.gov/2021047230

Hear the loud alarum bells—
Brazen bells!
What a tale of terror, now, their turbulency tells!
In the startled ear of night
How they scream out their affright!
Too much horrified to speak,
They can only shriek, shriek,
Out of tune,
In a clamorous appealing to the mercy of the fire,
In a mad expostulation with the deaf and frantic fire,
Leaping higher, higher, higher,
With a desperate desire,
And a resolute endeavor,
Now—now to sit or never,
By the side of the pale-faced moon.
Oh, the bells, bells, bells!
What a tale their terror tells
Of Despair!
How they clang, and clash, and roar!
What a horror they outpour
On the bosom of the palpitating air!
Yet the ear it fully knows,
By the twanging,
And the clanging,
How the danger ebbs and flows:
Yet the ear distinctly tells,
In the jangling,
And the wrangling,
How the danger sinks and swells,
By the sinking or the swelling in the anger of the bells—
Of the bells—
Of the bells, bells, bells, bells,
Bells, bells, bells—
In the clamor and the clangor of the bells!

—"THE BELLS," EDGAR ALLAN POE, 1849

CONTENTS

Illustrations follow page 150

FOREWORD
TO THE UPDATED EDITION

In the spring of 2007, I flew to Richmond to interview for a job. A pair of realtors had been recruited to give me a tour of the city, and as they drove me down Broad Street, on our way to Church Hill, one of them pointed out Monumental Church. The Greek Revival church, designed by Robert Mills, had been built on the site of a theater that burned to the ground on December 26, 1811. More than seventy people died in the fire, and their remains were buried in the church's crypt.

I was still years away from publishing my first novel, let alone my second, but I can recall being immediately taken with the story. Disaster narratives frequently have that effect on us; there is something deeply compelling about seeing how people cope in the most unenviable circumstances. Do they make moral choices? Come to better understand their own imperfect lives? Rebecca Solnit explores this phenomenon in her book *A Paradise Built in Hell*, writing: "Disasters provide an extraordinary window into social desire and possibility, and what manifests there matters everywhere, in ordinary times and in other extraordinary times."

I was attracted to the story of the theater fire because I am human, and also, I think, because I am a writer. A good story has a compelling plot, multidimensional characters, and a setting that conveys information about time and place, but also contributes to mood. The story of the Richmond Theater fire practically plotted itself—a simple mistake backstage became the inciting incident that forced a cast of flawed characters to make impossible choices, often with dire consequences. In fiction, we worry about not writing enough tension into a story, but there was little danger of making that mistake here.

In the years that followed my move to Richmond, I'd occasionally come across the odd story about the fire. In December 2011, a small group of historians and conservationists marked the two-hundredth anniversary of the theater fire with a special ceremony in the crypt of Monumental Church, and the *Richmond Times-Dispatch* reported on the event. In 2014, *Richmond* magazine's

Harry Kollatz, Jr., wrote a piece about the unveiling of Monumental Church's new terrace, which incorporates a time line of events relating to the fire. In 2017, ABC 8 News reported that Historic Richmond, the nonprofit entity that owns Monumental Church, had partnered with the Valentine Museum to offer daily tours of the church. Anytime I read anything about the fire, I was always left wanting more.

Thankfully, I wasn't the only one with an enduring interest in the theater fire. Meredith Henne Baker became fascinated with the catastrophe back in 2005 when she was a graduate student at the College of William & Mary. In the college's archives, she had discovered a sermon given by Rev. Archibald Alexander in January of 1812 at Philadelphia's old Pine Street Presbyterian Church and commissioned by a group of University of Pennsylvania medical students who hailed from Virginia and were left reeling in the days after news of the fire broke. In the sermon, Reverend Alexander acknowledged the personal losses these young men had suffered and expressed regret that so many of them had learned of the deaths of friends and family members via casualty lists, which ran in almost every major newspaper in the country.

Baker, who has always been interested in the intersection of religion and American culture, was captivated by Reverend Alexander's sermon, which she soon learned was not the only one of its kind. Ministers in churches as far afield as Boston, New York, and even London gave similar sermons in the weeks after the blaze. Many of them connected the tremendous loss of life in Richmond with the city's wicked ways—gambling, prostitution, even theatergoing—and urged people to return to church if they wanted to prevent other calamities of this magnitude.

To Baker, it seemed obvious that the fire had played an important role in the rise of American evangelicalism and the ushering in of the Second Great Awakening. Moreover, it struck her as surprising that an event that had made international news and inspired such conspicuous displays of religiosity had never been the subject of more concentrated scholarship.

Baker decided to write her master's thesis on the fire, and in 2007 she submitted "'MIRACULOUSLY SAVED': Richmond and the 1811 Theater Fire" to her thesis committee at William & Mary. She earned her degree, moved to Washington, D.C., and began working as a teacher and administrator, but became convinced that she wasn't ready to put the project to bed. Over the next several years, she continued to conduct research and wrote the proposal for a book-length work that Louisiana State University Press would eventually acquire. The press, which has a strong tradition of publishing southern literature and history, was the ideal home for the book.

In March 2012, LSU Press published the first edition of the book you hold in your hands. *The Richmond Theater Fire: Early America's First Great Disaster* was and is the only book-length study of the catastrophe and its aftermath. To tell the story of these true events, Baker returned to familiar sources like Charles Copland's diary—in which he recalls the death of his beloved daughter, Margaret—and Samuel Mordecai's *Richmond in By-Gone Days* (1856), but she also brought new documents into the conversation. Sermons by Rev. John Buchanan and Rev. John Blair helped her illustrate the long-lasting effects of the fire on theology; elegies and memorial poems published in the *Richmond Enquirer* and elsewhere gave her a window through which to see how people processed their grief; and articles about the fire that appeared in magazines and journals throughout the long nineteenth century allowed her to see how the story of the fire evolved in popular memory.

What Baker should be lauded for is not only her ability to cast new light on long overlooked sources, but her effort to put them in their proper context. Although the theater's audience was comprised of both men and women and included a large number of free and enslaved Blacks, almost all public accounts of the fire were written by white men of considerable power and prestige. White women wrote about the fire in personal letters, but, as in the case of Caroline Hommasel Thornton, those letters were not published until more than a century after the fire. Even the account of the enslaved black-smith Gilbert Hunt, which was put down on paper in 1859, was transcribed by a white man named Philip Barrett and thus cannot be taken at face value. Baker is always aware that white men—many of whom were trying to justify their own survival in the days after the fire—have controlled the narrative for a full two hundred years, and that the real story is waiting for us only if we are capable of reading between the lines.

When Baker's book was released, it was praised in the *Richmond Times-Dispatch*, Washington, D.C.'s WETA, the *Virginia Magazine of History and Biography*, and the *Journal of Southern Religion*, among other places. *Choice* called it the "best study yet of antebellum Richmond," which is an indication both of Baker's talents and the gap that exists in the literature. The years between the Revolution—when Richmond became Virginia's capital—and the Civil War—when it became the capital of the Confederacy—were years of both tragedy and triumph, but they are often overlooked.

For her efforts, Baker was recognized with the 2012 Phi Alpha Theta Best First Book Award. Within the community of historians, archivists, librarians, and museum administrators who study early Virginia, the book couldn't have come soon enough. "Knowing the history of the fire reveals so much about Richmond and the complexity of the city in the early nineteenth century," said Bill Martin, executive director of the Valentine Museum. "It's such an important period, and there's almost nothing written about it."

I'm embarrassed to admit that I did not discover *The Richmond Theater Fire* until the spring of 2020, when my first novel was months away from publication and the world had come to a screeching halt as a result of the spread of COVID-19. I was in the early stages of writing a second novel that was going to require a great deal of travel, and as the headlines grew increasingly terrifying, it dawned on me that I might not leave my house—let alone the continental US—for months or even years to come.

I had been fascinated by the theater fire since moving to Richmond all those years ago, and decided that if I was ever going to write a novel set in my own backyard, this would be the time to do it. During quarantine I read what I could about the fire, and it didn't take me long to encounter Baker's book; it was not only a propulsive read, but proof that—if I chose to set a novel in the days leading up to and after the catastrophe—I'd have plenty of material from which to draw.

Throughout the writing process, I have turned to Baker and her work again and again. Not only does she provide the facts—who was where, when, and how—but she places us firmly in early nineteenth-century Richmond. As readers, we are in the boxes of the theater on the night of the fire; in the funeral procession as it winds its way through Richmond's Court End neighborhood; and in the pews of Monumental Church on the day the new church is consecrated. The city's grief is felt at every turn, and it becomes our grief, too.

This is what good historical research does for us. It widens the lens through which we see and understand our past, opening the door for further study, broader interpretation, and the making of art—which is how we process what we feel about what we know. Thanks to the notable work Baker has done, scholars, writers, and artists will be telling the story of the Richmond Theater fire for centuries to come.

Rachel Beanland
Author

PREFACE

The Richmond Theater . . . was among the largest in America, and its destruction by fire forms one of the striking events of early American history.

—"FIRST THEATER FIRE," *Washington Post,* JANUARY 3, 1904

O
n the twelfth block of East Broad Street in Richmond, Virginia, where eastbound traffic noses down the steep hill toward the rail station, Monumental Church sits squarely on a scrubby green lawn like a domed white sepulcher, an isolated Greek ruin partially obscured by a temporary plywood walkway protecting pedestrians from the ambitious construction work on surrounding blocks. One October, I found parking a few streets away at the hospital garage and walked east in the sticky early autumn heat past John Marshall's family home, past the Egyptian building, until I reached Monumental. Jackhammers, hardhats, and the detritus of construction ringed Monumental Church as Virginia Commonwealth University augmented its campus up to the very property line of the old landmark. In the church's front lawn lay a few downed signposts. Next to a dirty, face-up "No Parking" sign lay the state-issued historical marker for Monumental Church, on its side, black script on a white background. The marker gave a few clues to the astounding story of a tragedy that forever transformed the capital of the South and led to the construction of this historic monument:

> Virginia Governor George W. Smith died here in 1811. Several survivors owed their lives to the bravery of Gilbert Hunt, a slave blacksmith. A committee chaired by Supreme Court Chief Justice John Marshall raised funds for the church's construction. Designed by Robert Mills and completed in 1814, the octagonal building served as an Episcopal church until 1965.

A year before, when I crashed a private tour for well-heeled Southern historical preservationists, we descended through a narrow, dark stairway to the arched walls and dirt floors of Monumental Church's subterranean vault.

The crypt rises in the center of the basement tomb, an enormous mound on a prehistoric scale. Using ground-penetrating radar, the Historic Richmond Foundation, owners of the site, had detected the locations of two oversized wooden coffins inside. The radar could not penetrate the coffins, but the foundation knew what was inside. Slave, free, schoolgirl, gentry, carpenter, governor, Jew, Catholic, father, actress, prisoner of war: the remains of nearly a hundred bodies lay in a cluttered heap, relics of those who attended the Richmond Theater one festive holiday night nearly two hundred years ago. Their lives ended suddenly, an eternal transaction taking mere minutes, and they fell, as a contemporary wrote, "in one promiscuous ruin."[1]

The Richmond Theater fire captured the public imagination in 1811 and held it for a hundred years before being gradually forgotten, no more than a footnote and a crumbling white memorial that once earned the wonder of the nation. The tragedy spawned a display of national mourning the scale of which had not been seen since the death of George Washington. Even in a day when destructive fires were frequent, this fatal conflagration horrified Americans like no other event in her young history. As Richmond questioned why the destruction had been visited upon it, the fire became a catalyst for religious transformation. This 1811 disaster led citizens to create change in a shattered city and to bring life out the ruins. How this prominent early republic city was transformed as a result of an unprecedented disaster is the subject of this book.

THE RICHMOND THEATER FIRE

PROLOGUE

In 1811, the day after Christmas, Caroline Homassel sat bejeweled and cheerless in box eight of the Richmond Theater, overlooking the stage where *The Bleeding Nun* was unfolding. A night of amusement at the theater was another of her friends' untiring efforts to cheer downcast Caroline. Her devoted companions, local belles Maria Mayo and Sally Conyers, sat nearby, as did another friend, Lucy Madison—niece of sitting president James Madison. Box eight was capacious, probably seating over a dozen theatergoers, all trying "to make my time pass pleasantly," as she recalled, providing distractions for her "crushed heart." Although her depression had lasted over a year, Caroline was not a characteristically despondent girl. That is, she had not been until Alfred Madison's sudden death the year before.[1]

Caroline had been born in Philadelphia in 1795. She took after her slight mother, inheriting her rich brown complexion, flushed rosy cheeks, chestnut curls, and hazel eyes. When a yellow fever outbreak in 1798 claimed two siblings and her mother, Caroline's dejected father put her in the care of her uncle John Richard and his wife, Mary Dixon Richard. He then fled to France and died eight years later. Young Caroline alternately referred to the Richards in her memoirs as her "parents" or as her aunt and uncle. For business reasons, the little family moved to Virginia's capital city, Richmond, which in 1801 "was then like a village, with only one church on Church Hill and one Baptist meeting house," as they discovered. Winsome and musical, Caroline brightened the lives of her adoptive parents, co-owners of the Gallego & Richard flour mills, and as a young lady made her mark as a vivacious favorite in the elite circles of Richmond society.

In 1809, soon after enrolling at the Hallerian Academy, Caroline attended a festive Fourth of July celebration on Richmond's Capitol Square. Proud Revolutionary War veterans turned out by the scores. The day was bright and the celebration stirring. Formal commemorations culminated in the delivery of an oration by one of Caroline's male classmates, the composed Alfred Madison, nephew of the president. Standing starstruck in the crowd, she was spellbound by his eloquence. Caroline immediately fell in love with him. She was then thirteen and Alfred about twenty years of age. When Caroline turned fourteen in October, with her parents' blessing, the two were engaged to marry. "Life was to us both a sea of gold without any alloy," she recalled, "until that fell destroyer came."

Shortly after moving to Williamsburg to attend the College of William and Mary, Alfred was diagnosed with "consumption"—tuberculosis of the lungs—and he died at age twenty-one. The loss shattered young Caroline, who became convinced with all the heartfelt certainty of an adolescent that she would never again experience happiness. "My earthly light was all gone—no sun, no moon, no stars, and I had no desire to live, which made my dear parents utterly miserable. . . . My health became seriously impaired by a blow too heavy for my frail body to bear, but all was darkness within and without, this world had then no charms for me."

It became her parents' mission to amuse and indulge their lonely daughter. They purchased her a harp, bought piano lessons, took her on trips, and gave her extravagant gifts of jewels. She believed that their gifts were a blatant attempt to distract her from drifting toward the church. "Of all other things, they dreaded my being, what they termed it, fanatically religious, and tried, by all this world's gems, to allure me to its pleasures once again," she later recalled. She remained depressed.

"My uncle thought exercise and traveling the great restorative," she wrote, and therefore Caroline was then sent to spend the summer of 1811 in Albemarle County at Woodberry Forest, home to General William Madison, Alfred's father. The cool air of this Blue Ridge Mountain retreat provided a pleasant alternative to Richmond's sultry, energy-sapping heat. Caroline and her hosts made frequent visits to scenic Montpelier, around three miles away, where she was an honored guest of the reserved President James Madison and his gregarious first lady, Dolley, at the mountain plantation where they escaped the miserable Washington city summers. Dolley Madison appeared to Caroline as "a most wonderful woman,—with talent, remarkable tact, a heart of love for all and but little education, but she knew by a mesmeric influence, it would seem, the one subject nearest all hearts, and approached them with success in winning their entire confidence and love." Upon meeting Caroline, Dolley gathered the dejected teenager in her arms and declared the young woman her little "Sweet heart."

After the first frost, when it was determined that Richmond's feverish summer temperatures could do no further harm to Caroline's health, Mary Richard rode in a carriage to Woodberry Forest to retrieve her niece, accompanied by young widower Philip Thornton, a Richmond doctor with whom Caroline had some acquaintance. Sometime on that return journey, Dr. Thornton revealed his love for her, perhaps tentatively. He was twice her age—thirty to her fifteen. Caroline rebuffed him as she did all her suitors, by saying dramatically, "I have no heart to give, it is buried forever." Thornton was undeterred and replied, "We are similarly situated." He had lost a bride after only a month of marriage. "I am willing to take a half heart, even," he avowed. He pressed his case again when they arrived in Richmond and throughout that autumn.

Caroline continued to ignore Thornton, but she could not avoid him entirely. That Thursday evening after Christmas at the theater, Thornton was among those seated with her in box eight. In a moment, the disaster that put Richmond on the map would shatter her ruminations and throw hundreds more into a religious crisis of their own. It would change Caroline's life forever, stealing her closest companions, propelling her into a surprising wedding, and resulting in a spiritual transformation that would scandalize her peers. Yet all then seemed safe and calm in the plush, furs, and velvets of box eight.

Caroline heard the cry of "Fire!"

1

CATASTROPHE

Duty . . . induced me to dispatch you a hasty account of the most calamitous event our city has ever been afflicted with.

—ROBERT GAMBLE, JR., TO U.S. CONGRESSMAN
JAMES BRECKINRIDGE, RICHMOND, VIRGINIA,
DECEMBER 27, 1811, AT 2:30 IN THE MORNING

The fatal night of December 26, 1811, the Richmond Theater should have been empty and silent. Had actor George Frederick Cooke shown up on time for a carriage ride in New York City, the fire may never have happened at all.

Cooke, one of the most celebrated and chronically inebriated actors on the British stage, performed for years at the Royal Theater in Covent Garden. Near the end of 1810, at the urging of actor and manager Thomas Abthorpe Cooper, the fifty-four-year-old thespian sailed to the States for a lengthy American tour and a shot at personal and professional redemption. But even after Cooke agreed to cross the Atlantic, Cooper had some trouble getting him to leave Liverpool. From a perch at his tavern, Cooke repeatedly turned away the carriages Cooper sent, arguing that departure was "inconvenient."[1]

When word reached the young nation that Cooke would perform on its boards, anticipation rose, and theater aficionados in the United States clamored for an opportunity to glimpse the legendary tragedian. Some fifty fans in Baltimore were trampled, none mortally, when ticket doors opened and the crowd "rushed in like a torrent."[2] In Boston, theatergoers, wrapped in blankets and thick wool coats and stamping their feet, huddled waiting outside the box office beginning in the wee hours of a frozen January morning to buy tickets.

Theatergoers in New York initially celebrated, then became disenchanted with Cooke during his lengthy stay there. The turning point in public favor came after a disastrously embarrassing benefit performance where Cooke, unrehearsed and stewed to the gills, repeated himself, recited soliloquies from the wrong play, and sputtered incoherent phrases.[3] "If you have heard anything of me you have heard that I always have a frolic on my benefit day," he protested weakly.[4] His violent and verbally abusive alcoholic binges became a matter of public knowledge, regularly shaming his managers, who had hoped that a change in surroundings would lessen the pull of his most unfortunate drinking habit. "As a man in private life, he is the gentleman, the scholar, the friend. . . . Such is George Cooke, in his sober hours; but when stimulated by the juice of the grape, he acts in diametrical opposition to all this," a fellow actor explained.[5] After what had been, overall, a successful and influential American tour, by December 1811 Cooke's behavior grew almost completely erratic. After a December 17 performance in New York City, he failed to catch his carriage to join the Placide & Green Company in Richmond, as was the mutual agreement.[6] Instead, he inexplicably arranged a trip north to Massachusetts, went on a terrific bender when trapped in New London during a snowstorm, and missed his own opening night performance in Boston.

Meanwhile, Alexander Placide and John William Green, managers of the Placide & Green Company along with their associate William "Billy" Twaits, learned that Cooke had never engaged the carriage waiting for him in New York. Perhaps they assumed that he was ill, that he would simply be delayed, and were not aware that this was a stunt that Cooke was wont to pull—just as he had when Cooper attempted to dislodge him from Liverpool. Although patrons in the North may have grown weary of Cooke's antics, the fact remained that he was an exceptionally famous artist, had never before toured in the South, and would be a sensation at the box office, drunk or not. His inclusion in the Placide & Green Company lineup effectively guaranteed them a triumphant and lucrative season.[7] Cooke, undependable Cooke, if he would come through for them, stood to cement the company's growing reputation and line their coffers well. And so the troupe waited, delaying their trip to Charleston, South Carolina, hoping Cooke would change his mind and meet them in Richmond. This meant extending their season several days until the evening after Christmas, when they put on what would be their final Richmond performance.

* * *

Placide & Green's fortunes had seemed to be on an upswing. The descendant of a 1794 merger between Englishman Thomas Wade West and Frenchman

Alexander Placide's then-competing South Carolina companies, the supercompany broke into small groups of dancers, concert performers, or acting companies that toured through small venues when not needed to perform in a larger town during a peak season, like Richmond during the legislative session or Petersburg during the horse races.[8] The units had a small touring group's ability to travel easily, with the advantage of a large group's top-quality instruments, scripts, sets, and costumes.[9] The Charleston supercompany offered the best provincial theater in the United States and had no real competitor in the South. Margaretta Sully West took leadership of the company in 1799 when her husband Thomas Wade West, at age fifty-four, plunged from his Alexandria, Virginia, theater's catwalk to the stage while examining fire damage.[10] John William Green assumed her managerial mantle around 1804.[11]

During the Virginia tours lasting from August through December in 1811, the small company performed two or three evenings a week at the local theater near the capitol and kept Richmond audiences entertained with an impressive forty-five different plays. Fans flocked to *Macbeth, Othello, She Stoops to Conquer,* and lesser-known dramas like *A Budget of Blunders.*[12] Placide & Green Company appealed to their patrons with visual effects and seemed to spare no expense in producing shows, advertising "new Scenery, Machinery, and Dresses" for the season and constant variety in their playbills. A new musical, *Black Beard, the Pirate,* amazed the audience in October with its "Grand Nautical Spectacle" and special effects: "The Revenge," a pirate's ship, "is seen on fire and sinks" in the final act.[13]

Though the company was enjoying a successful run in Virginia's capital, the year was in other ways not winding to an auspicious close for Placide & Green. In early December 1811, the troupe lost one of their most popular members, a petite and graceful brunette actress named Elizabeth Arnold Poe. Her astonishing range of roles and her perky song-and-dance routines made Poe a favorite in the eight years she toured through Richmond with Placide & Green. In 1810, an unnamed critic in the *Richmond Enquirer* raved about Poe's electrifying acting but confessed her personal charms were equally compelling to the male portion of the audience. "In regard to Mrs. Poe, for a reason which the glass will tell her, it is a difficult thing to separate the *actress* from the *woman;* no wonder then, if it should be also difficult to separate the *critic* from the *man.*"[14] The twenty-four-year-old actress fell ill during the autumn of 1811, most likely with pneumonia. The company mustered profitable benefit performances to raise money for her medical care and support.[15] Poe continued to worsen throughout the month of November, and her face grew sallow and thin as the disease progressed. She died in her rooms at the Washington Tavern on December 8, 1811, mere days before disaster struck her company, and was buried in an unmarked grave in Richmond's public cemetery.

There was some question about what should happen to the children Poe left behind, a small, poorly disciplined boy of nearly three and an infant daughter. Her husband, a former member of Placide's company and a shadowy historical figure, was probably dead. She had no family to speak of. The Mackenzies, a prominent Richmond family, took in Elizabeth's daughter Rose.[16] Wealthy, enterprising, and hard-driving Scotch tobacco merchant John "Jock" Allan and his kindhearted twenty-six-year-old wife Frances took in the boy. John had little interest in children, but Frances, who was adopted herself, had befriended an ailing Elizabeth Poe and fallen in love with her son. Frances's appeals swayed John, but his relationship with the boy would become a thorny one. It would not be surprising if the sudden loss of his second parent and the sensory impressions of the dark days that soon descended upon Richmond had deeply affected the dark-haired, clever boy, deepening the melancholy artistic vision that would later permeate his poetry and render him one of America's most groundbreaking and frightening authors.

As 1811 came to an end, there appeared unsettling signs, signs that made Virginians that December wonder aloud about the mysterious ways of nature—and the rumblings of divine wrath. On September 17, an annular eclipse had appeared in the sky, a bad portent. Then in November, America had been rocked by strange and sudden earthquakes, originating along the New Madrid fault line, which ran from southern Illinois down to Arkansas. The force of the quakes in Missouri caused the mighty Mississippi River to flow briefly backward and rang church bells in New England. Citizens as far away from the fault as Cuba, Quebec, and Washington, D.C.—where President and First Lady Madison feared the rattling White House was being burgled— felt the seismic activity, estimated to be as high as 8.0 on the modern Richter scale. The country would continue to rumble with aftershocks through February 1812.

Ominous feelings built when Virginians scanned the domestic and foreign news. The United States seemed to be in a very vulnerable position; war with Britain was imminent—it would be declared in June 1812—and the economic implications were sobering. In February 1811, President James Madison had levied another unpopular embargo against Britain, the third in four years, attempting to punish the British for their flagrant violations of international law against Americans. To Richmonder Benjamin Watkins Leigh, this was nothing less than an affair of honor between the two countries: "We have received a blow and we must strike one in return, or be forever disgraced," he protested after the "insult offered to our Navy, in the affair of the Chesapeake."[17] Yet the country seemed in no condition to go to battle; Madison's cabinet was unstable with its high turnover rates, the economy was worsening, and the nation's troops lacked training and operated under generally poor leadership. If war should come, victory was by no means certain.

But Virginians were an irrepressible lot, and the Christmas season was just the time to put oppressive cares aside and lose oneself in the festivities. While descendants of the Puritans in the North had never made much of Christmastime, Virginians with their Anglican heritage heartily celebrated the holiday. Richmond's population swelled in December due to the social season, which brought people into the capital from across the South. In an agrarian society, the overall pace of work, particularly for men, slowed during the winter, which became an ideal season for lengthy visits with friends and family, dances, and socializing.

It was also the time of year the state legislature held its annual session. In a 1904 retrospective, the Washington Post leafed back to the winter of 1811 in Richmond and stressed the significance of the social season in that locale. "Richmond and Philadelphia were in those days the two most important cities in America. While the meeting of Congress in Washington during the early winter of 1811 was a small affair in a small town, in the estimation of most Americans, the convening of the Virginia legislature and the opening of the social season in Richmond was in the Anglo-Saxon world second only to the opening of Parliament in London."[18] Many wealthy planters from distant counties in Virginia—or even other southern states—maintained a house in Richmond, relocating to town during the session.[19] Other visitors and assemblymen boarded in the city or lodged with friends.[20] Senators and delegates often brought their children of marriageable age to town in order to launch them into society, introducing them to suitable partners and business connections at dances, parties, and the theater, hoping to guarantee them a bright future. Parents had a narrow window: by February, the season would be over.[21] The 1811–12 season was the "gayest winter Richmond had ever known and often we went from one entertainment to another and even a third on the same evening. There was dancing for the young people and cards for the old," recalled one young woman.[22]

In 1811, a Philadelphia magazine praised Richmond for being a city celebrated beyond all others in the union for her cheerfulness and sophistication.[23] First Lady Dolley Madison had been caught up in the swirl of Richmond hospitality during the winters when James served in the state legislature, and she recalled her days there fondly. In 1812, Dolley wrote to friend Sally Coles Stevenson in Richmond, "I rejoice to find your health restored & that you will past the Winter in Richmond. I some times wish myself with you for a while, for I love Richmond, because there is so much soul, so much real kindness in its enlighten'd society."[24]

THE CITY

In 1780, Virginia had chosen a more central location for the seat of government than out-of-the-way Williamsburg and transferred the state capital to Richmond. Five years later, the state built the capitol building, designed by Thomas Jefferson, on Shockoe Hill, west of the original settlement on a nine-acre plot. This area, the "upper town," had a magnificent view of the James River Falls and the sweeping countryside on either side. The sunset caught the banks along the river transforming them into red hills ("Rouge-Mont," hence "Richmond") that reminded her earliest settlers of the hills in Richmond, England. By 1811, Richmond was a place of influence and importance, a burgeoning manufacturing center centered midstate at the James River Falls. Many of the nation's most prominent and powerful public servants in the colonial era and the early republic hailed from the state of Virginia—George Washington, Patrick Henry, Jefferson, James Madison—and most had spent time and established connections in Richmond.

Richmond was an isolated spot of urbanity in a very rural landscape of backcountry tobacco plantations, coal mines, and wheat fields. In 1816, tourist Henry Knight noted with surprise, "This state, called after the virgin queen Elizabeth, of glorious memory, appears like a new-settled, not an old one. You pass no stone-walls; but hedge, or *in-and-out* zig-zag cedar rails, or wattled fences, if indeed any, on the main roads. At the south, a few houses, though not incorporated, are called a town. "[25]

There were few towns of any material consequence in Virginia in these early years. This was attributed, noted visiting Scottish businessman James Melish, "to the circumstance of the state being so completely intersected with navigable rivers, that a market is brought almost to every man's door, and they have no inducement to establish large cities."[26] The manufacturing sites of Richmond therefore seemed all the more impressive to Melish, who in the fall of 1806 noted the prodigious flour mills, tobacco production, and extensive distilleries and breweries.[27]

In the ten years from 1800 to 1810, Richmond's population doubled to nearly ten thousand inhabitants. Nearly half of that number were enslaved blacks.[28] Around 1810, the growing city was divided into three wards— Madison, Monroe, and Jefferson—with most citizens concentrated in the high, central area of Madison Ward around the capitol. Like many of its native sons, Richmond was independent and hostile to centralized planning. Thus the city developed in a way that seemed somewhat haphazard, with little concern for a workable system of city services such as libraries or fire companies or passable roadways. Grassy lawns and tidy public spaces were rare; ramshackle homes made of leftover construction materials and tucked among the city's shops were not uncommon.[29] The disorderliness of Virginia's public works and roads struck northerners as downright immoral.[30] In its early years, an English visitor declared it "one of the dirtiest holes of a place I ever was in," and another claimed to have spotted a chasm in a main road large enough to submerge a hogshead barrel.[31] Before the terrain was leveled and bridged, the deep gulches, steep hills, swamps, flooding streams, and cliffs made Richmond an obstacle course—difficult to navigate by cart or on foot.[32]

That holiday season, a "CHRISTMAS ODE" to Richmond in the *Richmond Enquirer* gave a glowing estimation of the city. On his poetic tour through Richmond, the unnamed author first noted the capitol; from its hill, this creation of Thomas Jefferson modeled after the Maison Carrée in Nimes, France, was often the first sight to meet an approaching visitor's eyes. "Crown of the Hill, the Capitol appears! / And with colossal grandeur pond'rous rears."[33] Government buildings and courts clustered around the capitol, and this area, known as Court End, became the logical place for lawyers and their families to set up households.[34] Developers sold Court End land in large tracts, and a newcomer could purchase an entire city block, filling it with all the farm animals, outbuildings, houses, and offices his family might require. Although the houses of the upper classes were fine, even showy, they sat surrounded by streets that were no more than muddy footpaths, and Court End smelled of fenced-in pigs, chickens, and horses. As Court End land filled with homes, taverns, academies, and the theater, the town population expanded in a westerly direction, past Ninth Street, mostly on cleared acreage in a piney field in that area, purchased from Scottish entrepreneur and real estate magnate Thomas Rutherfoord, who lived there himself.

The poet then traveled about a mile and a half below the city, down Shockoe Hill, past the close quarters and cramped shops of the traders, artisans, and merchants clustered around Main, to the James River. The James, the poet wrote, possessed banks thick with primeval forests, its waters bearing ships with "every varied product of the soil / That makes the merchant rich— or pays the planter's toil." On the James yawned muddy Rockett's Landing, Richmond's port, a scene of constant action. Blacks "broke out" the cargo from incoming ships and loaded it onto horse-drawn wagons.[35] Coal yards, mills, and lumber houses surrounded the landing area.

Main Street ran at a southward diagonal from east to west—at most points less than a half-mile from the river. This thoroughfare of commerce for the six-horse wagons coming eastward from the Blue Ridge and north from the docks earned a stanza as well: "O! What a lively scene presents the street / When rattling drays with crashing wagons meet / When loaded carts and splendid coaches stop / And beaux and belles besiege the crowded shop!" The market on Main that Christmas in 1811 would have been piled with holly and evergreens, mixed among the produce, fish, and meats for sale.[36]

The poet also lauded the intellectual climate of the city: "Here learned Law, enlighten'd Justice shine / Wisdom and Wit and Lit'rature combine." Yet schooling remained the province of the wealthy. Some elites possessed impressive libraries and benefited from some form of private education, but tutors and books both often had to be imported from other states.[37] Virginia lacked a system of public education and had but one small public university, which served only male students. James Melish observed that in Virginia, "The means, in short, for educating the wealthy are ample, and extensively applied; but the system seems to be defective, so far as *the mass of the people are concerned*, and that important branch deserves the early attention of an enlightened legislature."[38] The state's "Literary Fund," established in 1810 to finance public education languished, with its revenues from fines and confiscations insufficient to fund mass education.[39] Thomas Jefferson feared that his beloved state would tumble into "Gothic barbarism" without a system to educate the common people.[40]

While the curricula lacked rigor, generally, citizens supported numerous private primary schools. Freelancing tutors scraped by, offering courses in evenings or at students' homes.[41] While options for girls were far more paltry than those for boys, at least ten girls' schools operated in Richmond between 1800 and 1820, many run out of private homes as an additional means of income for educated women whose family fortunes were declining.[42] The preeminent school for elite adolescents in Richmond and the largest, at over one hundred scholars, was Louis Hue Girardin's academy.[43] The program attracted the city's elite daughters and sons, drawing students from the far reaches of the state.[44] Although it flourished and faltered within a decade, the coeducational school was the finest in the city in 1811, with five instructors and an extensive course catalog. Boys could take classes in twenty-eight subjects, including Greek, Latin, geography, conic sections, bookkeeping, composition, and "Military fortification and Gunnery."

Headmaster Girardin was a dashing figure on the Richmond scene and a relative newcomer. He was born Louis-François Picot, most likely to a family in La Rochelle, France. By age twenty-two his avid and articulate royalist—then Girondist—sympathies enraged those in power, who condemned the young man to death by guillotine in 1793. He escaped from France and sailed to the United States, where, for fear of pursuit, he changed his name to Louis Girardin.[45] A writer and literary scholar trained in Rouen and Paris, the handsome Frenchman took work as a farmhand in Maryland before he was offered a position as a French teacher at Georgetown University. From that point forward, Girardin made his way in America with his intellect. He later took a professorship at the College of William and Mary, married Katherine "Polly" Cole, an Albemarle County, Virginia, native, and relocated to Richmond to raise two daughters and a son "on whom he doated."[46]

In existing records, Girardin's school at Eighth and Cary goes by several names: the Richmond Male and Female Academy, Haller's Academy, or, most commonly, the Hallerian Academy.[47] The octagonal building was originally Edmund Randolph's home, next to City Hall and Capitol Square, and was modified to create two separate entrances via different streets whereby the students could enter and exit, strictly separated by sex.[48]

Polly Girardin instructed the female pupils. It is not clear to what extent girls participated in the academic courses, although they probably took some, but the Girardins offered at least a sampling of art electives for the girls, including "Flower Drawing," dancing, handwriting, and music.[49] Caroline

Homassel, who studied dancing, drawing, and French there as a young teen, recalled her tenure at the Hallerian Academy in glowing terms. "It was the golden era of my existence, although it was my school days—but I was so happy!!" she wrote years later to her children."[50] Although her uncle had forbidden her to take piano lessons, fearing that she would pursue a career as a performer, he permitted Homassel briefly to resume piano studies under an adjunct teacher from the theater's orchestra, employed by the Hallerian Academy. She recalled, "I longed so much for his instruction that he was engaged for me, but he only gave me a few lessons when that awful catastrophe took place, and all was broken up, and I learned no more."[51]

In 1811, there also existed a private school for free blacks in Richmond, albeit fleetingly. The school founder, a free black named Christopher McPherson, had experience as a teacher and proved a clever law clerk for the High Court of Chancery, although his occasional prophetic, apocalyptic proclamations caused some colleagues to question his sanity. He planned to open the doors of his new school to black students of all ages, including slaves—if they obtained their masters' permission. He hired a white tutor whom he would oversee, arranged for a facility, and promoted the school in the newspaper. Notice of the school's founding provoked a vehement response. His school hurriedly closed, and McPherson was sent to the Eastern Lunatic Asylum in Williamsburg.[52]

"Trade is carried on here chiefly by foreigners, as the Virginians have but little inclination for it, and are too fond of amusement to pursue it with much success," remarked Isaac Weld, Jr., after visiting Richmond.[53] Virginia's passion for play, sport, and wagers surprised Henry Knight during his Virginia tour. "Accustomed from boyhood to athletic sports, in an infinite series, the Virginians are muscular and elastic in limb; and leaving draughts, whist, backgammon, and chess, for the evening; they are out at sling-fist, and sling-foot; or outjumping, or outrunning each other." Knight was shocked at the enthusiastic participation of respectable, grown men in marbles or ball games and their propensity to bet on everything; the outcome of one simple footrace he witnessed raised wagers of five hundred dollars.[54]

Card playing, gambling, and dancing, all reviled by the prevalent evangelical morality of the growing American middle class, were wildly fashionable in Richmond, cementing its reputation as a national center of vice in the eyes of some moralists. Fashionability trumped moral stigmas, and gambling was ubiquitous among all classes. The openness of it all surprised Dubliner Isaac Weld, Jr. When he alighted off his horse outside a Richmond tavern, the landlord's first question was, "What game are you partial to?" as he waved a hand in the general direction of a faro table, a hazard table, and a billiard table. "Not the smallest secrecy is employed in keeping these tables; they are always crowded with people," Weld noted with astonishment. "Perhaps in no place of the same size in the world is there more gambling going forward than in Richmond."[55]

Tonish ladies in Richmond's elite homes could be found gambling away in the parlor three or four winter evenings a week at the card game loo, quite the craze in the first decade or so of the century, while men played at whist in the smoking room. Stakes were most commonly trivial amounts, but a rising pool made even Richmond's most decorous ladies a little rowdy. Forbidden the male province of dueling, ladies resentful of losses or suspicious of foul play parlayed sharp insults, which sometimes led to shouting matches. In rare cases, mostly provoked by the discovery of a cheat, a few unnamed Richmond ladies had been known to lunge across the table to bring down a careful coiffure or tear a cap from some swindler's head in rage.[56]

In Richmond's tempestuous, profanity-laced, competitive climate, tempers could easily flare, firing hair-trigger responses to attacks on one's honor, and happy occasions could quickly turn into fatal ones. A city that contained half of the state's breweries, manufactured over a hundred times more swords than the rest of Virginia combined, and created over 60 percent of her guns was probably ripe for the rounds of fatal feuds that was her lot.[57]

Besides the ordinariness of duels, or "affairs of honor" as they were called, the frequency of common fights surprised visitors. A Baptist who grew up in rural Virginia matter-of-factly recalled that community gatherings were commonly marked by public drunkenness and fisticuffs. A muster day rarely passed without a few fights, and "a half dozen on court-day was deemed a very moderate number, and sometimes the excitement and the combats would become what was termed a 'battle royal,'" he recalled.[58] Richmond's lower-class pugilists were notorious for attempting to gouge eyes in their no-holds-barred brawls, for which purpose some male scrappers grew long fingernails. Weld described gouging in his correspondence. "To perform the horrid operation, the combatant twists his forefingers in the side locks of his adversary's hair, and then applies his thumbs to the bottom of the eye, to force it out of the socket."[59] Combatants also were known for another Richmond specialty: ripping out testicles. Weld encountered four or five men recovering from an amateur neutering during his tour through Maryland and Virginia.[60]

Use of strong drink was common, as there was no tax on distillation of spirits and consequently a very active market of providers and buyers.[61] Knight noted, "As to the *Diet* of the Virginians, I may tell you what I observe. Once for all, they are plentiful livers. The first thing in the morning, with many, is the silver goblet of mint-julap."[62] Even in a churchgoing man's house, one was likely to find five different kinds of wines and whiskey served with Sunday lunch.[63] Richmond's celebratory excesses, violent outbursts, and roughness made it an exciting city, but one that earned a national reputation for frivolity—and impiety. Overall, Virginians didn't seem troubled a bit by this.

There existed ample locations dedicated to play and amusement. Hundreds of spectators flocked in their finest to see the city's cockfights and legendary horse races at the three tracks. Virginians, no matter their race or economic status, were famous horse enthusiasts, and it is quite possible that Richmond was the greatest race center in early nineteenth-century America. The spring and fall social seasons even revolved around the goings-on at the race tracks.

The Haymarket Garden in a northwest corner of town was a popular spot for picnics, fireworks, games of quoits (similar to horseshoes except that metal disks were thrown) and ninepins, and masquerades. The flowered walks were brilliantly lit at night, leading to the ballroom, where an organ provided music for dances.[64] Richmond's frequent dancing assemblies and opulent balls supported Yankee tutor Philip Fithian's colonial-era observation that Virginians were downright fanatical about dancing. In his journal he recorded, "*Ben* is in a wonderful *Fluster* lest he shall have no company to-morrow at the Dance—But blow high, blow low, he need not be afraid; *Virginians* are of genuine Blood—They will dance or die!"[65]

One of the most popular places of public amusement was the Richmond Theater. The most famous actors and actresses on the European and American boards made stops in Richmond, where religious scruples generally did not disallow such amusements and they would be guaranteed a fine turnout.[66] Although it was drafty and shoddily built, in 1811 the Richmond Theater in Court End consistently drew large audiences. The theater stood on a block at the brow of Shockoe (sometimes spelled "Shockhoe") Hill at Broad (then H) and Twelfth streets, ringed by forty feet of open yard on each of its four sides, overlooking a great ravine to the east.[67] A Court End institution, the theater rested just north of Capitol Square, a block west from the First Baptist Church and a block east of the Old Market House. The first theater on that particular square of land appropriated the main building of Quesnay's

Academy, an ambitious and experimental French school which survived for a few years immediately following the Revolutionary War and briefly served as the site for Virginia's Constitutional Convention of 1788.[68] Thomas Wade West and John Bignall, English actors and theater managers, renovated Quesnay's Academy into a playhouse in the 1780s.[69] Quesnay's was hardly an ideal space; it was too large, and thieves found it so easy to break into that manager West squirreled away the company's stock of costumes in his rented rooms during Richmond tours, only bringing each night what was necessary for the evening's performance.[70] When the academy building burned in January 1798, taking nearly all the scenery and machinery with it, a call went out for a more convenient and less combustible theater, and on January 25, 1806, a small brick theater opened; the very building that theatergoers in 1811 attended.[71]

What the new Richmond Theater looked like must be pieced together from personal recollections, the city's Common Council investigative report, and the property deed. The two existing contemporary drawings of the property indicate only the outline of the building and do not illustrate any interior details. The five-year-old brick theater was not large—the deed indicated it was about ninety feet in length, fifty in width, and thirty feet high "in front," with offices, a green room, and a dressing room for the staff.[72] It held five hundred and was designed for intimate shows, family concerts, and chamber music. The front of the three-story building was bricked; it seems the other walls were as well. A large bull's-eye window hovered high above the entrance doors to the lobby and ticket window. The theater had two more doors for the stage and gallery. Although the lack of exits made some theater staff nervous, in the absence of fire prevention codes each builder was left to decide what safety features he would include and which corners he would cut.[73]

Inside, the narrow hall-like "lobbies" were dark and cramped, the stairways winding and constricted, and the doorframes so narrow that two people could not comfortably pass simultaneously. The ceiling was neither plastered nor sealed. Managers simply tacked a painted canvas tarp over bald pine roof boards oozing with resin. The ground level still had a dirt floor, and air crept through chinks in the walls. One of Placide & Green's actors deemed it not only the worst-constructed theater on the company's tour but the worst he had ever performed in.[74] A townsperson recalled that as the crowd was slowly retiring at the end of a play, numerous were the occasions on which someone speculated about the dire outcome should the building ignite.[75] If a fire broke out, ticket holders in the boxes, the best and most expensive seats, were in the greatest danger. Due to the theater's awkward construction, they would have to cram into the side corridors and descend a single, angular staircase either one or two flights, whereupon it would be necessary to then ascend a long passage to the street. The cheap seats would fare much better. The pit was a short distance from the outer door, and the small gallery for black attendees had a distinct entrance.[76]

While it bothered the managers to hear the actors and townsfolk disparage the place as a fire trap, there seemed little incentive to renovate it. The seats still filled.

THE EVENING OF DECEMBER 26, 1811

On that dark, windy night after Christmas, a festive holiday crowd flocked to the evening's variety show performance, a benefit for theater manager, tightrope walker, and audience favorite Alexander Placide.[77] Popular actors at this point in theater history were often given the privilege of having a "benefit night" at the end of the season, in which they received the proceeds from the evening's show. Such evenings often brought in the majority of their annual income. Records indicate that on December 26, 1811, the theater did a brisk business, selling 518 adult tickets for the pit and boxes, 80 children's tickets for the pit and boxes, and 50 gallery tickets. A delegate from Patrick County remembered, "From the pleasantness of the evening and the probability of a good play, we found an unusually full house."[78]

Gilbert Hunt, a thirty-one-year-old enslaved blacksmith, left the Baptist church that evening, a church to which he would belong for over fifty years, and saw the lights glimmer in the windows of the nearby theater. The sounds of laughter and liveliness seeped through its claptrap walls. Laws that formerly prevented blacks from meeting together at night had been revised, and beginning in 1805, Hunt could attend services after dark—as long as the worship was conducted by an ordained minister, or he attended with a white family.[79] It would be a short night for Hunt—the church service had gone late and he planned to wake the next morning at his usual early hour. The ring of his anvil was usually one of the first sounds to break the morning stillness in Richmond.

Behind Hunt, the scene would change quickly to one of terror, but he was too far away by then; he did not hear. Hunt was married, although it is not clear if his wife resided with him or at the Mayo home, where she was enslaved. He lived over his blacksmith shop near the city's main business thoroughfare, at the corner of Locust Alley and Franklin Street, but he was often at the Mayo home and went there after his meeting that Thursday to eat a late supper.[80] He probably hoped to see Louisa Mayo, whom he regularly met with after his day's labor, when she had completed her studies. Louisa, aged seventeen, was likely enrolled in one of Richmond's academies, and she shared her lessons with Hunt, an eager pupil. Like many others, she had gone to the theater that Thursday night with a group of friends.

Tonight, as was the case every night, the theater accommodated all social classes: gentry, slaves, free blacks, common workers, and disreputable types. Even runaways might find a harbor among the crowd. "Billy," on the lam from his owner in the fall of 1810, had "lurk[ed] about" Richmond and Petersburg, where he was known to have attended the theater in a yellow waistcoat, black fur hat, blue pantaloons and back strap boots, "pretending that his master was gone to the northward, and had permitted him to go at large till he returned."[81] Managers welcomed all classes to join in the raucous fun—as long as they paid—but the audience was segregated upon arrival. Types on or past the fringes of respectability sat in the gallery, paying twenty-five cents for a ticket. Middle-class theatergoers sat in the benches ringing the orchestra pit, and the wealthier attendees pressed their way up the single winding staircase and through narrow hallways (called "lobbies") to the lower and upper tiers of box seats on the second and third floors. Pit and orchestra seats cost a dollar, about the cost of a pair of shoes then, or roughly sixteen dollars in today's currency. All guests but those in the gallery entered at the south end of the building through the main door into a plank-floored foyer, no more than twelve feet wide. At the end of the foyer, they purchased tickets and presented them to a man named Thomas, perhaps a slave, before entering a narrow door and stepping down to the dirt floor of a semi-circular passageway.[82] Doors opened at six; the show typically began at seven.

In mid-Atlantic theaters, early republic audiences were blatantly disruptive. They sang along with the performers, puffed on cigars, wandered about the theater to mingle, occasionally hurled food on stage, talked or argued loudly with each other, and cheered or heckled the actors.[83] Richmond theater managers prohibited the wearing of men's hats, putting feet on seats or hanging them over fronts of boxes, loud conversation, disorderliness, and smoking among other violations, which means that these must have regularly occurred.[84]

A wheedling relative had probably strong-armed Michael Wall Hancock into chaperoning a large group of six young people to the show after dinner: three nephews—Peter, Alfred, and Nicholas—Hancock's niece, and her friends, the two Heron sisters. By the time Hancock's large party arrived, the theater was jammed full, and it was with difficulty that he procured seats for them among their friends in boxes seven and eight.

Hancock, making the way to his bench, probably noted George Smith, the newly minted governor of Virginia, among the audience with his family, his tall collar or "stock" secured with his distinctive stock buckle. After being appointed President Madison's secretary of state in April 1811, tall, dignified James Monroe had of necessity left his position as acting governor of Virginia in Richmond for Washington, D.C., with his wife Elizabeth and daughter Maria.[85] George Smith of Essex County took his place as interim governor for the duration of the year and was officially sworn in as governor on December 5, 1811. Smith hoped his term would be less dramatic than that of Monroe, whose planned—though never executed—kidnapping was discovered to be a key component of the infamous attempted revolt led by a Henrico County slave named Gabriel in August 1800. This would not be the case.

Thick, slow Tidewater drawls and twangy mountain vowels met clipped English tones and Scottish burrs in a Babel of accents. Uniformed army and navy officers mixed through the crowd, swords clanking at their sides.[86] "As it was during the session of the Legislature, and many had come from all parts of the State to attend the gayeties of the season, there were some of the most beautiful and excellent of Virginia's citizens in that building," noted Civil War–era historian John Little.[87] Large groups of girls from the city's most prominent families, dressed in their best winter gowns, settled into boxes with their friends and admirers.[88] Men that evening would have entered the theater in broadcloth coats with tall collars and Regency-style cravats created from yards of wrapped, starched white muslin. They probably wore winter hats and carried canes. Many civilian men entered with unconcealed weapons or "sword canes," walking sticks with covered blades. The younger men's hair would have been painstakingly mussed and the older men's pulled back in a queue. Women's fashion aimed for a neo-Grecian look. Soft, flat slippers were in fashion, worn in the evening with long, thin high-waisted dresses featuring low-cut necklines. A bonnet may have been perched on their piles of coiled hair, or a ribbon wrapped through their locks in imitation of Greek goddesses. To ward off the chill, Richmond's fashionable women would have put trimmed capes, wraps, or cloaks over their gowns. Later, the author of *Calamity at Richmond,* a dour Christian tract about the theater fire, would write, "Ah! how little thought the fair one whose curls were adjusted—whose garments, costly and elegant, were disposed, so as to produce on the spectator, the most impressive effect, that those curls were, that same night, to be crisped with devouring flame; and those garments to be denied the service of a winding-sheet!"[89]

Box eight held an assortment of Richmond's most distinguished citizens and unsurprisingly was the best seat in the house. Local belle Sarah Conyers, called Sally, sat with her two closest friends—tiny Caroline Homassel and popular brunette beauty Maria Mayo. They made a triumvirate of Richmond's most accomplished and celebrated debutantes. Dr. Philip Thornton, fifty-three-year-old former U.S. senator Abraham Venable, Charles Hay, along with business partners John Richard and Joseph Gallego and their wives, both named Mary, accompanied the young ladies in box eight. Richard and Gallego were as close as brothers, and both had adopted orphaned relatives: the Gallegos took in orphaned Sally Conyers and the Richards their niece Caroline. The girls considered themselves cousins, referring to one another's parents as "Aunt" and "Uncle."

Gallego was a Spanish emigrant from Andalusia who created a thriving business in flour production. His firm of Gallego, Richard & Co. constructed enormous mills along the James River.[90] He married American Mary Magee, and the childless couple formally adopted her niece Sally as their own. As the Gallegos grew older and Sally took her place as a captivating member of Richmond society, she became their comfort and pride.[91] Conyers, like her friends Maria and Caroline, possessed all the musical accomplishments appropriate for a girl of her age.[92] She read "polite literature," sketched well, and knew some French and Italian. She also spoke Spanish, probably learned casually at the table with her adoptive father, to whom she was very close. By her late teens, Conyers, with her pert nose, round cheeks, and frizzle of face-framing curls, had a flock of admiring beaux. Gallego believed she would make a wise match, despite a false start. In 1807, the whirlwind year of the Burr trial, Sally suffered a broken engagement with William Clarke Somerville. It is not known who ended it, but she would have been barely sixteen at the time.[93]

The company that would appear before them performed dozens of different plays in a month and welcomed new material and variety. It had probably been in October or November that Hallerian Academy principal Louis Hue Girardin confidentially presented John William Green with a dramatic script for his review—a translation of *The Father; or Family Feuds*, by French philosopher Denis Diderot. Girardin apparently received no remuneration, later writing, "No other advantage but admittance for myself and family was ever thought or spoken of."[94] "To enlist amusement in the service of morality was my sole object," he claimed, although, as a writer of growing renown, the cachet of having a successful script would have been a professional feather in his cap. The curtain for *The Father; or Family Feuds* rose on a capacity crowd of over six hundred theatergoers, a significant portion of Richmond's population to be gathered into a single place.[95]

Backstage, actor William Anderson complained to a crew member that the chandelier set piece hadn't been working properly. During rehearsal, he explained, all attempts to budge it "caused it to ride circularly round." Had it been repaired?[96]

* * *

Several accounts corroborate that Lieutenant James Gibbon, Jr., of the U.S. Navy arrived late to the theater. He was a dashing officer, the son of the Revolutionary War hero of Stoney Point, Major James Gibbon.[97] The well-connected major consorted with the likes of James Madison, Thomas Jefferson, and George Washington, and since 1800, he had been the collector of the Richmond Customs Port.[98] James the younger forged his own military reputation when he joined the U.S. Navy and sailed to Tripoli on the frigate *Philadelphia* in 1803, where he was captured and imprisoned by the Barbary pirates.[99] After America negotiated peace in June 1805, Gibbon and his fellow prisoners were released from capture, and when the officer returned to Richmond in 1805, his neighbors celebrated him with a grand public fete.[100]

Gibbon, once safely back home, had become enamored of Sarah Conyers, and the thoughtful blonde orphan with an upturned nose was the reason he forced himself to attend the theater that evening, despite a sense of foreboding, according to his sister, Mary Gibbon Carter. The latter befriended Conyers and later released an account of the Conyers-Gibbon romance she claimed was taken from her diary at the time. Several newspapers published her romanticized versions of the couple's story throughout the next century, as interest in the couple's tale still ran high.[101]

Gibbon and Conyers lived on opposite corners of Fifth and E, Conyers at

"Moldavia," an imposing former boarding house named after original owners Molly and David Meade Randolph. According to Gibbon Carter, the navy officer and Conyers did not meet until a November party in 1811. Conyers was barely twenty years old. By December, they were engaged, although there is some confusion about this in available records, complicated by the fact that engagements were customarily kept a secret.[102]

The affluent and merchant classes, especially during the legislative session, often incorporated a theater performance into an elaborate evening of entertainment.[103] The night began with an impressive and lengthy dinner at a private home around three o'clock, followed by a walk or ride to the theater.[104] There, friends colonized entire boxes of seats, causing significant background noise visiting and socializing with each other while performers were on stage.[105] "The theatre was a promiscuous gathering for a few hours, less attractive than the dining or dancing party, but one of the round of pleasures that occupied the time of the fashionable and the wealthy," recalled midcentury Virginia minister William Henry Foote.[106] Leading lawyer and man-of-letters William Wirt hosted a pack of friends on December 26 at a holiday dinner party in his candlelit home, including the family of his brother-in-law, merchant Robert Gamble, and friend John Wickham's extensive clan. If Wirt's dinner spread was as generous as the usual Virginia gentry meal, slaves probably set out relishes, a tureen of soup, and hominy (mixed corn and beans) along with six or more varieties of meats including a ubiquitous Virginia ham or piece of bacon. Company washed down the meal with whiskey, brandy, or other alcohols in decanters lining the sideboard.[107] While Wirt's party intended to attend the theater, the combination of food and animated conversation kept them longer at the dining room table than they had expected, and plans for the show were scrapped. "Our immediate relatives were prevented going to the Play by a dinner party at Wirts where we were detained too late for the performance," Gamble reported the next day to a friend in Washington, D.C. That wasn't exactly true: *almost* all at Wirt's home were detained. Three of Wickham's children, Julia and two brothers, excused themselves and slipped out onto H Street.[108]

Captain George Fleming of Louisa County had come to celebrate Christmas in Richmond with his old friend George Smith. That Thursday, a box of books had arrived from England and an excited Captain Fleming excused himself from the theater outing: he preferred to stay at home and look over the new volumes, he later recalled.[109]

U.S. chief justice and former secretary of state John Marshall had resided in Richmond since 1783 and served as chief justice from 1801 until his death in 1835.[110] This position required him to spend less than six months each year in Washington, D.C., or traveling around the country "on circuit" to hear cases. For more than half a year he could stay in Richmond. One chronicler noted, "Although his judicial decisions consistently ran contrary to the general trend of political thought in Virginia, the townspeople of Richmond never lost their affection for the man."[111]

A social gallivant, he frequently attended card parties, the theater, and events at the Mason's Hall, where he presided as grand master. Marshall took special delight in weekly outings from May to September with the Richmond Quoit Club, where thirty of the city's leading men discarded ceremony, imbibed from immense bowls of spiked punch, indulged in great quantities of food, rolled ten pins, and pitched quoits, a horseshoe-like game, near Buchanan's Spring off Clay Street.[112] Rev. John Buchanan of the Episcopal church, a lifelong bachelor, having inherited the property on the northwest outskirts of town from his wealthy businessman brother, played host to the gambols. Marshall found a partner with a "fondness for frolic" in James Monroe, his cabin mate at Valley Forge, with whom he attended plays and played billiards.[113] U.S. House speaker Theodore Sedgwick described Marshall as a unique mix of decadence and rationality—in a word, a Virginian. Marshall was "attached to pleasures, with convivial habits strongly fixed. He is indolent, therefore, [but] when aroused, has strong reasoning powers; they are indeed almost unequalled."[114]

"He was very fond of theatrical entertainments, and used to go to the theatre whenever the opportunity offered," recalled a man who spent his boyhood in Marshall's Richmond.[115] Considering Marshall's social propensities and love of a good show, it would have been perfectly logical for the judge to attend *Family Feuds* on the twenty-sixth, although he apparently did not. At least one account relates that his visiting son, Tom Marshall, in the company of a cousin, did attend.[116]

Local lawyer Charles Copland walked from his nearby home to the theater that evening to view part of the show.[117] He left early, a decision that saved the life of the outspoken, well-respected man with the second largest legal practice in town.[118] For several decades, Copland recorded the perfunctory details of his life in a small, red leather bound journal, "Diary of Charles Copland" embossed in neat gold lettering across the front. He was a penny-pincher and a meticulous record keeper: professional attainments, yearly expenditures and income, his children's dates of birth, and travel itineraries filled the pages in a neat, professional, uncluttered script. His entry for December 26, 1811, however, was highly uncustomary—nine pages of intense, emotional prose— and resulted in one of the most compelling firsthand accounts of the fiery disaster that consumed the theater that evening. "Four of my children were in the theatre, when the fire broke out. I was there myself in the early part of the night, but got tired of the play, and came home and was in bed and asleep when the fire commenced."[119]

Before falling asleep, Copland could have heard one of Madison Ward's night watchmen call the hour of ten and the "All is Well!"[120]

Even the playwright did not stay the full evening. Girardin's wife, Polly, and son, Louis Hue Girardin, Jr., entered a box seat with other family friends, but Girardin would not join them. "The state of my health was wretched," he later remembered, as he "labored under a complaint, whose attacks are often acute and sudden."[121] His descriptions may indicate he suffered from a severe claustrophobia that made remaining in the overcrowded theater a misery. Throughout the show he paced. He might have run his hand anxiously over his hair, cropped close in the front, a short beribboned queue in the back, while the troupe performed his play. As the curtain finally fell for *Family Feuds,* one can imagine that hearty cheers of congratulations and the wild whoops of his friends filled the hall. Perhaps he stood to be acknowledged by the grateful city who had taken him in. But this, the night of his triumph, the night that celebrated his wit and talent, would turn into his nightmare.

THE END BEGINS

A typical theatrical program of the day involved a full evening of entertainment, probably four or five hours in length, with dances and songs spaced between longer theatrical performances to appeal to the widest possible audience. Four short interim acts followed *Family Feuds* and preceded the second full-length show on the program—the pantomime *Raymond and Agnes: or the Bleeding Nun.* First, Thomas C. West sang a comic song, probably with the usual helping of double entendre; there followed a few numbers performed by the children of the theater troupe. Eliza Placide, daughter of manager Alexander, danced across the boards to the accompaniment of the tiny orchestra. Cornelia Thomas, the troupe's female vocalist, then took the stage for a solo, and, after the applause, a second Placide daughter took center stage in hard shoes to tap out a sailor's hornpipe.[122]

Amid the light tunes and laughter of this intermission, a triumphant but anxious Girardin slipped home, but he shortly returned to the theater. He approached Polly Girardin's box, where she sat with their small son, Louis, Jr., slumbering in her arms. Girardin proposed that he carry Louis home where the couple's two infant daughters, Adelaide Caroline and Mary Anne, already slept.[123] It was after ten o'clock in the evening. Polly told her husband that she would let the boy rest undisturbed until the end of the pantomime, observing that if he woke, he would "be delighted with the remainder of the exhibition."[124] The Frenchman acquiesced, kissed his little boy, and strode toward the door. Polly may have settled deeper into her box seat as the hornpipe concluded and the curtain rose on *The Bleeding Nun*.

In the lobby, Girardin met a former colleague, "generous, warm-hearted" David Doyle, a preceptor at another local private academy. Girardin proposed that the two men walk the short distance to his home, and they set out into the night air to "relieve our ennui by my fireside," he later recalled.[125]

As the final production of the evening, Matthew Gregory Lewis's popular pantomime *Raymond and Agnes: or, the Bleeding Nun* began. The melodrama starred the swooning hero, Raymond (played by Hopkins Robertson), whose lurid adventures commenced when his carriage broke down in a bandit-infested forest. The first act alone featured multiple murder attempts on the off-course hero, his escape through a secret passageway with a young, slightly drugged, and likewise lost Agnes, a sinister castle in the forest, and the ghostly apparition of a bleeding nun that haunted the castle rather punctually every fifth year. The sensational script concluded with the wedding of Raymond and Agnes—but Richmond theatergoers never saw the happy ending.

Before the second act, a junior stagehand lingering backstage heard a command barked to "raise the chandelier!" He bolted upright and went to work, obediently and mindlessly. Later, he claimed he could not identify who uttered the order. It was a man, it sounded authoritative, and the stagehand obeyed without delay, although the last remaining wick still flickered brightly on the chandelier.[126]

The man wrenched on a rope that wove through two pulleys inserted in the roof's collar beam. The candelabra slowly rose into the flyspace above the stage and rested at about fifteen feet below the beam. The stagehand anchored the lamp in place amid thirty-four hanging hemp canvas backdrops. Among the many large backdrop scenes painted thick with oils by professional artists Graim and West hung smaller flies and borders—peaked roofs, verandas, clouds, clumps of foliage.[127] The stagehand could hear the audience applauding. The candle slowly swung, veering closer and closer to the draping backdrops.

* * *

The Greenhow family, Robert, Mary Ann, and Robert, Jr., age twelve, heard the scene change bustle from their seats in the third box from the stage. The Greenhows hailed from Williamsburg, seat of the first playhouse in the British colonies, and apparently took their affection for the theater with them when they relocated. Not two years before, the family had moved from Williamsburg, where Robert managed his father's general store and sold everything from fresh garden seeds to secondhand grand pianos. Venturing westward to the capital to take advantage of its business opportunities, the nearly fifty-year-old merchant assumed proprietorship of a store under the sign of the Golden Padlock, perhaps a hardware store or general mercantile establishment.[128]

Displayed in their Madison Ward home were three small crayon portraits by French artist Charles Balthazar Julien Fevret de St. Memin, the portraitist *du jour* for Virginia's most distinguished families. Around 1807, St. Memin had drawn each Greenhow in sensitive, lifelike strokes.[129] The portraits reveal an interesting and handsome family. Black-eyed Robert Sr. faces his wife resolutely, calmly, and affectionately, looking younger than his years with long, unpowdered hair brushed back into a queue. Mary Ann's almost regal profile is softened by a cascade of ruffles from her collar and curled bangs peeping out from a bloused turban wrapped around her head. She looks every inch the confident, companionable woman described in her husband's warm letters. Young Robert's locks seem a bit unruly, but his collar is neat. Baby fat remains on his round cheeks. The family did not then suspect that their close threesome might suddenly be reduced to two.

Mary Ann sat in the first row, perhaps on a backless bench. Robert Sr. had pulled a seat directly behind hers so that she reclined between his knees. He wrapped his arms around her waist and rested his chin on her shoulder.

Tonight Mary Ann glowed with health, looking better than she had in months. After more than twenty-six years of marriage, the two were as affectionate as newlyweds and deeply in love. Robert Greenhow was convinced they enjoyed as much "connubial Bliss as ever fell to the Lot I dare venture to pronounce of any one pair!" She is the "friend of my heart, of my best & warmest affections," he professed to a colleague.[130] Robert Jr. sat beside them.

* * *

The flickering set piece suspended above stage caught the eye of the theater's property man, by the surname of Rice. Furious at the dangerous oversight, he grabbed a backstage carpenter and snapped, "Lower the lamp and blow it out!"

Thomas C. West rushed past in the wings, dressed as an "Old Servant," to commence the second act. He saw Rice motion at the lamp a second time and heard him order the carpenter to take some action. But then a stagehand across the way signaled to Rice, and other business drew him to that part of the stage. West assumed his place, securing a hoary wig on his head and readying himself to shamble in character onstage. Neither West nor Rice stayed to see that the flame was snuffed out. Four days later, the formal Committee of Investigation noted, "*This fatal lamp was not extinguished.* Here is the first link in the chain of our disasters!"

A few moments later, the head carpenter approached the stage and noticed an assistant carpenter attempting to let down the lamp, according to Rice's instructions. The assistant struggled with the ropes, which tangled and caught in a pulley. He tugged and the lit candelabra began to oscillate, just as Anderson had noticed in rehearsal. The carpenter jostled the ropes again, and the candelabra, still swinging in drunken circles, began to tip. The tiny flame touched the bottommost piece of a backdrop and set it alight.[131] Flames quickly licked up the hemp backing, flashing to the top of the scene. Within seconds, they had leapt the six-foot distance from the scenery to the pine ceiling, still covered with beads of rosin secreted in the previous summer's heat.

The workman's eyes widened and he scrambled into the carpenter's gallery, dropping wings, backdrops, and double back flats to the floor backstage, one after another, yet unable to distinguish the cords connected to the flaming canvas from the snarls of rope in hand. The flames shot along the underside of the roof with a roar. He fled for his life.

The second act began. Player Hopkins Robertson looked on as Thomas

Caulfield, "The Count," assumed a kneeling position onstage before a portrait of an elegant lady. Robertson suddenly spotted flakes of burning canvas gently falling to the floor. It was mesmerizing—a piece the size of a hand floated downward and, on contact, exploded in a soft spray of sparks. He was baffled—sparks were not planned for the scene. Another flake drifted past.

A bustle behind the curtain distracted West in the wings on the opposite side of the theater, but he "conceived [it] to be a mere fracas" among the stagehands, he later related. West heard the muffled cry of a crew member shouting "Fire!" and then another call out, "Don't be alarmed." Even if there were a fire, "little accidents of this description had often taken place" in the Richmond Theater, West recalled, and thus the situation gave him no serious apprehensions.[132] He put a shabby costumed leg forward and, as the "Old Servant," limped onstage.

Perplexed, Robertson tilted his head upward and watched flames spread in the flyspace, growing in a moment from the size of a handkerchief to the size of a bed sheet. He broke character, clumsily gestured to the audience, and blurted, "Fire!" Immediately the volume in the hall rose as audience members rustled out of their seats and bolted for the lobbies. A few women screamed and the sounds of crying and argument broke out.

West heard voices exclaim "Don't be alarmed" from behind the curtain. Afraid that a stampede would result from the panic and confusion, he repeated to the audience what he heard backstage and urged them to keep their seats.[133] While the general commotion in the house continued, some followed West's orders, pulled away from the crush in the corridors, and resumed their places, determined to wait and evacuate in an orderly way. John Lynch and Gibbon, leaning over the back of box eight, did not imagine they were in real peril. They quieted the apprehensions of the ladies, convincing them to remain in their seats.

Backstage, the rain of burning scenery intensified.

West looked behind the curtain and saw the whole backstage area wrapped in flames. Frantically, he tried to yank down burning pieces of the set, but he quickly realized his efforts to smother the growing firestorm were availing nothing. He dashed out the rear exit. Robertson ran to the box seats overlooking the stage and held out his arm to the ladies inside. "Jump into my arms—I can lead you to the private stage door!" he called to them, but they were frozen in terror and confusion. Compelled to at least save himself, he ran to the exit, but was cut off by the blaze.[134] The rear of the building still contained the fire.

Within five minutes, the whole roof had turned into a sheet of flame. The pantomime's backdrop looked like a transparency, behind which gleams of light showered. The curtain dropped, a very bright light emanating from behind.[135] The crowd at last knew the danger was real, and the festive atmosphere dissolved into sheer panic.

* * *

Three blocks south of the theater, in a flat above the Ellis & Allan firm's offices at Thirteenth and Main, lived the childless couple who took in the orphaned son of actress Elizabeth Arnold Poe.[136] Although this was not a legal adoption, John and Frances Allan had assumed all responsibility for the small stranger's upbringing and given him their surname. From that point on he was Edgar Allan—Edgar Allan Poe. The Allans were not known to be at the theater on the twenty-sixth, and the young boy was probably at home and in bed at this hour. But late that evening, through the glass windows of their apartment, they could have seen a low, horrid glow from the direction of the theater and heard the loud, despairing sound of incessant alarm bells, the sinking and the swelling, the clamor and the clanging, the bells that breathed out a tale of terror in the startled ear of night.

2

PANDEMONIUM

Being a stranger at the Theatre and ignorant of its construction I knew of no mode of escape except thro' the avenue I had ascended to the boxes. I found it blocked up by the crowd, and the light being very vivid, I discovered that the persons were principally Ladies: they were greatly alarmed and crying for relief, and entreating the crowd not to destroy them.

—JOHN G. JACKSON, DECEMBER 30, 1811

CONYERS SLUMPED, unconscious, off her bench and onto the filthy floor of box eight. As she lay motionless, Lynch and Gibbon stepped into action, reaching over the rear partition and pulling her out. Together they struggled further into the lobby, no more than a narrow hall, Sally between them, her head lolling over Lynch's left arm. Philip Thornton and Charles Hay began to quarrel over who would carry out Caroline Homassel until Thornton snatched her up and bore her tiny eighty-nine-pound frame into the hallway.[1] Women principally made up the crowd that filled the lobbies and, pummeled by the force of the mob, were at the greatest disadvantage. Long gowns hampered their movement; the crush lifted others off the ground and carried them helplessly along, shoes several inches from the floor. Desperate sounds, heartrending screams and pleading pervaded the lobbies for the two tiers of boxes, lit with the lurid brightness of the burning auditorium. Gibbon discerned that his friend could better lend assistance elsewhere and bellowed, "Lynch, leave Sally to me—I am strong enough to carry her, she is light and you can save somebody else." Lynch blurted, "God bless you, Gibbon, there is the stairs," and gestured toward a door about thirty feet away. Lynch then doubled back, pushing towards box eight to see if he could remove some of the other ladies inside.[2]

Like Lynch, Michael Wall Hancock pushed toward box eight to assist his niece and the Heron girls. By the time he arrived, each of his wards had evacuated, and the box stood empty, disrupted seats and abandoned reticules probably littering the floor.

Gibbon, with Conyers across his shoulder, continued to fight forward to the mouth of the staircase. It was about 11 o'clock.[3]

* * *

Turning to him at the first sight of the flames, Robert Greenhow remembered, Mary Ann was in terror, begging, "Save my child!" Robert's brother, Dr. James Greenhow, assured Robert he would take charge of Mary Ann's safety. Robert grabbed Robert Jr. and entered the crowded lobby. Mary Ann vanished behind him.

In the upper boxes, Gurden Huntington Bacchus stood with friends Maria Nelson, Mary Page, and Elizabeth Pendleton, reassuring them of the considerable distance between their box and the blaze. "The distance was such, that the fire could not possibly arrive so as to injure us in our retreat," he argued.[4] Nelson and Page seemed calm and collected about the situation, but Pendleton was not. She shrieked as her legs collapsed under her. Bacchus caught her mid-fall. "By stern advice and caution which I used, she revived, or recovered her faculties," he recalled. She recovered said faculties sufficiently to fly from the box while the other three continued to deliberate. According to Bacchus, "Miss Pendleton forsook us," but Pendleton's instincts were good: she would be the only of the three girls to survive. Less than a minute from the audience's first sign of fire, the scenery crashed down in a terrible blaze upon the stage, the vault of the theater collapsed, and the fire raced around the upper boxes.[5]

As realization dawned that there was no time to waste, the unprecedented rapidity of the fire caused even more people to pour out of the two tiers of box seats into the crowded corridors, pushing through the frantic, clawing mob toward the narrow stairwell, able to move no more than ten feet per minute—if at all. The official Committee of Investigation appointed by the City Council after the fire later recorded that of the 648 people on record as being present that evening "598 [those seated in the boxes and the pit] had to pass through one common avenue, and although all the spectators in the pit may have escaped, except a few who may have jumped into the boxes, yet the crowd in the lower and upper boxes had no other resource than to press through a narrow angular stair-case, or to leap the windows."[6]

Most legislators found seats in the boxes, but Patrick County delegate and lifelong bachelor Samuel Hughes, who had been "prevailed upon to accompany some of my acquaintances," found himself relegated to the pit and then apparently separated from his friends, possibly due to the seat shortage. This turned out to his benefit, as he relayed to his brother: "In consequence of my being so near the entrance of the pitt and flying to it immediately [I] was enabled to get to the outer door before the greatest crowd reached it."[7] It is not known if his "acquaintances" survived; although he wrote nothing of their fates in a missive to his brother on the twenty-ninth of December, Hughes is thought to have lost his fiancé in the fire.[8]

Almost no one jumped the short distance from the lower boxes into the pit to exit from the first floor and avoid the stairs. Survivor Jedediah Allen wrote that if patrons in the lower boxes had done this, "It would certainly have given room for the upper boxes [in the stairway], and by that means almost every soul would have been saved."[9] A house musician, the last to quit the orchestra, made his retreat from the pit through the semicircular avenue to the theater's inner door and was surprised to find it was almost empty, with ample room for more escapees. In the panic of the moment, however, the audience in the box seats thought only to leave through the avenue they had ascended.

Thomson F. Mason had been crouching outside box eight, talking with friends inside through the crack of a broken wall panel. Once the panic started, he stepped into the lobby and was swept away by the crowd. "The column of the crowd in which I was enclosed, bore me irresistibly, but slowly along towards the stairs [a journey of about ten yards]," he later wrote. "Still feeling no fears of being overtaken by the flames, I continued folded in my cloak and pressing my weight backwards, to give as far as possible an opportunity to those on the head of the stairs (where the pressure already seemed dreadful) to effect their escape."[10] In the narrow stairwell, the flow of human traffic had ground to a halt, and sufferers were immobilized. Leroy Anderson, a schoolmaster from Williamsburg trapped in the crush and holding his youngest daughter by the hand, later wrote of all the "amiable helpless females" stretching out imploring hands to him, crying, "Save me, sir; oh, sir, save *me*, save *me!*"[11] People who managed to force their way to the bottom of the stairs pooled in a pulsating mob at the doorway. In a tragic design flaw, the main downstairs inner doors opened *inward* toward the performance hall—the crowd's pressure pushed the doors solidly shut, despite the help that would-be rescuers offered from outside. The desperate scrambled over the fainting, feet skidding off heads and shoulders as they fought their way either up or down the stairs.

Fueled by adrenaline, Edmund Pendleton, Jr., Elizabeth's father, had been making good headway, his wife's arm locked fast in his own. Suddenly, someone tramped on the tail of his large, loose great coat, completely impeding his progress and all but throwing him backward. While he wrestled free, his wife was torn from him by the crowd, and he thought he saw her trampled with a number of other unfortunates. Pendleton was then wedged into a corner by the "prodigious crowd" until able to free himself and leap from a window.[12] Whether caught and trapped by their cumbersome clothing, manhandled after passing out, or directly trampled, many theatergoers were crushed to death within minutes.[13] Victims became nothing more than objects in the way, strangers threatening by their obstruction as the heat bore down and smells of burnt hair, turpentine, and paint grew noxious and thick.

Eighty children were present that evening. A pack of young schoolboys, all about twelve years of age, scuttled "under the elbows of the crowd" and all managed to escape.[14] Some survivors would surely have engraved in their memory the sight of small, panicked children, lost and jostled in the crowd without a mother or anyone to help, disheveled, crying in fear or silent in stark terror.

A lawyer was seen lingering in a box with two women, both in shock, immovable. He pleaded with them to flee as the heat and smoke became increasingly insufferable and his nose, eyebrows, and whiskers were badly scorched. Seeing they would not budge, his instinct of self-preservation drove him to a window near at hand, out of which he leaped, badly spraining a knee. The ladies kept their seats, and met their doom.[15]

As flames coated the underside of the roof, the bulls-eye window supplied oxygen from the fresh night air, sucking in a strong draft through the convection effect. Fire snarled through the seats and shot up the walls, licking up an entire painted canvas ceiling nailed to the underside of the roof and the lower boxes. Turpentine, resin, varnish, and hemp provided ample food for the fire's ravenous appetite as it moved from the back of the theater to the front, seeking out windows and bursting through the bulls-eye. Nearly the entire vault of the theater fell in "with considerable noise," one witness noted, its pieces landing in the pit and draping its skeleton around the gallery and upper boxes like curtains.[16] The theater glared with an angry orange light. Chunks of fiery debris showered down to the floor, bursting into a thousand fragments of fierce, uncontrollable fire.

From the doorway of box eight, Lynch saw flames flash across the facing of the upper boxes, shooting like lightning along both sides of the theater at the same time. Then a column of bituminous darkness descended and blackened the air with an opaque, sooty mass, tongues of vivid flame darting through like forked lightning in dark summer clouds.[17] Smoke billowed through the theater, expanding through the stairwells, through every avenue and room.[18] "All was now darkness in the lobby, and suffocation. I could not do anything," Lynch wrote.[19] Its suddenness shocked Thomson F. Mason: "Persons were no longer to be distinguished utter darkness prevailed—suffocation was fast approaching—for the first moment I was seriously alarmed," he recorded.[20] It became impossible to see even a few inches ahead, and to open one's eyes was to invite a horrible acidic burn. Breathing in the hot air source would have caused thermal injury to the upper airways of the people trapped in the lobby, damaging their mucous membranes. Men, women, and children covered their mouths with their hands, coughing and choking. Lurid sheets of flame caught the clothes of fugitives in the corridors, wrapping them in fire.

Mason struggled violently forward through the packed crowd, many dropping to the floor around him. His strength began to flag. One survivor wrote that he collapsed after inhaling the mixture for less than a minute, and only the fact that he fell through the floor into a shaft of fresh air revived him sufficiently to escape.[21] Carbon monoxide poisoning was setting in.

When inhaled, carbon monoxide binds to the hemoglobin molecule, preventing red blood cells from transporting oxygen. With the gradual loss of oxygen and a carboxy-hemoglobin level of over 10 percent in the bloodstream, victims may initially experience nausea or feel a pounding headache; at over 20 percent they may feel weak and drowsy. A presence of above 30 percent causes confusion, loss of memory, or agitation. Once levels reach 40 percent, the victim slips into a coma. The only treatment for an unconscious victim is oxygen, which explains how some who had already fainted survived.[22] Others similarly collapsed, and discovering chinks in the wall, they sucked hungrily at them for fresh air and shoved friends toward the cracks in the hopes of rallying them. Statesman Abraham Venable and an acquaintance by the name of Noland stood compressed near a window when hot and scorching smoke rolled in, sweeping over their faces like hot breath and coursing through their hair. The two were knocked down; Noland fell toward the window and was saved, Venable dropped the other way and died inhaling the toxic fumes.[23]

The smash and tinkle of broken glass was heard on one side of the lobby, then another. In the midst of the "awful horror and desperation that beggars all description," people trapped on the second floor and third floors groped their way along the side of the building toward windows, deliriously smashed them out, and regained coherence from the fresh air.[24] In an attempt to prevent the cold winter air from seeping through, theater managers had ordered casements to be boarded up, which added an additional obstruction to those pursuing a fresh lungful of air—boards had to be torn off by bare hands before the window could be opened. A wielded cane or balled fist smashed open a window in the lower box lobby near Mason, sucking in a cool stream of air, providing relief and hope to the crowd trapped in the blackened cloud. Those in the throng who had not already succumbed to smoke inhalation were "revived . . . to new exertion," surging from the stairwell toward the window, with a "universal scream of mingled joy and despair."[25] Mason was only a few feet from the broken glass, yet no one in front of him seemed to be advancing—he was trapped.

Robert Greenhow and his son would have experienced wild disorder, an assault on the body and the ear: panicked screaming and loud prayers, pleading with God in the belief that death was near. He suspected that for nearly four minutes he and his son were immovably planted in the midst of the pressing, overwhelming throng before being pitched to the ground and trampled as a roar of flame and hot, smothering vapor filled the air.[26] He and Robert Jr. gasped for air and drew in thick, abrasive smoke shot through with embers. The impact stunned him and he lost his grip on his son. "Father! I am dying!" Robert screamed, and his panicked voice was enough to rouse the father from a state of near insensibility. He seized his son's coat and secured him again in his hold. The two, still lying prostrate on a floor stained and slick with tobacco juice and saliva, were "kicked," in Greenhow's words, to the head of the staircase.[27]

For those trapped in the tunnel of the stairwell, the sounds of the strengthening fire roared in their ears as smoke darkened the air. Pressed against each other, perspiring heavily, they gagged and choked, coughing up black sticky liquid as the gritty smoke particles tore at their lungs. Their adrenaline used up and bloodstream poisoned, by scores they began to drop to the floor like their compatriots in the lobbies. Hunks of burning wood fell onto the steps and glanced off their dead and dying bodies. Those at the very bottom of the stairs could hear the muffled voices of people trying to help on the other side of the door. Whether chopped through, unhinged, or forced, once the doors finally gave way, those nearest the exit were trodden underfoot and pressed into the walls as the mass in the stair surged forward, bruising the people beneath them as they climbed forward, shredding clothing and tearing hair. Suffocation already had weakened many; the assault of the crush left many unable to rally themselves and move from the doorway. Although the fire advanced, many remained still, lying in a pile at the door's threshold.

Richard Dabney, a twenty-five-year-old local poet suffered "deeply burnt" hands and face when he refused to take the stairs as a matter of principle. "Seeing them strewed by the bodies of prostrated ladies, he thought sooner than injure them with his feet, he [would trust] his fate to chance, and accordingly jumped out of one of the upper windows," a friend recorded. Although critically injured, Dabney survived. [28] Few to none shared his scruples in their panic.

Greenhow, from the head of the stairs, rallied enough to give his body a "sudden impulse" that carried him, son in his arms, over the piles of hatted heads and tangled limbs. Once he reached the lower floor, he could see the external door and feel the fresh air. With his last remaining ounce of energy, he stumbled through the doorway into the night. After he regained his senses, he left Robert Jr. in place and ran back through the doors for Mary Ann. In the corridor a heavy rain of fiery debris blocked his path and he was forced to turn back. "Mary Ann was with Dr. Greenhow," he reassured himself. [29] Perhaps they too had escaped and were among the gasping, disheveled mass of broken-limbed humanity that circled the torched theater—he resolved to find them.

ATTEMPTED RESCUES AND ESCAPES

Fate's decrees seemed capricious: delaying departure from the auditorium could mean the loss of a life or could mean its salvation. Jedediah Allen initially felt no alarm and assumed that all would soon be under control, so he remained in place with his young daughter. "The vast number crowding for the stairs caused our stay," he explained, "and we [were] hindmost." From his vantage point low in the boxes, near the pit, he realized there were only a handful of people left in the house. Then, he heard a terrible crash. "All on a sudden the staircase gave way with the crowd, and left us alone." It became eerily silent and they heard no one until they gingerly entered a lobby and descended from a window. He recounted, "less than ten minutes after we left, the flames rushed out of the windows." [30]

Louis Girardin and David Doyle had walked no more than "thirty poles" from the theater, by Girardin's estimation, when a loud but confused noise burst on their ears. "I first thought it was the roar of mirth and applause," wrote the French instructor, but he then heard a distinct cry of "Fire! Fire!" behind him. When he and Doyle turned, "it was not a solitary curl of ascend-

ing flame, and undulating smoke, as is usual in the first stage of a conflagration," he recalled. A wide, bright sheet of fire swept over the roof, sliding down
the incline like a roaring wave.[31]

Girardin immediately sprinted to the building, "frantic" to protect his wife
and child and Doyle followed after. A short, fat man lay sprawled and comatose
at the entrance and another lay near him, "howling and writhing in agony."
Thinking only of Polly and his boy, Girardin jumped over them and charged
into the first passageway, empty save Girardin and "one or two wretches, who
probably like myself, had friends within and flew to their assistance."[32] He
proceeded into the second passage when he heard a tremendous crash above.

At the northwest window in front of the theater there appeared to Doyle
a number of ladies "most of whose faces I knew—I called to them to jump
out, they did and were all saved—even from a broken bone, yet some much
injured by the flames." He caught Ann Dent Hayes McRae, wife of foul-tem-
pered lieutenant governor Alexander McRae, when she lunged headfirst out
of the window.[33] Most of the women Doyle caught survived, although many
had clothes on fire, and several had broken limbs, painful burns, or suffered
"hideous contusions."[34] One "weighty lady," after ignoring pleas from below
to jump, unexpectedly fell from the window, landing on Doyle while he held
another lady in his arms. Neither of the ladies was severely injured, although
the force of the direct hit stunned Doyle, who "lay some time insensible."[35]

From below the crowd began to shout—a small boy of one or two years old
appeared in the window in his mother's arms. She released him, and the child
plummeted toward the ground. Someone rushed over and caught the boy,
unhurt. Paralyzed by the height, his mother could not be prevailed to leave
the window. A gathering crowd of hundreds watched her burn to death.[36]

Thomson Mason decided he would help himself to the window borrowing
the shoulder of someone next to him. He continued, "I drew my feet up and
was thrown by the united impulse of others, and my own exertions, with my
feet directly on the window sill, at the same instant fortunately seizing a broken fragment of the sash. I passed my head under it and reached the ground
without material injury—I left many behind me."[37] Meanwhile, actor Hopkins
Robertson found himself blocked from the stage door exit. He returned to the
stage box, hauled himself up, and followed the crowd pressing toward the only
other exit. Robertson was able to gain a front window, where he passed out
nearly a dozen females before throwing himself over the ledge.[38]

Near box seven, some twenty feet away from a forced-open window, Michael Wall Hancock caught a whiff of fresh air and pulled out his sword cane to make an escape. Using the cane as a pole vault to boost his ascent, he leapt to the partition between the lobby and his bench, and from there "mounted on the heads of the crowd betwixt me and the window."[39] By this time the house was in total darkness from smoke, but by groping, he reached the side of the window. The afflicting cries of those suffocating around him, of those on whom he literally stood, did not give him pause. At the window, he stuck his feet forward into the sill and pushed up the double-hung window's lower sash in order to slip out the bottom. But he was not the only one to clamor over his competitors for oxygen: he soon felt the lower sash crush his feet as those behind him with enough strength to do so climbed over him to leap from the upper part of the window. Every escapee kicked and bruised his back and shoulders, smashing his feet with the pressure of the sash as they dived out. He fell backward atop the piled humans behind him, one foot still wedged in the sill, and began to lose consciousness. Flames filled the lobby and rushed over his head. But around his shoe, a small gust of air penetrated the window and revived him enough to raise himself to a seated position. Those behind him being comatose and no longer able to keep him down, he with a last effort raised the sash, extracted his foot and jumped out. He landed dazed, his next sensible thought for his six wards. He had shouted, "Take care of *yourselves*!" to his nephews at the first alarm as they scrambled off their bench in the back of box seven, but he had not seen any of them in the crowd. Nor any of the girls.[40]

Behind him was the sound of a terrible crash, and then the thud of a falling body—John Lynch, from box eight, on fire. Lynch had been wedged in the crowd near the window only a few feet from Hancock, and there he turned into a human torch. "My hair caught fire (for my hat was gone,) hope deserted me; I was struck with horror at the idea of being burnt alive." But then, a glimpse of hope: the casement was finally clear of any obstruction. "I rushed towards the window, waving my hands as quick as possible over my head and clothes; this was a dreadful moment, I saw many drop down on each side of me suffocated. . . . I threw myself out, and providence preserved me."[41] Lynch was the last known to escape from that window.

* * *

Observers from the streets below saw fire puncture the bulls-eye window on the uppermost part of the exterior wall and flame breathe out like a dragon.

The inrush of fresh oxygen created an inferno, escalating the internal temperature toward wood's kindling point—the moment at which it explodes into flames. By this time, hundreds had gathered around the theater, filling the wide avenues of H Street and Twelfth Street, watching with horror those trapped at the windows inside.[42]

The editor of Richmond's *American Standard* newspaper ably exited the theater, being unencumbered with family and close to the door, and he immediately ran around to various windows "which were very high," he added, and "implored his fellow-creatures to save their lives by jumping out of them." Terrified and ignorant of their danger, those nearest the windows froze, he reported, "afraid to leap down, whilst those behind them, were seen catching on fire, and writhing in the greatest agonies of pain and distress. At length, those behind, urged by the pressing flames, pushed those who were nearest to the windows, and people of every description begun to fall, one upon another, some with their clothes on fire, some half roasted."[43]

Despairing persons lodged within a mass of humanity several yards from the windows would have felt the heat surge behind them, melting the wax in their ears, singeing their hair and blistering their skin. Of course they pushed impulsively, desperately, toward the casements ahead. Their force thrust those in front of them, ready or not, out the windows, and victims fell clinging to each other, slipping on the sill, and plummeting in flames, like comets. One woman vaulted out a window with her gown aflame. The editor, at great risk to himself, caught her before she reached the ground. He tore her burning clothes off of her body until she was "stripped . . . of her last rags" and wrapped her up with his coat, "protecting her nakedness," before carrying her from the scene.[44] She was later identified as Juliana Harvie, the teenage daughter of a family plagued by tragedy.

From the ground, onlookers saw Edmund Pendleton, Jr., stick his feet out the window, seat himself on the window sill, and ease himself slowly off, sliding along the wall by the seat of his trousers. He later described the logic behind this position: "If I could contrive my clothes to touch the wall as I descended, the force of my passage down would be somewhat broken. I soon experienced the happy reality of this experiment, for I landed on my feet, perfectly erect, and have never since felt the least soreness or inconvenience from my manner of escape." To his relief, he found that his wife, "the object which had thus far stimulated my exertions," survived, as did his daughter Elizabeth, although the girl's leg was badly broken. [45]

There were other strange sights at the windows: A man by the last name of Gordon lost consciousness and was separated from his family. His wife and tiny daughter managed alone to precipitate themselves out a window in a kind of dangling human chain—Gordon's wife clinging to a man ahead of her and the child clinging to her mother's mantle. Carter Page, a resourceful and fast-working man if ever there was one, saved his wife by splitting her pelisse—a coat-like dress typically worn over a longer cotton dress—into strips and tying the dress so as to form a rope. With this he got her down from the window, following her at the expense of a broken leg.[46]

Several box eight members gathered around a window amid the clouds of smoke. John Richard smashed out a shutter for their escape, and Philip Thornton quickly lowered Caroline Homassel down by her arms, suspending himself as far out the window as possible to minimize the distance of her fall. She stiffened in fear when she recognized below the dead and bloodied body of Almarine Marshall of Wythe, Virginia, who snapped his neck landing headfirst when diving from the upper stories. Charles Hay, who had seen his own way out, and Doyle positioned themselves below and caught Caroline. Thornton followed after dislodging himself from the sill where he had become partially caught; portions of his coat were completely burned through, providing proof of his near escape.[47]

* * *

After Gilbert Hunt returned from the First Baptist Church to the Mayo home, Louisa's frantic mother met him, crying that the theater was on fire—with Louisa inside. She begged him to go and find her daughter. The middle-aged blacksmith needed no urging to go to Louisa's aid. Hunt, by his own account, "loved her very much."[48]

Hunt ran to a nearby home to secure a mattress for cushioning the fall of the jumpers.[49] Unsuccessful, he returned to the blaze without a mattress, but with a stepladder. As others dragged bodies of the dead and living away, Hunt placed the ladder against the tottering walls on the eastern side of the building. He saw some shutters tremble, then splinter into pieces. A large head stuck out. The eastern window had been shuttered and strongly barricaded from the outside and crowds of anguished people were clustered, suffocating behind it. Dr. James McCaw, aged forty, "a man who might have been chosen by a sculptor for a model of Hercules," smashed out the sash, straddled the high window sill, and let down every female within his grasp; he held their hands firmly in his, gently lowered them as far as he could reach, and dropped them safely to the ground.[50] After capturing Hunt's attention, the two made a robust team rescue effort as McCaw dropped women into the powerful blacksmith's arms below.[51] The two saved nearly a dozen women, concluding with a rescue that tested Hunt's strength—the catching of McCaw's sister, "whose proportions were a feminine epitome of the Doctor himself," according to Samuel Mordecai.[52] The catch knocked Hunt backward to the ground, but both rescuer and rescued emerged unhurt. As the fire behind Dr. McCaw began to singe his clothing and his skin, he attempted an escape; the building's collapse seemed imminent. When the doctor dropped from the window, the last man to exit by this avenue, his sportsman's gaiter, a leather protector for his shins and ankles, caught on a metal projection from the wall. The doctor dangled helplessly by his pants, perhaps upside down, lacerating his muscles and charring his back. He ripped free, fell to the ground with a nasty thud, and screamed, "Will nobody save me?" Hunt rushed over and dragged him in the direction of the Baptist church, which was on the corner of H and Old Fourteenth Street. There, Hunt created splints for McCaw's mangled leg—it seemed that his thigh had been broken—out of fence palings and bound his wounds with handkerchiefs.[53]

By the time he exited the theater with a half-prostrate woman and made his way around the perimeter, Louis Girardin could spy people descending from the windows to the northwest and the south, but from the east window all was still. A ladder stood beneath the high window, probably left by Hunt. A woman draped in a pale garment leaned partially out, seemingly supported by someone behind her. His wife? He peered closer. No—Polly had not dressed in white that evening. Smoke rose from the cracks in the window and coiled above the woman's head. Drained of color, her half-lidded eyes and mouth barely moved. "Her attitude and looks evinced deadly faintness—perhaps she was breathing her last—perhaps," he wondered. Urging anyone behind her to assist her out over the sill, he climbed the ladder and exclaimed several times, "Let her down by the arms along the wall—I will receive her!" Silence. There were no signs of movement. Smoke continued to wend in strands through the shards of shattered glass. "I stretched my arms—roared like a maniac, "Let her down!" Hers would have been a long fall onto a frail ladder, "but what are considerations like those in such a case?" he asked in exasperation. "I might at least have broken her fall." Girardin did not stay longer. "Impatient at the fatal delay, distracted with alarm, harrowed up with desperation, I rushed from the steps—went round the house," he wrote later.[54] He had yet to find any sign of Polly or Louis Jr.

Contributing to the paralyzing horror of the evening was the tacit conviction of many inside and outside the theater that the fire was not an accident but rather a sinister slave plot to murder Virginia slave owners while they congregated en masse. "I speak from facts when I say that the night bell never tolls for fire in Richmond, that the mother does not hug the infant more closely to her bosom," wrote John Randolph after witnessing alarms in the state capital.[55] Only months before the fire, a Richmond editorialist wrote that a "disposition to rebel is most conspicuous in the slaves residing about Richmond."[56] After the 1800 discovery of an insurrection planned by an enslaved blacksmith named Gabriel from Henrico County, Richmond's whites lived with a perpetual undercurrent of fear that another slave uprising could occur at any time.[57] Stunned at the bravery and bloodthirstiness behind the attempted revolt as well as by the "fortitude" of the captured slaves once they were condemned to die, John Randolph noted with apprehension that the slaves "manifested a sense of their rights and contempt of danger, and a thirst for revenge which portend the most unhappy consequences [for Virginia]."[58] From this point forward, the capital regularly summoned the Richmond Light Infantry Blues or the citizen-organized Public Guard to augment the police force in times of suspected slave-revolt peril.[59] The capital city went on full alert in late 1808, when the Virginia militia received tips regarding a slave uprising planned during Christmastime. Then-governor Alexander McRae called the state military to the capital on December 19 and placed them on duty until New Year's Day.[60]

There were growing "Disturbances in Virginia" and a fresh rash of slave-instigated murders as late as 1810. In a June 25, 1810, letter, a Richmond correspondent reported: "On Saturday last a dreadful CONSPIRACY of the SLAVES took place at the Coal Pits. So Sudden and unexpected was the occurrence, that before a sufficient number of the patrole could be collected to disperse them, they MURDERED several FAMILIES! among which were Capt. Heth's, Mr. Gunliffe's and Judge Fleming's. The Governor has ordered out the Militia throughout the State:—and I fear there will be much bloodshed before tranquility can be restored. I am on the watch every night."[61] He added that armed citizens were ordered to call on a black but once before firing. One can imagine the terrible, nerve-fraying tension that wrapped the city.

Virginia House of Delegates member from Accomack County, Thomas R. Joynes, in Richmond for the legislative session, wrote to his brother Levin on December 27, 1811. "It was supposed when the fire was first discovered, that the house was intentionally set on fire, and that it was only the precursor of scenes still more tragical than the ones which has happened. It was supposed by many to have been the signal for *insurrection*, and that those who escaped the fury of the flames, might have to encounter an enemy more destructive than fire itself."[62] This would not have been implausible. Twenty years before, an eleven-year-old slave girl in Richmond was sent to jail after intentionally starting her master's house on fire. She intended to kill the family after a weaver who lived in the home "was cross to her."[63]

Enslaved malcontents were not responsible for the Richmond Theater fire, but some approved of its results. In April 1812, in Henry County on Virginia's North Carolina border, a slave named Tom went to trial for murdering his owner and participating in an insurrection plot encompassing slaves from several other counties. The hatred Tom and his enslaved accomplices felt toward slaveholders became evident when he reported that "the negroes in the neighbourhood said they were glad that the people were burnt in Richmond and wished that all the white people had been burnt with them—that God Almity had sent them a little Hell for the white people and that in a little time they would get a greater."[64]

The suspicion of slave intrigue in the case of the theater fire quickly faded. "There is now no doubt but that these fears were groundless. If there had been any intention of that kind, it would have been carried into effect when the flames were at their height, and all the inhabitants were collected there," concluded Joynes in his letter written the day after the fire. But during the blaze, the uncertainty would have added a new level of terror for those too afraid to leave the building and face a riot—but in too much danger to stay within.[65]

CHAOS AND CASUALTIES

"The fire flew with a rapidity, almost beyond example," wrote Thomas Ritchie. "Within 10 minutes after it caught, the whole house was wrapt in flames."[66] As the building transformed into an inferno, the frail wooden supports for the stairwell, where the majority of escaping theatergoers had congregated, collapsed. Dozens stood stranded on the upper stories, and the plunge killed most of those crammed into the stairwell. Merchant Joseph Gallego watched his wife plunge downward as the crowd pushed her to the top of the stairs at the very moment the structure fell. He was left standing on the platform above. In anguish and shock, he groped his way to a window which had saved his other friends and leaped to safety.[67]

Because of the darkness, people were not aware of the pit created by the collapsed stairs; they pushed others forward into the chasm and themselves fell into it, crashing and tumbling on top of the mix of victims and burning debris. Struggling through the lobby outside the first tier of boxes, U.S. representative from Virginia John G. Jackson's last recollection was that his feet were descending; had he fallen through the floorboards or stepped into the void? On impacting the pit floor, a strong current of fresh air reached his nostrils and revived him. He struggled to sit upright and saw people falling to the yard.[68]

One man by the name of Tucker reported that he heard the first cry of fire while walking "at the head of the brick-row," probably the exclusive stretch of townhomes about five blocks south of the theater and a block from Edgar Allan Poe's home on Main.[69] Similarly, others first heard word of the fire from someone shouting outdoors. At the sight of the orange glow, townspeople spread through the alleys and streets, like noncommissioned town criers, to rouse their neighbors, waking more who did the same until streets were filled with grim messengers, lanterns swinging, fists hammering frantically on wooden doors and window panes to stir the inhabitants to action.

Many also wrote of the incessant sound of tolling bells, probably from the nearby Market House, which drew hundreds to the site. Wherever a bell could be found, it was rung loudly, in an appalling sound that chilled the hearers. The 1837 rules for alarm bells may shed light on the course of action: the bell nearest the fire would strike to indicate the location, one for Jefferson Ward, two for Madison Ward, or three for Monroe Ward, and then ring furiously as the bells in the other wards continued to toll the number of the affected ward until the fire had ceased.[70] For a disaster of this scale, in such close proximity to the most populated portions of town, probably few remained at home.

On his way to the fatal site, Tucker, the man who had been walking the brick row, met with a volunteer fire-fighting brigade, identifiable by their hand-labeled hats, a "glaring flambeau" carried before them, and the engine they dragged behind.[71] Tucker quickly assisted in drawing the fire engine about ten or fifteen yards, the maneuvering of which would have been a terrific ordeal on rutted, frozen, unlit roads. At least one of the town's engines, little more than a hand pump with a leather hose, was present at the fire.

Considering the speed and intensity of the blaze, the engine would have been completely ineffective by the time it arrived at the theater. Firemen of the time fought fires externally, not typically entering buildings to confront flames at close range, so there was probably little that the volunteer brigade could do but stand and witness the destruction, pails in hand.[72] "Not a drop did I see poured on the raging flames," wrote one witness. "This scene we all had to witness, without the least means or power of averting or alleviating the sufferings of the victims in the smallest degree. Thus we beheld, like statues . . . the awful tortures of burning alive!"[73]

Sound asleep in his home across the road from the theater, Charles Copland awoke to the cries of fire, probably five to ten minutes after it began. As the lids lifted from his eyes, his room appeared lit by a dozen bright lamps—it was being "illuminated by the fire from the Theatre through the one window of my chamber," he wrote in his little leather diary. "Rising and going to my window I discovered the Theatre enveloped in flame." He threw on trousers and a shirt when he heard his daughter Elizabeth thundering up the stairs emitting earsplitting shrieks. His second wife, Heningham Carrington Bernard, twenty-five years his junior and only slightly older than Elizabeth, may have comforted the girl while Copland pulled on his boots.[74]

"When I got to my front door going out," he wrote, "I found crowds of people in the street coming from the Theatre, some of men bearing away their maimed friends who had suffered either from burning or broken limbs. On my way to the Theatre, I stopt at every group I met to inquire for my daughter Margaret and my sons William and Robert and after I got to the Theatre, I ran about in all directions making like inquiries, but could hear nothing of them." As the fire raged hotter, climbing to over five hundred degrees, faces ceased to show at the windows, and the flow of escapees slowed to a trickle from the front doors. Copland noted that the crowd had moved twenty or thirty yards from the theater, forced back either by the heat or by the fear of the walls falling on them. A wide-open space was left between the house and the crowd.[75] The area was being quickly cleared of the injured, who were farmed out to nearby houses or carted home on jerry-rigged conveyances.

Not able to locate his children, Charles Copland ran through the emptying yard and entered the theater by the main outward entrance door. Once he passed through the foyer to the interior door and reached the earthen floor of the circular corridor, he crossed into a surreal hell, eerily silent, brilliantly lit and laced with smoke: a deranged woman wandered helplessly toward the foyer, gesturing madly. He followed the dirty corridor and smoke to the stairs—or where the stairs used to stand. Lit candles in tin sconces flickered along the walls and the glare of flames radiated through the lobby, illuminating a ghastly sight in lurid brightness. He wrote it was "the most appalling sight I had [ever] witnessed"—a heap of girls in a tousled pile like maltreated dolls, young women who were first overcome by smoke and then trampled at the foot of the staircase. Of the roughly twelve women, some were dead but "some of them [were] manifestly alive, and which I discovered by the writhing of their bodies," he recorded. Copland could not accurately determine what had happened to them, but he suspected smoke inhalation, or possibly fright was responsible for their torpor.

And although the air was less hazy on the ground floor, the women still suffered the consequences of the air they had ingested in the upper stories. "I remember well that the smoke on the ground floor where I was, was not in such a degree as to endanger suffocation," Copland wrote. "It might however be in a degree sufficient to retard inspiration in those who had suffered from smoke before they got from the upper floor."[76]

Copland had only a few minutes in the burning building to choose a course of action and determine whom he would rescue. First he bore the madly gesticulating wanderer to the front yard and returned to carry out a woman who lay among the pile, "her arm extended and erect" as though imploring for help. Supposing that his daughter might be among the group of women at the stairs, Copland shouted "Margaret!" and continued to search for her. He supposed nineteen-year-old Margaret, in her cotton frock, may have been somewhere amid the pile of silk, wool, and flesh. "My daughter had worn to the theatre a cloth riding dress and . . . at the foot of the staircase, I passed my hand over the bodies of the females that lay prostrate before me, with a hope of discovering my daughter by the dress she had worn; for I had not time to examine faces, although there was a sufficient light. . . . While I was passing my hand over their bodies looking for a cloth dress, I frequently with a loud voice called my daughter, hoping by loud speaking to rouse her or some one of them, but the power of speech was gone or impeded. None spoke, but other signs of life were not wanting.[77]

Distracted by the realization that he had still not found Margaret or his sons, ages thirteen and eleven, his heart ached with the thought that all three were lost. There were no more accessible places to look. The stairwell grew brighter. "The roar of the fire above the crackling of the burning timbers, and the apprehension that my retreat to the outward door might be cut off by the falling in of the floor above me, all ignited, so affected me (I tell it to my shame) that I retreated from the foot of the stairway." Conflicted for leaving the scene when he may have rescued more of the injured, Copland finally, in anguish, ran to his house with the faint hope that his children might have escaped and returned home.

* * *

The stench of burning flesh, like overcooked meat, polluted the air. Several men ran inside, taking advantage of the last remaining minutes. Doyle entered the building's main lobby through the only outward entrance door, crossing a twelve-foot-wide plank floor to a smaller inner door where the ticket taker usually stood. Once there, he took a step down to the dirt corridor leading to the stairwell. He immediately encountered the asphyxiation victims' "blackened and lifeless bodies." Many would improve to be "in a fair way of recovery" within the week, but at that time, they were, to him, apparently dead.[78] Captain Henry Heth, who lost his family in the coal pit slave uprising of 1810, joined Doyle in carrying out several people, including a woman who miraculously was still speaking despite her devastating third-degree burns.[79]

Near the end of the effort, Girardin, too, evacuated several women. While he stood at the "fatal stair-case," he watched the back end of the building cave in. "Burning ruins fell down with horrid crash; volumes of suffocating vapour rolled onwards; lurid flames darted through them." He "with the utmost difficulty" retreated, dragging with him a "half prostate female" as hunks of burning building fell in around them.[80] By the time they evacuated, "destruction was raging with all its fury in the circular passage." It was a "fatal stair-case" indeed—the Committee of Investigation would later write of its critical role in the fatalities: "Even the relics of our fellow-citizens as they lay, pointed out the causes [of the mass casualties]. . . . They were found strewed in heaps at the foot of the narrow stair-case which led from the boxes—and though with less profusion, on the ground immediately *under* the lobby of the boxes above, from which lobby their retreat down the stairs had been intercepted by the crowd which choked them up."[81]

Outside again and unable to attempt any further rescues inside, Girardin sought out his wife and son amid the piles of wounded outdoors, where "miserable objects then afflicted my view! What mournful sounds lacerated my ears!!!" He noticed Juliana Harvie as she called out in "plaintive accents" that he mistook for those of his wife's aunt. When he approached the sound, he saw the girl lay dying in a cart. "God of mercy!" he cried with the shock of seeing her. Her condition "would have melted a barbarian's heart." While in the yard, ladies of his acquaintance spotted him and "rushed into my arms," he recalled. His aunt, sister, and mother, ecstatic at finding him alive, heard him sputter, "My wife! My child!!!" and, "looking on each other with consternation and despair," the whole mass of them broke into weeping.[82] None had seen Polly or the little boy.

From a window in a neighboring home, a resident saw a woman from Manchester, a town just over Mayo's Bridge south of Richmond, being helped along in excruciating pain, with her thigh broken. What he saw from his perch led him to claim that dozens, perhaps nearly a hundred more, suffered from shattered bones.[83] Leroy Anderson claimed the next day that "fifty others . . . broke their necks, or were crushed to death by those who fell on them from the same height." This was likely an exaggeration, but certainly many, though not killed, were "shockingly mangled," in the words of a contemporary, in their fall.[84] Judge John Coalter wrote, "I am told that the wretched half burnt females were crawling on their hand and knees in all directions from the smoking ruins in a state of frenzy—that one young lady who accompanied Mrs. Gov Smith was found in that state with a broken leg, as far down as the Bell Tavern."[85] John Richard, Samuel Dyer, and a "Mrs. Hatcher" were among the many with fractured legs; Mary Love Scott, whose husband represented Fairfax County in the House of Delegates, and a pair of local siblings—Juliana and Edwin Harvie—were among the more severely burned. A Richmonder named Fith had one side of his face, an observer noted, a "good deal burnt."[86] However, the causes of the most deaths were not burns or fall-related injuries but carbon monoxide poisoning and inhalation of the oily smoke, which is typical in large building fires.

* * *

Trampled hats littered the ground along with the other detritus of the disaster: spectacles, pocketbooks, leather shoes, and pieces of lost clothing. Reportedly several women emerged stripped to the waist, probably after having their clothes violently yanked from behind by fellow escapees.[87] As good Samaritans descended on the scene, dozens of wounded men and women would have hazily felt themselves lifted up and then deposited in a heap in carts, on mattresses, or on the browned grass outside, being unable to move themselves. Many, discolored by fire and smoke, were unrecognizable. All were illuminated by the dismal light that radiated from the building and brightened the windows of houses from blocks away. The wounded would have been carted away, miserable with pain, vomiting, and shivering. Burns damage the skin surface and disable the body from being able to regulate its own temperature—it is critical that victims be kept warm and dry, or else hypothermia can set in. Those with second-degree burns and fractured limbs had probably gone into shock—weak, skin pale and clammy, lips and fingernails turning blue.

* * *

On the grounds of the theater, successful Scottish tobacco merchant Thomas Rutherfoord had questioned bystanders and learned that his neighbor Thomas Wilson's daughter was safe, but Wilson's wife, Lucinda, was still unaccounted for. Wilson, a future Richmond mayor, had stayed home that evening, and in his house on the westernmost part of town about twelve blocks away, he was as yet unaware of the catastrophe. Rutherfoord rode to Wilson, and in his thick brogue convinced the man, who "seemed bereft of reason" upon hearing the news, to accompany him to the scene. Rutherfoord described the pandemonium. "On our arrival there we found nothing but confusion. Many persons, like ourselves, were looking for lost relatives of friends, and unable to give answers to the inquiries which were made."[88] Crowds gathered eagerly around survivors still able to speak, still able to stand, as the near-victims relayed their stories of escape and the dire predicament of those still inside the glowing walls.

Besides the adult males who arrived with their buckets ready to assist as volunteer fire fighters, curiosity seekers by the score also came to watch the fire. Throughout the eighteenth and nineteenth centuries, a good blaze could prove the best show in town, and invariably attracted innumerable gawkers, as postcards and illustrations of famous fires readily attest. Although fires were common, fatalities were not, so it was usually a harmless spectacle—unless the spectators got in the way of the blaze. This was also not uncommon, as people sought out the best vantage point for the free exhibition, heedless of rescue attempts, fire hoses, and stored gunpowder.

Witnesses attempted to describe the scene outside the theater: "Women with dishevelled hair—fathers and mothers shrieking out for their children—husbands for their wives—brothers for their sisters—filled the whole area on the outside of the building. . . . Others were frantic and would have rushed to destruction, but for the hand of a friend. Almost the whole town rushed to the fatal spot."[89] In a commemorative sermon, Rev. John D. Blair of Richmond later prompted his audience to remember that night. "And from those who escaped from the house or ran thither upon the alarm of the Bells, you heard the frantic cries, the anxious inquiries, Where is my wife? Where is my husband? Where is my child? Where are my parents? And from some, already fatherless, Where is my dear mother?"[90] The costumed cast and orchestra added to the surreal turmoil of the crowd. Placide later wrote, "We had just time enough to save ourselves, dressed as we were," and thus, milling around outside in the chaos were a Bandit, a Woodman, a Countess, and (most horrifying) the Bleeding Nun.[91] Perhaps a musician wandered past, clarinet, flute or violin grasped tightly in hand.[92]

Escapees found shelter from the cold in neighboring houses, and the wounded were carried there for treatment.[93] This only added to the complications for those trying to track down family members. Girardin went back and forth between the theater and his home no fewer than four times that evening.[94] Theatergoers might be trapped, or in a random neighboring home, on the floor of the nearby Baptist church, or safely at their own residence.[95] "It is scarcely possible to imagine any thing more awful than the suspense with which the friends of those who were missing must have awaited their return during the night, or more distracting than their horror on finding that all traces of them were destroyed," sympathized a Philadelphia theater magazine.[96] Family members were torn in the final seconds—should they begin an exhaustive survey of the homes or plunge into the building in case their loved ones had not yet been rescued? Either way, it would have been no use for Rutherfood and Wilson to search for Lucinda Wilson—she was already dead.[97]

Then a twenty-five-year-old Jewish bachelor, Samuel Mordecai had earlier that evening reached Richmond from a "Christmas jaunt in the country," hoping to obtain a seat for *Family Feuds*. He and his friends arrived too late, all seats were taken. Dejected, he retired to the home where he was lodging until he woke to the sound of screaming and followed the pandemonium to the theater. When he approached the first clearing near the capitol, he nearly stumbled over a bruised lady lying on the grass, apparently in a swoon. He tried to lift her, but in horror realized she was dead, and laid her lifeless body back on the ground. Mordecai afterward learned that she had leaped from a window, but before she could be moved away, she was crushed by those who followed her.[98] Several paces away lay a gentleman so terribly excoriated with ferocious third-degree burns that Mordecai could do nothing for him. Death mercifully put an end to the man's tortures within a few hours.[99]

* * *

The winds blew high, and flames moved quickly over the parts of the wooden and brick building still left standing, greedily consuming all that was left.[100] Supports for the building fell into an ocean of molten flame. Doyle thought it might have been no more than six minutes from first appearance to last person saved.[101] No conclusive duration was ever established.

By one in the morning, the scattered members of box eight were either dead in the ruins or making their slow way home. Dr. Thornton carried shoeless Caroline Homassel all the way to her dwelling in his arms, while her adoptive father John Richard's mill hands carried him aloft on a blood-stained mattress. The broken white bone from his compound thigh fracture probably poked through his torn trousers.[102]

Stories of close calls spread quickly. One woman from the Couch family, caught after leaping off a sill, was mostly uninjured after her ordeal. Stepping into the crowd, she saw burn victims being carried away and heard the chilling screams of those driven nearly wild with anxiety and pain. Although her home was almost a mile away, she would not admit anyone to accompany her on her walk back, "seeing so many objects in distress, who had a greater claim to assistance than she had," as one townsperson remembered. Her intentions exceeded her fortitude and "before she went far she was near falling a victim to her humanity, for, from the great exertions of body and mind necessary to her preservation—her spirits failed her."[103] She crumpled, exhausted, in the street. Difficult to traverse for those in hale health, navigating the poor roads home would have been a nightmarish pilgrimage for the wounded. In winter, mud was often ankle deep and in some places up to the hub of a cart wheel. Sidewalks started and stopped here and there, "and wo to him or her who, on a dark night, deviated from the right path," recalled Mordecai.[104] Someone found the cataleptic woman in the early hours of the morning and carefully roused her. "She must have lain probably lifeless, in the street that night, had not a gentleman fortunately seen her, and after reviving her, brought her home."[105]

The mother of a twelve-year-old schoolboy was wintering with her family in Richmond and lodging at a boardinghouse. A group of his young friends persuaded her and her husband to come to the play that evening. Country folk, they generally eschewed the theatre, but found themselves attending along with around ten fellow boarders. The group splintered apart after the cry of fire, and the mother found herself at the stairs. The dense mass of humanity thrust her upward and, according to her son's account, "she was carried, in a reclining posture, to the bottom on her feet, and then the outer door, just before her, afforded ready egress." As she stumbled out the door, she glimpsed "a heavy old man lying on his back, beneath a window, perfectly dead." She used to say to her son that "the look of agony in that ghastly face haunted her for years."[106] Finding an acquaintance, she left a message for her husband, should he not have already emerged from the theater, and set off alone for the boardinghouse, more than half a mile distant, impatient to find her son and husband there. "She lost shoes, bonnet and cap," recalled her son, who was following not far behind. "When I reached the parlor, she had arrived, and, with her hair streaming over her shoulders, was recounting some of the terrible scenes of the fire. She was the first to reach the house."[107] Her husband, a "stout heavy man," watched the staircase give way and "the masses of frantic beings went rolling over each other to the floor." He stumbled away from the gaping hole, reached a window "by a violent effort" and dropped himself out safely. The boy's half sister survived, although a fall from the window shattered her right ankle and lamed her for life. Her elderly maternal grandmother, "heavy and helpless," made no effort to escape and was burned to death. Fear appeared to deprive her and many others of the power to move.[108]

Another survivor woke up in his own bed after being discovered at some distance from the playhouse. His last memory was being compressed in the staircase while hugging his two children to his chest, one under each arm. Neighbors conjectured that he had been wedged up and forced along unconsciously, like a fishing bobber, atop the crowd until deposited outdoors. From there, he had somehow been borne home to his bedroom, where he awoke to gratefully discover his children and wife alive.[109]

* * *

All night the building burned like a furnace, spraying showers of sparks into the night air. By dawn, flames had consumed Samuel Myers's home to the immediate west and reduced the theater to rubble. The playhouse was nothing more than a few blackened, crumbling walls surrounded by mounds of charred bodies, bone fragments, and smoking timbers. To have broken down brick and mortar, the temperature of the fire had probably climbed over one thousand degrees Fahrenheit.

Crowds filled the streets as though it were noontime. Candles flickered in all the houses. Richmond slept little that night. A friend of the *Petersburg Intelligencer*'s editor wrote, "G—! what havock ensued! Our houses are all hospitals; our streets lined with parents lamenting the loss of children—children shrieking for parents just perished—wives lamenting lost husbands, and husbands wives!—In short the picture of gloomy wo is heightened beyond any conception of fancy."[110]

Manager Green's daughter Ann Morton Green, called "Nancy," was the only casualty among the Placide & Green Company's cast and crew. She happened to be an audience member that evening, not on stage. Because the Greens did not expect her to be in attendance that evening, they were confused as to her whereabouts in the bedlam following the theater exodus. Young Henry Placide, being led home by his father, reported seeing Green exhausted and leaning against a fence, overlooking the "mass of smoking destruction." He reportedly heard the manager exclaim "Thank God! I prohibited Nancy from coming to the house to-night. She is safe."[111] He had not wanted Nancy to occupy a paid seat on a night when the house would be crowded. Unbeknownst to him, as the story goes, Nancy's teacher Mrs. Gibson had purchased Nancy a ticket so that she might attend with other girls from Gibson's boarding school.[112] Legend relays that when Frances Willems Green discovered her daughter was not at their boardinghouse, she rushed into the street, still in the wraithlike costume of the Bleeding Nun, and began hammering on Court End doors, seeking out her daughter in the houses where Nancy usually visited. She flew from house to house, drifting like a white apparition down Marshall, Clay, and Eleventh Streets, appearing in neighborhood doorways, startling inhabitants in her costume, smeared with artificial blood.[113]

And it was real tragedy, for Nancy Green, by one account, had progressed as far as the inner ticket door of the theater, having "bustled" her way through the burning theater while holding the hand of her friend, a Miss McMurdo. The two were moving toward the exit when a would-be rescuer in the foyer grasped McMurdo's free hand and pulled her out violently, forcing her to let go of her companion. Green was heard to scream, "Ah! Don't leave me!" before a volley of smoke blindingly rushed in.[114] It was thought that in the resulting darkness, Green could not locate the stair that led to the exit and fell as she attempted to find it. She died of suffocation, probably no more than twenty feet from safety.

Girardin repeatedly circled the building, peering into the ruins and sifting through the crowds before he fled to his nearby home for a final time to see if his wife and son were there. They were not. His brother-in-law was probably waiting, hovering within the door, bracing himself to share the news. In the crush, Polly's brother had taken her and her son under his protection, but the three were repeatedly separated. After her second attempt to recover her son, who had been torn from her, Polly disappeared from her brother's view. It appeared, in the words of a reporter, "that this excellent lady fell a victim to maternal love!" At his brother-in-law's news, Girardin wrote that his worst "fears were realized; and all remaining hopes vanished."[115]

After ensuring his son's safety, Robert Greenhow dashed back to the theater to find Mary Ann, but he was repelled by "Death & destruction."[116] In a state of frantic distraction, he paced outside the theater for hours, searching for her in the blackness and ash, even when there were plainly no more survivors.[117]

Copland's was a tainted joy. When he crossed the street to enter his home, his household slaves were probably moving about at the windows, tending to the wounded; proximity to the theater meant it likely that the injured were brought into his home too to await medical attention. Upon entering his house, mud on his feet, reeking of smoke and perspiration, his heart rose in a sudden rush of relief. The evening certainly had its moments of overwhelming joy and close embraces when one thought lost was found. Such a scene unfolded in Copland home that evening when Charles's eyes met those of his two exhausted boys. There was William. And there, Robert. But then followed a moment of debilitating despair—no Margaret. Copland penned a final sentence in his diary entry for December 27, 1811: "I found my two sons but my daughter was no more."[118]

* * *

The death count left Richmond—and all of America—in shock. Not only was this a powerful blow for the population of a high-spirited town, but also it was likely America's first disaster with large-scale civilian losses. Jeremiah Jeter, a young boy living in rural Virginia when news of the Richmond Theater fire sped across the state, explained in 1891, "We now hear of the sinking of a noble ocean steamer, with hundreds of valuable passengers on board, and hardly deem it necessary to inquire for her name, the latitude in which she sunk, of the causes of the direful catastrophe. It was far otherwise when the theatre was burned. The whole country was filled with amazement and sorrow. For weeks it was almost the only theme of conversation for hundreds of miles around the scene of the disaster."[119] Newspapers from New Hampshire's *Farmer's Cabinet* to South Carolina's *City Gazette* dispatched reports of the fire in exhaustive detail into the early months of 1812, and the event attracted international interest. The work of healing and restoration—as well as the search for the disaster's cause—began the next day.

3

LOSS

The disaster & grief seem to be universal. None has entirely escaped. Very many years
will pass away before the town recovers from the gloom, into which it has been plunged.
—JAMES MONROE, JANUARY 1, 1812

The public mind is estranged from everything save the horrible catastrophe at Richmond.
—*Petersburg Intelligencer*, DECEMBER 31, 1811

A s the sun rose, Richmond's residents, haggard and strained, returned to H Street with tools to sift through the smoldering rubble of the theater. Delegate Thomas Joynes nearly lost his life in the fire but was drawn back to the grounds the next morning. Later that Friday evening, he wrote to his brother in Accomack County, "I have this moment returned from the place of this melancho[l]y catastrophe, where great quantities of human carcases are to be seen which were not entirely consumed by the fire."[1] George Wythe Munford wandered with other boys to the ruins and watched men with rakes, shovels, and spades upturning and removing the charred remains of the dead from the immense pile of ashes where the ill-fated staircases had given way, It was more than young Munford and his companions could handle. Unaccustomed to such sickening sights, the boys fled the scene in amazement and horror.[2]

John Coalter, a judge on the Supreme Court of Appeals in Virginia, was not in town for the holiday, but he apparently arrived soon after. To his father-in-law, distinguished jurist St. George Tucker, Coalter wrote: "The wretched survivors were all next day engaged in drawing the half-consumed bodies from the ruins, many of which they were able by one means or another, to identify."[3] For the most part, the remains within the crumbled walls were unidentifiable and could scarcely be disentangled for individual burial.[4] A letter to the editor of the *Mercantile Advertiser* reported that men digging out bodies found "they are so burnt to a cinder, that but one out of those taken out has been recognized."[5] Incinerated bone fragments littered the area and crunched underfoot, disarmingly recreating the sounds of the oyster shell walkways so common in Tidewater Virginia. The commingled ashes and bones were poured into sheets and laid in the aisles of the Baptist church until final arrangements could be made.[6]

Plans for commemoration began before the coals had even cooled. The men who sat on Richmond's Common Council, the city's governing board, met the morning of December 27. Likely red-eyed and haggard from a long, sleepless night, they planned a response to the emergency. By the end of the meeting, William C. Williams, the Common Council president, signed into effect a multi-part ordinance and a course of action. Establishing a burial committee was one of their first steps. They authorized leading citizens Dr. John Adams, William Hay, Jr., Gabriel Ralston, and John G. Gamble to form the Burial Committee, which would oversee the collection of the remains. In addition to directing the interment of the victims' ashes, which were "to be collected and deposited in such urns, coffins, or other suitable inclosures, as they may approve," the same committee was requested to regulate the time and order of the funeral procession.[7]

That afternoon, the Common Council met at the capitol with a large number of Richmond and Manchester citizens led by Mayor Benjamin Tate, and the group created three additional committees: one consisted of twelve men, "proper persons," assigned to visit the houses in each ward and Manchester, administering an impromptu census to determine how many families were affected and obtain an official death count. The second, headed by John Marshall, who had a way of being roped into nearly every civic fundraising effort, would begin a collection, "in concert with a committee from the Common Hall," for the building of a suitable monument. The Committee of Investigation was then commissioned to examine the causes of the fire.

The Burial Committee reported the discovery of identified bodies to family members, an unpleasant duty. One of the early discoveries was a young girl's corpse wearing a double gold chain, attached to a locket, with the inscription, "The gift of grand papa." Leroy Anderson, and probably other families of missing teenage daughters, received a communication from the Burial Committee of the finding, which Anderson gratefully remembered was made "in the kindest and most delicate manner." He knew immediately that it was his daughter Margaret. "My own child, dear little innocent, had buckled [it] round her neck that morning," recalled Anderson. "By this, *her* beloved relics were distinguished."[8] William Temple of the Burial Committee offered to return the locket to the Anderson family upon their request—otherwise it would stay with her remains. They also offered that she could be returned to the family for private burial. Anderson wrote back to Temple, thanking him for handling the matter with such sensitivity. "For your kind and tender attention accept the gratitude of a weeping father. Let the chain remain on her dear neck—I wish it not removed."[9] He requested Margaret's burial with her friends in the mass grave although he was one of the few who could have exercised the option to have her interred in a family plot. He would explain why later, to his friend, U.S. representative Matthew Clay.

Governor George Smith's body was another of the few identified. A Richmond resident witnessed what was left and wrote, "His remains I saw taken from the ruins (which was designated by a stock buckle which he wore,) a crisped lump."[10] Maria Nelson's body was identified by her engraved brass watch.[11] According to several accounts, jewelry also identified Sally Conyers and Lieutenant Gibbon, neither of whom had escaped from the theater alive.[12]

Gibbon's valor and assurance that Lynch could "leave Sally to me" could not surmount the effects of carbon monoxide, nor the limitations of a handicap that went unmentioned by Gibbon's eulogizers. Only years later in an offhand comment by Richmond historian and doctor John P. Little would it come to light when he dryly noted that Gibbon, "had lost an arm in the war with Tripoli, and being thus crippled, was unable to render proper assistance to his charge."[13] After widespread newspaper accounts reported that the naval officer and the blonde orphan were found in the ruins holding each other tightly, their tragic romance captivated the nation's imagination and spawned saccharine poems for decades. Probably due to the effusive verses and subsequent fictional accounts, the pair became a critical part of the 1811 theater fire legend and two of its most memorialized victims. A century later, they were among a handful of the dead still remembered.

* * *

Blacksmith Gilbert Hunt returned to H Street the next morning, still hoping to locate Louisa Mayo. He recalled later that his heart shuddered at the things which met his eye—the pile of "half-burned bodies," lying there together. "Some of them were so badly burned that it was almost impossible to recognize them. Others were almost uninjured; yet life had left their bodies, and there they lay, cold, and stiff, and dead."[14]

"I never found my young mistress," Hunt reported to his biographer, who noted the teardrops standing in his eyes.[15] Hunt would remember Mayo for instructing him in the alphabet and the Scriptures—as he put it, "teaching me my book every night."[16] Only a small percentage of slaves achieved some degree of literacy, and learning from white children was one of the chief ways in which slaves became literate.[17] To an enslaved man or woman, literacy was a tool for self-determination; it provided a sense of self-worth, and it opened a path to liberation.[18] It is not surprising that many slave owners—particularly after the Nat Turner rebellion in 1831—had a strong interest in keeping their slaves illiterate, and several southern states passed harsh laws forbidding reading lessons for free blacks, mulattos, and slaves. Virginia's, issued in April of 1831, forbade meetings of free blacks or mulattos for the purpose of mutual literacy instruction and forbade whites to instruct members of either group in reading or writing or to receive compensation for educating slaves. In 1849, slaves, free blacks, and mulattos were all forbidden from "assemblage for the purpose of instruction in reading or writing, by whomsoever conducted." Although few were actually prosecuted under these laws, whites acting as teachers could be fined up to a hundred dollars or confined in jail for six months.[19] Gilbert Hunt became a prominent black leader in Richmond, a successful business owner, and a free man—there is no doubt that his ability to read contributed to his accomplishments and set him apart. Her contribution to his achievements would be Louisa's legacy.

The theater grounds remained a place of activity for several weeks. While the poor and slaves probably pulled salvageable pieces of wood from the ruins to use as winter fuel, little boys, servants, morbid tourists, and other curious townsfolk sorted through the rubble to uncover souvenirs from the blaze. Well into January, postings appeared in the *Enquirer* advertising lost and found items at the site: a large bunch of keys, a red morocco pocketbook, silver spectacles. The Burial Committee deposited all gems, watches, and valuables they'd uncovered with a member of the committee, "to be delivered to the relatives of the deceased when called for."[20]

LETTERS OF LOSS

"Every thing we see around us seems shrouded with grief," lamented Rev. John Blair in a sermon following the fire. "Every surviving citizen of Richmond

& Manchester wears today the badge of woe & on whatever sign we turn, whithersoever we direct our steps, we behold the deeply distressed mourners going about the streets."[21] All that was unknown in the first twenty-four hours created a great strain. Friday morning and throughout the weekend, relatives and friends sought to locate the missing and injured. Men and women wrapped themselves in overcoats and trudged through the winter streets, paying calls to friends, gathering in the taverns, hoping to glean information about acquaintances. An observer in Richmond wrote, "During the next day, two persons could scarcely meet without exchanging expressions full of solicitude; 'Have you lost any of your family?'—'Is your family safe?'—'I am glad of it, I am glad of it!'"[22] The dozens of local taverns and coffeehouses, with their walls of messages and placards and collections of newspapers, probably served, as they always did in a time of crisis, as hubs of information.

The post delivered hurriedly written letters the next day to notify friends and family of the losses—and the salvations. Throughout Virginia was universal gloom; in every part of the state were some who had lost a friend or a relative in the disaster.[23] Dispatches from Virginia traveled via horse or boat to the major cities of Boston, New York, Philadelphia, and the U.S. capital, where the Virginian president and his administration had many a connection to the affected city. The news took two days to reach Washington, D.C., and three to reach Philadelphia. On December 30, in his commonplace book, physician and eminent revolutionary Benjamin Rush noted, "This day the awful news of the burning of the Theatre in Richmond reached [Philadelphia]. . . . It took place on the 26th of this month."[24]

"During the gleeful Christmas days" of 1811 in rural Bedford County, Virginia, young Jeremiah Jeter had learned of the Richmond Theater fire from an uncle, who bore the news from the post office. "It made a profound impression on my boyish imagination," he wrote. "Of a theatre I had little or no knowledge, but I had a vivid conception of the horrors of being consumed in a burning building. No event in all my early years produced such a deep, pervasive, and enduring impression in the State as did the conflagration of the theatre and the deplorable sufferings and losses by which it was accompanied."[25]

From Richmond, grief radiated like a starburst throughout the world, tracing lines from victims to their relatives in Great Britain, colleagues on the Continent, fellow planters and lawyers in Tidewater and Piedmont Virginia, and into the American frontier, where hardier kinsmen had ventured. Some victims' loved ones were impossible to reach, like Englishman Patrick Gibson, a talented flutist and business partner of Thomas Jefferson's nephew George who was visiting the European continent.[26] Gibson also ran a girls' boarding school in Richmond from his home, "Spring Hill" on Leigh Street, with his wife Eleanor Sanderson Gibson. Eleanor had perished in the fire.[27] Those overseas might wait five to ten weeks before learning their family members' fates.

John Coalter calculated the losses for his father-in-law St. George Tucker in Williamsburg the Sunday morning after the fire: "We have seen a list of sixty odd of the victims and are told that double that number have fallen. . . . Great God!" After listing the fates of as many family friends as he could remember he added, "I feel as if I was too fortunate in being absent from this danger; and that the deep distress which I must witness and participate is much below my share of the general Calamity—God avert such from me and mine!"[28] Coalter's nearly frantic brother-in-law Henry St. George Tucker in Winchester, Virginia, penned a late January letter to St. George Tucker filled with gratitude upon discovering that Coalter and his wife lived. "I glanced rapidly over the names of persons whom I had known and respected and who were no more. . . . Thanks be to gods, we have been saved from the great misery of giving to lament a relative lost by so fearful a death!"[29]

Merchant Robert Gamble fired off two letters to his friend, U.S. congressman James Breckinridge, in Washington, D.C., posting the scanty information that he had in those first hours. It seems he penned the first missive on "Friday night 2. O clk." amid the confusion of the still-burning fire. Having missed the stagecoach that set out that night with the news, he dispatched "one of my Troopers" to deliver the message to Breckinridge "that your mind might be relieved."[30] He listed around fifteen known dead but remarked this was a "very inconsiderable part of those now known to be lost." Later that same Friday, Gamble penned a second letter to Breckinridge, hoping "my letter will relieve you of the apprehensions you must have felt by merely getting the rumour without any of the particulars," and providing an expanded list of the dead. He admitted the city might never know exactly how many had died. "Upwards of 60 are I understand known to have perished of course from the number of strangers now in Town many are yet unknown."[31]

Dr. Phillip Barraud had extensive connections across the state; he had practiced medicine in both Williamsburg and Norfolk and apprenticed under

Dr. McClurg of Richmond during the Revolutionary War. He and his wife, the musically gifted Anne Blaws Hansford, daughter of a Williamsburg physician, moved in 1799 from his snug white home in Williamsburg to Norfolk, where he assumed superintendence over the Marine Hospital. While many of his closest associates had lived through the theater fire, their poignant letters overwhelmed the doctor. "[The] day before I got your last letter in a Hand Bill by the Southern Mail," Barraud wrote to his dear friend St. George Tucker from Norfolk on December 31, "I can by no means describe to you the half that [the letters have thrown] my mind into, for the last two days I am almost incapable of performing my usual occupations, as of thinking of any other subjects."[32] Greenhow's plight in particular must have affected him—Dr. James Greenhow, brother to Robert, had been his medical protégé.[33]

With regret and fatigue, Leroy Anderson, the schoolmaster of a female academy in Williamsburg, pulled a chair to his desk Friday the twenty-seventh to pen a bleak letter to Matthew Clay, Esq., his friend and a fellow widower.[34] At the time, Clay, a Danville, Virginia, native and Revolutionary War veteran, was in Washington, D.C., serving his eighth term in the U.S. House of Representatives. The men's daughters Margaret Anderson and Mary Clay, probably in town for the social season like many others, attended the Thursday play with Sally Gatewood and Lucy Gwathmey. The four girls had been inseparable friends, all about sixteen years of age.

Anderson began: "I have a tale of horror to tell; prepare to hear of the most awful calamity that ever plunged a whole city into affliction. Yes, all Richmond is in tears: children have lost their parents, parents have lost their children. Yesterday a beloved daughter gladdened my heart with her innocent smiles; to-day she is in Heaven! God gave her to me, and God—yes, it has pleased Almighty God to take her from me." He dispensed the crushing news: "O! sir, feel for me, and not for me only; arm yourself with fortitude, whilst I discharge the mournful duty of telling you, that you have to feel also for yourself. Yes, for it must be told, you also were the father of an amiable daughter, now, like my beloved child, gone to join her mother in Heaven."[35]

Anderson told of how he had been separated in the confusion from his two daughters and sister. He had never found his precious Margaret or her best friend Mary. After five paragraphs, unable to write any longer, powerless to capture the "horrors that language has no terms to represent . . . awful, shocking, maddening scene," he closed. "Oh, sir, you can have no idea of the general consternation—the universal grief that pervades this city—but why do I speak of that? I scarcely know what I write to you. Farewell. In haste and in deep affliction, Leroy Anderson."[36]

Grappling with the sad news of the fire delayed important legislative information and affected Clay's legislator-constituent communications. In a late January letter, he begged forgiveness of his constituents for the lateness of his correspondence with them. He explained he had suffered a "dreadful affliction with which I have been visited in the agonizing loss of a beloved daughter, who perished in Richmond on the fatal night of the 26th Dec., last, a night of sorrow and distress, which the lapse of no time can efface from my heart." The news he delayed was word of the impending War of 1812.[37]

Outside the Scottish fishing town of Kirkcudbright, James Brown awaited a letter from his son William, a highly respected bachelor and merchant.[38] William's letters arrived regularly in Scotland, written in a neat hand, sealed with dark wax. Like his two brothers in Richmond, James and John, William had done well for himself after immigrating to Virginia, and he sent money earned at his Lynchburg business to his family.

James received a letter in a different hand in February 1812. This letter was on a large nine-by-fourteen-inch piece of linen folio paper, folded into a small rectangle and sealed as his son William's always were. But the lettering was hasty and tall with dramatic swaths of ink, very unlike his son's hand. James broke the seal. It was from his grandson, William Black. The unmarried William Brown had gone to spend the holidays with his family in Richmond. Black wrote to his grandfather that he was "sorry to have to relate the panefull knews of the death of your much esteemed son William, in the night of the 26th Decer. The Theater caught fire & in making his escape throe one of the windows of the second story he being so much injured by the fall that he only survived a few moments—upwards of a hundred persons lost there lives, there is no doubt but the knews of his death most be panefull to you & family but more so to those relations he has left in this country."[39]

Scottish immigrants to Virginia, William Smart and his sisters Mary and Ann were left orphans in their new country soon after arriving in 1799. A local woman took in Mary and a silversmith named William Rogers took on William as an apprentice. William's sister Ann went to live with the Nelson family in Richmond, where she probably helped to run their boardinghouse. William sent a letter to his "respected relations," Scots who lived in London, in January, assuring them that both he and his sisters were safe. William noted that the dead included "two girls living at the Nelsons, Maria Nelson and Mary Page, two young ladies out of the family in which my sister lives, & had she been in town would most certainly have accompanied them, fortunately she was on a visit to my sister Mary, who now lives in the county of Louisa."[40]

An Elizabeth Page also died—she may have been a relation to Mary. Robert Gamble, in his personal catalog of the dead, parenthetically listed reasons for each victim's death or short descriptions to aid his correspondent in distinguishing them, such as "Widow" or "killed getting out" or "Anderson School." After noting the death of "Mrs. Page," Gamble wrote: "fat."[41]

TALLYING AND REPORTING THE LOSSES

Facts were still muddy that first weekend after the blaze, the number of losses and the names still pure conjecture; estimates of the dead ranged from fifty to several hundred.[42] The *Enquirer,* in an early report, stated on December 31 that the city still had at least fifty unclaimed remains and a skull count of over two hundred, although on the twenty-eighth, they had published the official list of the dead and missing commissioned by the group of Richmond citizens, which listed only sixty-one dead.[43] A correspondent of the editor of the *Baltimore Federal Gazette* recorded that the death count was "supposed to be nearly two hundred, from the number of sculls taken out of the building," and a widely published letter from Richmond to a correspondent in Boston judged that one hundred and fifty perished.[44] The condition of the recovered bodies and the fact that victims continued to perish from their injuries for the next few months made an exact count difficult, but by the first week of January the city arrived at an official number: seventy-two identified dead, sixty-six of whom were white, six black.

The American public was eager for lists of names, numbers, details, and ranks. Yet the victim lists collected by the citizens' committee and those printed in newspapers across the country lacked information basic by today's standards. Females were known mainly by their surnames, and married women's Christian names were almost never provided on the lists. "Two Miss Trouins" or "Mrs. Thomas Wilson" often sufficed. What bits of identifying information the list provided were haphazardly tacked on, as is illustrated by "John Welch, a stranger, nephew to Sir A. Pigott, late from England,"

"Pleasant, a mulatto woman," "Nuttle [Nuttal], Carpenter." Precise ages were not provided on the lists; but then, that information may have been a mystery even to close family members or a person him- or herself. In an 1809 letter to his father in Scotland, fire victim William Brown had asked in an earnest postscript: "In your next please mention the day, month & year I was born not being intirely certain that I know my age."[45] Obituaries made age a matter of conjecture, indicating that even the close friends and family who wrote them were uncertain of loved ones' ages: in the *Enquirer,* when they met their deaths, Charlotte Raphael was "about five years old" and Benjamin Botts "was in the 36 or 37th year of his life."

Obituary notices, most tributes penned by friends or admirers, trickled into the *Enquirer* office. The lengths ranged wildly, as did the tone. Usually labeled simply, "For the *Enquirer,*" contributed obituaries often incorporated poetry and usually included elaborate descriptions of the deceased's talents, qualities, hobbies, and even mannerisms. With few exceptions, the reader-contributed obituaries were written for young women, but not many were written at all. In total, fewer than twenty victims had their passings noted by an obituary.

An *Enquirer* correspondent defended the publishing of special tributes but understood the opposing view: "There are those perhaps, who deeming the disaster to be of such a character & vastness as must abrogate discriminations of distress and degrees of estimation, or who influenced by the deep sense of their own severe issues and affliction, will have objection to seeing individual victims of the late appalling and mournful catastrophe, distinguished by particular testimonials and a separate tribute of sorrow. . . . It must be difficult too for attention in a season of universal desolation to find place for delineations of individual merit, or the expression of personal distress."[46]

Several cities released special edition papers to keep up with reader fascination. Richmond's *American Standard,* for example, issued a single-sheet "extra" edition on December 27 with a wide black mourning border, containing a list of the dead, the Common Council statement, and a narrative by the editor. One correspondent noted the difficulty of obtaining new stories in Richmond that week:

> We have taken uncommon pains to collect an authentic narrative of the events of this disastrous night; we have requested the aid of every person who *we had heard* was capable of furnishing any information, and

to whom the subject was not too tender to be mentioned; yet it is with some pain we have failed in our efforts. . . . There were few persons so cool and collected as to be able to illustrate the horrors of that night. . . . Some who have promised to reduce their narrative to paper, have been prevented from doing so by their engagements or their feelings.[47]

The correspondent longing for more firsthand accounts could wheedle none from Richmond's grieving population.

Most readers outside and inside Richmond received particulars about the disaster not from personal letters, but via newspapers, even in the nation's hinterlands. In May 1812, one Virginian wrote to her brother in Louisiana territory, "No doubt, the papers have long since furnished you with accounts of that ever memorable catastrophe, too horrible for me to attempt a description of!"[48]

John O'Lynch, a printer from Richmond, began collecting reports from various committees and newspapers, compiling them into a slapdash chapbook, more of a souvenir pamphlet, to be released mid-January. About a half-dozen more such books would be cobbled together in the next few months, most relying on the body of O'Lynch's *Narrative & Report of the Causes and Circumstances of the Deplorable Conflagration at Richmond from Letters and Authentic Documents* as the prototype, and usually pinning a diatribe in the front against the theater or a polemic with the author's theological take on the Richmond calamity.[49] The little pamphlets, printed on uneven sheets of paper and bound with simple stitching, were priced for wide circulation at about twelve cents apiece and became a main source of fire news for the international audience.

Reminiscent of the "last confession" pamphlets printed about convicted murderers, these popular volumes presaged similar books churned out on the American presses after other high-profile catastrophes in subsequent centuries. In their critics' opinion, such works reeked of opportunism. "The first thought which strikes every reader of this pamphlet, will be the motive of its publication—the subject matter of it has been published in all the daily papers, whence the whole contents are copied, word for word—all, save the luminous unparalleled prefatory address," an editorialist in Philadelphia's *The Cynick* magazine sarcastically wrote. At worst, he thought these volumes profited from and trafficked in "publick grief" or were "the attempt of some holy miscreant to vent his disappointed and pestilent humour against pleasures which he is forbidden to enjoy."[50]

* * *

Theater fire victims were overwhelmingly women—most either teenagers of debutante age or mothers.[51] A nineteenth-century historian wrote, "Most of the dead were females of the higher walks of life: their position in the boxes, their helplessness and terror, their inflammable dresses, all combined to render them peculiar objects of injury."[52] Perhaps pointing to this fact, the *Massachusetts Baptist Missionary Magazine* of March 1812 called the fire "a catastrophe . . . unparalleled in its destruction of domestic happiness."[53]

In the newspaper and personal letters, nearly all males who died reportedly did so attempting to save a stranded female or a child. This is not likely true but rather a defensive default setting in the face of the sad facts: fifty-four of the dead were female, eighteen were male. That two out of three victims were female threw into question Virginia's reputation for male gallantry.

A much-imitated engraving of the burning theater by Benjamin Tanner of Philadelphia sensationalized the fire, but was rooted in true, first-person descriptions.[54] Men hang from flaming casements; fire belches from the bulls-eye window. A mad tangle of people fills every unshuttered windowpane and, knotted together, struggles through the door. Bystanders forcibly prevent a man and a woman from reentering the building, while others embrace gratefully, having found each other in the yard. The escapees are in disarray: half the men have lost their hats; women are coatless, hair waving wild, feet bare on the winter ground. Victims, pale and naked, are carried from the scene on makeshift stretchers and slings made of cloaks. Ladies wander deliriously, eyes rolled upward in distraction, and enough hands are in the air to cause suspicion that a revival meeting is about. It is a bloody bedlam. And in the lower right-hand corner, a group of composed men, hats and coats on, calmly observe the action, pointing and conferring among themselves. One holds what appears to be a fire bucket, but it hangs at his side. The group seems even to block the way of a man fleeing with a bloodied baby in his arms. In other, derivative versions, the men lean forward as though intending to walk toward the building, but when partnered with the printed record, the testimony of Tanner's picture bears out.

Eyewitnesses reported that the behavior of the theater's men was often less than commendable. Some openly admitted it. Michael Hancock, the sword-wielding survivor who monopolized the window, later begged oblique apology for his actions, "All ceremony was forgotten in conforming to the first law of nature," he rationalized.[55] In a letter to the editor of the *Enquirer,* Gurden Bacchus, who had assumed responsibility for three women, wrote, "The flame and hot smoke of turpentine and paint reached my hair, my right ear, and curled round my head.—I inhaled it, my nose was burnt, all reflection was selfishness, I sprang to the window and leaned about 12 feet from the house and about 30 feet from the ground."[56] Two of his female companions perished.

Ann Dent Hayes McRae, wife of a distinguished statesman, wandered without assistance in the dark, left entirely to her own devices until part of the building plummeted next to her and she had enough light to see a window opening. Her sister Delia Hayes was repeatedly trampled, but a gentleman at the landing of the stairs pulled her from the mass of insentient women at the staircase and saved her life.[57] Miss Couch, the "delicate young lady . . . without any particular protector" later found collapsed on the road, attempted to make her way to the window during the fire when "she was several times thrown back by inhuman selfish men," according to one troubled observer, before she made her own escape with a last desperate effort.[58]

When Representative John G. Jackson, who plunged into the pit when the stairway broke, became conscious, he discovered a woman was clinging to him, unable to stand. She was a stranger, but he picked her up bodily, straining to see through the smoke as he determined the way from the pit to the lobby door. Although he cut a helpless figure with a full-grown woman in his arms, he could not obtain any assistance from the men in the theater. "In this effort to find the way out I saw several gentlemen running to and fro to whom I addressed the enquiry 'which is the way out?' but obtained no answer," he later wrote. Moments after he located the door, the roof fell in behind him, making further rescue attempts nearly impossible. Yet he knew that in the minutes before the collapse, more could have—and should have—been done by the nearby men. "I do not know if any or how many got out after we did, but I am confident that if those from without had ran in," he conjectured, "many who fell by the suffocation and were burned before they regained strength to rise would have been saved."[59]

Provocatively, a Baltimore newspaper insinuated that if the fire had occurred in Baltimore, the numbers of men and women lost would not have been so disproportionate: Maryland's men would have behaved far more gallantly toward the fairer sex.[60] This launched a printed scuffle between Maryland and Virginia over chivalry. Editor Ritchie of the *Enquirer* took issue with Baltimore's "illiberal insinuation," although, he admitted, "we are not so much bigotted in favour of the people of this city as to think that in the midst of so tremendous a scene so apt to shake reason on her throne by the contention of the passions, there might not have been some individuals who too readily listened to the laws of self-preservation." Yet such men were only a small part of the story, Ritchie contended. "We may say, on the other hand, that there were proofs of as gallant and heroic devotion to the cause of woman and of virtue as any city can boast of."[61]

The ever-pragmatic Ritchie denied that the imbalanced death ratio was anything but a result of physical causes. His first reason was that the men gave the best box seats to women and instead took their own seats in the pit, from which it was easier to escape, as was the case with Delegate Samuel Hughes. Ritchie argued, "The disproportion in the number of those who have perished is scarcely greater than of those who sat in the boxes." Yet, each male survivor who published an account in Ritchie's paper (and only men published accounts of their survival) held a box seat.[62] Ritchie also contended that men were physically unable to help the women when the pressure of the crowd separated the men from their companions and that children were the men's rescue priority, less so their wives, who were then left to their own devices.

Male eyewitnesses printed in Ritchie's own paper proffered proof of cowardice. David Doyle, writing in to the *Enquirer,* suggested Richmond's men saved themselves at any expense, even if this meant injuring women. He reported that many women had been "frequently knocked down" during their journey out of the theater and others were ignored in their distress. "I received *all the ladies* from that window and no man assisted one of them," he wrote with amazement at the numbers of "unfeeling men."[63] A male survivor who lost his mother to the flames described victims of the mob in a chilling scene of desperation, "In one wretched group, eight mothers of families, who were forced into a corner by the croud—their clothes on fire they clung franticly together; and thus embracing, were seen to sink into eternity!!!"[64]

Mindful of the controversy, at least one man demanded vindication in print. On January 7, John G. Jackson, the young delegate from Harrison County (in what is now West Virginia) who had provided a statement about his escape in the January 2 *Enquirer,* requested the editor correct his story. As

Jackson initially related, he met Mary Love Scott when they were both halfway to the stairs, and he encouraged her to be calm. It would seem the Scott family was unhappy with Jackson's egregious omission of *Mr.* Scott. The accusations of incivility perhaps had already formed enough of an angry undercurrent that Richard Scott, a vocal delegate, was anxious to have his gallantry affirmed. "I was not so explicit in my statement concerning the burning of the Theatre as I should have been," Jackson apologized. "Mrs. Scott the lady I referred to, was all the time I saw her attended by her husband. I request a favor of you to insert this explanation so that if any erroneous impressions have been made they may be corrected."[65]

In his red diary, Charles Copland recorded that he entered the building three times. The first two times Copland carried a woman outside to the yard. "Spectators," as he referred to them, met him part way in the yard and from there took the women into their care, but even after seeing that Copland was successfully rescuing live victims, "no one followed me" into the theater, he wrote in exasperation. Copland described his work as a solo effort, ringed by an interested and largely idle audience, and at the time he left, there were still more women abandoned and helpless in the lobby.[66] But it is certain that more rescue attempts happened after Copland left the lobby. G. Tucker, eyewitness and rescuer, related that he and others helped evacuate women from the very lobby Copland had entered. He and several other "very active" men set about helping the women lying limp and half-naked in the landing. Tucker began by picking up the smallest, and he carried her to the outer door. Several other men joined him in relaying the ladies out, and they succeeded in removing all those who were unconscious on the lower flight of stairs.[67]

Over time, residual embarrassment over episodes of ungallant behavior was almost completely eclipsed by the stories of selflessness and courage (however apocryphal) enshrined in memorial and literature. In 1859, biographer Philip Barrett broadcast the fine examples of sacrifice among the outbreaks of base self-interest. "But, in the midst of terrors which roused the selfishness of human nature to its utmost strength, there were displays of love in death, which make the heart bleed with pity. Fathers were seen rushing back into the flames to save their children; mothers were calling in frenzied tones for their daughters; and were with difficulty dragged from the building; husbands and wives refused to leave each other, and met death together; even friends lost life in endeavouring to save those under their care."[68]

Some of the men who played the hero's role that day later chastised themselves for not doing more. Despite his bravery and numerous successful rescues, Charles Copland was plagued with guilt and dark memories of the helpless women he left alone.[69] But other men were filled with a sense of pride in their acts. The indefatigable tutor David Doyle wrote to Ritchie, "The most pleasing part of my life was that which I spent in the act of preservation."[70]

* * *

Slaves may have taken advantage of the theater fire's confusion to slip out of their owners' oversight and escape to freedom. Trying to stem the inexhaustible tide of runaways was a never-ending pursuit, and local newspaper classified sections posted notices about runaway slaves in every issue, almost without exception. Slaves didn't always run north, away from Richmond; they often stayed in the area, where they had friends, family, or a spouse. In 1811, James Semple offered ten dollars for anyone who would apprehend "old Isham, about 60 years old, a tall black man, with one glass eye." The indignant owner wrote that Isham ran away "without even a word" and he suspected the man was "lurking . . . in Richmond."[71] In 1812, a man named Dick ran away from the Dunns in Tappahannock, Virginia, about a fifty-mile journey from the capital. Dinah Dunn suspected Dick fled to Richmond as "the said fellow has a wife in the town of Richmond, at Mrs. Robert Vonard's." She offered fifteen dollars plus travel expenses for anyone who would return him.[72]

When the call of fire and the crush of the crowd began on December 26, blacks in the gallery, like everyone else, left by the way they entered. "The coloured people in the gallery, most of them escaped through the stairs cut off from the house. . . . The pit and boxes had but one common avenue, through which the whole crowd escaped, save those only who leaped through the windows," remembered an eyewitness.[73] The gallery-sitters thus exited with far less fuss and obstruction. Once they emerged, all was chaos outside. It would not have been surprising or impossible for a slave to bolt in the midst of the confusion. Who would notice? The work of rescue and nursing the hundreds of injured would have absorbed the masses surrounding the theater. The night watch would have been obligated to tend to the fire under the presiding warden.[74]

On the initial death count list, Nancy Patterson, a "woman of colour," has an interesting addendum after her name—"supposed to have perished." An enslaved male, Philadelphia, was listed not as dead, but "missing." In the darkness and disorder, it may have been that Nancy Patterson and Philadelphia took stock of their situation and slipped into a Court End alley; escaping that evening not only from death but also from slavery.[75]

* * *

Besides the grisly nature of the event in Richmond, the disaster engaged the public imagination in America and Europe for another reason: its victims were principally wealthy, notable, and significant. "It was a catastrophe, in many respects without precedent," reported an 1894 article in the *Washington Post,* "considering that of the 600 people who had assembled on the occasion . . . not less than a tenth of the number fell victims to the conflagration, and among these were many of the most distinguished citizens of the town."[76] Over 90 percent of the victims by some estimations were members of the upper classes. One Richmond elite wrote in a panic to a friend in Washington, D.C., in the hours after the fire: "The Richmond Theatre has been burnt & in it very many of our most respectable & valueable citizens all yours are safe so are Mr. Wickhams most providentially & Mr. Monroes friends."[77] Because of the victims' status and its international impact, in 1908 the *Washington Post* registered the Richmond Theater fire as one of the nine "Great Fire Disasters of the Past," although it had the fewest casualties by far of the international events on the roll.[78]

Sixty-five years after the Richmond Theater burned, another tragic fire claiming four times the number of victims occurred in Brooklyn in December 1876—the worst of the thirty-odd serious theater fires inflicted on New York City that century.[79] A thousand people had congregated in the house; three hundred perished. Yet commentators considered the disaster less consequential than the inferno in Richmond. After all, the attendees in New York were not citizens of note, but rather the kind of people who would attend the lowbrow entertainments exhibited in Brooklyn: "depraved and fast young people, and the coarse and vulgar . . . of all ages," inferred the *New York Observer,* a Presbyterian magazine. In the *Observer's* judgment, even though Brooklyn's catastrophe was "one of the most shocking events in the history of the drama," it did not merit the attention due the Richmond fire. "The Richmond fire, in [1811], is terribly conspicuous in the list because of the social position of those who fell victims, the Governor of the State being among them." In the case of the Brooklyn fire, however, "among all those hundreds burned, not one, except the two actors [Mr. Murdoch and Mr. Burroughs], were persons of distinction in the community, and on that account the social effect of the tragedy is less powerful." The journalist added halfheartedly, "But they were all somebody's friends."[80]

* * *

Perhaps the greatest blow in 1811 for Richmond—for the whole state of Virginia—was the loss of its leader, Governor George William Smith. A collaborator and peacemaker, the former state legislator from Essex County took firm political stands while leaving "not one enemy behind," according to his heartfelt obituary.[81] Most accounts concurred that he emerged from the fire alive. They also reported that he looked around in search of someone and then reentered the burning building, where he met his death. The person for whom the forty-nine-year-old father was searching remained unclear. Editor Thomas Ritchie of the *Richmond Enquirer,* an escapee of the blaze himself, wrote, "It is not certainly known whether he had . . . rushed again into the flames to save his child!"[82] Whatever his object was, the governor's reentry meant an unfortunate death.

Without Smith's guidance, the executive branch nearly fell apart in the week after the fire. Peyton Randolph, the senior member of the Executive Council and interim governor, submitted a rather desperate memo to the legislature on December 31, 1811, regarding Smith's death. "This unhappy occurrence . . . has left the Executive Department in such a state of disorganization as to create serious doubt whether under the existing laws, there is any [one] competent to discharge the important duties which belong to that branch of the government. Feeling myself great reluctance to exercise powers which are in any degree doubtful, it will not be deemed improper of me to suggest the expediency of supplying the vacancy, as soon as possible."[83] The Virginia Constitution directed the legislature to choose the governor and his council, not a direct vote by the people of Virginia.[84] On January 3, 1812, the beleaguered General Assembly elected Speaker of the House James

Barbour, a wealthy Presbyterian lawyer and the delegate from Orange, to take Smith's place for a one-year term. Not a month previously, Smith had defeated James Barbour in the gubernatorial election by joint ballot of both houses of the legislature.

The much-lamented George William Smith did not receive a personal tribute in the news until a full month after the fire. After an embarrassing public silence on the executive branch's loss, a writer floridly protesting his unfitness took up the task of writing an obituary in the *Enquirer*. "I awaited in anxious solicitude for this fond evidence of affectionate regard. Unfitted as I am for such a subject not from a want of inclination to do it justice but from want of ability to pourtray it in its proper colors, I approach it with presentiments that peculiarly disqualify me," he wrote, before recalling his subject's courage and mental vigor.[85]

The governor was, however, recognized through other channels. In a brief handwritten resolution dated December 27 and adopted on December 28, the legislature of Virginia had expressed "profound sorrow" over the loss of Governor Smith as well as the other "worthy and meritorious citizens" who perished in the flames.[86] For a month, the state legislators wore black crape armbands in special memory of the statesman.[87]

Releasing a resolution from a meeting at the Eagle Tavern on Tuesday the thirty-first of December 1811, Richmond's Nineteenth Regiment, over whom Smith, a colonel, had been commanding officer, went one better than state legislators and declared they would wear their black armbands for two full months in Smith's memory.[88] Although the regiment desired to confer upon him a military funeral with full honors, they demurred, suspecting that another memorial observance might prolong "sensations which are already too afflicting."[89]

INVESTIGATION

With public anger simmering and questions of blame beginning to surface, the Common Council established a Committee of Investigation to inquire into the fire's causes.[90] The council chose committee members with a reputation for rationality: real-estate investor and glass-factory owner Samuel G. Adams, who was acquainted with fire prevention in a high-risk environment; lawyer William Marshall; and editor Thomas Ritchie of the *Enquirer*. After two days of climbing through the wreckage and pigeonholing Placide & Green employees, the committee released the report on December 30.[91] They had discovered the cause, beyond a doubt. Within days, national newspapers had spread the report to all corners of the United States.

Placide & Green company manager Alexander Placide knew his theater company stood liable for the carnage and destruction, and he was eager to clear the company's name, however possible, lest he be ruined. Early on the twenty-seventh, he desperately submitted an allegation to the *Enquirer*, suggesting that the fire was a result of arson. "Last night about 700 persons were in the theatre, at my benefit . . . alas! The audience suffered beyond the power of language to express. . . . This has been the work of some worse than vile incendiary, as two attempts had been made before, during the night, which were frustrated by the guards of the theatre."[92] Arson was, at the time, a fairly common source of Richmond's fires, and factories and businesses often made fine targets. In October 1810, a hefty portion of city pillar John Mayo's property, including his stables and granary, was destroyed. The investigators reported, "There is too much reason to apprehend that it was the work of some diabolical incendiary. On Sunday night another attempt was made at the same place. . . . It was happily discovered and extinguished without its doing much injury."[93] Earlier that May another suspicious fire had destroyed the Merchant Mill on the James River Canal with all its contents.[94]

Even so, the Committee of Investigation's exhaustive report did not confirm Placide's allegations. In fact, when they interviewed nine employees, every eyewitness watched the chandelier start the fire. Placide's arson theory was the assertion of a man anxious for exoneration. Surprisingly, however, it appears that neither individuals nor the city pressed charges against the Placide & Green Company, and records do not indicate that Richmond's leaders held the stagehands responsible for the fire. Instead, the Committee of Investigation astonishingly absolved the company from all blame, declaring, "We cast not the slightest imputations upon the Managers or any of the regular Comedians of the stage—their positions at the moment as well as other circumstances, forbid the idea, that the order [to raise the lit lamp] ever passed their lips; yet the act was done."[95] It appears that, not being able to identify the person who gave the order, the Committee refused to assign responsibility to the company at all.

According to their report, the unidentified man who gave the insistent order to raise the lamp issued the order repeatedly with such a commanding voice that the stagehand apparently never thought to question the directive, although the stagehand "[did] not pretend positively to recognise him."[96] There is the slightest chance it was a member of the audience, anxious for the next act to begin, although it is unlikely that the audience would have even been able to see the lamp suspended so high on the beam. In the estimation of nineteenth-century historian John P. Little, the stagehands had not proceeded as they ought. "Those who saw the danger, had no coolness or presence of mind to aid others, but fled in dismay, and left the audience and the actors to their fate. As most of the performers were playing near the orchestra, the greater part of the danger was obscured from them and from the audience by a curtain; and the first notice of the danger was by the fire falling upon some of the performers."[97] The citizens of Richmond may have felt that the theater company was trying to cover itself and not expose the perpetrator to the justice he deserved. Though the Common Council did not censure the company, Placide & Green were obliquely penalized when the council declared the populace was forbidden to "exhibit any public show or spectacle" or "open any public dancing assembly" within the city limits for the space of four months. Placide & Green's season had officially ended.

A TROUPE BANISHED

Based on an open letter to the people of Richmond penned by the Placide & Green cast and crew, there must have existed some unsettling public resentment against the company. The December 31, 1811, *Enquirer* published the letter after the city declared the four-month suspension on entertainment. Confessing they were an "innocent cause" of the fire, the company bewailed the turn of sentiments against them. "From a liberal and enlightened community we fear no reproaches, but we are conscious that many have too much cause to wish they had never known us. . . . In this miserable calamity we find a sentence of banishment from your hospitable city. No more do we expect to feel that glow of pleasure which pervades a grateful heart, while it received favours liberally bestowed. Never again shall we . . . view with exultation the benevolent who fostered the fatherless, and shed a ray of comfort on the departed soul of a dying mother [Elizabeth Arnold Poe]."[98]

The whims of magistrates had before spelled the end of a company's career in Virginia. In 1774, the First Continental Congress declared theater performances a source of idleness and dissipation, banning them as an activity too frivolous for wartime. Consequently, Williamsburg's theater closed, and her troupe, the American Company, left the mainland and set sail for Jamaica. (Despite the absence of professional players, both British and American military men performed amateur theater, with George Washington himself approving a production of *Cato* among his officers.)[99] Their fate sealed by the dictates of the 1811 ordinance, the Placide & Green Company, too, sailed out of Virginia.

After packing their trunks and vacating the boardinghouse rooms they had held since August, the majority of the troupe traveled east to Norfolk, Virginia. There, they arranged for passage on the first ship downriver that could take them to their home base of Charleston, South Carolina. (Unfortunately, as it turned out, the ship they chose was the sloop *Experiment*.) Misters Placide, Green, Twaits, Robertson, Young, and Clark did not sail with the others. They remained in Richmond for several more days, most likely to settle the company's accounts for good—they apparently did not expect to return to Richmond for some time.[100]

Jurist and playwright St. George Tucker forwarded a script to William Wirt in December 1811, hoping that Wirt would pitch it successfully to the Placide & Green Theater Company, as Girardin had done with *Family Feuds*. Wirt replied to Tucker in late January 1812 that he obviously couldn't proceed with their plan.[101] He explained that John William Green, the most likely man to review the script, was unable to do so because "the loss of his only daughter, a fine young girl, who perished in the flames of the theatre, had placed his mind in such a state of distraction that he was incapable of business during the very few days that he was here after that catastrophe."[102] Placide wrote, "[We] saved nothing—my music, scenery, wardrobe, every thing, fell as prey to the flames."[103] But the fire had taken even more from Green; it spelled the death of Nancy and also the end of his marriage.

The twenty-one company members who bought passage on the *Experiment*, a sixty-year-old Norfolk-based ship, set sail into the ocean that cold January, preparing to round the Virginia coast and sail south along the eastern seaboard to South Carolina.[104] But early in the journey, something went horribly awry. Perhaps due to an error in judgment, or foul weather, or the general practice of the time to run down ships and machinery, their vessel wrecked in the Atlantic. The sloop was a total loss—it was all Captain Hall could do to preserve the lives of his passengers, at which apparently he succeeded. Once they arrived in South Carolina around the twentieth of January, the Placide &

Green Company released a public thanks to Captain Hall. They absolved him of any culpability and thanked him for the preservation of their lives.[105]

What had begun as a most fortuitous season was turning into an interminable horror of fire, death, and shipwreck. Was the company somehow cursed, the more superstitious among them wondered? The troupe could only hope that a change of location would bring good fortune and a fresh start. Manager Green and the five other men who had delayed their Richmond departure joined the rest of the cast and crew in Charleston. With almost no time for pause, they began to prepare for a new season. The theater musicians returned to Norfolk, where they performed a benefit concert to defray their travel costs from Richmond.[106]

Nancy Green, buried under the orchestra pit, was not the only actress to stay behind in Richmond. A second actress remained in the city: her mother, Frances Willems Green. Why she did not move to Charleston is not exactly known. Some surmised that she could not bring herself to leave her daughter's remains. Mordecai claimed that John William Green "became dissipated," deserted her, and left the distraught and destitute mother to fend for herself.[107] Whatever the case, when Placide, Green & Twaits opened in Charleston that January 31, Frances Green sat mourning in Richmond, alone in an unwelcoming city with no means of support.

4

MOURNING

[The Richmond Theater fire] not only converted many a stately Virginia home into a house of mourning, but sent a thrill of horror through the whole country. It was the first great holocaust of this character in our annals.

—"ANNIVERSARY OF A HOLOCAUST." *Washington Post,* DECEMBER 26, 1894

On an occasion this horrific, elaborate expressions of public ceremonial grief were in order. In the early republic, the death of prominent persons (like George Washington, James Madison, and John Marshall) meant, as a matter of course, a day of public mourning, closed businesses, memorial gunfire, bell ringing, and a funeral oration.[1] The memorialization of the theater fire victims followed the same solemn script. The mourning ceremonies provided welcome predictability in the chaos of sudden loss and created occasions for social support in a time of tragedy.[2] By honoring the victims of the fire in the same manner as the nation's greatest heroes, the Common Council indicated both the Richmond victims' status and the enormity of the tragedy. The council's official observances were intended to show respect for the victims and soothe the grief of the friends and relations of the deceased.[3]

First in the schedule of events was a mass funeral initially to be held on the twenty-eighth, a Saturday. The Burial Committee originally planned for the unclaimed remains to be transferred by means of a solemn procession originating at the Baptist "Meeting-House" next to the theater site and ending at the public burial plot of Henrico Parish Church (now St. John's).[4] This would have required a frigid ten-block march eastward on H Street, part of it up a steep hill and all of it on substandard roads, significantly limiting potential participation.[5] Additionally, it became clear that the sheer quantity and state of the human remains rendered them impossible to move.

While sorting out how to proceed, the Burial Committee decided to postpone the funeral by a day.[6] William Marshall, brother to Judge John, reported to the Council on the twenty-eighth that many family members objected to having the remains transferred across town, and he made a motion to change the burial plans. In their meeting at the Washington Tavern, the Burial Committee agreed that, regarding the dead, "it would be more satisfactory to their relations that they should be interred on the spot where they perished, and that the site of the Theatre should be consecrated as the sacred deposit of their bones and ashes."[7] No matter how workers sifted through the debris, they were bound to leave human remains on the site or accidentally discard them with the rubble from the building. Many of the human remains they discovered fell to ashes upon the slightest touch.[8] The Burial Committee agreed to change the funeral plans, purchase the ground on which the theater had stood, and convert the site into a cemetery and an undetermined sort of memorial.[9] The funeral would thus be conducted in the most populated portion of the city, and the theater site would be forever consecrated to the victims' memory.

The second event scheduled was a January 1 holiday of prayer and fasting, proposed by the Richmond citizen's group headed by Mayor Tate. They requested the city's most beloved ministers, John Buchanan and John D. Blair, whose joint congregation of Episcopalians and Presbyterians had been most directly affected, to prepare and deliver a funeral sermon for the occasion as a public service.[10] Additionally, citizens were asked to join Virginia's executive branch and the House of Delegates in wearing crape for one month "in token of the deep sense universally entertained of this severe visitation" and to cease all "shows, plays, public balls or assemblies" within the city for four months.[11]

COMMEMORATIONS

Organized by the Burial Committee, Richmond's mass funeral for the theater fatalities was held three days after the fire, on Sunday, December 29, and had all the trappings of a state funeral. Citizens, clad in black (if they owned it), but at the very least wearing a black armband, gathered in the downtown streets on that winter day. From a balcony on Main Street, a witness could have observed participants—thousands of them—slowly arranging themselves in a prescribed order. Carriers conveyed previously exhumed remains, ensconced in urns and coffins, to the head of the line. Clergymen, most likely numbering fewer than ten, followed immediately behind the caskets. "Mourners and ladies" were next: this group consisting of children and families who suffered a direct loss, as well as townswomen clad in their winter cloaks and gloves. Then came a phalanx of local notables: the city's Executive Council, the directors of the bank, the judiciary, members of the legislature, the Court of Hustings, and Common Hall members, clean-shaven, dark hats pulled low, swaths of fabric wrapped about their necks in elaborate white ascots, and canes in hand. Those bringing up the rear were "citizens on foot," and finally "citizens on horseback," who wished to express their sympathy and support.[12] Every business's door on Main, every market stall near the water, was closed, every window shuttered. Bells clanged slowly from the Market House in town, and could be heard ringing faintly from Henrico Parish Church to the east. The bells would ring for weeks as townspeople continued to expire from their injuries.

The procession began on Main Street, near Edward Trent's home, where Elizabeth Patterson died after being treated for her injuries. A report noted that she had been "overwhelmed by the crowd."[13] Patterson's shrouded body was carried to the front of the procession among the line of mourners and the march began, with the scuff and crunch of thousands of leather shoes on mottled roads. As the procession filed past "certain sorrowful houses" along the way, it continued to integrate corpses—the remains of those who had died of their injuries in the days after the fire. The body of Juliana Harvie, whose brother would also shortly die of his wounds, was assimilated by her grieving family and neighbors. At the cross street leading to the bank, the crowd turned north up Capitol Hill, marching like weary soldiers. Near the capitol, "the bearers of two large mahogany boxes, in which were enclosed the ashes and relics of the deceased" joined the march.[14] The procession slowed two blocks northeast of the capitol building on what is now east Broad Street, between Twelfth and Old Fourteenth streets, and slowly encircled the site of the fire.

Once the whole assembly arrived at the theater site, they pressed close in to surround the area where the orchestra pit once stood, and Rev. John Buchanan led a service for the dead without aid of amplification. Those on the far side of the crowd may have been scarcely able to hear. Remembered a friend, "He had a good voice for public speaking, and managed it pretty well, though his manner was rather dignified than animated."[15] After his homily on the brevity of life and seeking comfort from the Lord, with the coarse grating of ropes, pallbearers slowly lowered the urns and mahogany boxes into the pit, and all victims—slave, free, children, leaders of the community—were buried in a common grave on the spot. Shoveled spadefuls of dirt and cinders slowly covered the boxes.[16] A participant at the funeral wrote, "The whole scene defies description. A whole city bathed in tears!—How awful the transition on this devoted spot!—A few days since, it was the theatre of joy and merriment—animated by the sound of music and the hum of a delighted multitude. It is now a funeral pyre! the receptacle of the relics of our friends!"[17]

Those who subsequently died of fire-related causes were also interred on the theater grounds. The brief obituary on January 4, 1812, of John Schaub indicates that the young man died at the offices of Charles Beck & Company of his injuries and was buried in the crypt in a funeral overseen by the Burial Committee.[18]

The very day of the mass funeral, Representative Matthew Clay, apparently unapprised of the Common Council's proceedings, posted a letter to Leroy Anderson requesting that "if the person of his daughter [Mary Clay] could possibly be designated," her body could be preserved until he arrived in Richmond. Clay did not wish her remains deposited in a mass grave, but interred in a family vault where her mother and sister lay, as had been the custom in Virginia from colonial days. His wife, at only thirty-one years of age, had died the previous May.[19] Mary had been sixteen for exactly two weeks when she perished with her friends in the fire.

Anderson, who did not receive Clay's letter until the thirty-first of December, gently informed Clay in his response that Mary had not been recognized among the corpses. "Your beloved Mary, on that fatal night wore no ornament that could resist the action of the devouring element. It was the same case with [her companions] the amiable Miss Gatewood and Miss Gwathmey," Anderson relayed. Margaret Anderson had been one of the few identified, but after "mature reflection," Anderson decided not to inter his daughter in the family plot, as was his initial design. Anderson wrote to William Temple,

No, my dear friend, I have no wish to separate the remains of my beloved child from those of the amiable and dear companions, in whose embrace, perhaps, she died. Side by side they sunk, together their immortal spirits took flight, and it is even a sort of melancholy satisfaction, that their dust will mingle in one common tomb, social even in death. Under different circumstances, it would perhaps, have been a mournful consolation to deposit her dear relics near those of her departed mother; but on the present occasion, no private arrangement of individual feeling seems so welcome and consolatory as that which the humanity and benevolence of a sympathising society is preparing, to honor the memory of all.[20]

In any case, by the time Clay's letter arrived in Richmond, it would have been too late for Anderson to have made alternative arrangements to accommodate Clay's request.

* * *

The mourning pattern of procession, day of prayer, corporate church service was repeated in most of Virginia's principal towns, even those which had suffered no direct loss, as an act of solidarity with the capital. On January 5, the ship flags over Norfolk's harbor were lowered to half-mast. Norfolk's citizens, dressed in "weeds of mourning," crowded the Market Square and adjoining streets to honor the dead. "Never did we behold so great a concourse of people assembled at once on any former occasion in this Borough, and since the funeral rites in honor of WASHINGTON, the nation's savior and benefactor, never on so mournful a one," reported a dispatch from Norfolk. "Every heart was touched with sorrow;—it was not the empty pageant of a volatile crowd, fond of novelty and parade, but it was the solemn ritual of real mourners."[21] Norfolk also held a Catholic mass on the ninth of January, "performed at the Roman church for the souls that were victims to the fire at the Richmond Theatre," inviting all in the area to attend, for Richmond had no permanent Catholic priest.[22]

On the official day of humility and prayer on Wednesday, the first of January, 1812, the city's shortage of churches became glaringly obvious. Although the city ordinance requested that Buchanan and Blair deliver a New Year commemorative sermon at Henrico Parish Church on Church Hill, after the proclamation was issued it became evident that one building was not sufficient to host the predicted crowds. A scramble ensued to find adequate space—where could the city possibly house all the mourners? Every building that had ever hosted divine service was utilized, and at least eight services were held at locations like the Henrico Parish Church, the Baptist meeting house, and the new Methodist church. Morning and evening services were held in the hall of the capitol building and the old Methodist church, a modified stable on Main Street. Every service was "filled to overflowing."[23]

Of all the homilies delivered that day in Richmond, Blair's sermon—given by the Presbyterian minister at Henrico Parish Church—is the only one remaining, handwritten and archived with his personal papers. He chose as his foreboding text: "Prepare to meet thy God, O Israel," from Amos 4:12. "In the memory of the oldest of us, there never has been a more awful warning of the uncertainty of human life than this which is given us now," he read solemnly to those in his audience. "A large number of our relatives, friends & neighbours have been torn from us by the most furious of all the elements & in a moment hurried into eternity. Can anything present to our minds a more striking memento of the precarious tenure on which we hold our lives, or a more powerful motive for us to comply with the admonition in the text, to be upon our guard & "prepare," as we know neither the day nor the hour in which the Son of Man cometh?" Early nineteenth-century Richmond was no stranger to mortality, he granted, and her citizens had seen many go to meet their God. "But never has the call been addressed to us with so loud a voice, or in a manner so impressive as on the present melancholy occasion. And while we mingle our tears together on every recollection of our dear devoted friends who our tears cannot recal[l]—it will be prudent in the living to profit by this solemn scene of general woe." How could one profit from such catastrophe? "Nothing would better become us than to humble ourselves before the God of Heaven . . . for we are a sinful people a people *laden* with iniquity."[24]

Judging by the spate of sermons issued after the fire, Christian leaders were concerned that God would visit another disaster on America if her people were not introspective and repentant about the shortcomings in their own lives. The theater fire became a sobering catalyst for introspection. On the twenty-third of January 1812, the city of Winchester, Virginia, also observed a day of "fasting and humiliation," wherein Rev. William Hill gave a message at the Presbyterian meeting house about the Richmond fire. As Hill wrote, "If when God sends judgments upon others we do not take the warning; if, when instead of reflecting upon ourselves, and trying our own ways, we turn our eyes from the sight, and shut our ears upon the voice: then we leave the Almighty no other way to awaken us, and bring us to the consideration of our evil ways, but by pouring down his wrath upon our own heads, that so he may convince us that we are sinners, by the same argument from which we have concluded others to be so."[25]

It was the hope of local ministers that the people in the pews, crouched over wooden kneelers on New Year's Day, were thinking of their own sins and resolving to live more holy lives. The day of fasting and prayer was meant to be more than a spiritual exercise—it was meant to affect people's hearts and change the way their days were spent well past the first of January. Hill preached, "But in vain should we profess our penitence, if we should continue in our former practice of sin. We must be conscious that we are all chargeable with many sins and misdeeds; if so, we are but masking the matter with our Maker, and practising the merest dissimulation to pretend to fast and humble ourselves before him, without a reformation."[26]

Richmond's Jewish community, which sustained serious losses in the fire, also held a service on January 1. Samuel Mordecai, eyewitness to the disaster, wrote and presumably delivered an address entitled, "A Discourse in the Synagogue in the City of Richmond, January 1, 1812, in consequence of the loss of life occasioned by the burning of the Theatre on 26 December 1811."[27]

* * *

The Common Council's four-month prohibition on amusements spelled the swift end of the city's celebrated winter social season. Violators of the moratorium would incur a fine of six dollars and sixty-six cents for each hour of disrespectful revelry they hosted.[28] In terms of today's purchasing power, those six dollars and sixty-six cents would have a value of nearly one hundred dollars. Probably not enough to dissuade the insistent, but, restrained by good taste, Richmond seems to have abided by the regulation.

In light of the scope of the disaster and the nationwide observances and gestures of condolence, religious leaders seem to have expected that other American theaters would respectfully close, at least temporarily, to honor the dead. However, most cities did not observe even a day of abstinence from public amusements. One editorialist in a Congregationalist religious magazine called the *Panoplist* wrote in indignation that local theaters held no observations whatsoever in January. "It was supposed by many persons that the Boston theatre would be shut on the Monday evening after the foregoing intelligence reached this town; so great was the impression made on the minds of people generally by the melancholy tidings. But it seems the actors could not forego their profits, nor the votaries of pleasure their accustomed enjoyments, for a single night."[29]

Irritated ministers all over America berated their congregations for continuing to attend the theater after such an obvious warning to avoid the place. A preacher in Pennsylvania wrote, "To the shame of this populous city and to the astonishment of every reflecting mind, whilst the burning ashes of our brethren at Richmond are presented to our view . . . the citizens of Philadelphia are rioting in mirth and dissipation, and the Theatre groaning under the weight of its attending votaries."[30] Rev. Archibald Alexander, Princeton Seminary's first professor of theology, a conservative Presbyterian and native Virginian, supposed Americans' "infatuated devotion to pleasure, in the midst of threatening judgments, and public calamities, is a certain indication of a people being ripe for ruin, and a sure forerunner of it."[31] What would it take for recalcitrant America to learn her lesson? Alexander believed participation in public amusements was not only disrespectful of the dead but also denied the living adequate time to contemplate the spiritual significance of disaster.

* * *

On December 30, 1811, in the United States House in Washington, D.C., a Republican representative from Virginia stood to address the chair. His colleagues quieted and strained to hear him. In a low, hoarse voice owing as much to a lingering illness as to the solemnity of his message, John Dawson recounted the events of the twenty-sixth in Richmond. This had been "a great national calamity," he announced, owing to the status and civic promise of the victims, not to mention their personal connections to the United States legislature—by this he meant the loss of Representative Matthew Clay's daughter Mary and Governor George Smith, a former House member. Dawson offered a resolution that the House don black crape bands for thirty days.[32] (Irritated by the vaguely deistic language urging them to submit humbly to the "decrees of fate" in Dawson's resolution, the *Panoplist* grumbled, "No mention is made of God or Divine Providence, in the remarks or the resolution; though such mention ought to have been made in both. . . . Such heathenish ignorance ought not to have been expected in one of the high legislators of a Christian Country.")[33] The House unanimously adopted Dawson's resolution.

That same Monday, U.S. senator Stephen R. Bradley of Vermont, a Democrat-Republican like Virginian President James Madison, proposed a similar resolution, also quickly approved, in which the U.S. Senate would wear crape "in testimony of the national respect & sorrow for the unfortunate persons, who perished in the city of Richmond in Virginia on the night of the 26th in the present month."[34] William Branch Giles, the Virginian who had assumed his childhood friend Abraham Venable's Senate position upon Venable's resignation in 1803, had prepared a Senate resolution as well, memorializing his friend's judgment and integrity. However, tending to "the sick chamber of a beloved wife" prevented Senator Giles from presenting his enthusiastic resolution (it contained no fewer than nineteen exclamation points).[35]

The theater fire was not a matter of mere local importance but a calamity of a magnitude "unknown in the annals of our country," as Richmond's Common Council stated.[36] Expressions from the national legislature confirmed the enormity of the disaster. A speaker before the Virginia legislature declared that in the days following the disaster, "The sympathy which was excited was as general as the calamity was awful. It drew forth the feelings of a nation. It caused us to feel that we were all of one family—from Boston to Savannah, the sentiment spread with a rapidity, unprecedented in the American Annals. The Congress of the U[nited] States, the venerable sages of our country condescended to bend over us and join in our grief."[37] The U.S. legislature, on behalf of the entire United States, spent January of 1812 wearing black for Richmond's theater fire. Washington City, as the nation's capital was then known, also suspended plans for winter balls and parties.[38] Naval school midshipmen at the Washington Naval Yard unanimously resolved to wear black crape for the month of January "in testament of the respect and sorrow which they feel for [the victims], but particularly for Lieut. J. Gibbon of the U. S. Navy."[39]

In colleges, legislative offices, and private homes up and down the Atlantic coast, Americans tied or sewed small, hemmed lengths of black crape over the upper arms of their suit jackets, uniforms, and dress sleeves every morning and removed them every evening. The badges of grief respectfully granted weeks of remembrance to those whose deaths had taken mere minutes. This small action, so universally adopted, deeply affected the survivors. Three Richmond men who had lost wives and children gratefully thanked the American people in a widely circulated public letter for wearing the "sable badge of sorrow" in commiseration and sharing in griefs "which throughout the world, bind man to man, make of each nation a family, and of all nations a vast aggregate of kindred, congenial beings."[40] As one poet wrote, "Surprised we heard from all our country round / the plaintive echos of our grief resound / Cities and towns and villages combined / and in our tears and lamentations joined."[41] Through acts of grief and condolence, the young nation functioned like a family.

It was a contentious time, with interparty rivalries and the nation on the brink of war. When Ruth Baldwin Barlow, wife of the American minister to France, received the latest news from Washington City and Virginia after its slow trip across the Atlantic, she sent a note to her friend First Lady Dolley Madison on March 4, 1812. The Madisons had by this time received word that their niece Lucy, a houseguest of John Richard's family in Richmond, was among the living, suffering only a dislocated wrist in her escape.[42] "We are lamenting over the sad news from Richmond—it must have caused you a mellancholly winter," Barlow wrote, adding, "We are very glad to hear there is such a spirit of union in public affairs—we hope things will yet go right here & that good may come out of evil."[43]

In Virginia, the city councils of Norfolk, Falmouth, Fredericksburg, Smithfield, Winchester, and Alexandria offered resolutions, as did the legislatures of Ohio and Massachusetts and the judges of North Carolina's Supreme Court. Citizen groups from Raleigh, North Carolina; Savannah, Georgia; Charleston, South Carolina; and Zanesville, Ohio, sent condolences.[44]

In the more than fifteen resolutions on record, the most common means of expressing official commiseration included days of prayer, the wearing of crape, suspension of amusements, a day of closed businesses, and an officially commissioned sermon for the public. Petersburg and Alexandria, Virginia, both canceled public balls and "dancing assemblies" for the space of a month. Smithfield, Virginia, famous for her hams, went even further than this. In addition to observing a day of "Devotion and Prayer," Smithfield established a committee to receive contributions for the sufferers "in need of pecuniary aid," which was not explicitly addressed in other resolutions.[45]

Men's groups in major American cities spearheaded memorial efforts. The "Young Gentlemen" of New York City met on College Walk on a Sunday morning and proceeded to the Presbyterian Church on Wall Street, where Rev. Dr. Samuel Miller preached a robustly antitheater sermon "at the request of a number of young gentlemen of the city of New-York, who had assembled to express their condolence with the inhabitants of Richmond."[46] Soldiers of the Navy Yard in Washington, D.C., met to commemorate Richmond's tragic deaths. Early in 1812, a group of "young gentlemen" met at Boston's Exchange Coffee House "and resolved to express in a public manner their sorrow for the late melancholy calamity in this City [Richmond]—a committee was appointed to make suitable arrangements."[47]

Philadelphia in particular launched a series of elaborate commemorative events on behalf of victims, sponsored chiefly by two fraternal groups: the Virginia students at the University of Pennsylvania Medical School and the "Assembled Youth of Philadelphia" organization. Modeled after the University of Edinburgh in Scotland, the medical school at the University of Pennsylvania was the foremost in the country for about 150 years after its creation in 1765. The lack of a medical school in Virginia meant that gentry parents had to send their young men north for training as physicians. Besides its prestige, the University of Pennsylvania became an attractive choice for the strongly parochial Virginians because of numerous Old Dominion connections, particularly in her faculty.[48] At the University of Pennsylvania, as at Yale and Harvard, Virginia's sons formed a tight cadre—a Virginia subculture in a northern school. The Richmond Theater fire became an important occasion for them to display their solidarity. Meeting on New Year's Day, 1812, Virginia-born students commissioned a sermon from Rev. Archibald Alexander, to be delivered on January 8. A native Virginian and former president of Virginia's Hampden-Sydney College, Alexander was a natural choice. His family's elevated pew at Third Presbyterian Church in Philadelphia often seated several Virginia students of medicine during the winter season, and he retained a deep connection to friends in his home state.[49] The young medical students issued a public expression of sympathy for publication in the Richmond newspapers, resolved to wear crape for a month, and arranged for the Wednesday assembly, after which Alexander's discourse would be put into print. During his sermon, Alexander noted that a fair number of his addressees had been directly affected. "To many of you, this sad catalogue of death, presented the names of much esteemed friends and intimate acquaintances; to some, of beloved relatives; and alas! to one or more, the first intelligence of their misfortune, was conveyed by the distressing sight of the *endeared name of a sister!*"[50]

An attendee called it "one of the largest assemblies I ever saw in Old Pine Street Church."[51] Nearly a hundred of the medical students who heard Alexander that day hailed from Virginia, yet Virginians were hardly the only men present—over five hundred young men from Philadelphia joined the University of Pennsylvania medical students from Virginia to show their sympathy. The Assembled Youth of Philadelphia group issued one of the more extensive sets of resolutions regarding Richmond after the fire, testifying that "the recent calamity at Richmond is infinitely the most awful of its kind that has ever occurred in our country."[52] In a meeting at the circuit court room on the sixth of January, hundreds of men assembled, "publicly expressing their feeling sense of the late distressing occurrence at Richmond."[53]

FINANCIAL SUFFERING

After a destructive Newburyport fire on May 31, 1811, the citizens of that Massachusetts town lost around 250 buildings, estimated at over a million dollars' worth of damage in the currency of the time. The Baptist church, the library, taverns, barns, printing houses, the post office, law offices, more than ninety private homes, and nearly all the dry goods stores were swallowed whole.[54] Unaffected residents had not been able to provide more than "the immediate necessities of the sufferers," so via an agent, the town's selectmen presented a petition to Connecticut's governor Roger Griswald, pleading for his state's assistance that June. "Such is the magnitude of the disaster," they wrote with a certain degree of discomfiture, "that we are compelled to look for more permanent succor from abroad." At a meeting of the governor and council of the neighbor state Connecticut on July 3, the council passed a resolution recommending that Connecticut's churches should take on the relief effort. After services on the second Sunday in August, the council unanimously urged Christian congregations to "contribute for the relief of their suffering brethren in *Newburyport.*"[55]

It seemed a natural conclusion: churches could quickly reach a large percentage of the populace, possessed the necessary infrastructure to administer charity, and had the ethical mandate to carry it out. This type of arrangement made sense in a state with an organized system of churches, which Virginia lacked after the disestablishment of her state church in 1787. Richmond had no such infrastructure for meeting the needs of her citizens. Instead, those bereft of support after the theater fire had to rely on individual donations or assistance from outside municipalities. It does not appear that the city sought help from other states as Newburyport had.

In the past, the local governments of Virginia had assumed financial aid responsibility after a notable fire. On the morning of January 9, 1787, an inferno fought by a feeble bucket brigade endangered the capitol and treasury buildings and swallowed between forty and fifty homes, warehouses, and stores worth over a half million dollars: far more than Richmond itself could muster to rebuild. After the *Virginia Independent Chronicle* issued a repeat appeal, nearly every Virginia county convened a committee and contributed something.[56]

In a list published a year after Newburyport's fire, contributors to the destitute had included not only parishes, but also individuals, organizations like the Martha's Vineyard Baptist Society, a private academy, and Quakers in New York and New Hampshire. In all, over fifty cities, societies, individuals, and organizations contributed toward the relief of the injured and impoverished victims.[57]

No such organized solicitation or donation effort is apparent in the case of the Theater Fire, strangely, and no committee was established by the Common Council to aid the newly destitute. It seems evident that the contributions that did come in were not sufficient to meet the needs of many families for whom the financial consequences of the fire were ruinous. In only one case, a death list indicated the victim's economic importance: "William Southgate the only prop of the family of Wright Southgate, dec[eased]."[58] Although most of the victims were not the chief wage earners in their homes, a handful of families found themselves in severe financial straits after the breadwinner died. Thirty-six-year-old victim Benjamin Botts, for example, maintained sole fiscal responsibility for around a dozen people. After Botts married Jane Tylor of Dumfries, their family quickly grew to include four sons and one daughter. Then it expanded further when Benjamin's newly widowed sister came to stay in the Court End house with her brood of children. Benjamin's elderly mother moved in as well.[59] Botts's portrait by St. Memin shows the handsome young lawyer with a shock of longish dark curls, wide trimmed sideburns, and a calm expression in his eyes. The weight of his responsibility gave Botts gravity far beyond his years, by a friend's account.[60]

Born into a poor Virginia family, Botts was not accustomed to the advantages enjoyed by most of his neighbors, the city's elite in Court End. According to his vivid obituary, the patronage of distinguished lawyer and statesman General John Minor of Spotsylvania County, near Fredericksburg, and his own diligence resulted in Botts's passing the bar in 1794 at age eighteen. This paved the way for his climb to the upper echelons of the Virginia bar, considered by most at the time to be the most brilliant in the entire United States. His shining moment, the moment that proved beyond a doubt that the industrious, penniless boy from Dumfries, Virginia, had arrived, was his selection to the defense for former vice president Aaron Burr's treason trials in 1807.

There was a self-possession and firmness about him that commanded respect, and without question he excelled at whatever he set his hand to. The *Enquirer* reported, "When he spoke, he seemed always to communicate the result of previous reflection. This circumstance gave him great advantage in colloquial debate. He appeared to be convinced that he was in the right: and so imposing was his manner, that those who were not informed upon the point under discussion, generally took it for granted that he was so. . . . Mr. Botts was a man of sound judgment and a good lawyer."[61] Botts's prestige and client base increased after Burr's exoneration, and at the time of Botts's death, the young lawyer was representing multiple cases in the Federal Court, the Court of Chancery, and the Court of Appeals in Richmond.

On December 26, Benjamin and Jane attended *Family Feuds*. They were last seen standing together in a lobby outside of their box. On her way out, carried in Philip Thornton's arms, Caroline Homassel passed Botts, who she said stood rooted in place against the crush of the crowd. Botts held his wife firmly, and in confident tones Homassel heard him assure Jane, "There will be time for all to get out."[62] There was not.

John Minor, Benjamin Botts's old mentor from Spotsylvania County, came to the rescue of his protégé's family, pro bono. On January 7, 1812, he posted an advertisement in Richmond: "The death of my much loved friends, Mr. and Mrs. Botts . . . devolves on me the sacred duty of rendering every aid and service in my power to their Orphan Children." He offered to finish Botts's professional business in the courts, even if that required a removal to Richmond.[63] But some more unusual allies came to the rescue of the Botts family: his vociferous opponents from the Burr trial. A group of local lawyers, including William Wirt and George Hay, promised to join John Minor "in the discharge of this duty," taking on additional Botts cases pro bono, "whenever not engaged on the opposite side," of course.[64] Botts's clients could expect some disorder with the transition, but they were truly getting a dream team of lawyers to assume their cases. All of this was done in the name of helping Botts's dependents, who must truly have been in a desperate spot. Minor confidently believed that all who had not kept accounts current with Botts "will pay the fees due with increased alacrity . . . when assured, that they will all be applied to the use of the children of the deceased." And just in case they forgot, Minor reminded them of their overdue payments several times a week in a paid advertisement in the *Enquirer*.

The Harvies, a prominent local family living in William Byrd II's former

Richmond townhouse, met further financial distress with the loss of siblings Edwin and Juliana, who died in the days following the fire of their severe injuries. Since 1806, the extended Harvie family had lost seven family members to untimely deaths. The *Enquirer* recounted: "Poor mourners, deeply indeed have ye drunk of the cup of affliction. Within five short years ye had numbered among the dead, the venerable *John Harvie*, the distinguished *Lewis Harvie*, the amiable *Mrs. McCraw*, the interesting little boy, of *Dr. Brockenbrough*. But by one blow, the distressed mother, *Mrs. Harvie*, has lost her noble and high-souled daughter, *Juliana*, her excellent son *E. J. Harvie*, and that sweet little girl *Mary Whitlock*, her beloved Grand-daughter!!! Reader, conceive if you can, what you never can have felt."[65]

The family patriarch was Revolutionary War veteran Colonel John Harvie, who served as a delegate to the Continental Congress in 1777, where he signed the Articles of Confederation. Once Virginia's secretary of the commonwealth, he became the register of the Land Office and died unexpectedly in his home, "Belvidere," as the result of an accident in February 1807. His eldest son, Lewis, was next in line to assume leadership of the family. A gifted young lawyer and member of the Executive Council of State, Lewis assumed his father's mantle as a leading patriot and orator of his day. He far eclipsed his younger brother and fellow lawyer Edwin in attainments, ambition, and prestige. Edwin was quieter, and rather an unremarkable sort, who, the *Enquirer* reported, "loved private life" and "though young and animated . . . was not ambitious. He had never sought for the distinction which popular favor confers."[66]

Only two months after his father's accident, in April of 1807, Lewis died tragically at the age of twenty-five of a lingering illness. After his death, the *Enquirer* mourned, "He seemed destined to render service to mankind. . . . Lewis Harvie was an extraordinary and excellent young man."[67] After the deaths of both father and older brother, the more retiring Edwin stepped into the role of family leader. He served as executor of John's estate, handling lingering court issues and managing the family landholdings. At the Eagle Tavern, Edwin auctioned over eight hundred acres in Chesterfield, and he advertised for a new overseer to manage the remaining land and the family's slaves. "Belvidere," an expansive home with lovely gardens about one mile from the capitol, was even put up for a short-term lease by Edwin and his mother, Margaret, in July 1811.[68] Edwin, however unassuming he may have been about his role, did much to keep the family finances together, as is evidenced by the way everything fell apart after his death that December night.

In the February 6, 1812, *Enquirer,* a notice appeared. "On Wednesday the 12th of the present month will be sold to the highest bidder, at the house in which the late Edwin J. Harvie, esq. resided, all the Household and Kitchen *FURNITURE* of the decedent." The furniture was "nearly all new and elegant." His widow, Martha, even sold his horse, saddle, and bridle.[69] Harvie neighbor Dr. John Brockenbrough became administrator of John and Edwin's estates in February 1812 and publicly requested debtors to pay their debts back to the men's estates quickly.[70] With the family's financial security in jeopardy, Edwin and Juliana's brother Jacquelin Burwell Harvie resigned from the navy at the age of twenty-three and came home to support what was left of his family.

He took up more quiet work as a businessman and, in 1813, wed cousin, neighbor, and childhood sweetheart Mary Marshall, daughter of the chief justice of the Supreme Court. The nuptials occurred the day after Mary turned eighteen years of age; the timing suggests that John Marshall may not have granted his permission for the match. Historians surmise that feisty Mary acted on her decision to wed Harvie the moment she could legally do so as an independent under Virginia law.[71] However awkward their marriage's start, Jacquelin did both the Marshall and Harvie families proud. Making the most of his situation and continuing the family's commitment to public service (something in which Edwin, for all his charms, did not excel), Jacquelin became a city alderman and eventually a state senator.

Governor George Smith's family did not escape hardship after the fire. His wife Lucy F. Smith was left with eight children from his previous marriage to the deceased Sarah Adams, and she must have found it necessary to obtain an infusion of cash to sustain the household. By January 28, Smith's valuables were scheduled for auction. "All the Household and Kitchen furniture of the late GEORGE W SMITH, Esq, consisting of a tableboard, a Mahogany Settee and Chairs, Bed-steads with Curtains, Tables, Chairs, Table and Tea China, &c. &c." were for sale as well as three of the family's household slaves.[72]

This auction was deemed necessary despite an act of the Assembly passed on January 21 allocating monies to the Smith family—the only example of state aid to victims of the Richmond Theater fire. Smith had acted as lieutenant governor from April 3, 1811, through December 6 without compensation, as no act of the legislature had made provision for this role. But since "the Legislature is disposed to do ample justice to all persons for services rendered, and more especially to the said George William Smith, for the many important duties performed by him," the Assembly authorized the auditor of public accounts to pay $1,946.39 to Smith's family, "being the difference between the salary of the Councillor and Governor" for the eight-month term Smith served as interim governor.[73] George's widow, Lucy, received a third of the money, and the remaining two-thirds went to trustees John Adams and Samuel G. Adams for the four Smith sons—Richard Lee, George William, John A., and Thomas. The funds were to be spent "in such way as the maintenance and education of the aforesaid children may seem to require, and shall account to them, as they shall respectively arrive to the age of twenty-one years, for one equal fourth part each, of the nett balance in hand, after the maintenance and education of them as aforesaid."[74]

A correspondent, encouraging locals to donate to the newly impoverished, wrote in the *Richmond Enquirer*, "No scene ever offered such fine scope for the benevolent (in secret) to prove to an all-wise God, that his merciful goodness and bounty to us is not bestowed in vain."[75] Victims' homes were placed on the market, furnishings auctioned off the block, and a dry goods store liquidated. The surviving partner of one enterprise bluntly explained: "In consequence of the melancholy death of Joseph Jacobs, the firm of S & J Jacobs is dissolved."[76]

The Jacobs family, members of Richmond's vibrant, assimilated Jewish community, had lost more people in the fire than any other Richmond family. The January 4 obituary for the family lamented, "How poignant must be the anguish—*how unutterable the grief,* of those who have to deplore the loss of FIVE dear relatives—swept off by this sad catastrophe!"[77] Killed were family head Joseph Jacobs, "a man of strict honor and great benevolence of heart," his "lovely" seventeen-year-old daughter Eliza, a "sweet" four-year-old granddaughter Adeline Bausman, and his two nieces, Zipporah Marx (sometimes Marks), the "amiable and affectionate" mother of four, and Charlotte Raphael, a "very promising child."[78]

In order to assist the fire orphans, one school created a novel solution. The Cornelia Academy, a boarding seminary for young women, suffered a deep blow with the loss of six pupils in the fire, among them Lucy Gwathmey, Mary Clay of Danville, and Judith Elliot of New Kent County.[79] In "just tribute to their memory," and acknowledging the serious disadvantages that parentless girls faced, the school launched a scholarship program for six orphaned females in memory of the students who had perished. The superintendent requested nominations for scholarship recipients and solicited donations to fund the effort. The selected orphans would be trained as professional teachers with the hopes that they would be able to earn a living teaching other female orphans "the benefits of mental culture." Ann Camp, affiliated with the school, even offered to adopt one child and anticipated that others would also extend their arms to such girls, left unable to support themselves.[80]

On the fourteenth of January a contributor to the *Richmond Enquirer* celebrated the donations that had, by that time, been bestowed on the victims' families. "To cast the eye . . . over the late disastrous event in this City, will harrow up every soul; but what consolation we have, that (save, it is believed a very few exceptions) though a load of grief may last for life; yet no conflict with the world can arise from want of Fortune to the surviving relations. Such have been the workings of Providence."[81] Based on the auction notices alone, it is clear the correspondent paints too rosy a picture. His own letter provided an example of a family still suffering, unaided: that of Nuttal, a carpenter. The carpenter had met his wife when she was an indigent woman with several children, all too young to work. His heart went out to her, and the inexhaustible, industrious man tenderly cared for the entire brood.[82] With his death, the widow found herself in the same desperate financial situation that Mr. Nuttal had helped her to escape, and now eviction was imminent. The correspondent stated, "The rent of the house became due on the 1st of the month and the disconsolate widow of this unfortunate victim, expects every day, that her little belongings will be sold for the rest, and herself afforded no shelter but the canopy of Heaven."[83] The author, describing himself as a poor man, gave the Nuttals' address (in a tenement near a tavern) and petitioned for the wealthy to give. Relief must have come. In September 1812, Nuttal still lived in Richmond and had upgraded her lodgings to a home that also housed the law offices of Henry Hiort.[84]

The Monument Committee began posting donation solicitations publicly on the fourteenth of January, requesting that all subscriptions be sent to an account at the Bank of Virginia. All aid coming into the city for destitute families and for the construction of a memorial came from private donors or city councils, like that in Smithfield, Virginia. Although the Monument Committee had solicited donations for nearly three weeks, by the sixth of February 1812, the Virginia legislature had yet to put monies from state coffers toward aid or a memorial. The deadline was closing in: subscriptions would be closed by the first of March so that planning could begin and a budget be created.

That the state of Virginia had not contributed and would not contribute something toward the memorial was unthinkable to many, including a

delegate who stood before the legislature, persuading them that funding the
memorial was not a local governmental concern, but an issue of state. He
reminded the Assembly that they themselves had seen the victims—from all
parts of Virginia—overwhelmed by the fire, had experienced the "general grief
which covered our state," and yet had not donated to the monument. "Will you
not express the feelings and the generosity of the State at large, by a national
contribution?" he asked.[85]

Delegate Samuel Hughes informed his brother in Patrick County in a letter
that "the members of Legislature have all escaped without the loss of a single
life though many of them wounded in the flight from windows, though there is
no one hurt from our part of the country and none but what are likely shortly
to recover."[86] The man addressing the legislature suspected this as the reason
why the delegates and senators were not taking the donation drive seriously:
no legislator was "mingled in these holy ashes," and all who had been present
escaped death. But, he reminded them, the chief magistrate was dead, whom
both houses had days before elected, and thus they should bear some sense of
obligation to the drive and connection to the cause. The speaker closed, "Join
in this pious purpose. Contribute one or two thousand dollars towards the
projected monument. It is not the pelf, the money that we ask for—we do not
want it—the monument will rise without it. But we ask it as the expression
of the national feeling . . . that the same stone which covers the ashes of our
countrymen should bear stampt upon it the munificence of private feeling
and the sympathy of a great State.—I ask it, as a man; as a Patriot; and as A
VIRGINIAN." With that he closed, and left it to their consciences as "Sons of
Virginia" to do the right thing.[87]

Among the appropriations specified in the Acts of the Assembly for the
1811 session were 8,500 dollars for capitol repairs and three thousand dollars
for the completion of the governor's house, as well as funds for a fireproof
roof for the Armory, and ammunition for state defense. The Acts of the
Assembly do not indicate that any state monies were allocated for the theater
fire memorial.[88] The city of Richmond did donate five thousand dollars to the
effort, which the Monument Committee used to purchase the land for the
memorial.

A February 12, 1812, letter from Samuel Mordecai in Richmond to his
sister Rachel in North Carolina indicates that much more could have been
done for the victims. "The Sensations of distress, piety and charity, which the
dreadful disaster here in December, caused to be so strongly felt (but of which

still more was said) appear to have almost subsided," he wrote, "even in those who had greatest cause for affliction—except in a few instances we see the same undivided attention paid to the accumulation of overflowing wealth."[89] Richmond was getting back to business.

FIRE FIGHTING IN RICHMOND

Until 1859, when Richmond created the first paid fire department, the city relied exclusively on volunteers to fight conflagrations, as was standard in early republic America.[90] The "Union Fire Company of Richmond," one of the first volunteer fire companies, was incorporated in 1797 and consisted of thirty-six local notables. The roster also included the names of men whose families would later sustain grievous losses in the Richmond Theater tragedy: Thomas Rutherfoord, Joseph Gallego, and James Heron. Members of the Union Fire Company had to live between Shockoe Creek and the western bounds of Richmond so they would be able to quickly reach fires in the most populated portion of the city. Members were also under obligation to be perpetually at the ready. Their rules, printed on a large broadside intended for posting in every member's home, specified: "Upon any alarm of fire, every Member not sick, nor out of town, shall repair with his Buckets to the place in danger, and endeavour to extinguish the same, in such manner as the Captain or Assistants shall direct."[91] For equipment, Union possessed a simple hand-pumped "engine," axes, ladders, and hooks that the company maintained corporately. The company lent out buckets to members, who were required to return them if they should move outside of Richmond. A member provided, at his own expense, a hat with the word "Union" in black and two long hemp bags for salvaging items in homes and stores.[92]

Volunteers in the company oversaw and organized the community bucket brigades, directing lines of people to the nearest water source: the James River canal, private wells, public waterworks, or Shockoe Creek, which wended its way across Main uncovered.[93] Volunteers also functioned as cheerleaders once the extinguishing effort was underway. Union members drilled eight months of the year and held an annual meeting at the Rising Sun Tavern in Shockoe Valley.[94]

A report from a fire in November 1798 gives us an idea of how the fire-fighting process usually transpired. First the "Alarm of fire sounded," perhaps bells, or shouting neighbors running door to door with the news. Conscientious townspeople turned out that November and saved several houses with "great exertions," preventing the fire from extending up the street. However, it rushed in the other direction and consumed eleven more houses.[95] Richmond carpenters cut down buildings adjacent to the Gilberts' flaming house in 1788 and thus prevented the spread of fire throughout the neighborhood. Neighbors slapped out roof fires with wet blankets and knocked off flammable wooden shingles as two engines shot a steady stream of water at the blaze. Although preservation of property was the fundamental work of fire fighting at this time, not rescuing endangered people, one man climbed a ladder—perhaps belonging to the fire company—to convey the silversmith's wife, an invalid, out of a window, to the joy of onlookers.[96]

A Benjamin Latrobe sketch of the Market House on Shockoe Hill in 1798 shows two men pulling an early fire engine, which was a simple wheeled hand pump with curved handles that spewed water in the direction of the fire when engaged by teams of men. In 1803, volunteers in the Philadelphia Hose Company attached leather hoses with copper fittings to the engines and forever changed fire fighting. Richmond subsequently adopted the new hose technology, and by 1811, Court End had a community bucket brigade, at least one engine, a leather hose, and a hook-and-ladder truck on hand, all owned by the Shockoe Fire Company, one of several that had been added in the city. Other neighborhood fire companies in Richmond probably had an engine as well. The Union Fire Company kept theirs in a kind of shed, "under a good lock," for which the elected officers had keys, hung up in some public place in their houses, so as to be easily accessed in case of an alarm.[97] In the first decade of the nineteenth century, the new city waterworks in Richmond conveyed water from a spring on westerly Libby Hill to the market via wooden pipes, and it funneled various Shockoe springs waters into a public basin, about twenty feet square, near the capitol.[98] The new water mains included fire plugs, a kind of oversized cork in the water main. Engines required constant filling by bucket brigade or "plug" to operate. During a fire, a plug would be "uncorked" and the fire fighters could tap directly into the main as a water source with leather hoses. (Plugs were not proper hydrants; America's first real pressurized fire hydrant would not exist until 1817.) The first test of this innovation was in November 1810, during a three-building fire in the lower part of town. A reporter noted, "The great importance of Doctor Adams' water works to this city, was very apparent on this occasion; a plug being opened in the street a few yards from the buildings on fire, afforded a plentiful supply of water, which would not have been obtained in any other way than by forming a line to the river, a distance of at least a quarter of a mile."[99] Instead of requiring fifteen minutes to fill the engine with water by bucket, a hose attachment could do the same work, sucking water from the main, in ninety seconds. Hose companies with 120 men could deliver the same amount of water as eleven thousand men with buckets, dramatically reducing the number of labor needed to extinguish fires and saving thousands in property damage.[100]

On January 13, 1812, smoke began to pour out of a store near Main and Fifteenth streets. Citizens formed a bucket brigade line to a water source because a plug was not accessible, but assembling everyone in the bitter cold outdoors took over forty minutes. By that time five tenement houses had burned.[101] To experience such a loss so few days after the Richmond Theater fire led many to conclude that the city's disorganized approach to fire fighting required a complete overhaul. Exasperated citizens identified a number of serious problems, beginning with the equipment. The engines were neglected and in "bad order," while hoses, ladders, and hooks were neither present in sufficient numbers nor distributed well across the city. The companies were not provided with the hats and clothing they needed.[102] Richmonders themselves were the other problem. Their indifference had led the companies to become understaffed and undisciplined. Sentinels guarding saved furniture frequently deserted, and incapacitated officers did not arrange for a second-in-command. "All [seem] willing to give directions and none to follow them," noted one correspondent to the *Enquirer*.[103] City managers had left the law that all citizens keep fire buckets in their homes unenforced, and they had not imposed the fines that the wardens deserved for their inattention.[104]

Sewell Osgood, the hero credited with stopping the progress of the January blaze, recommended that Richmond establish volunteer fire companies of forty "strong, able men" who would function as a dedicated demolition team, tearing down houses to stop the spread of the fire.[105] To that end, a young mechanic in Richmond solicited "mechanical young men of the city of Richmond" to meet at the capitol for the purpose of establishing a new hose and fire company. "As our city has been of late visited with such dreadful calamities by fire, it is hoped that every enterprising young man will not be backward in joining so valuable an institution," he wrote.[106] The term "mechanic" in the early republic designated a man who worked with tools, a craftsperson—a man not engaged in agrarian work and not a merchant. Fire-fighting machinery required brawn to operate and technical skill to maintain, two tasks for which the average mechanic was well suited. The manpower to operate an engine, for example, was considerable, requiring brute strength and strict timing as teams of men steadily pulsed the twin levers (or "brakes") to generate water pressure, sometimes for hours. Companies created work groups to cycle through rotations lasting five to fifteen minutes, but it remained an exhausting effort. Additionally, technical competence made for good firefighters. Artisans and mechanical types constantly experimented with the equipment, testing ways to make the apparatus more effective. Cleaning and maintaining the various hoses and moving engine parts, a recurring task, required a basic knowledge of machinery and aptitude for engineering.[107]

Apparently, some Richmond citizens took offense at the mechanic's post—not because they opposed a new fire company, but because they weren't "mechanicks" and still wanted to help. In a lengthy apology following the notice, the lead mechanic wrote he "expected that every person who was under the age of 45, or strong able bodied men, would consider themselves as included in that notice, neither did he intend it to be particularly partial to any other persons but mechanicks." He made it clear, however, that young, mechanically inclined men were the type he *preferred* in the company, because he supposed that the mechanics of the city of Richmond "possessed not only the means, but also the energy to establish so valuable a society."[108] His presupposition was correct: nationally, thousands of reliable, hardworking, middle-class mechanics were organizing innumerable fraternal and relief organizations.

Thomas H. Palmer, the editor of the *Historical Register of the United States*, scrutinized the city's fire safety protocols, such as they were, when he paid a visit to Virginia in 1814. Palmer noted the Common Hall had elected a warden for each of the three city wards—Jefferson, Madison, and Monroe. Wardens set each ward's regulations and codes regarding allowable types of stoves and chimneys, and they determined which dangerous trades would be prohibited. When a fire lit up shop or home, wardens rallied to the site, where they then directed the engines and led the extinguishing and rescue efforts, conspicuous in special hats. Homes could be blown up at the warden's discretion, and he could imprison any obnoxious, interfering types in the local guardhouse or a large cage until the alarms ceased. As a final resort, he could also direct the engines to play with full force on those who continued to interfere with his orders.[109]

By 1816, the four existing voluntary brigades in the city consolidated to form the Richmond Fire Society, and the city acquired its first hook-and-ladder horse-drawn truck. Another interesting change had occurred as well—the demographic conversion of the fire company from an elite undertaking, as indicated by the Union Fire Company member rolls in 1787, to a middle-class laborers' effort. The 1816 rolls contained among their thirty-odd names a few prominent merchants but included a greater variety of laborers—a machinist, a leather dealer, a bookseller, a manufacturer, several builders, and an apothecary—among their numbers.[110] The names of the elite now rested on the rolls of the "Mutual Assurance Society on Buildings against Fire of the State of Virginia."[111] The rich insured against fire—the middle class fought it.

Richmond's slaves were also involved in local fire-fighting efforts, and in an experience eerily parallel to the theater fire, Gilbert Hunt again proved his courage in a famous fire rescue.[112] In 1823, architect Benjamin Henry Latrobe's renowned Richmond penitentiary caught fire. Hunt, who forged chains and cuffs for the prisoners, heard the alarm sound at around ten at night, and he ran for the jail to assist—his biography records that he was a member of the fire company at the time.[113]

Although he described the prisoners trapped inside the walls of the prison as "cutthroats . . . and rogues," Hunt felt instant compassion for them. "If you could have seen the poor fellows countenances, lighted up by the red light of the flames, and heard their piercing cries, you couldn't have helped doing something," he explained.[114] Seeing that it was impossible to get any water and the uncontainable fire had cut off the only jail exit, Hunt and fireman Captain Freeman made a human ladder and cut into the wall, allowing prisoners to escape the burning building through a sizable hole. Hunt reported, "We handed them down, one at a time, to the soldiers, who kept them from getting away. During all this time the flames were spreading like wild-fire over the whole building. But I was perfectly reckless; in fact, I forgot all about the fire, though the flames were hissing, and popping, and the flakes falling all around me."[115] No convicts were lost.

Mordecai vigorously contended that the smith should have received manumission at the hands of a grateful community. If not for his coolheaded rescues at the Richmond Theater, then he ought to have been freed for his intervention at the prison.[116] Noting that the elderly Hunt, for reason of poverty, was still doing backbreaking smithy work in his mid-seventies, Mordecai exclaimed, "Surely Gilbert deserves [at least] a pension for his services!"[117] Hunt did die a free man, but his manumission would be a result of his own diligent labor, not a gift from the public.

5

RECOVERY

Fom the end of December through the month of January, Richmond's doctors made round-the-clock home visits to patients, trying their best to treat the ubiquitous post-disaster broken bones and burns. Dr. Philip Thornton, who kept three horses at the ready in order to pay all the house calls necessary, was particularly attentive at Caroline Homassel's residence. Convalescing under that one roof were Caroline's aunt Mary Richard, who suffered a sprained ankle; Mary's niece Rosanna Dixon, who nursed numerous cuts and bruises; Caroline's friend Lucy Madison (her former fiancé's sister and James and Dolley Madison's niece), who had dislocated her wrist; and patriarch John Richard, who both dislocated an ankle and snapped his leg at the thigh in a compound fracture. The household mourned young George Dixon, Rosanna's brother, who had not survived. While Caroline was traumatized, she sustained no major injuries.

Thornton, in every moment where he was not needed at another home, came to the Richards to sit by John's bedside and investigate his progress, as attentive as any son. John's recovery was slow: it would be three months before he, permanently crippled, could again use the leg Thornton had set.[1] During those three months, Caroline found her heart warming toward the doctor she had spurned at Woodberry Forest, and she accepted his proposal of marriage. To her children, Caroline later wrote, "[Thornton's] devoted attention towards my idolized parent was most acceptable to my feelings, and whilst many said I married your father from gratitude for the preservation of my life, it was more from that tender, devoted attention to my beloved uncle, which was so appreciated by me, and seemed to merit some return."[2] Because she did not feel for him the overwhelming ardor she had carried for her former fiancé, Alfred Madison, Caroline wrestled with her motives until the eleventh hour. "The day before I was married my conscience almost said, 'you are doing wrong,'" she recorded, "but I did feel his tenderness and attention to my beloved uncle deeply."

On April 25, 1812, Dr. Philip Thornton and Caroline Homassel wed. The Richards bestowed on their daughter an elaborate trousseau and laid out an extravagant spread of confections for the guests. However, "the sadness of all hearts induced a quiet wedding," remembered Caroline, "and it was in accordance with my feelings and those of my uncle [her adopted father John Richard] and uncle Gallego."[3] The bride wore Mary Gallego's pearls, in memory of her gracious dark-haired "aunt" who perished in the fire. Caroline's bridesmaids included Maria Mayo, Betsy Gibbon (Lieutenant Gibbon's sister), Agnes Nicholson, and Lucy Madison, sister of Caroline's former fiancé. The absence of Sally Conyers in the bridesmaid's party was painfully conspicuous; she had been a central member in this coterie of young friends.[4]

Instead of leaving for a wedding trip, the newlyweds remained at Homassel's home for a month before traveling north to Thornton's family home in Rappahannock County. There Homassel met her husband's parents, as well as his nine brothers and multiple sisters, none of whom had apparently been present in Richmond for their nuptials. Philip's siblings spoiled her and called her their "French sister." His mother "was almost my beau Ideal of perfection," she wrote, and "we were united indissolubly." His imposing father was not so welcoming, and she never did feel she could overcome his "great reserve."[5]

After a prolonged stay, the couple made plans to return to Richmond, where Thornton's medical and surgical services were still required. The resources of the city were scarcely enough to meet the need of a mass casualty event. There were only around twelve doctors in Richmond in 1800, although numbers had probably increased by 1811. The most prestigious and civically active doctors in town were longtime Richmond residents Dr. McClurg and Dr. Foushee; the first was the father-in-law of lawyer John Wickham and the second the father-in-law of editor Thomas Ritchie.

An out-of-town physician with prescient timing, Dr. Bohannan, took a room over Ryan & Wilkins' Auction Store by the Market Bridge the first week in December 1811. He offered general medical care, surgery, and midwifery, and would "attend and furnish Medicine for the Poor, gratis."[6] Many physicians were not wealthy because, like Dr. Bohannan, they did extensive pro bono work. One Dr. Currie, however, had more business savvy, if less compassion, and was known for only taking on paying patients, which was unusual.[7]

To provide the necessary remedies and elixirs, the city had around three apothecary shops.[8] Patent medicines for afflictions such as venereal diseases, worms, and freckles could also be obtained at Samuel Pleasants' Printing Office and Bookstore.[9] Richmond's free blacks and whites were also likely to practice folk remedies, which may have been as effective—or noneffective— as anything prescribed by a doctor in the early republic, before medical practitioners had professional standards.[10]

In what was a great misfortune for the community at a time when quality medical care was a critical need, Dr. James McCaw, one of the city's foremost physicians, had been completely sidelined by injuries sustained after he plummeted from a window of the theater. A report stated, "His assistance as a physician and as a friend, would have been a balm to the woes of many; it may not be deemed presumption in saying, in the loss of his aid, some lives have been lost. The injury he has received [to his leg] is not incurable, but it is such as to neutralize his useful services for a long time."[11] Both a general physician and surgeon, McCaw had keen judgment and self-possession that made him equal to any emergency in his profession.[12] A graduate of medical school in Edinburgh, Scotland, McCaw had a more rigorous education than the other practicing physicians in Richmond, most of whom likely learned their profession through an apprenticeship or perhaps from self-instruction alone—nearly anyone so inclined in the early years of the nineteenth century could call himself a physician, hang out a shingle, and make a full-time career of treating infirmities.

The night of the fire and his narrow escape, McCaw assumed he had suffered a thigh fracture in his plunge to the ground, but upon examination there were no broken bones. Instead, the torturous pain he experienced exuded from multiple lacerated muscles in his leg.[13] Months of misery followed. McCaw apparently refused to be touched or moved, and he did not permit the removal of a single piece of his clothing for several months. When a caretaker or family member finally peeled off his crispy shirt and trousers, they saw that the garments McCaw had worn since the disaster were burned clear through his flannel underwear to his skin. It was then detected that he had a massive cicatrix on his back, perhaps fused to the fabric, indicating that he had suffered all those months from an extensive, entirely untreated burn.[14] The doctor may have healed others through proven skill, but his decisions relating to his own medical care did precious little to further his own recovery. McCaw eventually recuperated enough to resume his medical practice, which he went on to maintain for fifty years, but he carried the mark of the Richmond Theater fire with him forever. The vigorous Hercules of a man walked the rest of his life with a pronounced limp.[15]

PHYSICAL AND PSYCHOLOGICAL CURES

One begins to grasp the agonizing convalescence in store for burn victims upon apprehending the medical treatments utilized in the early republic. The prevailing medical philosophy of the time was known as "heroic medicine," and its advocate in the United States was preeminent medical practitioner and patriot Benjamin Rush. The ideas behind heroic medicine were as old as the first-century Greek physician Galen and emphasized restoring natural balances of the four bodily fluids through bleeding, purging, laxatives, and blistering. Depleting excess fluids, it was believed, held the key to healing everything—including burn wounds, for which hydration is crucial.

On January 4, 1812, Richmond's Dr. James Lyons, owner of a large and lucrative Richmond medical practice, published a timely article in the *Enquirer* entitled "Best Remedy for Burns." He took much of his advice from the 1792 book *Medical Facts and Observations* by David Cleghorn, a brewer from Edinburgh, Scotland. Cleghorn had become something of a lay expert on burn treatment after years of treating workers who had suffered burns in his breweries, and he had come to the conclusion that the "best remedy" was not the common practice of enemas but a topical application of cold vinegar.[16] Lyons submitted the article as a public service to Richmond's doctors and those administering home treatments to inform them of how best to employ the healing liquid. "The burnt or scalded part [of the body] is to be kept constantly wet with the Vinegar, by linen cloths which have been well soaked in it," Lyons advised. "Where the part can be immersed in the Vinegar, it is a preferable way of using it. . . . It cools & reduces the inflammation surrounding."[17] Unfortunately, immersing a severe burn in cold liquids can also cause shock. In medicine at that time, it was commonly believed that by creating a sensation or symptom akin to, but milder than, that which caused the injury, one could treat the disease or wound. This may explain the use of vinegar, which burns acutely on tender skin. "The smarting is no doubt a little irksome," Lyons admitted, "but it is worst at first, and, at any rate, goes off immediately upon discontinuing the vinegar." Unfortunate, then, for his patients that he prescribed its application for hours at a time.

Although modern doctors advise against the application of ointments or adhesives to a burn, Dr. Lyons had no reservations about their ample use. He also prescribed poultices made of chalk powder and lard, making the suggestion to "scrape the chalk on all the excoriated parts as soon as they begin to discharge" in order to absorb the excretions. If a chalky poultice was difficult to keep on a certain part of the body, Lyons made a thickly spread plaster of white lead and covered it with a dressing through the day, revisiting the chalk powder treatment in the evening.[18]

The Hallerian Academy's drawing instructor, a man by the name of Poisson who suffered burn wounds on his head, did not see Lyons until almost five days after the accident. Poisson had attempted to treat himself at home with topical applications of turpentine. He experienced a great scare midweek when his fever spiked and he became frighteningly feeble. Poisson then visited Dr. Lyons, who examined his wounds. The doctor wrote, "All the top of the head was in a crust. . . . The inflammation was so great that a heat was felt by holding a hand three or four inches above his head."[19] That substances like turpentine had been poured on the man's charred head is not surprising; a salve for burns, in Benjamin Bates's *Virginia Almanack* for 1812, incorporated not only "half a pound of thick turpentine" but a pint of linseed oil and a pound each of beeswax, rosin, and deer tallow. This mixture was to be stirred with a stick in a new earthen vessel over a slow fire until well blended before application.[20] Other American folk remedies for burns included applying bicarbonate of soda, sulfate of zinc, carbolic acid, Irish potatoes, or raw beaten eggs to the affected area.[21] (Vinegar, at least, has some astringent and antimicrobial qualities, although application to the skin is not usually advised by modern health practitioners.)

Fluid replacement is the first step in the modern treatment of burns. When skin is burned, large quantities of fluid pour into the tissue and accumulate in the body; therefore it is critical that victims take in fluid. Dr. Lyons demonstrated some inkling of the need for hydration when he prescribed tamarind water for Poisson's thirst and prepared a glass for him. Poisson promptly poured it on his head, and Lyons surmised that this was probably of more benefit than if he had taken it internally. Poisson then received the vinegar treatment, having his head thoroughly wetted, and Lyons reported improvement after only twelve hours, stating "[Poisson] is relieved beyond his expectation."[22]

Lyons's lengthy article closed with a rather unbelievable statement: "From this Method, Mr. C[leghorn] observes, that his cures are almost always effected without leaving any mark or scar."[23] Contrary to Cleghorn's assertion, most of Richmond's burn patients would have certainly sustained some disfigurement. Before the age of skin grafts, victims of second-degree burns could expect lifelong problems with their burned skin. The epidermis growing over the burn would be poor quality and easy to slough off. This would mean that Richmond's fire casualties with hand and arm burns might never again be able to engage in manual work. Because of the thick, rubbery scars, the wounded would probably have a severely limited range of motion, not able to easily bend their arms or pick up objects with their fingers. In 1831, Cincinnati physician Daniel Drake performed a case study on his own injuries and described the sensations of a serious burn to the hands. Drake's blistered hands ached for at least five weeks, and the inability to use his appendages aggravated his nerves further. Violent neuralgia lasted for eight months and appeared episodically even two years later. It could manifest itself as a dull ache or an acute, radiating pain. More commonly, Drake "could only compare it with the imaginary effect of millions of fine, red hot needles, running in all directions through the new flesh."[24]

Blistered areas, an immediate symptom of second-degree burns, presented another problem. They can fill with liquid to over a half-inch in height and vary in size from a quarter to an area larger than a handprint. Modern doctors recommend debriding them, although it is critical that they be kept clean. Because Lyons believed the chalk and the vinegar needed to come into direct contact with the raw, burnt flesh, he too advised opening blisters, "with a pin or lancet in different parts, and gently press the water out of them with a linen cloth. . . . New punctures . . . must be made at every dressing, whenever matter is seen lurking."[25] One can only imagine the rampant infection and soreness experienced by the victims. Lyons also advised scab picking on the second or third day as soon as the skin "can be separated from the sore without irritating it."[26]

Second-degree burns not properly treated can develop into third-degree burns. In a third-degree burn, nerve endings are destroyed, so the skin loses all sensation and appears dry, not moist. Skin may take on a waxy, grayish appearance, it may take on brown, pink, or white hues, or it may appear black and leathery. The entire depth of the dermis is baked solid and loses elasticity in a third-degree burn, and it may swell profoundly as the skin hardens. When this occurs in the extremities, it restricts the pulse; thus treatment requires slicing the skin open with a scalpel and allowing it to spread in a procedure called an escharotomy to release the fluid buildup. Although the wounds may not bleed initially from the incision, they gradually will. Thus it becomes necessary to dress the wounds and apply pressure. Skin burned to this extent will not heal—the epidermis and dermis clear through to the subcutaneous tissue have been destroyed. In 1812, few options beside opiates and alcohol existed for assistance in enduring the pain of such an injury.

Considering the numbers that escaped via the windows, there were also lacerations and bruises to treat. Survivors had used brute force to smash window panes, sustaining bleeding fists and limbs from the broken glass. Others had been shoved to the floor in piles of sharp shards in their attempt to jump out windows and sustained cuts of their own. Bone breaks were also common and would have been treated using splints or traction. John Richard's injuries from his thigh fracture developed into a long-term tribulation. A few years after the fire, he relied entirely on a carriage and horses for transportation. "His dislocated ankle and broken leg . . . kept him from walking with pleasure," Homassel Thornton noted.[27] A teen-aged girl with an ankle injury suffered agony for weeks as she convalesced in a home near the theater. A younger brother recalled that a year elapsed before his sister—who had shattered her ankle jumping out a window after watching her grandmother burn to death—could walk again, and she too was lame for life.[28]

Many survivors would have sustained inhalation injuries from the thick, poisonous smoke that filled the theater. Inhalation injuries, which were even more common than burns, may have produced bronchospasm in many of the theatergoers and rescuers, with symptoms similar to an asthmatic attack or a severe sore throat. The damage to the respiratory tract could also, in time, have led to pneumonia and even respiratory failure. It is doubtful that the prevailing remedy for breathing difficulties would have been ultimately helpful: Bates's *Virginia Almanack* for 1812 advised asthmatics and people with respiratory problems to inhale smoke from a stinkweed or thorn apple, breathed through a pipe. "The smoke, as well as the saliva [should be] swallowed together. The patient will find relief on smoaking the first pipe," he assured.[29]

* * *

"The Bells, for days toll'd for the whole community—for Richmond was in mourning," remembered Caroline Homassel Thornton. "Many hearts, withered, & died."[30] The psychological wounds of the fire were as deep and scarring as any third-degree burn, and the losses almost more than some could bear. The death count alone did not make the event so horrific and psychologically traumatic; it was its unexpectedness and the helpless nature of the victims it selected. Dr. Phillip Barraud of Norfolk, who had ample Tidewater connections in Richmond, wrote to a friend, "The Field of Battle presents no such spectacle to the mind. Men around well set for action, against each other, are expected to produce courage and Death. All parties are prepared for horrible events." The night of the twenty-sixth had presented a far different scene. "But here in the Moments of Festivity and Joy—at a Time when (in confident security) all the sportive and inocent passions of the soul were afloat, to find a Gulf of Fire, traveling with the rapidity of Lightening. . . . One feels stunn'd with the Immensity of the Picture."[31]

By New Year's Day, Secretary of State James Monroe in Washington, D.C., had received word of the fire and read a preliminary list of victims. To his family's relief, he learned that daughter Eliza Hay and her husband George were safe. Still the news cast a dark cloud. "You have heard of the dreadful calamity which has befallen the town of Richmond," James Monroe wrote to friend and fellow Revolutionary War veteran Paul Bentalou of Baltimore in his thick, black scrawl. "It has overwhelmed us all with affliction. Our daughter was fortunately not at the theater, nor have any of our immediate relations fallen victims; but we have had many near friends cut off by it."[32] Years later, when she became the de facto first lady during her father's presidency, Eliza had a reputation for being cold and inhospitable, but in 1811 one catches a glimpse of a woman whose sense of obligation to be present with her anguished friends was thought to threaten her very health. "Our daughter's situation, being advanced in her pregnancy, exposed her to much danger, from mere sympathy and a participation in the affliction of others, & there was much to bear for her on that account," wrote the worried future president. The morning that he penned his missive to Bentalou, the Monroes had received a letter from George Hay with the heartening report that Eliza's "spirits are more composed." Monroe breathed a sigh of relief and added to Bentalou, "We hope she will do well."[33]

Mourning rituals and visitation absorbed a great deal of the public's time in the first month of 1812. Lawyer William Wirt apologized to an out-of-town friend for an overdue letter on January 29, writing that he, like many in Richmond, had been preoccupied throughout the entire month with paying calls to the sick and families of victims. "The receipt of your letter [in late December] was followed doubly by the conflagration of the theatre and a consternation which suspended all business and all duties but those of offering consolation to the afflicted survivors of that most awful and dreadful calamity," he explained.[34] Between his legal caseload and the raft of commemorative activities, Wirt had neither time nor nerves in January for more than a scribbled letter of more than three or four hasty lines.

Hallerian Academy headmaster Louis Hue Girardin, while a combatant during the French Revolution, had witnessed piles of corpses and mangled bodies outnumbering those of the Richmond disaster. "But you may believe me, even then I did not experience half the horror which tortured me on the fatal night of the conflagration," he wrote. Absent were the emotions that make a hundred deaths seem somehow understandable in wartime. "Sentiments, such as party spirit, rational animosity, etc. rouse and support the physical and moral energies—but here, nothing stimulated, nothing invigorated, and everything palsied, unnerved both body and mind."[35] Seventy-two men, women, and children: disease could carry that number away easily, but usually disease brought a warning—some symptoms to presage the demise. Virginia historian John P. Little wrote of the fire in the 1850s, "It was the most awful stroke that ever afflicted Richmond; worse than pestilence, and more unsparing than war, the flames carried off in one red burial, those who made the dealings of many homes; and by the suddenness and awful horror of the calamity, made grief more loud and sorrow more bitter, than if another and milder form of death had been sent. Richmond became, like Ramah of old, a place of comfortless mourning."[36]

In 1854, the *New York Observer and Chronicle* reprinted the account of a minister in North Carolina who lived in Richmond during the fire. He provided an unexpected insight into the psychological effects of the theater fire on average citizens. Apparently grown at the time of the fire, the young minister lived in Richmond with an engaged older brother, who tried to induce him to attend the theater on December 26. "During the day which preceded the fire he approached me, handing me a dollar [the price of a ticket], and saying he supposed I wanted to attend the theatre in the evening. On my leaving home to reside in the city, my mother had charged me not to go to the theatre; this I told him, adding, I can't disobey my mother.—Upon this, he took back the dollar he had given me, expressing much contempt for my course. I was willing indeed, and even anxious to retain the dollar, but not as the means of violating my mother's command."[37]

The elder brother attended the performance with his fiancé while the minister went to sleep, not learning of the fire until the next morning. The fiancé died that evening; the brother narrowly escaped. The minister wrote of his brother, "This bereavement was to him a source of overwhelming grief, and he kept his room closely for nearly a month afterwards. He never subsequently said aught to me in reference to the theatre."[38] Memories drove many to silence, despite the possibility that dialogue might provide relief. Lawyer Charles Copland recorded in his diary, "The sad catastrophe of this night my feeling has hindered me from making a subject of conversation; but I have often wished that I knew the recollections (if any) which the two ladies I rescued, had of the scenes of that night."[39]

One can imagine the despair hovering over Richmond. Unpublished correspondence dating from the early months of 1812 describes widespread symptoms of depression, although the word was not in common parlance then. Survivors and friends expressed to each other their loss of interest in normal activities, feelings of helplessness, slipping work performance, sleep difficulties, and feelings of guilt—all symptoms of depression—as they grappled with the consequences of the fire.

While some correspondents expressed their anguish in writing, simply and without commentary, other sufferers seemed determined to remind themselves to think on spiritual truths that lent perspective to the misfortune. In her troubled frame of mind, it took Susan Bowdoin several months even to answer her mail, as she indicated in a May 11, 1812, letter to her dear brother in St. Louis, Missouri—then part of Louisiana. A longtime houseguest of the St. George Tucker family in Williamsburg, Virginia, Bowdoin described her spirits as "considerably dampened by the too shocking! Calamity at Richmond in Dec. which destroyed so many acquaintances, & fellow Creatures—." Two surviving friends had recently stopped in to see the Tuckers on their way home to the eastern shore, she noted. "Our dear Maria [Teackle] Parker, with her Husband, had a fortunate escape from the window of the Theatre. . . . The horrors of that scene, had wrought a great change in Maria's spirits, as you might easily conceive." Bowdoin, a dedicated Episcopalian, saw purpose in the misery. "These afflictions my dear Friend, are wisely ordered, to wean us from a World, where, our existence it should be remembered, is only, a state of trial & preparation for a better Life! In the last six months, we have been dayly reminded of the uncertainty of our stay here."[40]

The voids left in her friends' absence and her new frame of mind made the social rounds of cards and parties supremely distasteful to Homassel Thornton. Her husband, at "great injury to his practice," determined to alleviate her ennui by taking Caroline and her injured father-in-law on an extended vacation to improve their health. "We had a charming trip to the springs," Caroline recalled, "and visited first the Hot, and then the White, then the Sweet and returned by the Salt Sulphur." As much as a preventative as a curative, a trip to the springs allowed Virginia gentry an escape from stagnant urban humidity, the spread of summer disease, and the tensions of everyday life. The resorts that clustered around the hot springs in Virginia featured luxury residences for guests, dining, and recreational outings. Escaping Richmond's social frenzy for a more bucolic setting seemed to settle Caroline. "The scenery, variety and pleasant company, and friends I made at each place made it delightful, and I returned the first of October, after a frost to Richmond, greatly improved in health and spirits," wrote Caroline.[41]

In a letter from his lodging place in Georgetown dated the sixteenth of January 1812, Congressman John Randolph of Roanoke had written an eager letter to preeminent actor and personal friend Thomas Abthorpe Cooper in New York regretting that the two had not been able to meet in person that winter and putting forth plans for a reunion. As much as he anticipated a trip out of state and mingling with Cooper and his associates, Randolph balked at actually attending one of Cooper's performances. "A great part of my inducement to visit New York is . . . to be away," he wrote, "for, after the late dreadful occurrence at Richmond, I should hardly be able to look on any theatrical spectacle with pleasure."[42]

* * *

The depressed Charles Copland did not leave his home for days. His silent isolation even led friends to believe that Copland was dead. On Sunday, December 29, Judge John Coalter wrote a letter to his father-in-law in Williamsburg reporting that no one had heard from Copland in three days. "Margaret Copeland was consumed, and her Father also, it is said, in attempting to save her, this (his name) not being with the . . . list, I hope he may only be amongst the wounded."[43]

In east central Ohio, Copland owned nearly three hundred acres of wilderness and an isolated cabin along the Muskingum River, which son Charles Jr. oversaw. "Suffering much this year under a nervous affliction and finding no cure from medicine, I was advised by Doctor McClurg to travel and amuse myself in the best way I could," he recorded in May 1812.[44] Therefore, Copland, his wife, and son William set out from Richmond for an extended trip on the twentieth of May. They arrived on the family property road weary, no doubt, after their long journey, but were instantly enchanted by their simple wilderness hideaway with its own freshwater spring. The watershed hosted teems of wild game—deer, elk, river otters, bears, and panthers. Bald eagles and dark flocks of passenger pigeons traversed the sky above acres of beeches, pine, elm, tulip trees, and a carpet of ferns.

Copland's small vacation home was built of round oak logs, the floor of plain oak planks. He did not record that the family brought any slaves; instead they managed the chores themselves, finding it immensely restorative. Copland built a chicken coop, rode horses, and received visits from far-flung neighbors. "I was constantly employed in one thing or another and I have often thought that I enjoyed in this humble cottage as much happiness as human life is capable of," he remembered fondly. The peacefulness of nature, novelty of the excursion, and distance from his home—next door to the disaster site— afforded an effective respite. "It was to me a place of rest and of comfort, and there my health continued to improve every day."[45] After five weeks in Ohio, Copland felt rejuvenated enough to return to his home in Richmond. His retreat from Richmond, journey included, totaled over eleven weeks.

Ellen Mordecai visited Richmond during the second anniversary of the fire. "Louisa, called here this morning," she wrote to her brother Samuel. "She had just come from Mr. Pickets [sic] and mentioned *Mr. Galligo* [sic] was there who being invited to stay to dinner said if there was no company expected he would, for home is *too dreary* for me—And who would not have indulged the gloom he must have felt, nor sought for company when on this night he lost his wife and niece."[46] Joseph Gallego never recovered from that loss. His festive home was an empty place without Mary and Sally. "Oh! What a scene of desolation did that elegant mansion present," recalled Caroline Homassel Thornton, "what a seeming mockery to the broken heart, the appliance of wealth in every form and shape, and who could describe the anguish of his widowed and childless heart, for all was gone that made life dear to him."[47] Gallego's slow decline ended with his death in July 1818. Seven years later, "Jock" Allan, whose fortunes were rising, bought Moldavia, Gallego's home. His ward, Edgar Allan Poe, lived there for a year before leaving to attend the University of Virginia. A persistent, fictitious rumor survives that Poe's parents died in the fire. Poe started the rumor, and the couple most certainly did not.

After losing wife and son, Louis Hue Girardin became nearly suicidal. The *Petersburg Intelligencer* published one of Girardin's private letters, penned when in a raw state of grief, arguing with himself over whether or not he should remain alive. On one hand, "an imperious, a sacred duty calls upon me to live," he declared. "My two daughters remain, the one scarcely able to feel because she does not fully comprehend her misfortune, the other calling with heart-rending cries for the nourishment which a mother's breast lately supplied. . . . Be it so, then—Let me live—But—thou, merciful God, who art compassionate to the newly shorn lamb, sustain me, a wretched desponding mourner beneath this heaviest load of accumulated affliction and woe!" A few pages later, he again shored up his resolve, but wondered what kind of parent he might be in his distraught state to his motherless children. "I must live—live for my daughters—but where shall I find even a smile to reciprocate their innocent, infantine caresses?"[48]

Girardin's deeply troubled emotional condition led to the closing of his prestigious school. On January 9, he announced a brief leave of absence, explaining in the third person that the "heavy pressure of calamity, alas! Too well known, does not permit him immediately to resume his professional duties." David Doyle and Francis Power, the latter previously a "Teacher of the English Branches" at the Hallerian Academy, would instruct Girardin's pupils until he was able to return.[49]

Early in January 1812, Girardin solemnly put his classrooms in order, probably lining books along the shelf, straightening chairs, and forcing himself to draft lessons he had no heart to teach. But when the week finally approached during which he planned to resume tutoring, he found that he could not. When Girardin moved his family to the capitol area in Richmond in 1810, he had prepared to dedicate himself to the area and to his Hallerian Academy pupils.[50] But after burying his wife and son in the ruins, it became impossible for him to stay in Court End, to smell the stale smoke from the wreckage on H Street, to compose his tortured mind, preoccupied with the plight of his daughters, enough to instruct a classroom full of young students.[51]

Two small posts by Girardin advertising his large brick house near the capitol for rent appear near the end of January.[52] Girardin was leaving town for good. On the fourth of February, he permanently retired from the Hallerian Academy.[53] Citing his disquiet mind, an "obstinate malady," and "horribly distressing" circumstances, Girardin recommended his students transfer to Power, a graduate of Dublin University, and promised to render up student accounts and adjust them "fairly and amicably."[54]

The folding of the Hallerian Academy was the final upset for the popular school; most of its problems in 1811 had been related to personnel. Mathematics instructor John Wood had suddenly quit and opened a competing public school.[55] French teacher Charles Fremon, by student Thomas Atkinson's account, was an "exquisite fop" who offered lessons in French, spelling, reading, and elocution for a over a year at the Hallerian Academy until he began instructing a married, upper-class female pupil in a subject not taught in any school.[56] His affair with Mrs. Anne (sometimes Anna) Pryor happened in her home, where Fremon was boarding, right under the nose of her much older husband, a Revolutionary War veteran and local businessman.[57] In December 1811, an outraged John Pryor petitioned for divorce from his wife, stating on the record that in June "by the stratagems of a certain Charles Fremon, her affection was perpously seduced, so far as to be concerned in a criminal intercourse with the said Fremon." With Fremon, Anne left the state. Notwithstanding the divorce request of both parties, the court rejected John Pryor's petition.[58] Anne and Charles's son, known as John Charles Fremont, was born in January 1813 in the state of Georgia. He became an adventurer and abolitionist, and he served a short term as a Democratic senator from California before the fledgling Republican Party elected Fremont their first presidential candidate in 1856. His campaign slogan: "Free soil, free labor, free speech, free men, Fremont." He had by this time married Jessie Benton, a senator's daughter, and lost some of the social stigma he carried as a child of "free love." The Fremon-Pryor affair at the Hallerian Academy caused a sensational Richmond scandal in 1811 and did not reflect well on Girardin's school.

Francis Power had been steadily working with Girardin in Richmond since late August of 1810 and was a man on whom Girardin could rely to guide the school forward in his absence.[59] The new downsized academy would educate only "young gentlemen" and offered half the courses advertised in 1810. It relocated to "The Little Capitol" on H Street and ran for at least two more years.[60] David Doyle's new school, which met in Joseph Gallego's yellow house, took on some of Girardin's male pupils as well. If demand were present, Doyle offered to hire a teacher for females in a separate part of the building.[61] It would seem, overall, that Girardin's female pupils were more likely to be set adrift without tutors than the males after the fire and subsequent closing of the Hallerian Academy.

ELEGIES AND POETRY

In the face of mass suffering, a sense of compulsion settles on some to assist however they can in order to comfort the mourning. One of the most interesting means in the wake of the fire was through the writing of original poetry, most of which was excruciatingly bad. From the available manuscripts found accompanying the poems, elegies served a cathartic purpose for the writer and were offered as a means of succor to the reader. Richmond Theater fire–themed elegies, monodies, and odes appeared in newspapers and journals and were circulated among friends for decades following the fire. The stiff formality and predictable conventions made elegies easy to satire, but participating in familiar, structured means of expressing grief comforted many Americans. In the poem, an author often explained what he or she understood as the purpose of the fire, described the event, and memorialized particular victims and heroes. It usually ended with poetic advice for the reader.[62] Out of fashion by this time in England, elegies remained popular expressions of sorrow in America well into the nineteenth century. Amateurs did not shy from the challenge.

Rev. Thomas Bomar lamented victim Abraham Venable, Richmond's bank president, in a particularly awkward verse.

Now let Virginia's bank with sorrow tell,
How she has lost poor Abram Venable;
His hand must now in silent dust be still,
And never more can sign another bill.[63]

The theater fire deeply affected St. George Tucker, one of Virginia's leading judges and law professors. Tucker had studied under George Wythe, framer of the Constitution and signer of the Declaration of Independence, and in turn Tucker tutored William and Mary students in law. Letters from grieving associates and relatives poured into his Williamsburg home for months after the fire, providing dramatic details about painful losses. Tucker wrote an elegy within a week of the disaster, which he sent privately to affected friends and also to several newspapers. Included among his original drafts is a letter to the editor of the *Richmond Enquirer*, written on January 8, 1812. Under conditions of anonymity, Tucker stated that his purpose for publishing the poem was to "in some small Degree, contribute to solace the affliction of such of the unhappy sufferers in the late Calamity, as still survive; and soothe the Grief of some of those who lament the loss of their dearest friends, or connexions."[64]

Meditation on poetry seems to have been a way to combat the longings and lonesomeness of a new widower in the early republic. On January 3, 1812, Tucker mailed a draft of the elegy to his old friend Robert Greenhow, who mourned his wife Mary Ann. Although the poet had "not yet had time to revise and correct it, as perhaps I may, hereafter. I send it to you in its present state, because, if it should happen to touch the chords of your feelings, it may possibly contribute to soothe your afflictions."[65] Tucker shared it because he found poetry of medicinal value in his own experience. He lost his first wife, Frances Bland Randolph (mother of John Randolph of Roanoke), in 1788 when she was only thirty-six, and Frances left him with several young children to raise. In his pain, Tucker found writing poetry purgative and memorizing it restorative. He wrote to Greenhow:

I have felt affliction, keenly; and have felt relief by first giving vent to my agonies, in writing something of the kind, which I committed to memory, and repeated to myself, when *alone*, and especially *when in Bed*, and unable to close an Eye. In such a situation I have been relieved by frequently repeating what I had written, or something of the same kind, which I had read, and got by heart, for the same purposes. And if it be not too great presumption in me to offer you advice in such an Occasion, permit me to recommend the same course to you.[66]

John Marshall inscribed a short tribute to his wife—"the solace of my life!"—in 1832 on the first anniversary of her death. Poetry had aided him, too, in his bereft state. "More than a thousand times since the 25th of December, 1831, have I repeated to myself the beautiful lines written by General Burgoyne, under a similar affliction, substituting 'Mary' for 'Anna:'

> Encommpass'd in an angel's frame,
> An angel's virtues lay;
> Too soon did heaven assert its claim
> And take its own away!
> My Mary's worth, my Mary's charms,
> Can never more return!
> What now shall fill these widow'd arms?
> Ah me! My Mary's urn![67]

More than two weeks after the Richmond Theater fire, the *Enquirer* announced two new victims: Mary Love Scott, wife of Richard M. Scott, delegate from Fairfax, and John Alcock's son, whose name was not given. Neither were remembered on the memorial or even included on the official death tally. Perhaps for this reason, Richard M. Scott contacted Tucker by letter on May 15, 1812 (the day after Tucker's elegy was published in the *Alexandria Daily Gazette*), hoping to commission a few additional stanzas specifically honoring Mary Scott and her family. "The indulgence my Dear Sir which you have extended to me on this, as well as every other occasion, emboldens me to impose upon your kindness so far as to solicit from you at your leisure an Epitaph, and also an Elegy, on her whose loss I mourn. She was the best of human beings, and the best of wives, indeed Sir, too much cannot be said in her praise," wrote Scott.[68]

Although Tucker did his best, the effort presented a challenge. Scott "requested me to introduce the characters of his decease'd lady's brothers, and five sisters, in the Elegy," recorded Tucker in exasperation. But the lines did not come easily and the effort to compose something suitable took over a month. Strikethroughs and annoyed annotations indicate Tucker's frustration with the process. In the space above the stanza draft he wrote: "I sent him the following lines, which are miserably bad, but they are the best I could compose." And following the stanza: "Unless I can make something better of them I shall probably throw the above into the fire. June 28. 1812."[69]

* * *

By the third week of January, the winter chill had frozen the swirling waters of the James River into sheets of solid ice. Townspeople struggled to keep their homes tolerably warm, especially for the invalids still recovering from the theater fire, in what was becoming the coldest winter in several years. Law clerks in frustration tried to scratch out documents with ink frozen in the pot. In recognition of the cold, the *Enquirer* urged charity to the "aged, the orphan, and the distressed."[70]

During the freeze, tremors rocked Virginia. On the twenty-third of January, two earthquakes shook beleaguered Richmond, with strong vibrations felt on Shockoe Hill. "Some persons were rocked in their chair. Some staggered as they stood. Hanging keys oxcillated. Doors and windows flapped. Bedsteads and tall articles of furniture were moved to and fro. Those who were at breakfast saw a violent ripple on the surface of tea & coffee. A few ran out of their houses in great alarm," reported the *Enquirer*.[71]

Fresh speculation about the meaning of the tremors erupted across town. First the fire, now an earthquake? Had Richmond done something to anger God? *Enquirer* editor Thomas Ritchie felt compelled to quash the rampant superstition. "Whether they are the tales of the nursery or of old women; whether we are told of the fate of nations in an eclipse or of a friend's death in the winding-sheet of a candle; whether it be a dream . . . they are equally at war with the lessons of philosophy," he argued, pleading for a more scientific understanding. "Where is the connection between the sign and the event? What is it that links them together? Where is the cause or where the effect?"[72]

Yet the idea persisted that the fire was an act of God with an important lesson for America.

6

JUDGMENT

May theatres all be done away,
Thro' all Columbia's shore,
The buildings put to better use,
And plays be seen no more.
—"THEATRE ON FIRE. AWFUL
CALAMITY!" BROADSIDE, 1811

A wide black mourning border rings a nine-by-eleven-inch broadside distributed after the fire. Penny broadside publications often followed a sensational event, memorializing a comet, murder, or shipwreck in stanzas of amateur poetry intended for singing. This particular broadside featured lyrics about the Richmond Theater fire.

An evening in December last,
Th' six and twentieth day,
The people there with joyful haste,
Did go to see a play.

When in the midst of joy and mirth,
The house it caught on fire,
Hundreds envelop'd in the flames—
There many did expire.

People of ev'ry sect and age.
Of dignity and state
Were hurried from this mortal stage—
How dreadful to relate!

Ye thoughtless, gay, both old and young—
To sacred things attend;
And think how many ways death comes,
To bring us to our end.

A crude woodcut of the theater is printed top and center. Thick, jagged lines emanate from the roof, ending in a pair of dark clouds that loom over the structure.[1] These could be flames shooting out of the building, producing high billows of smoke. But they more strongly resemble angry clouds striking bolts of lightning into the theater. This interpretation would have been historically inaccurate but in line with the theological beliefs of clerics who insisted divine anger caused the disaster. Americans in the early republic often understood natural events and disasters to be imbued with meaning—a divine cause and an instructive purpose lay behind all events.

In 1711, a hundred years prior to the Richmond fire, Puritan divine Increase Mather preached a sermon entitled "Burnings Bewailed" after a destructive conflagration roared through Boston and authorities traced responsibility for the fire back to a "wicked drunken Woman."[2] The redoubtable minister asked if God had not brought this fire upon Boston on account of the failures of Massachusetts's lax Christians. *"Many are Departed & Degenerated from those Holy Principles, which in our First & Purest Times, NEW-ENGLAND was distinguished by,"* he lamented.[3]

Many understood the fire as a call for repentance and revival and sought to discern why this unexpected tragedy had transpired. If God orchestrated the event, and many believed he did, what was he saying to America? What about the new republic angered God? And of what did Americans need to repent? An ink-and-paper flood of sermons, editorials, pamphlets, elegies, and heated newspaper opinion pieces churned around possible reasons.

The ways in which Virginians and Americans perceived the tragedy help us to grasp early nineteenth-century perceptions about the purpose behind natural disasters—perceptions that remain part of the American consciousness today. The discussions also illuminate another interesting topic: About which things did early republic Americans feel shame? For what omissions and commissions did they believe God might rightly visit judgment on them?

At the same time, rationalist voices challenged the providential reading of the fire, and Christians debated the conflagration's theological significance, making for a vigorous debate over the spiritual meaning—if there was one—of the disaster at the Richmond Theater.

Unitarian schismatic George Richards, in his theater fire sermon, concluded that although America was "the hope, the strength, the pride, the bulwark of this western world," American leaders lacked mercy for the most deserving among them: the men who had delivered the nation from tyranny.[4] This he considered a reason for God's judgment on the nation. The U.S. government had not properly supplied for "the war worn soldier" after the Revolution and had left the soldiers' widows and orphans in poverty.[5] Legal reports in the Richmond newspapers feature regular petitions for military pensions from veterans in dire straits. The government had failed to promptly deliver on pension promises and, in the case of enslaved black veterans, promises of manumission.

In 1812 while Richmond publicly honored Commander Stephen Decatur with a lavish public dinner and a handsome portrait, other, less distinguished veterans traveled to the legislature, cap in hand, to plead for basic aid. Wounded Revolutionary War veteran William Gentry of Hanover stood before Virginia's Committee of Propositions and Grievances, forced to broadcast his infirmities, directly related to his time in the military under Harrison's Artillery Regiment: "From the fatigue and exposure of his health, whilst in the service as aforesaid, he is rendered unfit for labor; that, from pains and weakness in his hips and knees, it is with difficulty he can even walk," reported the House of Delegates. The incongruously named Gentry was "POOR, possessing no property whatever," and he and his four children were "praying therefore relief from the bounty of his country."[6] That heroes would have to beg seemed shameful.

The hardships were more than some veterans could bear. On Richmond's Capitol Square during an evening parade of the Public Guard of the State in February 1819, Colonel William Tatham, an old and impoverished soldier, took his station with other veterans near the artillery during a gun salute. The moment a guard applied the match to it, Tatham intentionally stepped in front of a nearby cannon. The blast tore him apart. Mordecai called him "either very eccentric or deranged, and moreover poor," any of which reasons could have been related to what has been called battle fatigue or post-traumatic stress disorder and may have driven him to suicidal desperation.[7]

George Richards and Ann Tuke Alexander, an English Quaker abolitionist, believed that God had punished Richmond specifically for embracing African slavery. Richards asked, "Has eternal justice no claims in behalf of twelve millions of Africans, who have been annually sacrificed . . . to the demon of commercial avarice, the spirit of European luxury; and the genius of American Indolence?" It was no wonder, if slavery grieved God, that Richmond would be a special target. Tuke Alexander noted that Richmond was "notorious" for its slave trade, a trafficking she had witnessed firsthand during a tour of the United States from 1803 to 1805.[8]

Robert Sutcliff, a Quaker tourist from Sheffield, England, was astonished by the contrast in quality of life between slave states and free states in America. He found particularly disgusting the predatory sexual escapades of the white Richmond male. "From my own observations, and the information I received from an inhabitant, Richmond appears to be a place of great dissipation," he wrote, "chiefly arising from the loose and debauched conduct of the white people of their black female slaves." He added in astonishment, "It frequently happens here, as in other places, that the white inhabitants, in selling the offspring of these poor debased females, sell their own sons and daughters, with as much indifference as they would sell their cattle. By such means, every tender sentiment of the human breast is laid waste, and men become so degraded, that their feelings rank but little above those of the beasts of the field."[9] Other visitors like Josiah Quincy, Jr., who passed through in the 1770s, noted in shock: "It is far from being uncommon to see a gentleman at dinner, and his reputed offspring a slave to the master of the table. I myself saw two instances of this. . . . The fathers neither of them blushed or seem[ed] disconcerted. They were called men of worth, politeness and humanity. Strange perversion of terms and language!"[10]

Traveling northward on the road out of Richmond, Sutcliff met an "active, industrious couple," milliners and drapers by trade and recent émigrés from Scotland. Despite establishing a lucrative business, the entrepreneurial family packed their trunks and moved out of Richmond, convinced that staying permanently in the city would "be attended with almost certain ruin to the morals of their children."[11] They tried to acclimate to the customs of the place—but were moving north, "where they would not be tried with the contaminating influence and effects of this unhallowed system of slavery."[12]

Sutcliff's drapers were but a small number of the immigrants, Quakers, and poor whites who eventually left the state in the early years of the nineteenth century—most for western lands—in order to secure their family's prosperity and escape the ways in which the canker of slavery diseased and devalued labor.[13] Some claimed you could even perceive the moral difference in the diseased geography of slave-holding Virginia: Federalist Samuel White of Delaware claimed during a Senate debate in 1804, "As you travel south, the instant you arrive to where slavery is, you find the lands uncultivated, the building decaying and falling into ruins and the people poor, weak and feeble."[14] Sutcliff remarked that in Virginia, "as a matter of course, poverty and wretchedness seem to abound."[15]

Tuke Alexander believed there would be hope that God would relent of his destructive visitations if Richmond's slaveholders and citizens repented of their wickedness toward blacks. "Should these pages ever cross the Atlantic," she wrote from England, "and meet the eye of any of those who witnessed this awful visitation [the destruction wrought by the fire], may such, in particular, be thereby induced to take warning, and to attend to the prophetic exhortation of 'Seek ye the Lord, while he may be found; call ye upon him, while he is near. Let the wicked forsake his ways, and the unrighteous man his thoughts; and let him return unto the Lord, and he will have mercy upon him, and to our God, for he will abundantly pardon.'"[16]

"The general impression was that the burning of the theatre was a clear manifestation of its divine condemnation," recalled Virginian and Baptist minister Jeremiah Jeter, a boy at the time of the fire.[17] American Christians held positions on theatergoing that ranged from tolerance to hostility, but certainly after the disaster in Richmond, the loudest voices in the public square were those who criticized the stage and theatergoers and saw it as the reason for Richmond's "punishment" by fire. Richmond's destructive blaze resulted in a groundswell of preaching against the theater in 1812. "The Calamity which we lament, ought to be employed, among other purposes, as an occasion of entering a solemn protest against a prevailing, but most unchristian, and most baneful Amusement," lectured Rev. Samuel Miller of First Presbyterian Church in New York City.[18] *Zion's Herald,* a Methodist lay publication, wrote, "We must conclude that the Theatre is the object of his great displeasure. To deny this, would, in effect, be to deny the providence of God. That most calamitous event, the burning of the Theatre at Richmond, and the losses of theatres by fire since that period . . . are tokens of the Divine displeasure, too manifest to allow us to hesitate."[19]

To religious critics, the company the theater provided and the insidious immorality learned within its doors would undo the careful training of godly parents. "I am persuaded it is my duty to declare . . . all those who encourage this sinful practice of plays, &c. are not worthy in this respect to be called Christians, because they promote . . . the cause of Satan," railed independent minister Rees Lloyd.[20] The theater seemed a direct rival, a competitor for their parishioners' time, money, and affection. Particularly galling to a clergy convinced of the theater's vileness, the stage actually had moral pretentions and backers who vigorously argued on behalf of its instructive power for good.[21] Evangelical ministers viewed it as a very grave threat; the sweeping clerical condemnations of the theater from the first half of the nineteenth century are described by a historian of American theater as immoderate, irrational, marked by desperation, and even violent.[22] Despite their vociferousness, the pastors' arguments ultimately proved ineffective, as evidenced by the cultural acceptance of the theater, and even its appropriation by Christians, later in the century.[23]

The vehemence of opinion can be explained partly by the belief of some ministers that not only souls were put at risk by avid American theatergoing but the existence of the American republic itself. If it were the case that theatergoing encouraged habits in direct opposition to republican virtues of high-minded morality, thrift, and personal industry, then even the civic-minded who were not particularly religious had reason to develop serious reservations about the propriety of attending.[24] Renouncing the theater then took on a larger significance—no longer should renunciation be a religious compulsion, but a civic duty.[25] Rees Lloyd even argued that plays undermined the republic's ability to defend itself: "[Plays] make no man a better soldier, but rather make him more mercenary, idle and effeminate."[26]

If this were the case, then it seemed appropriate for national leaders to become involved in ending the institution of the American theater. Lloyd warned American congressmen: "The place [the Richmond Theater] was not far from the seat of government; this might have been, to warn our rulers to take notice of leading vices that bring calamities and accidents upon the nation; to warn them not to be unconcerned of their duty, to discountenance such vain amusements by law and example."[27] Lloyd's advice was an exception; only a few ministers recommended legislative action or stricter government regulations for American theaters; most recommended a simple boycott.

Who, specifically, spoke out against the theater? Northerners, Calvinists, and evangelicals produced most of the extant printed religious commentary about the Richmond Theater fire. Printed sermons were, of course, only a fraction of the sermons actually delivered on this topic, although they usually represent the most influential of them. Of the twenty or so surviving printed sermons and religious pamphlets from the fire, nine were printed in Philadelphia. Two came out of Baltimore, two from New York City. Massachusetts issued three: two from Boston, one from Ipswich. Only two sermons by Virginia ministers are represented: one from Alexandria and one from Winchester, both by Presbyterians. Geographic region did not seem to make a significant difference to theater criticism generally speaking, however; throughout the first decades of the nineteenth century, southern ministers were as likely to attack the stage as those from the West and North.[28]

While denominations and even city of print are not always provided, Presbyterians are the best-represented religious organization according to available records, delivering seven of the existing postfire antitheater sermons. Other denominations were represented by two Methodists, an "Independent Minister," two Congregationalists, a Unitarian, a Quaker, and an Episcopalian. (The Unitarian, George Richards, and the Episcopalian, George Dashiell, were schismatics within their denominations and did not espouse views representing their larger denominations.) Less representation in print is to be expected from denominations such as the Baptists and Methodists, who placed a high priority on extemporaneous preaching and did not leave the written record of sermon notes and drafts that other denominations would. Sermons may not have been remembered sufficiently enough to recreate in writing if no written notes or draft existed. It could be done with some trouble—when Jeremiah Jeter, a Baptist, gave a message against the Richmond Theater, several men asked for a copy to distribute. Because he had preached from "not very copious notes," he had to reconstruct it as best he could from memory.[29]

Historian of early nineteenth-century theater David Grimsted remarked that although tone and emphasis might differ among critics, Catholics, Quakers, Episcopalians, Baptists, Congregationalists, Presbyterians, and Methodists who attacked the stage drew from the same arsenal of arguments. The religious attack on the stage essentially was made with one voice.[30] Throughout the first decades of the nineteenth century, there were a few urtexts from which nearly all ministers—regardless of denomination— sourced their antitheater arguments. The first was the influential "Essay on the Nature and Effects of the Stage" by John Witherspoon, a leading Presbyterian clergyman and signer of the Declaration of Independence, and the second, the writings of John Tillotson, a seventeenth-century archbishop of Canterbury. In 1789, Lindley Murray, a Quaker, compiled a list of famous men who had uttered quotes against the theater, including Plato, Tacitus, and Rousseau, in his pamphlet *Extracts from the Writings of Diverse Eminent Authors . . . Representing the Evils and Pernicious Effects of Stage Plays and Other Vain Amusements.* Murray's list was frequently quoted in sermons and articles regarding the Richmond Theater fire as well.[31]

Witherspoon's lengthy invective sought to prove that "PUBLIC THEATRICAL REPRESENTATIONS, either tragedy or comedy, are, in their general nature or in their best possible state, unlawful, contrary to the purity of our religion; and that writing, acting or attending them, is inconsistent with the character of a Christian."[32] While he provided many reasons as to why Christianity and the theater were incompatible, he emphasized the following: the theater put Christians in the way of temptation; rather than being a "school of morality," it taught ungodly morals that corrupted the audience; actors and actresses had "foul, polluted" minds and lives (although he admitted "never having exchanged a word with one of that employment in my life"); theater attendance was an "altogether unnecessary" cost and undermined thrift; and attending a play was a misuse of the time entrusted to us by God. The disquieting conclusion he suggested was that dying in (or after attending) a theater could possibly endanger one's soul.[33] After the fire in Richmond, these six major themes were echoed in sermons and articles by Christians of many creeds. Witherspoon's criticisms of theatergoing corresponded with evangelical values then gaining in ascendancy, as well as with republican civic virtues as they were then widely understood, and thus appealed to men of the cloth from a wide range of denominations.

THE LURE OF THE CORRUPTING THEATER

"'Lord, lead us not into temptation,' is a petition which we are taught to offer up," wrote Witherspoon. "But how much do those act in opposition to this, and even in contempt of it, who make temptations to themselves. And are not stage-plays temptations of the strongest kind, in which the mind is softened with pleasure, and the affections powerfully excited?"[34] Another Presbyterian minister agreed that theaters exposed men, women, and children to immorality that might tempt them to stray from an obedient Christian walk. "I am constrained to declare myself an enemy to the amusements of the theatre, as they are in use in our day," wrote Rev. William Hill. While theater had the potential to be a force for virtue and patriotism, as it had been in Greece and Rome, Hill considered the unregulated theaters in America to be "little better than schools of vice.[35] He preached that American theater had "fallen into the hands of the most abandoned and licentious wretches and prostitutes, with few exceptions."[36]

Prostitution was indeed a part of American theater culture in the first half of the nineteenth century. In his 1833 classic *History of the American Theatre,* actor William Dunlap disapprovingly referenced the "American regulation of theatres, which allots a distinct portion of the proscenium to those unfortunate females who have been the victims of seduction."[37] A Baltimorean described his local playhouse as a "very exchange for harlots," a "Flesh-market" where "male and female prostitutes [in] the front boxes rendered the scene of actions fit only for a brothel."[38] It is known that audiences in Baltimore, Norfolk, and Richmond theaters regularly included prostitutes, drunks, and other socially unsavory sorts.[39] From Boston to New Orleans, theaters offered a prime location for "ladies on the town" to make initial contact with prospective clients or arrange a meeting with existing clients. Because of the patrons they attracted to the theater, prostitutes were sometimes given discount ticket prices or admitted for free. Managers in most theaters allowed prostitutes the run of the top row of gallery seating—infamously known as the "third tier." The women would often arrive in their seats by a separate entrance a few hours before the rest of the house opened.[40] Theater historian Claudia Durst Johnson considers the widespread existence of the third tier—a practice that colored theater policy for over fifty years—the most irrefutable argument the church possessed against the theater as an institution that encouraged and facilitated immorality.[41]

The Baltimorean recalled that twenty years earlier, theater managers and theatergoers would have censured a prostitute who left her seat in the back and dared "shew her face" in the lower boxes. But social rules had changed by 1812. "The front boxes of the theatre are almost exclusively devoted to women of the town. The lobbies swarm with them," he stated indignantly.[42] This incursion would have been particularly offensive; the physical separation of prostitutes from the boxes and better seats in the house allowed many religious theater patrons to justify regular theater attendance. They sat apart from the prostitutes and their clients and did not patronize the in-theater bars that fueled the rowdy atmosphere of the third tier. Just as a passenger in a first-class ship cabin could not be held responsible for indecent acts in the steerage, respectable theater patrons could argue they had nothing to do with the behavior of disreputable theatergoers. However, disgraced women infiltrating regular theater patron seating demolished the dividing wall between the groups, acknowledging the fact that disgraced women often found clients from among the more respectable classes and requiring respectable women to interact with their rouged and fallen counterparts.

* * *

Rev. Robert May, a twenty-one-year-old missionary from Suffolk, England, was biding time in Philadelphia the winter of 1811. The previous March he had sailed from England to the Quaker city and then set out on a ship bound for India, his ultimate destination, in the month of May. But storms grew violent over the Atlantic that spring and forced the ship back to Philadelphia's port. Robert May remained in the city with his wife through the fall and winter, waiting for the winds to blow favorably, waiting for the day when he could set foot in India.[43] While stranded in Pennsylvania, May began to teach in local Sunday schools and was much in demand as a children's speaker.

When the sad news from Richmond arrived in Philadelphia in December 1811, the fate of the six "dear little children" who perished along with "no less than thirty-six young persons, in the prime of life," seized his imagination and plunged him into a gloom which happenings at his own home only exacerbated.[44] The winter of 1811, death visited his home and "snatched from me a beloved child."[45] His baby's life had been cut short, and Robert May had an ominous sense that his own life would be brief. Diseases had claimed the lives of many missionaries to India. His ship's delays emphasized the perilous conditions he faced on his way across the Atlantic. And now the theater fire had shown that no child was truly safe, even when surrounded by adults, even when at play. And so May drafted a sermon, a pleading discourse about the Richmond Theater fire for his young listeners, in the hopes that they might be spared from corporeal, and eternal, death as a result of this disaster in Richmond.[46]

Keeping him ever on task as he penned a new sermon was the sight of a graveyard outside his window, peppered with stones, stretching over bleak, wintery hills. As a boy of seven or eight, he had read *Janeway's Token for Children*, a seventeenth-century Restoration-era text recounting the "joyful deaths" of small children, and it had converted him. May's own writings were deeply influenced by Rev. James Janeway's morbid, dramatic style, which ostensibly readied youngsters for the reality of death in a time of high child mortality.

His sermon carried this message to children in the aftermath of the fire: "Avoid, as you would a serpent, the amusement of the theatre. The haunts of the theatre lead down to the gates of eternal death."[47] May described the six children who met an early death in the burning ruins of the Richmond Theater fire. "I think I see their burnt and mangled bodies, wrapped carefully up, and carried to their houses of mourning from the house of mirth. I see them but in part. Their half burnt bodies and their smoking bones!"[48] He imagined a ghostly child cautioning the living.

> I have a message from God unto you. Shun the theatre: avoid the haunts of Satan, the destroyer of your souls. . . . Five weeks ago, I was in life, blooming, healthy and gay. I thought, like many others, that there was no harm in attending on the amusements of the theatre, and from persuasion and example I was confirmed in my opinion. That very afternoon, I laughed at a young lady for saying that "the theatre was a very improper place; that many had been ruined, body and soul, by attending at such places of amusement." Ah, my young friends, I wish I had felt the force of her observation. . . . Suffocated with smoke, I fainted and fell, blazing into the pit, and was crushed and covered with the burning ruin. . . . My state is now unalterably fixed forever. Attend to the warning. Behold the displeasure of a holy God . . . and remember that "the end of these things is death."[49]

May and a cadre of similarly minded clerics portrayed plays as a gateway sin. Passing one's time in a theater would cause a slide into iniquitous mire, vacuous habits, and eternal damnation. Rees Lloyd purported that theatergoers "depart from virtue to vanity; from consideration to rashness; from a tender conscience to hardness of heart; from prayer, to swearing, cursing, and blasphemy; from meditating on the works, word and perfections of God, to meditate on gambling, and a crowd of vanities; from hearing the preaching of the gospel, to hear foolish and lewd speeches of play actors, the infernal noise of swearing and cursing, of horseraces, puppet shows, and gambling; is not this a sufficient proof that these things are a desperate spiritual evil?"[50] Rev. Archibald Alexander lamented a pious girl, "a modest and amiable young lady," who had been, he believed, derailed from spiritual progress by the theater. He wrote, "On a visit to Virginia last summer, in company with a pious mother, at a solemn religious meeting . . . she appeared to be deeply interested and to enter very devotionally into the exercises of the day." However, the "gaities and dissipation of the metropolis" claimed her in the end, through the siren call of the theater. Alexander grieved, "Alas! in looking over this melancholy list (if I mistake not) I find her name enrolled. She perished in the flames on the fatal twenty-sixth of December!"[51]

The stridency and hyperbole of May's addresses to children can be off-putting, but his complaints about the theater's inappropriateness for children were not groundless. Theatergoers in Philadelphia, May's temporary place of residence, whose families accompanied them to a show, often regretted bringing the children. The subject matter on stage was far less repugnant than the behavior of the audience. Several Philadelphians wrote to a local theater magazine in 1810 to protest the appalling behavior of their fellow attendees and urge the community to create reform through more attentive managers and stricter laws. "Our theatre, gentlemen," one wrote, "has sunk to the worst state imaginable of licentiousness and savage riot. Don't mistake me—I don't mean behind the curtain; but before it."[52]

A father complained that when he brought his family to the pit to see Thomas Abthorpe Cooper, "the whole time the blackguards were throwing down various kinds of things upon our heads. Scraps of apples, nutshells in handfuls, and what is worse something I can't well name—some about me said that brandy or strong grog was thrown down—it might be so once;—but it was not exactly that which fell on me and my family." He saw Cooper a second time in *Macbeth,* but went alone, leaving his wife and daughter at home. The fellows seated above were as bad as before, and if he hadn't worn a hat, he supposed his head would have been badly injured by a forcefully hurled hickory nut.[53]

Another father wrote, "I look upon a playhouse to be a very good thing, often keeping young men from worse places, and young women from worse employment. But if our playhouse goes on as it does, it will soon be a worse place to go to than any I allude to." When he brought his family to a play, his wife pleaded with him to leave on their little girl's account when one man in the gallery "spoke smut and roared it out loud. . . . I can't write such filthy words as was spoken the whole evening," he wrote in revulsion. "It is not the players you ought to criticize, they behave themselves—but it is those vagabonds that think they have a right to disturb the house because they pay their half dollar a piece."[54]

* * *

Actors and actresses were almost always portrayed by enemies of the theater as scandalous libertines. "It is beyond all dispute that damnation shall be the end of actors on the stage, and gamblers," Rees Lloyd maintained, "except they are brought to Jesus by repentance, and true conversion."[55] Why were actors and actresses such despicable specimens? Witherspoon wrote that "the life of players is not only idle and vain, and therefore inconsistent with the character of a Christian, but it is still more directly and grossly criminal," claiming that immersing themselves in their subjects, they were "infected," and eventually assumed the character of the villains, charlatans, and worldly subjects they portrayed, leaving them with "no character at all of their own."[56]

Critics feared that ladies risked corruption by exposure not only to the prostitutes who populated the theater audience but also to the women who performed on stage. Actresses defied accepted definitions of appropriate behavior for women. They had abandoned the domestic sphere, and many had no permanent home to speak of. They recited, danced, and sang before mixed crowds. They had frequent, familiar contact with men—travelling with them, performing love scenes with them, and changing costumes in the same general area.[57] While some actresses engaged in affairs and scandalized the public with their behavior, many actresses were simply women—often raised in the church—who lived lives of propriety but were compelled to perform on stage in order to support themselves and their families. Pervasive prejudice caused even these actresses, careful to live in a manner above reproach, to be considered suspect.

Anna Cora Mowatt performed on stage in the 1840s and was for years a Richmond resident. As a child in New York, she attended divine services twice every Sunday and eventually became a Sunday school teacher in a church where her minister "disapproved of theatres; he pronounced them the "abodes of sin and wickedness," she recalled. "I determined that I never would enter such a dreadful place. My sisters went now and then with our father; but, in spite of my decided passion for plays and for acting, the thought of the imaginary monsters of evil, which I was certainly to behold, kept me away."[58] She eloped at fifteen and, forced by her husband James's business failures to take a profession, she wrote a play entitled *Fashion*. After its success, she embarked on a series of public readings and began to act on stage when her husband's risky land speculations spelled the loss of the family home. Despite a "flood of remonstrances from relatives and friends—opposition in every variety of form," Mowatt had resolved to pursue a career as a performer.[59] "My views concerning the stage, and my estimate of the members of dramatic companies, had undergone a total revolution," she wrote in her autobiography. "Many circumstances had proved to me how unfounded were the prejudices of the world against the profession as a body. . . . All I heard of their private histories, convinced me that I had formed unjust conclusions. Rather, I had adopted the conclusions of those who were as ignorant on the subject as myself—who, perhaps, cared as little as I had done to ascertain the truth."[60]

When respectable ladies socialized with actresses, which they did, it was most often under circumstances where they would be viewed as benefactors and the actresses as the objects of their charity. Mowatt relayed the tale of a dancer whose arms had been horribly burned "almost to the bone" in a theater accident. Ballet girls were looked down upon even by other members of their acting company, yet when the dancer was wounded, she received charitable visits from the wealthy and fashionable, whose coaches filled her humble alleyway.[61] This scene was also replayed in Richmond when Elizabeth Arnold Poe fell ill in 1811. Her chambers became a popular destination for local society ladies, who lavished her with food and attention, sending cooks and nurses at their own expense, as her health declined.[62]

Actress and fire victim Nancy Green's closest associates included the daughters of Richmond's leading lights, indicating that the troupe members socialized with local elites during the 1811 season. Local dignitary William Wirt had promised her an original "sentimental drama," as he indicated in a letter to his friend Judge Dabney Carr.[63] Yet complete integration into polite society was something that eluded nearly every actor or actress in the early nineteenth century, according to their personal accounts. Even in Virginia, a relatively friendly locale for performers, a strange dynamic existed wherein stage players were admired but were also subject to social slights and offensive behavior.

On a Wednesday night in October 1811, an umbrella-toting man in dark clothes lingered outside of actor Thomas C. West's boardinghouse around six in the evening and waited for West to leave for work. West's wife, an actress, was left home alone. In an indignant notice published afterward, West, the son of Thomas Wade West, wrote, "knowing of my absence from home on the business of the Theater, [the man] forced his way into the house and insulted my wife," and he offered twenty dollars for clues to the man's identity.[64]

Leaving the theater completely behind was one of the only ways for an actor or actress to gain acceptance into society's acceptable social circles. The *New York Times* reported that actor Thomas Abthorpe Cooper's "associates were gentlemen of wealth and fashion, and he was ever a welcome guest at the houses of our most eminent citizens."[65] Although local gentry admired Cooper, the actor crossed a significant line when he married into New York's high society. American upper classes appreciated the theater, praised actors and actresses for their skill and charms, but preferred to keep public performers in the bracket of friendship and acquaintance—not family. On June 11, 1812, Cooper wed pretty, brown-eyed Mary Fairlie, a young New York society belle and the daughter of Mary Yates Fairlie and Major James Fairlie, who had served with distinction in the Continental Army. Mary's parents, appalled that their "brilliant" daughter would marry an actor, refused to attend the wedding. Mary Yates Fairlie, in particular, found the prospect unthinkable. Not only was Cooper a thespian, but he was a widower with children and Mary's senior by thirteen years—hardly the man they had dreamed of for their daughter.[66]

Mary died young, but not before delivering Thomas a daughter, Priscilla, in 1816, and a son, James Fairlie Cooper. After Mary's death, Cooper was left to his own devices in managing the finances and raising the children. His grief over his wife's demise was only exacerbated by the knowledge that his popularity in America was waning and that supporting his family was becoming a more nerve-racking enterprise. By the time Priscilla reached the age of seventeen, the family's state of financial affairs had become particularly grim. Although Priscilla showed a proclivity toward acting and offered to assist the family by touring with her father, Cooper resisted the idea. A biographer notes, "Cooper had always protected his daughters from theatrical life, which he, like any gentleman of his time, considered unsuitable for young ladies of breeding."[67] Further consideration, and perhaps the serious nature of his indebtedness, caused him to rethink the matter and in time decide that young Priscilla, despite the temptations of stage life, was mature and prudent enough to uphold her good character.[68]

Priscilla—who, Katharine Hepburn–like, entered the profession as a lady born and bred—was a resounding success. Critical reviewers praised the young Miss Cooper, and like her father, she became an acclaimed favorite of the American stage. A series of shows at the Bowery Theater brought father and daughter back to New York City, home to Priscilla's Fairlie grandparents. Although Maria Yates Fairlie later expressed regret for the "worldly pride" that prompted her actions, she refused to receive either Thomas or Priscilla at her home. The very thought of Priscilla, her own flesh and blood, onstage thoroughly scandalized the conservative grandmother.[69]

Priscilla received quite a different reception several years later from the genteel Tyler family of Virginia. Following her performance of Desdemona to her father's Othello (probably in 1837) at the Richmond Theater, Robert Tyler, son of former governor of Virginia John Tyler, scrambled backstage. Completely smitten by the dark-haired young actress, Robert sought out Thomas Cooper and asked permission to pay his addresses to Priscilla. Although the Cooper fortunes had not radically improved and Priscilla's profession was that of a traveling actress, the Tyler family approved of the match and welcomed the actress. Priscilla affectionately called Robert's gracious mother, Letitia, a devout Episcopalian, "mother" or "Lizzie." Five months after Priscilla's April baptism at St. James Episcopal Church in Bristol, Pennsylvania, Robert and Priscilla were married there on September 12, 1839, and the bride never returned to the stage.

Mowatt stopped performing and married into Richmond's distinguished Ritchie family in the 1850s after nearly a decade on stage. A Richmond neighbor, author Marion Harland, was soon to marry a minister. Harland wrote of Mowatt's arrival, "It went without saying that an ex-actress was out of my sphere. The church that condemned dancing was yet more severe upon the theatre. True, Mrs. Ritchie had left the stage . . . but she had trodden the boards for eight or nine years, and that stamped her as a personage quite unlike the rest of 'us.'"[70] Yet Mowatt's response to repeated social humiliations was one of such grace that Harland found herself completely won over, and the two became close friends.[71]

A Baptist clergyman wrote, "It is not denied, that some performers have been respectable; but it is notorious, that, as a class, they are every where considered as unfit companions for virtuous people. Their amusing talents may sometimes gain for them an admission into good society; but they are rarely treated as intimate friends. The wit, and still more, perhaps, the wealth, of Garrick, raised him to the society of such men as Johnson, Burke, Goldsmith, and Reynolds; but it is plain, that they felt very little respect for him."[72] The suggestion of impropriety always lingered; professional actors in the early nineteenth century were never unreservedly accepted by polite society, a fact of which they were keenly aware.

A WASTE OF MONEY AND TIME

That alleged aiders and abettors to American moral decline should be so generously recompensed caused further dismay. In January 1810, visiting celebrity John Howard Payne trod the Richmond boards for eight nights. The tremendously popular baby-faced Payne, about eighteen years of age, had enjoyed a smashingly successful debut in 1809 and, fawned on by his adoring fans and smitten critics, had become a vain, rude, American star. After his Richmond performances, which included the roles of Hamlet and Romeo, the *Enquirer* noted in astonishment that the boy had pocketed 1,700 dollars in only ten days. The writer pointed out that Richmond's distinguished and overworked Court of Appeals judges earned that much only after a year of public service, and he feared the Richmond public's extravagant expenditures on plays reflected poor priorities and lack of civic sensibility. "Is it because men care more for their amusements than for solid, substantial services?" he asked.[73]

A cadre of twelve New York City Presbyterian ministers reckoned that the theatrical establishment in New York earned annually the sum of sixty thousand dollars. In a group letter they asked, "Can you christians contemplate this spectacle without horror? A city enjoying the law and the gospel of God, bestowing 60,000 dollars per annum, on an immoral association of play actors, whose trade consists in demoralizing the habits and corrupting the taste of your sons and your daughters."[74] Money spent on entertainment seemed to violate the republican virtue of thrift. Prominent English actors like George Cooke and Thomas Abthorpe Cooper earned at their height exorbitant incomes similar to Payne's. The same rebellious colonists who had worn homespun and drunk vile tea substitutes during the Revolutionary War were now lavishly enriching British coffers.

Tuke Alexander regretted that many who could scarcely maintain their families spent precious funds on playhouse tickets, attempting to imitate the higher classes who ought to have been setting a more virtuous example.[75] Methodist publisher John Watson noted that the upper classes suffered the most from the fire disaster and suggested that a more modest lifestyle had its own rewards.[76] Witherspoon reminded Christians that they would have to render an account to God on Judgment Day for how they spent their money, reminding readers that even "the greatest and richest man on earth hath not any license in the word of God, for an unnecessary waste of his substance, or consuming it in unprofitable and hurtful pleasures."[77] The theater, he believed, siphoned off not only the money but also the energies of elite citizens with great capacity to do civic good.

Many a minister, as existing sermons record, hoped that the Richmond Theater fire would lead Christians to stop squandering away their time on meaningless activities. Lloyd protested that one should not be ambivalent about amusements such as "stage-plays, horseraces and gambling," for losing or wasting any portion of time in trifling amusements must be evil.[78] The type of activity was almost irrelevant in this line of reasoning—even innocent recreations could become evil if they wasted time. (Lloyd, for example, seemed to nurse a particular venom for puppet shows.) Applying a traditional Puritan perspective on recreation, Miller declared that its purpose was not to "kill time," but to refresh the body and mind and to prepare them for the performance of duty.[79] Witherspoon argued that recreation was like sleep, necessary for refreshing the body but sinful in excess. "When plays are chosen as a recreation, for which they are so exceedingly improper, it is always in opposition to other methods of recreation, which are perfectly fit for the purpose, and not liable to any of these objections," he maintained.[80]

Many preachers reminded their audiences that they would each be required to give an account of their stewardship on Judgment Day.[81] James Muir, the chaplain of George Washington's Masonic Lodge, had presided at the late president's funeral and was pastor of the Alexandria Presbyterian Church.[82] He too chose to weigh in on the matter with a commemorative sermon. The victims had suffered, Muir counseled, "*that we may be warned* by their sufferings. If after such warning, any of you persist to lead unprofitable, careless, dissipated lives; and thus to murder the few days which God has given you on earth, to prepare for heaven, you must be speechless when you stand before his bar, not having one single excuse to offer for your conduct."[83]

These ministers held the bar relentlessly high—not a single moment should be wasted. Miller wrote, "To spend an hour *unprofitably*, or even in a *less* profitable way, when a mode of spending it more conformably to the will of God, and more usefully to himself and others, is within his reach, will appear to such a one quite as criminal as many of what are called gross sins, and quite as sacredly to be avoided."[84]

A fixation with "redeeming the time" reflected northern, Puritan values and countered traditional Southern approaches to recreation. Virginians embraced the notion of "killing the time," and gentry families relished regular, conspicuous leisure.[85] Historian David Hackett Fischer noted that Virginians were less consumed than New Englanders with finding a godly purpose for every moment.[86] Reproofs to "improve the time" after the Richmond disaster most often came from northern ministers and Presbyterians, whose culturally influential Calvinist way of viewing time imbued each minute with sacred meaning and responsibility. "I am perfectly sensible that all this [criticism of amusements] will be called, by some, 'the dark and scowling spirit of *Calvinism*,'" preached Miller, a Presbyterian, "that it will be stigmatized as 'the cant of that *puritanical* austerity, which aims at being *righteous overmuch*.'"[87] A more customary Virginian response would be that of Richmond's Rev. Buchanan, who agreed that it was a Christian's duty to call off attention from "light pursuits" to those that were of eternal consequence, yet he did not condemn amusements. In fact, in a sermon perhaps preached in the wake of the fire, he maintained the writer of Ecclesiastes did not prohibit mirth, "requiring us to wear a perpetual cloud on our brow, and to sequestrate ourselves from every cheerful entertainment of social life."[88] Instead, one should balance times of socializing and recreation with times of service and reflection.

* * *

A "good death," an ideal death, for early republic Americans happened at home among family. In this peaceful setting, the dying man or woman had opportunity to confess his or her faith before gently expiring. A calm, composed scene of death provided the surviving family members with assurance that their loved one was indeed a Christian, bound for Heaven. After the passing of his wife, Sarah Missanau Moore, in Richmond, Episcopalian minister Richard Channing Moore sent the news of her "good death" to one of his sons. "The tranquility and composure with which she met her dissolution forms another evidence to the many I have heard of the power of a saving faith, and of that belief in the promises of God which inspires the soul with confidence, and the mind with perfect assurance in His word." He continued, "It was evident that she was engaged in prayer, after which she raised her eyes to heaven, and exclaimed, 'Come, Lord Jesus, come quickly!' She died without the movement of a finger."[89] When Rev. Jeremiah Jeter's wife, Sarah Ann Gaskins Jeter, died in Richmond, the Baptist preacher wrote that he did not know how such calmness, joy, and perfect self-possession could be accounted for in one facing the prospect of certain death "except on the supposition that she was sustained and cheered by divine grace." "The hour of her death was the hour of her triumph and rapture," he recalled. The way in which one died, therefore, was the supposed capstone of a life's testimony and the confirmation of one's Christian character—for Jeter's wife, he believed, "her death was a fitting end of her life of unostentatious and fervent piety."[90] When Baptist deacon Daniel Trabue of Powhatan County, Virginia, died in

1819, his obituary reported that this pillar of his church "calmly *fell asleep in Jesus,* without even a struggle or a groan."[91]

It was not an uncommon belief that an unquiet, sudden death, not to mention death in a place of dubious entertainment, presented serious questions about one's eternal salvation. "I would much rather meet death in any other place than a theatre," missionary Robert May wrote, as though the location of one's death could tip the eternal scales against paradise.[92] A lingering question after the Richmond Theater fire seemed to be: had theatergoers died outside a state of grace, unable to profess Christian belief before their lives were snatched away? Would God's displeasure in their final act bar them from heaven? The eternal implications of dying in a theater were a matter of solemn inquiry to Christians from many denominations. The idea that a Christian could fall from grace and lose hope of heaven by committing this sin was intriguingly articulated not only by historically Arminian denominations but also by Calvinists (Presbyterians, Congregationalists, and most Baptists), whose theology upholds the eternally secure salvation of the redeemed and the impossibility of falling from a divinely bestowed state of grace. Death in a state of disobedience, to the Arminian Methodists, would give reason to question the validity of a man or woman's faith. Their insistence on holiness and simple living for their members meant that "backsliding" could put one outside a state of grace and in need of repentance. For Calvinist denominations, like the Presbyterians and some Baptists, death in a state of disobedience meant that the victims were not walking in Christian obedience and hence, were not—and perhaps had never been—true Christians.

Witherspoon asked, "Is the theatre an amusement which will be remembered with complacency by any man when he comes to die? Or is it a place from which any reflecting man would be willing to be called to the bar of God?"[93] A Congregationalist publication warned, "Thinking, as we do, that the theatre, as it always has been and probably always will be conducted, is an unlawful amusement . . . we earnestly request our young readers to reflect on their exposure to sudden death, and on the importance of engaging in no amusement from which they would be unwilling to be removed into eternity."[94] "You know," chided Baptist Robert Turnbull, "that after you have been at the theatre, the thought of God and of eternity is unwelcome, and that you feel unprepared to die."[95]

Others disparaged the "bad death" as a bogus fear and argued that the means of one's passing meant little in relation to one's ultimate spiritual destination. In his postfire sermon, Presbyterian Archibald Alexander relayed a tale of a dying infidel and his protégé to illustrate a bad death, one devoid of peace and solace. In his story, the protégé could not erase the memory of a godless teacher's unsettling deathbed scene. He swiftly renounced the tenets of infidelity and acquainted himself with sacred scriptures, "which he found to contain *the true secret of a peaceful death,* as well as a happy immortality."[96] In response to this, a critic wrote, "Have we no instances of the disciples of Fox, or Buddah, Brama . . . dying in peace & certainty of salvation? What does this prove?"[97] After the fire, a Methodist asked rhetorically, "Who would be willing to close the career of mortality in the very act of displeasing his Maker and his Judge! Who in a Theatre would be content to give up the ghost?"[98] An exasperated critic of the sermon replied, "Would our author like to die in his bed, if he could help it?"[99]

It is obvious that Richmonders believed the victims had died "in the Lord," despite the horrific circumstances and unexpected speed of their demise. During the memorial service for the victims, Buchanan dwelt upon Revelation 14:13, "I heard a voice from heaven saying unto me, Write, from henceforth blessed are the dead who die in the Lord; even so, saith the Spirit, for they rest from their labors."[100] Rev. John Durbarrow Blair, in his sermon at Henrico Parish Church, expressed belief that even without the opportunity to profess their faith before death, Richmond's deceased could still enter heaven. "May the God of mercy pity & support [the survivors], & apply to their wounded hearts some balm of consolation. Let them & let us all indulge the consoling hope that the God of mercy, who has declared that he 'will have mercy on whom he will have mercy,' pitied their distress & graciously lent an ear to their supplicating importunate Call, in the hour of their extremity."[101]

Louis Hue Girardin, Leroy Anderson, and Patrick Gibson, three men who lost wives and daughters, expressed their hope in a public letter to the city of Richmond: "We humbly trust that the spirits of our departed Relatives, have been wafted to the bosom of the Father of love, of the universal parent of mankind—transferred from fleeting, chequered, and fugitive scenes, to the blissful abode of undisturbed and eternal rest!"[102]

JUDGE NOT

The most frequently cited verses in sermons about the Richmond tragedy were Luke 13:1–5, in which Jesus responded to two disasters. During Passover, while the Galileans offered animal sacrifices, Pilate, Roman governor of Judea, ordered his soldiers to invade the temple and butcher the worshippers.[103] A second tragedy occurred when a tower, probably on a ridge overlooking Jerusalem's Pool of Siloam, toppled to the ground and crushed eighteen people to death. When asked about the two tragedies, Jesus denied vehemently that the victims somehow deserved their fate. "Suppose ye that these Galilaeans were sinners above all the Galilaeans, because they suffered such things?" He inquired, then answered, "I tell you, Nay: but, except ye repent, ye shall all likewise perish. Or those eighteen, upon whom the tower in Siloam fell, and slew them, think ye that they were sinners above all men that dwelt in Jerusalem? I tell you, Nay: but, except ye repent, ye shall all likewise perish."[104] The application for the early republic was this: the disasters of Galilee and Siloam, just like the Richmond fire, "befalleth the righteous and the wicked, and in temporal calamities, the good and bad is equally involved," as Rev. James Muir put it.[105] If Jesus himself exonerated the victims and excoriated the survivors, it would be the utmost in pride for anyone to "impute aggravated offence to the unhappy sufferers."[106] Rev. William Hill believed this proceeded "from laying down this mistaken principle, 'That God always deals with men in this world according to their actions, and that one might judge of a man's state, from the rewards or punishments that follow him, in this life.'" He did allow, however, that God might issue immediate and remarkable punishments on notorious sins, as in the case of Ananias and Sapphira in the book of Acts, as a mark of his displeasure. "But unless the case be remarkably clear and obvious, it is more becoming creatures possessed of such limited power as we have, to be cautious and modest," he cautioned.[107]

Samuel Gilman, as a poet and future Unitarian minister, also warned against blaming the victims in a "Monody on the Victims and Sufferers by the Late Conflagration in the City of Richmond, Virginia," every bit as protracted as its lengthy title might imply:

> But, though the world a lesson here may see,
> There is no censure, Richmond, meant for thee.
> . . .
> Is suff'ring then a signal for reproach?
> Inhuman hearts, that dare such doctrines broach!
> How then can that be piety, which sees
> In some clown's heedless blunder—God's decrees!

How weak the eye, how circumscrib'd the span,
That find a special judgment—in the lot of man![108]

More common among ministers than the idea that God specifically punished Richmond's theatergoers was the concept that the theater fire was a universal warning to repent. "It is taken for granted that all strokes of this nature are leveled at the society in general, and not at particular persons as such, and consequently every judicial execution of this sort is strictly and properly a punishment of national and social guilt," wrote a self-described "Theocrate."[109] Rev. Joseph Dana, who led the Congregationalist South Church in Ipswich, Massachusetts, near neighboring Newburyport—which had also suffered a devastating fire in 1811—asked his Massachusetts congregation after the destructive blazes in Newburyport and Richmond, "Are there no neglectors of God in Ipswich? No slumbering Christians here? . . . Is there not sin enough here, to invite it—unless we repent?"[110] Instead of casting stones, he and others asserted that Americans needed to look at themselves critically, repent of their sins, and begin living consecrated lives. John Buchanan, probably preaching after the fire, said, "Contemplate the lifeless remains of what once was fair and flourishing; bring home to thyself the vicissitudes of life; recall the remembrance of the friend, the parent, or the child whom thou tenderly lovedst . . . let the vanity, the mutability, and the sorrows of the human estate rise in full prospect before thee; and though thy countenance may be made sad, thy heart shall be made better."[111]

Hill noted, "Men are apt to multiply and aggravate the faults and miscarriages of others, that their own may appear the less. . . . And because there can be no greater evidence that a man is a great sinner, than for him to be declared to be so, from heaven, many are forward to interpret the remarkable judgments of God upon others, as an argument of their being more notorious offenders."[112] This was certainly the case in Rees Lloyd's sermon, where he quoted from Romans "the wages of sin is death"—and then listed only sins related to entertainment.[113] Hill, a Calvinist, emphasized God's sovereignty and omniscience, advising Christians to be cautious and modest, since they were "creatures possessed of such limited power." For "there is nothing which occasions more mistakes about God and his providence, than to bring him to our standard, and to measure . . . the ways and methods of his providence by ours."[114]

When Rev. Samuel Miller preached his Richmond Theater fire sermon in

New York City, he pronounced, "It was not the work of chance. A righteous God has done it. His breath kindled the devouring flame. . . . He ordered and controuled all the circumstances attending the melancholy scene."[115] But when ministers like Miller across the country declared the fire a punishing act of God, they did not go unchallenged. Protheater pamphleteers responded in print and newspapers, publishing rebuttals and editorials defending the theater and its votaries against defamation and protesting the argument that God sent the fire as punishment.

Some objectors attacked the doctrines in magazines, as in the case of the anonymous critic of Watson's *Calamity at Richmond* in *The Cynick,* a Philadelphia magazine of theater criticism. The reviewer called the Methodist author "wicked and silly," a "holy miscreant" who made others' grief a "publick pastime" and exploited the victims by publishing for profit an opportunistic book of mostly unoriginal material.[116] Defending his lengthy criticism of Watson, the author explained "when a man presses on the ignorant and addled, mischievous and unfounded bigotries, introduced with the whining, canting obsequiousness of a hypocrite, and all the solemnities of religion, devoid of its essence and divinity, it is necessary, if possible, to unmask the traitor, and expose his real intentions."[117]

In the Boston magazine *The Polyanthos,* a critic of Methodist Elijah Sabin's discourse reminded Sabin that a man "in a house tiled with glass, should not throw stones at his neighbor." Apparently Boston's theaters were not the only place where young people might encounter immoral company; while Sabin called the theater "a school where all kinds of amorous intrigues are taught," the critic accused Methodist midnight lectures of being "sad begetters of bastard children" and Methodist conferences of being "snares to allure silly girls to seduction."[118]

Finding Rev. Archibald Alexander's sermon to be "cold, inanimate, and mechanical, unkindled by the gentle beams of heaven born Sympathy," a commentator who called himself "Gregory Gravity" wrote a long preface in the front matter and extensive comments in the margins of his pamphlet copy of the sermon.[119] His critiques were largely religious in nature, although he did not spell out which denomination he may have been a part of. He probably intended to circulate the annotated document among friends and connections.

"Gravity" thought Alexander a "bigot" plagued with "middle-aged imbecility" whose sermon lacked the compassion by which Christians should be recognized. Gravity did not even mention the theater; his concern lay with what he perceived as a misrepresentation of Christianity and an insensitivity to victims and their families. He accused Alexander of being "guilty of the most unthinking cruelty by reciting with seeming indifference the fate of those who were so suddenly called from life, by insinuating that the manner of their death precluded all consolation, and by nagging the unhealed mind back to the misery of sorrow in turning its attention thus coldly to the change in the appearance of those who are now *I* hope in heaven."[120] As an example of Alexander's "unfeeling" prose, he pointed to the preacher's dramatization of a Richmond fiancé discovering his intended bride transformed from a theatergoing beauty to "a frightful and deformed skeleton!" Raising the point that immediate family members of the deceased were among Alexander's audience, "Gravity" asked incredulously, "Is this the language of consolation? . . . Is this the comfort to be derived from religion?"[121]

Worse yet, Alexander declared the calamity a "*judgment from heaven*" and thereby left the survivors and victim's families to feel they had been the object of special wrath, estranged from God's love. (In the portion where Alexander called the theater fire a "distressing visitation of Almighty God," the critic circled it and wrote, "How do you know?") "Gravity" sarcastically queried, "Is it by indirectly insinuating that the sufferers are now writhing in unending torments that you expect to tranquillize the heart of the mourner, and to turn his thoughts to a reliance on his God?" Christianity's God, "Gravity" maintained, was remarkable for his compassion and kindness—he "pardons the Sinner" and "softens the heart." God did not sit, "Gravity" argued, "like a tyger triumphant among the carcases of the helpless . . . insatiable even in the midst of destruction." He directed his final sentence to Alexander: "If you be a Christian you are either led astray by mistaken zeal or I am unacquainted, and hope always to be so, with the doctrines of Christianity!"[122]

Thomas Ritchie, the tall, aristocratic editor of the *Enquirer*, also contended that divine will had nothing to do with the tragic fire on rationalist grounds. (Although Ritchie would not join a church in Richmond, his wife, an Episcopalian, did.)[123] Champion of traditional Virginian entertainments and friend of the theater, Ritchie managed most of Richmond's public balls and frequently attended the Placide & Green productions. He even witnessed the destruction of the theater himself, managing to escape from his seat the night of the twenty-sixth.[124] His son William Foushee Ritchie would later marry into the theater, wedding socialite actress Anna Cora Mowatt in 1854.[125]

After the spate of comets, eclipses, tornadoes, and earthquakes in Virginia throughout December and January, many Virginians believed that these were "portentous signs."[126] "The distress & Consternation by this melancholy Event [the Richmond Theater fire] must long prevail," Williamsburg resident Mary Andrews exclaimed on January 20, 1812. "It has been an Eventfull period as there has been three shocks of an Earthquake have been felt here thank God there has been no further Damage than making several people very sick at Stomach during the time of it but I fear it may have been more calamitous at other places."[127]

Ritchie wrote, "To the eye of the bigot, there seems to be a mysterious sympathy between the revolutions of the moral and physical world. But truth abjures such absurdities. . . . Away then with these chimeras! They are only worthy of those ingenious days of witchcraft."[128] To counter the idea that Richmond and her theatergoers had been singled out for divine punishment, in mid-January of 1812, Ritchie outlined in the *Enquirer* the source of the fire in an investigative, scientific manner, quoting from the 2,732-word official report of causation. The fire had been traced to defects in the construction of the theater, he pointed out.[129] A live flame, due to human carelessness, set scenery on fire. The building was flammable, the exits were few, the smoke was thick, and thus the casualties were many.

Yet Americans lived by heavenly signs and folk wisdom, and lunar patterns governed everyday activities. Almanacs, the best-selling publications of the early nineteenth century, often dispensed advice based on astrology and natural phenomena. Hog slaughtering should be avoided during the waning moon lest pork wither away in the barrel; butter making should be done under an auspicious sign.[130] Such convictions were earnestly held.

Even leading minds took portentous signs seriously, including one of Ritchie's nemeses, eccentric U.S. representative John Randolph of Roanoke. During February 1812 deliberations in Washington, D.C., regarding war with Great Britain, baby-faced bachelor Randolph warned his fellows of the clear "signs of the times," including eclipses, earthquakes, comets, and the theater fire—which he deemed one of "the most desolating visitations of God"—in order to discourage the United States from entering into combat. In his shrill voice he protested, "Can these be the harbingers of any good?"[131] The ancient republics, he claimed, whom America sought to model itself after, would have quailed at launching acts of aggression in such an inauspicious time.

Ritchie dismissed the statesman as a "Sooth-Sayer" and asked in umbrage, "Is this cant the *harbinger* of a sound unsophisticated politician?" The editor suggested, "Let us have a new *department* to be called the College of Augurs—who may tell us the fate of measures not by the force of reflection, but by the feeding of *chickens* of the entrails of *calves*.—It would save us a world of arguments and of words." He nominated Mr. Randolph to be the "chief haraspex."[132] After a February 7 morning earthquake hit Richmond, Ritchie snorted, "More food for Mr. Randolph's imagination!"[133]

Countering the notion that Richmond was somehow accursed or deserved its misery, Ritchie invited his reading public to "open the pages of history, & see whether this is the only City, which has been afflicted by so severe a visitation—whether this is the only people, whom "the paths of *pleasure* have led to the grave!"[134] Ritchie emphasized that although the fatal night in Richmond was unequalled in the annals of American history, it was not without parallels in the old world."[135] This he illustrated by accounts of deadly fires in European theaters pulled from *Luckombe's Tablet of Memory*, a text frequently reprinted in American newspapers after the theater fire.

Montpellier in France, had a booth wherein a play was performing, fell, and killed 500 persons. July 31, 1786.

The Theatre at Mentz, was destroyed by fire during the performance, on the falling in of which many were crushed to death; and 70 were burnt. Aug 1796.

Saragossa in Spain, had 400 of its inhabitants perished by a fire, that burnt down the Play-House. December 1778. [136]

Ministers cited the statistics above as well to prove the dangers of theatrical amusements. But disproving these statistics as evidence that God hated the theater, Ritchie included accounts of deadly *church* disasters:

Bourbon-les-bains, in Bassigni, France; had the vault under the Church give way, during the celebration of mass, which occasioned the death of six hundred persons. Sept. 14, 1778.

The floor of a Meeting House of Methodists at Leeds, gave way, when 16 women, a man and a child, were killed, and near 30 persons dreadfully wounded. May 25, 1796.[137]

Building-related disasters were no argument against the stage, Ritchie argued. A concurring *Enquirer* editorial mailed from New York stated:

> If such accidents only happened to Theatres and Dancing Assemblies, I will allow they would then have some room to plead in support of such a horrid opinion; but as such dreadful conflagrations have happened to the assemblies in Churches (so called,) and Meeting Houses, where the object of meetings was to perform solemn Worship . . . surely they would not say, that these cases were also judgments from on high! I think that people of all sects ought rather to tremble and shudder in contemplating on the subject of such uncharitable and monstrous doctrines.[138]

This spurred an exchange over God's agency in the fire. A *Virginia Patriot* reader took issue with Ritchie's explanations. "All the means with which God in his providence suffers the children of men to be afflicted, are so many rebukes as signal tokens of God's displeasure against us as sinners," the subscriber maintained.[139] The debate picked up speed and venom in the *Virginia Argus* and *Virginia Patriot* that February when Harvard-educated lawyer Oliver Whipple of Georgetown submitted an open letter to Richmond's mayor denying the fire was an act of God's vengeance. Whipple criticized those "hard-hearted" people who, while saying the fire was God's work, "class themselves among professing Christians."[140] Two weeks later, one such "hard-hearted" Christian, labeling himself "a Friend to Sound Doctrine," scoffed at Whipple. "It certainly is a dangerous and unevangelical doctrine to say that sinful mortals, hurled away, by an act of Providence, in the midst of gaiety and mirth, are like the prophet Elijah,—on a chariot of fire, translated to the heavenly domains."[141] A critic lambasted the "Friend to Sound Doctrine" a week later for lacking "delicacy, sensibility, and sentiment."[142]

* * *

The belief that the theater was a "school of vice," the presumed bad character of performers, theatergoing's role in encouraging a lack of industry and thrift, and the presence of prostitutes in the nearly ubiquitous "third tier" caused the theater to come under increased scrutiny and rebuke in the decades following the theater fire, even among Christian denominations that had previously tolerated or ignored theatrical amusements. By 1837 Baptist minister James D. Knowles could write, "There is a gratifying unanimity of opinion among pious men, respecting the tendency of theatrical amusement. They are so uncongenial with the feelings of a pure heart, and so hostile to the cultivation of true piety, that no man could, in this country, maintain the character of a serious Christian, who was in the habit of visiting the theatre."[143]

Clerical hostility continued throughout the nineteenth century, even as the general public's condemnation of the theater ceased to be widespread and theater attendance increased after the Civil War.[144] Moral dramas like *The Drunkard*, a temperance drama, in the 1840s; *Uncle Tom's Cabin* in the 1850s; the Mallory brothers' Madison Square Theatre productions in the 1860s; and *Ben Hur* in the 1890s attracted religious people to the theater and challenged preconceptions about the theater as a fomenter of immorality.[145] By the close of the nineteenth century, in many Christian circles, theater attendance had lost the tremendous stigma it once held.

"View of the City of Richmond from the Bank of the James River," by Benjamin Henry Latrobe, May 24, 1798. The theater is to the right of the capitol building on Shockhoe Hill. Courtesy of the Maryland Historical Society, Baltimore, Maryland (1960.108.1.3.34).

Actress Elizabeth Arnold Hopkins Poe, mother of Edgar Allan Poe. Library of Congress Prints and Photographs Division, Washington, D.C. (LC-USZ62-62316).

Cutaway of prospective Richmond Theater by Benjamin Henry Latrobe, ca. 1797. Library of Congress Prints and Photographs Division, Washington, D.C. (LC-USZC4-102).

Front of prospective Richmond Theater, northwest and southeast elevations, by Benjamin Henry Latrobe, ca. 1797. Library of Congress Prints and Photographs Division, Washington, D.C. (LC-USZC4-100).

Last week of Performance this Season.

Mr. Placide's Benefit.

Will CERTAINLY take place on
THURSDAY NEXT,

When will be presented, an entire New PLAY, translated from the French
of Diderot, by a Gentleman of this City, called

THE FATHER;
OR,
FAMILY FEUDS.

Monsieur Durbeson,	Mr. GREEN,	Police Officer,	Mr. UTT,
St. Albin,	YOUNG,	Duchesny,	HANNA,
Commodore,	THAITS,		
Germed,	ANDERSON	Cecile,	Mrs. PLACIDE,
Le Fon,	BURKE	Sophia,	YOUNG,
Philip,	ROSE	Clara,	Miss THOMAS,
La Brie,	DURING,	Mrs. Herbert,	Mrs UTT.

At the End of the Play,

A COMIC SONG,	By	Mr. WEST.
A DANCE,	By	Miss E. PLACIDE.
SONG,		Miss THOMAS.
A HORNPIPE,	By	Miss PLACIDE.

To which will be added, (for the first time here) the Favorite New Pantomime, of

Raymond and Agnes:
OR, THE BLEEDING NUN.

Raymond,	Mr. ROBERTSON,	Count of Lindenburg,	Mr. CAULFIELD,
Theodore,	ROSE	Don Felix,	CLARK,
Jacques,	ANDERSON,	Countess of Lindenburg,	Mrs. CLARK,
Old Servant,	WEST,	Margaretta,	PLACIDE,
Baptist,	PLACIDE,	Spectre of the Bleeding Nun,	GREEN,
Robert,	THAITS,	Marvianna,	Miss THOMAS,
Claude,	BURKE	Agnes,	Mrs. YOUNG,

A description of the principal Scenes in the Pantomime. Raymond discovered at the Banks, is intercepted by the servants of Don Felix, who informs him it is in this wish he should get upon his travels: Theodore, his favourite domestic, intreats to accompany him. Scene—An Hotel and Content; a promise and Mons and Frais—Chorus, departing from the Convent of Agnes, the neighboring Count Lindenburg. Raymond and Theodore enter, refreshments from the travel, and prepare for their journey, under the guidance of Claude, out of a Bandit detailing the neighboring Forest. Scene—A Forest at Midnight, with a distant Hotel. Enter Raymond, one of the Bandits, disguised as a woodsman. The Carriage with Raymond and Theodore is here to break down, Claude pointing to the Hotel, intreats them they may there find Shelter for the night. Scene—The inside of the Hotel. Margaretta and her child alone. Raymond and Theodore are impeached by Bandit. Theodore is shown to his room by Margaretta. Robert and Jacques. How to these? everything, making a Perfect obedience to Raymond. Scene—The Red Room prepared for Raymond; who are wishing to precipitate the Bay of Raymond from the assassins, conveys a pillow there, with blood upon his bed, thereby to inform him of his danger; the innocent herself. Raymond refuses to rest, but is preserved, by finding the lonely pillow, and struck with horror, falls into a Swoon. Robert enters, attempts to murder him, is prevented by Margaretta, and Raymond at her request acknowledges. The Lower Apartments of the Hotel. Robert discovers his father and brother of the murder, they fixed attempt on the life of Raymond, who is brought in by Margaretta. A time escapes without Agnes, when is also benighted in the Forest, which the Chief attempts to overcome. Succour is prepared, Quarry are mixed with the wine, Agnes refuses, and calls into a Swallen. Margaretta sees Raymond to a drink, but in pain out the Confidence of the assassins, Baptist finds Robert and Jacques to sleeve the Rosemary wine here priced, and departing Raymond to rest, are carried to murder him. Raymond enters the room, and makes him aware; through which, by taking last in the hands of Margaretta, who points out a secret avenue, through which by taking last wish, Raymond, Theodore and Agnes escape. Scene—Interior of Lindenburg Castle. The latter murder of Agnes, the late Countess proving in in the hands of a Nun. The Spectre appears

showing the picture with agitation. Knocks to induce respiration for the murder. Agnes thought in by Marvianna, is introduced to the picture. Consults, the weather convinced of ...lity, and offers him her picture which he regards with horror. Scene—The chamber of Agnes. Portrait of a Nun with a wound on her heart, hung, dragged and a ruffian on her wrist. Acknowledgment of Raymond, is discovered kneeling her portrait. Raymond enters the portrait, draws himself at her feet, and points the promise of her hand, he implores an explanation of the bleeding Nun, she indulges him, on the satisfaction of a justice which prevails the castle every this year. The Count and Countess approach, and in anger leave Raymond to wait the castle. Scene—Outline of the castle. Raymond about to depart, is resisted by the Spectre once more him. A paper follows his Agnes from the Castle can be a stern ring of the Nun, with the following resolve: When the castle bell tells one, we must not like the Bleeding Nun. Scene—Outside of the Castle as fetters. Raymond enters, the clock fixes one. The passing Agnes, the Apparition of the Nun comes from the Castle. Raymond, imagining it Agnes follows it rather. Twelve approaching, he most by Agnes, or the Spectre of the Nun. Agnes hid in the apparent neglect of Raymond, they resolve to confine it, when suddenly rembling, a third resolves the faith, bearing the following inscription:—Prevent the death of the murdered Agnes.—Scene—The Mountains. Bestja, Jacques and Claude, the Robbers, all carried at the grave of Baptist. They plan on Agnes enter. Agnes is interred and borne into the cavern. Scene—Theodore and Margaretta meet Raymond, and inform him of Agnes being seized by the Robbers. They resolve to their relief. Scene—Inside are Agnes. The three Robbers sell Les to Agnes. No intimation flies of Robert, she attempts to stay her. Marvianna, he slain a the cavern. At the instant Raymond, Theodore and Margaretta rush in. Robert Jacques fall by the sword of Raymond, and Claude of the hand of Margaretta, who rescues the weapon of Robert. Scene—A distant Mountain, Raymond arrives at the Castle. Scene the sail—An illuminated Hall.—The union of Raymond and Agnes are joined.

Placide and Green Company playbill for the fatal performance the night of December
26, 1811. Courtesy of the Library of Virginia, Richmond, Virginia.

Louis Hue Girardin, by Charles Balthazar Julien Fevret de St. Memin, 1807. Courtesy of the Library of Virginia, Richmond, Virginia.

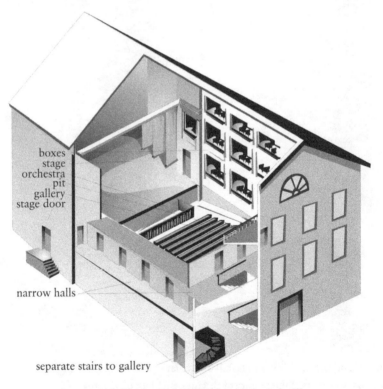

boxes
stage
orchestra
pit
gallery
stage door

narrow halls

separate stairs to gallery

Diagram of the 1811 Richmond Theater, by Bob Oller.

Mrs. Robert Greenhow, Sr. (Mary Ann Willis), by Charles Balthazar Julien Fevret de St. Memin, ca. 1808.Virginia Museum of Fine Arts, Richmond, Virginia; gift of Mrs. William R. Scott, photo: Katherine Wetzel, copyright © Virginia Museum of Fine Arts.

Robert Greenhow, Sr., by Charles Balthazar Julien Fevret de St. Memin, ca. 1808. Virginia Museum of Fine Arts, Richmond, Virginia; gift of Mrs. William R. Scott, photo: Katherine Wetzel, copyright © Virginia Museum of Fine Arts.

Robert Greenhow, Jr., by Charles Balthazar Julien Fevret de St. Memin, ca. 1808. Virginia Museum of Fine Arts, Richmond, Virginia; gift of Mrs. William R. Scott, photo: Katherine Wetzel, copyright © Virginia Museum of Fine Arts.

PLATE XII

THE BURNING OF THE THEATRE IN RICHMOND, VIRGINIA, ON THE
NIGHT OF THE 26TH DECEMBER 1811,

By which awful Calamity upwards of one hundred of its most valuable
Citizens suddenly lost their lives, and many others, were much injured.

Published Feby. 25th. 1812, by B. Tanner, No. 74 South 8th. St. Philadelphia.

fell, made it a lash with which to scourge the vices of the day or a weapon with
which to attack the theatrical profession.

Such an event did not lack its heroes, and it is a privilege here to record the
rôle played by Dr. James D. McCaw, bearer of a name then as now honoured in
Richmond; the conduct of the gallant James Gibbon, son of the hero of Stony
Point, who kept his "rendezvous with Death" with his fiancée, the beautiful Sally
Conyers, whom he endeavoured to save; and the paternal love of the generous and
gifted Smith, who, reëntering the flaming building to seek a beloved son, perished

41

"The burning of the Richmond Theatre, on the night of December 26,
1811." Copy from the original Tanner aquatint. Illus. in Alexander W.
Weddell, *Richmond, Virginia,* in Old Prints. 1737–1887, plate 12. Library
of Congress Prints and Photographs Division, Washington, D.C. (LC-
USZ62-54502).

PLATE XIII

Frontispiece from "An Account of the Awful Calamity . . . 1812."

"In the midst of life we are in death." Frontispiece from *An Account of the Awful Calamity, 1812.* Imagined scene of firemen fighting the blaze at the Richmond Theater. Illus. in Alexander W. Weddell, *Richmond, Virginia,* in Old Prints. 1737–1887. Library of Congress Prints and Photographs Division, Washington, D.C. (LC-USZ62-54503).

Gilbert Hunt. Courtesy of the Virginia Historical Society, Richmond, Virginia.

Governor George William Smith.
Courtesy of the Library of Virginia,
Richmond, Virginia.

Sarah C. Conyers, by Charles Balthazar
Julien Fevret de St. Memin, 1808.
Courtesy of the Library of Virginia,
Richmond, Virginia.

Charred Chater & Livermore brass pocket watch, used to identify fire victim Maria Nelson. Courtesy of Virginia Historical Society, Richmond, Virginia, photo: Meg M. Eastman.

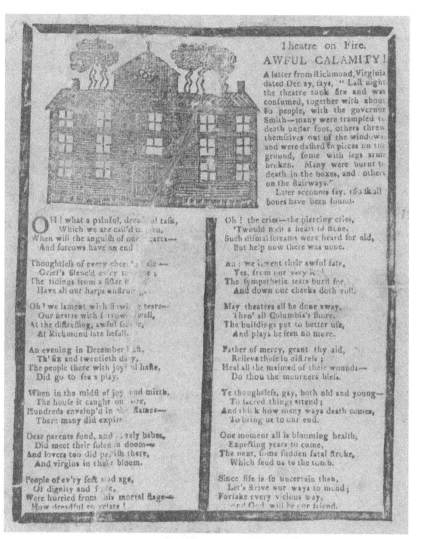

"Theatre on Fire. Awful Calamity!" Commemorative broadside, 1812. Courtesy of the Virginia Historical Society, Richmond, Virginia.

Rev. John Durbarrow Blair. Courtesy of the Library of Virginia, Richmond, Virginia.

Rev John Buchanan. Courtesy of the Library of Virginia, Richmond, Virginia.

Matthew Clay, by Charles Balthazar Julien Fevret de St. Memin, 1800. Courtesy of the Library of Virginia, Richmond, Virginia.

St. George Tucker, by Charles Balthazar Julien Fevret de St. Memin, 1808. Courtesy of the Library of Virginia, Richmond, Virginia.

John Marshall, by Charles Balthazar Julien Fevret de St. Memin, ca. 1807. Library of Congress, Prints and Photographs Division, Washington, D.C. (LC-USZ62-54940).

"A Representation of the New Church at Richmond Virginia," promotional print of Robert Mills's design for Monumental Church by William Strickland, 1812. Courtesy of the Library of Virginia, Richmond, Virginia.

Monumental Church, ca. 1865, photograph. Library of Congress Prints and Photographs Division, Washington, D.C. (LC-B811- 3369).

Exterior photograph of Monumental Church, ca. 1987. Library of Congress Prints and Photographs Division, Washington, D.C. (HABS VA, 44-RICH, 24-1).

The original commemorative sarcophagus monument in the Monumental Church portico lists the names of known fire victims, photograph ca. 1987. Library of Congress Prints and Photographs Division, Washington, D.C. (HABS VA, 44-RICH, 24-14).

Rev. Dr. Richard Channing Moore. Library of Congress Prints and Photographs Division, Washington, D.C. (LC-USZ62-58497).

Rev. John Holt Rice. Courtesy of the Library of Virginia, Richmond, Virginia.

Thomas Abthorpe Cooper, by Chester Harding, ca. 1822. Library of Congress Prints and Photographs Division, Washington, D.C. (LC-USZ62-87870).

William Wirt, by Charles Balthazar Julien Fevret de St. Memin, ca. 1807. Library of Congress Prints and Photographs Division, Washington, D.C. (LC-USZ62-119242).

Richmond, from the hill above the waterworks, ca. 1834. Library of Congress Prints and Photographs Division, Washington, D.C. (LC-USZC4-4539).

Portrait of Caroline Homassel Thornton, ca. 1812, artist unknown, Richmond, Virginia. Private collection.

Portrait of Philip Thornton, ca. 1812, artist unknown, Richmond, Virginia. Private collection.

7
REBUILDING

Oh! Let that sympathy, let the intensity of our own grief, long continue!—Let the pious monument rise, & perpetuate a mournful, yet sacred, sentiment!
—AN ANONYMOUS SURVIVOR, *Richmond Enquirer,* JANUARY 23, 1812

Indeed, throughout the lower parts of Virginia, that is, between the mountains and the sea, the people have scarcely any sense of religion, and in the country parts the churches are all falling into decay. As I rode along, I scarcely observed any one that was not in a ruinous condition, with the windows broken, and doors dropping off the hinges, and lying open to the pigs and cattle wandering about the woods; yet many of these were not past repair. The churches in Virginia, excepting such as are in towns, stand for the most part in the woods, retired from any houses, and it does not appear that any persons are appointed to pay the smallest attention to them."
—*Isaac Weld, Jr.,* TRAVELS THROUGH THE STATES OF NORTH AMERICA: AND THE PROVINCES OF UPPER AND LOWER CANADA DURING THE YEARS 1795, 1796, AND 1797

In 1811, Richmond had only four church buildings for a population of ten thousand people. As the oldest congregation in Richmond, the Episcopal Church had maintained a presence at the Henrico Parish Church on Church Hill since 1741.[1] The rutted roads and steepness of the grade made the trek to church a miserable one, especially in poor weather, so services were held there, on average, only three times yearly between 1789 and 1814, and by most accounts were poorly attended.[2] Merchant Thomas H. Drew moved to Richmond at age sixteen. "I came to this city on the 1st of November, 1800," he wrote. "At that time the only Episcopal church in this city was the old parish church, now called 'St. John's,' of which the Rev. John Buchanan was rector. It was opened every Christmas day, Easter-day, and Whit-Sunday, when the sacrament of the Lord's supper was administered to the Episcopalians, and persons of other denominations that chose to unite."[3]

Joint services of the Episcopalians and Presbyterians had been meeting in the capitol building since before 1791.[4] Most of the attendees represented the gentry classes of the city; a few came up from the business district south of the capitol.[5] Leading citizens formed the choir, which led the service music and hymns in lieu of an organ.[6] On alternating weeks, Richmond's beloved "Two Parsons," Rev. John D. Blair, a Presbyterian, and Rev. John Buchanan, an Episcopalian, led services, using the antique colonial speaker's chair as a pulpit.[7] The situation was convenient for the famously collegial ministers, each of whom had preaching obligations outside the city in rural churches. Blair held a full-time pastoral post at Pole Green Church in Hanover, twenty-three miles away.[8]

Rev. John Buchanan, poor when he arrived in America, had inherited a fortune from his brother James, a successful Scottish entrepreneur in Richmond. John had earned a Master of Arts in Edinburgh, dabbled in law, and showed an utter ineptitude for business while attempting to assist his brother. Noted his obituary in 1822, "His own inclination concurring with the advice of his brother to study divinity, he returned to Great Britain for the purpose of being invested with holy orders."[9] Of middling stature and inclined to be stout, the courtly and well-mannered Buchanan returned to Virginia's shore in time to experience the Revolutionary War and the troubled tenure of Episcopal bishop James Madison.[10] Amid the upheaval and anti-British animosity, he found no immediate employment as a clergyman of the Episcopal Church.[11] For ten years Buchanan lived with lawyer and state treasurer Jaquelin Ambler, tutoring Ambler's daughters, before a position opened for him in Henrico Parish. During his residence in Richmond, James died, and John came into five hundred acres of land along with several houses and empty lots in Richmond.[12] John Buchanan sold much of it before 1812 and gave liberally of the proceeds to his friends, particularly to Blair, who had a large family. Blair unfailingly was given the payment from every wedding that Buchanan performed.[13] Buchanan also gave quietly to those in need. "He had a large property and a large heart," wrote Anne Rice, friend to Buchanan and wife of Presbyterian pastor John Holt Rice, "and as he had no family to provide for, he delighted in ministering most liberally to the wants of the poor." Buchanan requested that Rice alert him immediately if she came into contact with someone in need of pecuniary aid. "I did it frequently, and with perfect freedom, and always found him ready to assist me to any extent that I might desire," she wrote with admiration.[14]

Blair and Buchanan's gentle ecumenicalism had arisen from necessity.

Neither of them were zealous proselytizers; this would have been likely to disturb the peace or interfere with the interests of the other minister while the two men shared responsibility for a single congregation.[15] Denominational affiliations seemed to matter little. The son of a Methodist minister accompanied Blair as a chorister in the Sabbath services at the capitol.[16] Blair and Buchanan invited to their shared pulpit other ministers, like Methodist Thomas Coke, who preached several times at the capitol in the 1790s, and the Baptist preachers who spoke to an overflowing crowd during the Dover Association conference in 1810.[17]

Methodists, Baptists, and Disciples of Christ were all known to hold services in the capitol building in the early days of Richmond, and the Abbé Dubois said the first mass there in 1791.[18] The Hall of Delegates in Richmond, although the largest available space in the city, was not commodious enough to hold more than a few hundred people, and the services were "not largely attended," according to church historians.[19] It is impossible to determine an exact count of the joint Presbyterian-Episcopal congregation size. To begin with, there exist no vestry records for the capitol building congregation, although some exist for St. John's church during Buchanan's tenure. In what was indicative of the general denominational disarray in Virginia's Protestant Episcopal Church, no one had bothered to create any specifically for the capitol congregation.

The Protestant Episcopal Church, as a result of religious disestablishment in Virginia and its connection with the Church of England, suffered severe setbacks after the Revolutionary War, both legally and in terms of its reputation.[20] No longer enjoying the privilege of being a state church after 1784, the Episcopal Church was forced to battle for its glebe lands and found itself in an environment of religious freedom in which it was ill-equipped to compete. Having no experience in self-government or self-support, it did not fare well. In 1805, the Richmond Enquirer observed that the Episcopal Church had been thrown "with all the satiety and indolence of old establishments, into a fair and fearful competition with the novelty and zeal of the present sects. What other predictions then could have been formed, than that they would gradually see the proselytes of their church passing over to the communion of more animated though less enlightened ministers?"[21]

There were over ninety Church of England clergymen and 164 churches and chapels in Virginia at the outbreak of the Revolutionary War in 1776. Only twenty-eight clergymen and seventy-two functioning parishes remained at the war's end in 1787.[22] Visitors noted the crumbling, formerly beautiful edifices of country churches and were surprised to see cattle wandered through empty, doorless chapels with birds roosting in the rafters. In one parish, locals reportedly transformed the unused marble baptismal font into a watering trough for horses.[23] Although the numbers of clergy slowly climbed in consequent years, by 1811 only forty Episcopal churches in Virginia were able to support a minister.[24]

Virginia was unusual in that she had a bishop of her own; in the first decade of the nineteenth century, only four acting bishops served in the United States.[25] The bishop of Virginia, James Madison (a cousin to President James Madison), held the post from 1790 to his death at age sixty-two in 1812. He was nearly six feet tall and thin, a gentleman of respectable character and a popular preacher famous for his eloquent deliveries.[26] He also had a heart condition and was incredibly overworked. Madison served simultaneously as bishop, president of William and Mary College, a professor of mathematics and moral philosophy, a board member at the local insane asylum, and the rector of James City Parish.[27] As a practicing scientist, he additionally took on important cartography projects and published research on physics, geology, and biology.[28]

During Madison's tenure as president, William and Mary College was experiencing great difficulties, Madison's teaching load was a heavy one, and subsequently his academic duties absorbed much of his time and flagging energies. He had been trying for years, without success, to leave the college and his obligations there.[29] Although the college produced a number of national leaders under Madison's tenure, William and Mary was under fire by Virginia's Federalists, scraping and begging for every penny of support, and rife with student misconduct. Madison struggled to fill teaching posts and retain his professors. Although there were usually no more than about fifty students (all male) attending the college, they raised enough hell to besmirch William and Mary's name all the way to New York, where the *Post* criticized its rowdy collegians.[30] Student misbehavior included drunken, obscenity-spouting students stumbling down Duke Street, breaking up wooden carriages and other personal property and tossing bricks through the glass windows of Williamsburg homes.[31] They even decapitated the statue of Lord Botetourt in the center of the college grounds. President Madison unhappily reattached the nobleman's marble head by himself.[32]

While he must have been disturbed at his students' lack of respect for the college and its history, what probably proved most disconcerting to Madison was the violent animosity some students demonstrated toward the Episcopal Church. Madison tried to inculcate piety by requiring daily morning prayer attendance of all students at the college, but even his masterfully sonorous readings of the prayers and scriptures could not make their messages stick.[33] During his tenure, a coterie of William and Mary's collegians broke into the Bruton Parish Church, smashed church windows, and caused significant damage to the pipe organ. During a second raid of the stately brick building, students destroyed the communion table and took armloads of prayer books and Bibles outdoors, strewing them across the churchyard. The pulpit they smeared from one end to the other with fresh human excrement. On another occasion, the students stooped to a chilling new low in their attempts to desecrate the sacred ground and climbed over the low brick walls around the churchyard on Duke of Gloucester Street to rob a grave. A townsperson later discovered a female corpse, whom students had disinterred from the Bruton Parish cemetery, abandoned on the floor of an empty house "in a situation too shocking to describe!!!"[34]

With a large majority of its students and faculty—including Madison—embracing Jeffersonian republicanism, the College of William and Mary was said to be a hotbed of radical, irreligious thought by its Federalist critics. Edmund Randolph, a William and Mary student who would become governor of Virginia, U.S. secretary of state, and the first American attorney general, claimed that, in his experience, some professors encouraged spiritual skepticism. As a student, young Randolph had expressed tentative doubts about the truth of Christian doctrines and consequently was praised by a respected teacher for his intellectual promise and independent thought.[35]

Evangelicals judged Madison severely during his lifetime and in subsequent years for what they saw as a lack of moral rigor. Evangelical Episcopalian and future bishop William Meade spent some time with Bishop Madison when visiting Williamsburg in February 1811 for his ordination examination. While breakfasting with the bishop, a disapproving Meade pointed out that a neighbor was restocking his ice house on the Sabbath. Madison, untroubled by the activity, responded that such work was permissible on the Lord's Day. Meade also learned with shock that the bishop had allowed students at William and Mary to debate both the existence of God and whether Christianity had been "injurious or beneficial to mankind."[36] As the two men rode to the ramshackle Bruton Parish Church for Meade's ordination service—attended only by a small handful of Meade's family and associates—the young minister disapprovingly noted that Duke of Gloucester Street was filled with Madison's college students and their hunting dogs, ready for a day of sport.[37] Rumors that Madison was a freethinking unbeliever at the end of his life—probably based on the state of the church during his leadership, the escapades of his rabble-rousing pupils, and his politics—were even circulated.[38]

"Ill health and much occupation, together with the necessity of taking my usual exercise, always defeated my intentions," the sickly bishop wrote to a student in 1811.[39] These burdens of a heart condition (which would eventually cause his death) and a plate of responsibilities full to overflowing resulted in Bishop Madison's provision of minimal oversight to the ministers in Virginia's Episcopal parishes. College work so consumed him that Tyler recalled Madison could spend only school vacations—a few months out of the year—carrying out diocesan duties and visiting individual parishes.[40] This lack of contact meant he couldn't even identify the men under his leadership; Madison was not able to provide a required current list of practicing diocesan clergy to the Episcopal General Assembly after 1801.[41] Although he ordained more clergy in the first decade of his episcopate than any other Episcopal bishop of his time, he called but a single convention of ministers during his twenty-two-year term.[42] This is certainly not how he wished to lead. Sore pressed to do adequate service to his responsibilities as bishop, he sought to have an assistant appointed in 1805 to help with the burden of serving the parishes of Virginia. The request was not granted.[43]

George MacLaren Brydon, former historiographer of the Diocese of Virginia and an evangelical, blamed Madison's lack of oversight for the generally poor quality of the day's ministers. "Owing to the collapse of discipline during the period, it was disgraced by the incoming into the State of ministers, some perhaps with forged credentials, who on account of unworthy and immoral lives had been forced out of other Dioceses."[44] Of the hundred or so ministers who served during the years 1784 to 1814, around fifteen publicly dishonored the church with their behavior—about one out of every six ministers.[45] (More recent research puts the number closer to one wayward minister out of ten, no better or worse than their contemporary British compatriots.)[46] Brydon, often quoting from fellow evangelical Bishop Meade's multivolume *Old Churches, Ministers, and Families of Virginia*, provided some examples of "unwatchful shepherds."[47]

Dr. James Chambers of Augusta Parish moved to Kentucky, after which "he was completely secularized, making no attempt to exercise his ministry," and was killed in a duel. Rev. William Lewis Gibson from Fairfax Parish was part of a vicious church split in Alexandria and later was dropped from the ministry on account of intemperance. Rev. Samuel Gray of Botetourt Parish died in the parish poorhouse "the miserable victim of drink." Rev. James Kemp served "for want to those that were better" and "drank to excess." Rev. Samuel Low, a gigantic man and powerful orator, occasionally preached in Richmond. Low, it was discovered in 1808, had abandoned his wife and was cohabiting with a woman he had not married, but even this was not enough to secure his dismissal. He simply disappeared after the Diocesan Convention in May 1813 and died a short time after. Rev. Elkanah Talley became a Universalist and drank himself to death.[48]

Madison diagnosed the problem with his ministers as a lack of "fervent zeal, without which the great ends of [our] ministry can never be accomplished."[49] He proposed that ardent ministers who lived exemplary lives might have prevented the indifference and falling attendance of Virginia Episcopalians. "Our Church is blessed with many truly pious and zealous pastors," he preached to his priests at a clergy convention in the last decade of the eighteenth century, "but, at the same time, I fear there is too much reason to apprehend that the great dereliction sustained by our Church hath arisen, in no small degree, from the want of that fervent Christian zeal, which such examples ought more generally to have inspired." The rising evangelical sects were remarkable for the religious enthusiasm of their preachers, and their vigor drew converts. Madison urged his parish priests to "be renewed, I entreat you, in the spirit of our vocation, in that holy, fervent zeal which should be the distinguishing characteristic of every minister of the Gospel."[50]

Although Madison championed zeal about a half-dozen times in his sermon, it is doubtful that many were able to drum up enthusiasm for life as a parish priest. Meade recalled that after his ordination, tales circulated "that there was something unsound in mind or eccentric in character, at any rate a want of good common sense" about him to have made the mistake of joining a church with such "fallen and desperate fortunes."[51] Salaries were so low that over one-fifth of the priests in those years, like Bishop Madison himself, held other jobs, which diverted them from the work of monitoring their parishes, some quite extensive in size. Most preachers who had second jobs worked as tutors, professors, or headmasters. Rev. Needler Robinson, for example, oversaw a parish in Norfolk County, but Meade reported, "His time and labours were chiefly devoted to a school from the first. Although he lived for many years after our Conventions in Richmond were renewed, he never attended them."[52] Others, stretched to serve congregations spread miles apart, could not attend as diligently to their work and parishioners as they may have wished.

Nineteenth-century Episcopalians who chronicled their denomination's early history in Virginia, such as Bishop William Meade and Rev. Dr. Francis Hawks, tended to be evangelical reformers, and their accounts became the reference of choice for researchers and historians like Brydon throughout the twentieth century. These clergymen tended to portray the Episcopal Church as broken almost beyond repair from the mid-eighteenth century through the first decade of the nineteenth, when evangelicals like themselves gained influence within the denomination. This latter was principally due to the selection of an evangelical bishop of Virginia following on the heels of Richmond's theater fire and Monumental Church's construction. For example, Brydon wrote darkly that Madison's tenure was "the most difficult period of the history of the Episcopal Church in Virginia," an era of "absolute collapse and hopelessness, from which it revived in 1814 with the election of Rt. Rev. Richard Channing Moore of New York [an evangelical] as its second Bishop."[53]

These same critics argued Madison's despondency led to an entire remission of effort on his part.[54] Evangelical bias notwithstanding, there is no question that the Episcopal Church in the years under Bishop Madison's leadership was troubled and faced grave challenges. But those who knew Bishop James Madison personally would not have agreed that he was lazy, religiously apathetic, or careless about his responsibilities to the diocese or the college. As former students like tenth U.S. president John Tyler and Colonel Charles Stewart Todd, a U.S. minister to Russia, remembered, Madison was a profound preacher and fatherly scholar who educated the state's leading minds while simultaneously holding together a floundering college and the remaining fragments of Virginia's Episcopal Church.[55] Madison may at times have felt he was one of a meager handful of people committed to the sustainability and future of his church, and he may have doubted that it could long survive; yet he continued to serve the church to the best of his ability.[56] He worked under great disadvantages and often alone. Congestive heart failure finally claimed Madison's life in March 1812, and the bishop was buried under the floor of the William and Mary College chapel. Although no revival or reversal of the Episcopal Church's fortunes happened on his watch, what work Madison was able to accomplish may have prevented the church's collapse into complete ruin and irrelevance in Virginia.

A NEW CHURCH, A NEW BEGINNING

In early 1812, the Episcopal Church in Virginia found itself in need of a bishop and also in need of a serviceable church in the Commonwealth's capital city. In the first decade of the century, an interdenominational community organization—the Association for Erecting a Church on Shockoe Hill—had labored to raise funds for a dedicated place of worship in Richmond. Members, many of whom were Episcopalians, hoped to establish a church in an accessible and populated part of the city, closer to the capitol. After years of sporadic and inconsequential donations, by fall of 1811 the association remained at least three thousand dollars short of their target.[57] At the same time, the Common Council–appointed Monument Committee, headed by John Marshall, was appointed to receive contributions and to make arrangements for erecting the monument to the theater fire victims.[58] Contributions had not been as munificent as they had hoped, and on February 8, they ran a notice to the public warning that a paltry memorial might be all they could construct with what had been donated to date. "The size and form of the Monument to be erected over the remains of the victims to the conflagration of the Theatre, lately consumed in this city, will depend on the sum subscribed for that purpose, and as it must be extremely desirable that arrangements should be promptly made for commencing the work, it will be necessary soon to close the subscription."[59]

Sacred purpose joined secular purpose on February 17, 1812, when the Association for Erecting a Church on Shockoe Hill united with the Monument Committee. The motivation for merging the projects may have been financial; it was more economical to have one structure serve both purposes (the church could house the monument) and more efficient for the two groups to work toward one fund-raising goal.[60]

John Marshall took the helm on numberless civic projects over his lifetime, including pledge drives and lotteries funding the Richmond Masonic Lodge, the national Washington Monument, and, years later, another theater in Richmond. His service as chairman of the committee that built the faulty brick theater in 1806 may have made his appointment as chairman of the Monument Committee all the more appropriate—a means of making atonement, perhaps.[61] The black-eyed judge's ecumenical Monument Committee consisted of William Fenwick and Thomas Taylor, both Episcopalians; Joseph Marx, a Jew; and Benjamin Hatcher, probably a

Presbyterian.[62] The group decided that the land best suited for the new church and memorial would be the very land where the destroyed theater had once stood.[63]

After officially joining, the Monument Committee and Association to Erect a Church merged their resources into an aggregate fund and split the cost of the property; two-thirds to be paid by the church association, one-third by the Common Hall committee.[64] The chamberlain of the city donated five thousand dollars from the funds of the corporation for the purchase of the lot, although the voucher proving this donation was destroyed during the U.S. occupation of Richmond in 1865.[65] The first step, once the committees decided to appropriate the land, was to buy it from the trust of its former owner, Margaretta Sully West, the recently deceased tragedian, theater company manager, and widow of theater manager Thomas Wade West, of West & Bignall fame.[66] From the scanty financial and legal records available, it seems Richmond courts decreed West's trusts failed due to nonperformance of covenants to the subscribers to the theater. Therefore the theater trustees (which included William Marshall) sold the property at public auction, and the joint committee (led by William's brother John Marshall) purchased it for $4,500, apparently unopposed.[67]

The joint committee raised the capital for the Monumental Church project by selling subscriptions to the church at twenty-five dollars a share, not an uncommon way to finance a large civic building. The committee "placed in my hands a paper soliciting contributions both for the church and monument," recalled Thomas Drew, who promptly began courting Richmond families for subscriptions. The most generous donation Drew solicited—two hundred dollars—came from Joseph Gallego, a Roman Catholic.[68]

Committee members were also expected to donate, and John Marshall made one of the first pledges. He added a provisional rider stating that he would contribute the amount to the monument only if twenty-five other contributors matched his amount. While this rider may have been Marshall's attempt to challenge townspeople to match his gift, his friend Charles Copland took deep exception. When the list of donations was publicly released, Copland pledged a gift of fifty British pounds. Listed with his gift amount was an oblique reference to Marshall: "Charles Copeland now subscribes what he always said he would subscribe and no more. He does not trammel his subscription by annexing any conditions." Perhaps due to a pang of guilt for his harshness or at the suggestion or more tactful friends, Copland added,

"This expression will not be taken (as it is not intended) to blame any one for annexing a condition to their subscription."[69] Whatever awkwardness may have been created by this pointed message was eventually smoothed over between the two friends, and twenty-three years later, Copland served as a pallbearer in Marshall's funeral.[70]

Besides the subscriber system, funds for the church and monument arrived from other outside sources. A Pennsylvania theater even donated toward the construction of the new church. Victor Pepin and Jean Breschard, Philadelphia circus owners, met in their city's public chambers and declared their intentions to hold a benefit performance at their new building, the Olympic Theater, with all proceeds going toward the Monumental Church.[71]

* * *

The structure to be erected, the church association proposed, should first be approved by a majority of the joint committee and at least "three of the relatives of the deceased."[72] The standard account told in local histories and even in Historic Richmond Foundation (which owns Monumental) documents claims that the joint committee solicited submissions for the best design, a keen competition between the country's finest architectural minds ensued, and the subsequently famous Robert Mills of South Carolina won out. However, this is not true. No public notices of a competition or contest exist; that was a later assertion by Mills. Selecting the monument design was actually a haphazard process, marked by a lack of good communication and tainted by professional rivalry between Mills and his mentor, Benjamin Henry Latrobe.

After his arrival in America in 1796, tousle-haired, bespectacled British architect Benjamin Latrobe made Richmond his home and set up an office at Quarrier's Court on the canal near Seventh Street.[73] In 1798 he moved to Washington, D.C., where he was selected to become the first national surveyor of public buildings. In this capacity, Latrobe found himself responsible for key architectural projects like the construction of the Supreme Court quarters at the U.S. capitol and collaborating with Dolley Madison to redesign the White House.

But in his Richmond days, it seemed he might make the city his permanent home. Latrobe participated in local politics and wrote for the local theater.[74] He became well acquainted with Thomas Wade West, owner of the theater, and was commissioned in 1797 to create a new theater design for West, who envisioned an enormous entertainment center: a combination conference hall, theater, and hotel. Instead of scattering cast and crew in boardinghouses across the city, West's company could lodge in one place, conveniently adjoining the theater. A more spacious building could store his expansive collection of set pieces and costumes (not possible in the current structure), and because of the neighboring hotel and tavern, it would be continually habited and a less-attractive spot for the vandals who targeted empty buildings and stole costumes from the company's stock.[75] Latrobe generated several beautiful sketches of the proposed complex, which he envisioned as a massive four-story pink stuccoed building, the front studded with forty-two large windows and a grand entry door. West, sadly for Latrobe, would never build the pink entertainment wonderland; at over $27,000, it was too expensive for practical consideration.[76] Yet his design was so compelling and forward-thinking that plans to construct a theater according to Latrobe's sketches and diagrams were briefly resurrected in the 1960s.[77]

On the side, Latrobe had also instructed a few promising American students, like young South Carolinian Robert Mills. The latter had also studied with James Hoban, designer of the White House, and had lived as a student-in-residence with Thomas Jefferson at Monticello.[78] Mills, whose parents were Scottish immigrants, married well, wedding his sweetheart, Eliza Barnwell Smith, on her expansive northern Virginia plantation, Hackwood, on October 15, 1808.[79] His reputation and business grew in the years following his marriage, and Mills began to receive more commissions. By 1812, his designs for a jail, multiple residences, and a few churches had been either constructed or were underway.

Latrobe knew, once word of the theater's burning reached Washington, D.C., that city leaders would insist such a disaster merited a large-scale commemorative structure. He immediately contacted the mayor of Richmond, Benjamin Tate, and proposed, unsolicited, to construct a monument. Subsequently in January, he corresponded with city leaders John Wickham and John Brockenbrough about his design, sending letters through the speaker of the U.S. House, Henry Clay, on his journeys between Washington, D.C., and Richmond. Latrobe completed, as requested, a draft of a square church with two towers fronted by a pyramid. His letters indicate he was unaware of any public competition.

Henry Hiort, a lawyer and contractor in Richmond, also contributed a sketch in February to the Monument Committee (it is not clear if it was solicited), which was roundly praised in the *Enquirer*. Latrobe became aware of this competing plan but held such confidence that Tate and the committee would choose his design that he set about hiring contractors for the monument project.[80] After all, he was America's leading public architect—it was an honor for someone of his stature to even consider this project for Richmond. Hiort was no more than a local who could draw. Architectural design was a largely misunderstood field in the early republic, with no academic architectural programs available to train professionals in proportion, acoustics, and the science of design. Therefore, public building and monument competitions regularly resulted in submissions by scientists, painters, and administrators, and the winners not infrequently had connections to the committee members.[81] Those who made architectural design a profession, like pioneers Mills and Latrobe, found it to be a financially volatile field lacking standardized payment scales and professional respect.

Meanwhile, John Brockenbrough, who was most likely an original member of the Shockoe Hill church-building association, contacted twenty-nine-year-old architect Robert Mills and solicited a design proposal. Brockenbrough did not inform Latrobe of this.[82] Perhaps the committee wished to procure a less-expensive design. Whatever the committee's intention, its communication methods caused a mighty rift between master and protégé.

Once notified of the need for a monument, Mills gleaned some information about the committee's desires—and possibly Latrobe's proposal—courtesy of his father-in-law, John Smith. Certainly Smith had a personal interest in seeing his son-in-law succeed financially and gain a commission in the competitive and uncertain field of architecture. In a friendly conversation, Latrobe had unguardedly shared plans with General Smith, not realizing until later that Smith could—and probably did—pass this information along to Mills. Smith also passed on a tip on February 25, 1812, that the committee now wished to include a church to the monument. Within two weeks, Mills had submitted a design incorporating both. The committee then contacted Latrobe, requesting a second design so that his final proposal could be compared with that of Mills, whose draft of a steepled church was the front-runner. Latrobe was incensed when he discovered Mills's involvement and even more angered when he noticed the similarities between their proposals, as described by the committee. Latrobe responded, "I feel exceedingly reluctant to enter the lists against my own professional child,—contrary to the established rule of the profession, even in cases of actual and profitable benefit, especially when the principal on which Mr. Mills has made his design, is my own idea communicated to him; though much modified."[83]

The extent to which Mills may have directly borrowed from Latrobe and the degree to which their years of working together resulted in similar thoughts cannot be determined, but both designs included a church structure fronted with a thirty-two-foot-square columned portico containing niches and a monument to the victims. Both embraced Egyptian themes, Mills's in the decorative details, Latrobe's in a forty-eight-foot-high stepped pyramid atop the portico. Both designs featured funerary urns and marble tablets recording the victims' names. Latrobe wryly noted the remarkable coincidences in his deliberately restrained correspondence with Mills. "It is also singular," Latrobe wrote to Mills in May 1812, "that you should propose inserting marble panels into freestone margins exactly in the same manner in which I had proposed without being informed of my intention." If Mills had received insider information about Latrobe's plan, the sheer audacity of the plagiarism baffled his architectural mentor. Latrobe added, "It is however impossible to suppose that you were so informed because you would hardly have waged war against me in my own armor."[84] In a reply, Mills protested that he had not known of Latrobe's marble panel plan, nor that Latrobe had been communicating with the Richmond committee. Latrobe did not directly call Mills disingenuous but presumed that Henry Clay may have shared information and General Smith had been the primary informant: "[If you claim] you did not know . . . & were wholly unapprised of my intentions as to the mode of recording the names of the sufferers, although your father in law told me that he should write to You on the subject, before you sent in your different plans, then all ground of offence is certainly removed, & nothing remains but the astonishment that in so novel a mode of setting Marble in Freestone as Your and my method certainly are we should both have invented the same thing at the same moment." This was a great stretch for Latrobe's imagination, but, he wryly added, "Such an extraordinary coincidences [sic] do actually happen sometimes."[85]

Mills undercut Latrobe with an estimate of $35,000, which Latrobe found completely unrealistic in light of Mills's expensive building materials.[86] Nevertheless, in May 1812, the joint committee confirmed that they would use Robert Mills's design. The committee awarded Mills the commission and a prize of five hundred dollars. On the twenty-sixth, Latrobe wrote sadly to Mills, "I take this occasion to express my regret that after knowing that I Had been consulted on the Monument once proposed to be erected at Richmond You would have transmitted to them a number of Ideas and drawings, which rendering decision difficult has I believed defeated the object. I am far from supposing you intended me an injury yet you have not only injured but disgraced me because I had already made a conditional contract with respectable men, whom I have had to disappoint with an explanation not very creditable to myself, namely that your plan was preferred." Undercutting a competitor and borrowing his design was a form of professional disrespect "which no inducement of profit could have made me guilty toward you," Latrobe insisted to Mills. Latrobe claimed he was incapable of "permanent displeasure," but the incident would spell the end of Latrobe and Mills's working relationship.[87]

Perhaps the committee's preference for Mills had to do in part with Latrobe's political leanings. His satire "The Apology" had parodied Federalists, and Latrobe, as a good friend of Aaron Burr, had been subpoenaed for Burr's treason trial in 1807. That Monument Committee chairman John Marshall, prominent Federalist and the judge over Burr's trial, might view him with suspicion is certainly possible and has been suggested by one Richmond theater historian.[88]

* * *

The ruins had remained in place for over a year, crumbling and weed strewn: a public eyesore. Save what had been picked over by memento seekers, the site looked just as it had on December 27, 1811, until March 1813. At that time, the city paid Christopher Tompkins fifty-five dollars to pull down the walls of the theater and those of a house next door, which had burned as well.[89] He may have had to work around laborers on the theater site: construction for the new church was already underway amid the wreckage.

Mills traveled between Philadelphia and Richmond from 1812 to 1814 to meet with the committee and provide drawings for the contractor, Isaac Sturdevant of Boston.[90] By May 1813, the walls of Monumental Church had been erected, workmen were shingling the dome, and the interior was being painted.[91] The committee had grown anxious about the construction expenses, which Brockenbrough wrote to Mills "they fear will exceed their means."[92] Fund shortages meant that the steeple tower and the large allegorical sculpture of mourning Richmond among the ruins were never installed and important features—like the monument itself—were delayed. Instead of the sculpture, builders constructed a triangular attic on the portico in 1816 and later installed the sarcophagus monument.[93]

Monumental took five years before it was completely finished, three years longer than most of Mills's churches. Its first fire insurance policy from the Mutual Assurance Society of Virginia in 1818 shows that the completed church was valued at thirty thousand dollars.[94]

SYMBOLISM

As the first anniversary of the fire approached, Mills had written to close family friend Sarah Zane in Philadelphia about the status of his memorial building. "From its present progress, I hope it will be ready for divine service to be held within its walls before another year runs its important round. I wish to produce in . . . this building all that effect which the importance of its use demands, and which the peculiar circumstances which have occasioned its erection require, to strike the senses."[95] Strike the senses it did; Mills's hybrid neoclassical memorial and house of worship was an eclectic architectural mix that departed from traditional American churches both in the interior and the exterior. Mills believed America needed an innovative architectural "language" for its public structures, not fawning imitations of ancient cathedrals or civic buildings from the Old Country. In an unpublished autobiography, he wrote, "I have always deprecated the servile copying of the buildings of antiquity; we have the same principles and materials to work upon that the ancients had, and we should adapt these materials to the habits and customs of our people."[96] Mills's key innovation was the auditorium-style sanctuary, oriented toward the pulpit rather than the altar. He recognized that preaching was assuming a more central role than music or ritual or Eucharist in evangelical Protestant churches, and he made the pulpit—not the altar—the orientation point for church design.

Not all appreciated his innovation. Evangelical Episcopalian historian George MacLaren Brydon wrote that the people of wealth who donated toward Monumental's construction wanted "a very impressive building, different in architectural type from anything in America." The structure was to be a classic example of grief for their dead, and hence it lacked typical church features. "They wanted a mausoleum alone—and got it!" Brydon exclaimed. He credited the later formation of St. Paul's Episcopal Church, an offshoot of Monumental, to the congregation's ("or the most devout of them") desiring to meet in a church which not only had more seating but "looked like a Church."[97]

The Carrara marble monument stood in the middle of the portico, inscribed with the names of all the fire's victims. Parishioner Thomas Drew claimed that the sculptor, without order or authority, created the monument and brought it to Richmond complete, prevailing on the vestry or committee reluctantly to receive it. "It was not entirely approved by them, and even some of the names were inaccurately spelt," Drew recorded.[98] A Roman urn, an honorific symbol of death, sits atop the monument's platform. Although cremation was virtually unheard of in America at this time, crematory urns, which recalled the Roman republic, were very fashionable as funerary images from the end of the Revolutionary War through the 1820s. They appeared on objects from gravestones to needlepoint and were a generic image of mourning, rather than one typically related to fires. However, in this particular case, the urn, a receptacle for human ashes, was a fitting symbol of the holocaust that claimed Richmond's victims.[99]

The engraved names were arranged according to the victims' status. Men, who made up the smallest percentage of the victims, were featured on the side of the sarcophagus facing Broad (or H) Street, indicating their importance and significance. Women's names covered the remaining three sides. Although the bodies of blacks and whites lay entwined beneath the building, the sculptor kept their monikers distinctly separated on the sculpture; the names of blacks and mulattos are found inscribed into the base of the monument.[100] It makes an interesting, unintentional statement: although separated and relegated below white townspeople, the black citizens provided the foundation upon which the others rested—and truly, in a city with a 50 percent enslaved population, Richmond's black labor supported the city.

As a cost-saving measure, Mills stuccoed the exterior walls (a favorite faux finish of Latrobe's) and incised lines into them to simulate more expensive masonry.[101] However, his choice of Aquia sandstone may have served to inflate the cost. Thomas H. Drew complained, "The cost of the building was much increased by bringing the stone, which proved to be of an inferior quality, from the mouth of Acquia [sic] Creek, on the Potomac, when we had an abundance of the very best granite on the canal within a half mile of the city."[102]

Inside, the building was spacious, bright with natural light, and austerely decorated with simple, federal-style altarpieces and unpainted wooden benches. Steam heat rose through decorative grates in the floor. Although parishioners would later install Tiffany stained-glass windows in the church, as Mills designed it, the light entered a clean, light space through large clear-glass windows. The walls were painted a light salmon shade (probably tinted with clay) and woodwork a cool gray. Four exquisitely constructed cantilevered staircases appeared to float to the balcony, where rows of free benches overlooked the auditorium-style sanctuary. Light from unexpected sources occurred frequently in the design. The final result was a memorial that alluded to Christian faith springing phoenix-like out of despair.[103]

Mills was an intensely evangelical Christian, a Presbyterian, and while in Richmond he attended the capitol church, which had grown to a "very large assembly" by the time of his stay.[104] The extent to which his beliefs influenced his design or the projects he undertook has not been examined by his biographers and historians but is a topic deserving of some attention. He probably relished the opportunity to turn the site from a place of entertainment to a place of worship. It was also Mills's hope that the building would further Christian activity in the state capital and that he could thus play a role in the city's redemption. Mills wrote to Zane in 1812, "You will feel interested to know how the Monumental Church progresses, as through divine providence I trust its use to the sacred duties of religion will be advanced."[105] He described his plan for an apocalyptic altar painting of an annihilated Richmond, with Monumental Church in ruins and a crowd therein ascending to heaven. Such a painting, Mills believed, would remind Richmonders of the Resurrection and encourage them to prepare their own souls for death."I humbly pray, that the awful visitation with which he has visited R[ichmond] may redound to his glory in the salvation of all its inhabitants," he wrote.[106]

* * *

Arguably, as the chief financiers and the groups suffering the greatest casualties in the fire, the Presbyterian and the Episcopalian contingents in town, both of whom met in a joint service at the capitol, could lay claim to the building. The two groups were virtually indistinguishable at this point, continuing to attend one another's services throughout the years between 1812 and 1814, with baptized Episcopalians sitting under the new Presbyterian minister's preaching and Presbyterians taking communion from Episcopal priests.

After considering various schemes for the proprietorship of the building—

common to all denominations, exclusive to one, or occupied by two—the church's subscribers chose to make it an exclusive congregation but then had to determine the denomination of the new church structure. Subscribers were about evenly divided between Episcopalians and Presbyterians, but Rev. Blair held back from pressing the Presbyterian claim to the building and encouraged the Presbyterians to follow his ambivalent lead. At the end, the final decision threatened to become acrimonious and was close enough to have been decided by a single subscriber's vote.[107] "The majority might have been carried for Mr. Blair and the Presbyterians if he had pressed his claims with the diligence others pressed theirs," noted a later Presbyterian minister, somewhat sullenly.[108] Not until the seventh of February 1814 did the subscribers finally vote for Episcopal consecration, only weeks before the church doors officially opened for the beginning of a special diocesan convention.[109]

The town bells rang on May 4, 1814, rousing Richmonders to the first service at Monumental Church. Entering the new memorial church that Wednesday proved to be an emotional event, according to the *Virginia Patriot*, for nearly every attendee had an immediate connection to a theater fire victim.[110] After a subsequent special convention, on Sunday, May 8, the Reverend William Meade preached in a service that officially admitted Monumental Church into the diocese. Monumental was then consecrated on November 13 in a service led by their new rector and bishop, Richard Channing Moore.[111]

Through the building of Monumental Church, Richmond's theater fire victims—at least a few of them—achieved a romantic, almost legendary status, and the site became a place of pilgrimage for visitors. Tourist Henry Knight penned a note to his brother after a visit to Richmond and Petersburg in 1816, where he made sure to visit the disaster site "where the awful fire appalled the Theatre, and crowded above three score of shrieking victims from the scenes of time, into the scenes of eternity; and among them the governor, and a brave officer and his beloved."[112] Monumental Church also propelled Mills's career forward. He later received commissions for other civic monuments, most famously the Washington Monument in the District of Columbia.[113] While overseeing Monumental's construction, he also garnered numerous contracts for Richmond-area homes, including the stately Brockenbrough House. Fifty years later it became the "White House of the Confederacy," home to Jefferson Davis and his family. The devastation in Washington, D.C., during the War of 1812 had showed government leaders how critical was the fireproofing of public buildings. When the United States needed construction for its rapidly growing capital, Mills was one of the few men in the nation with those skills. When applying to Andrew Jackson for the position of "architect to the public buildings" in Washington, D.C., a position he obtained and held through seven presidencies, Mills made particular reference to his designs "of a fire-proof character," which had become his special trademark.[114]

Before the church opened in May 1814, the Monument Committee held a public sale for its one hundred ground-floor pews. More than a way to insure choice seating for one's family, such sales raised significant amounts of money for new churches. The auction excited great local interest and made national news. To indicate their support for the memorial effort, Catholics, Jews, and assorted Protestants joined the crowd "with a spirit of liberality" and bid for pews alongside Episcopalians.[115] At the end of the day, the committee grossed $25,345 as a result of the sale. All the best pews—those centrally placed and nearest the pulpit—went for over three hundred dollars each, some climbing over five hundred dollars in the "amiable competition." By admission, the pews were "very narrow, and not capable of admitting commodiously more than five or six persons each," but still they garnered a healthy price.[116] Charles Macmurdo and John Brockenbrough, active donors to the church effort, enthusiastically bid on each pew until it reached the price assessed as its value, which is how Macmurdo ended up with nearly a dozen pews of his own.[117]

The pew deeds registered in the clerk's office of the Hustings Court record that pew buyers included individuals from several families who had lost loved ones in the fire: Charles Copland, Robert Greenhow, and James Gibbon, Sr.[118] John Marshall also purchased a pew, the narrow proportions of which proved to be dreadfully uncomfortable for the tall man. William Meade remembered, "Not finding room enough for his whole body within the pew, he used to take his seat nearest the door of his pew, and, throwing it open, let his legs stretch a little into the aisle. This I have seen with my own eyes."[119] Marshall's wife was a devoted member of Monumental Church and probably the reason for her husband's regular attendance. Although Marshall consistently took a seat in his pew with Polly, the judge never became a communicant of the church.[120]

Although he supported the Episcopal Church financially, Marshall was wary of joining what he saw as a sinking ship. When Meade asked Marshall for a donation to a proposed theological seminary around 1814, Marshall gave liberally, yet "he could not refrain from saying, that it was a hopeless undertaking, and that it was almost unkind to induce young Virginians to enter the Episcopal ministry, the Church being too far gone ever to be revived," as Meade recalled.[121] Yet Marshall would live to see a remarkable change.[122]

RICHMOND: A CHALLENGING PARISH

The destruction of the theater played a key role in reestablishing the struggling Episcopalians as a strong presence in the religious life of the city by bestowing on them a permanent building. But the death of Virginia's overstrained bishop, James Madison, in March 1812 also paved the way for denominational changes.

In May 1812, a remnant of active Episcopalian laymen and ministers called an emergency convention in Richmond. In the April general Protestant Episcopal convention in New Haven, Connecticut, national Episcopal leaders declared the Virginia branch of the church was "so depressed, that there is danger of her total ruin, unless great exertions, favored by the blessing of Providence, are employed to raise her."[123] Wrote one Episcopal divine of Virginia's spiritual state, "It must be evident that she can be raised, as a Church, from her present depressed condition, only by the blessing of God on the labours of a pious and zealous clergy, who, faithfully fulfilling their ordination vows, inculcate her evangelical doctrines, and steadfastly adhere to her apostolic order and primitive worship."[124]

Hoping for a rescue, the Virginia convention chose a new bishop, Rev. Dr. John Bracken. Bracken, a grammar school master, took over the presidency of William and Mary and was elected to the bishopric of Virginia, holding James Madison's prior posts. He was ill-suited for both. "The new Bishop looks more like a tavern keeper than a divine. Indeed, I am told he has nothing divine about him but the name," wrote an unimpressed Williamsburg visitor.[125] Within a few months, Bracken declined the office and excused himself from all responsibilities as bishop.[126] He turned in his resignation, no doubt as overwhelmed by his adjunct duties as his predecessor Madison. A special committee then chose Rev. Richard Channing Moore, the fifty-two-year-old rector of St. Stephen's in New York City, as Virginia's new bishop.[127] Unfortunately, the struggling denomination could offer no salary for the position. The convention therefore proposed a dual opportunity: those of (unpaid) bishop of Virginia and (paid) rector of Monumental Church—two jobs with the salary of one, probably totaling less than Moore had earned in New York.

Moore, who had studied languages at King's College, now Columbia University, practiced medicine for several years in his mid-twenties before he took orders for the Episcopal ministry in 1787. His own conversion experience came while waiting for a haircut at a New York barbershop. Paging through a Bible, he happened on the passage in Acts where Saul, broken and blinded, asks "Lord, what wilt thou have me to do?" The verse resonated in Moore's soul, and he adopted it as his own burning question. He later ascribed to this encounter the "turning of his life to Christ with full and serious purpose," and the experience redirected him from medicine to the pulpit.[128]

On January 27, 1813, Rev. William Wilmer of Alexandria, Virginia, had begged Moore to visit Richmond and tried to convince him of the strategic importance of the mission. His timing was critical: the Episcopal church needed to install a minister while the memory of the fire was still fresh. "The inhabitants of that place have, I hope, derived some advantage from their calamities, and are desirous of obtaining a man of zeal and piety," Wilmer wrote. "It would be a great pity that these poor lacerated lambs should fall into the hands of an unfaithful Shepherd. Besides this, Richmond, in its relation to the other parts of Virginia, is in an infinitely important situation; it is the heart, and if it be unsound, the body and extremities must of course be unhealthful."[129] Moore probably raised his white, overgrown eyebrows at the daunting prospect, but he did not reply in the negative. The hardships and financial shortcomings were not enough to deter him, "but as the way appears to me so obscured by doubts, I dare not venture to comply," he replied.[130] Moore was the first man of evangelical persuasion to be elected to the Episcopate in America, and he would be serving as bishop in a diocese other than that in which he resided.[131] Yet Virginians were encouraged by a proven history of church growth. Under his leadership, St. Stephens had grown from thirty families to around four hundred congregants in five years.[132]

Urban ministry presented immense challenges—challenges probably unappealing to a minister like Moore, nearing retirement age. "If a country parish, with its homogenous society, fixed character, simple unsophisticated habits, and peaceful seclusion from the dissipations and vices of fashionable life, holds out the greater promise of personal comfort and happiness, it must be admitted that the large and crowded city opens a wider field of usefulness to the able and faithful minister of Jesus Christ," read Moore's memoir.[133] Although Richmond resisted becoming the kind of industrialized metropolis developing in the North, it was still a city, and as far as some ministers were concerned, urbanity loomed as a dangerous threat to belief. As Moore's memoir recorded, the din of incessant occupation and the bustle of traffic combining with the "pageantry and vanity of wealth" were thought to distract the attention and thoughts of men from the themes of morals and religion. "There the enemies of our faith are combined in most formidable numbers," it warned, stating that ministers in cities had to be endlessly engaged in close conflict with "the world, the flesh, and the devil." But cities also presented the greatest reaping for the harvesters. "Is the Gospel to be preached to sinners? In large cities they are found in the greatest numbers," the author continued.[134]

Eventually, Moore accepted the position and introduced an evangelical period of Virginia Episcopalianism that lasted for the next seventy years.[135] The gentle-eyed, double-chinned minister with flowing white hair arrived in Richmond in June 1814, with his wife, Sarah. "The ancient Episcopal churches, which were once so predominant, are mostly in a state of dilapidation. The rank reeds rustle round their doors; the fox looks out at their windows," noted British tourist Henry Knight after Moore's arrival. "But, as a new bishop has been lately consecrated for Virginia, it is hoped that the churches will soon be re-edified."[136] Indeed, under Moore's leadership, Richmond's Episcopal Church annals recorded steady growth.

At Moore's consecration service in Philadelphia in 1814, Rev. John Henry Hobart uttered his regret that few parishes in Virginia enjoyed the regular ministrations of a clergyman, declaring that "in many places the liturgy is scarcely known, but as some antiquated book which was once used by their fathers."[137] However, the "dreadful experience" of the theater fire had made Virginians "ready and desirous to return to that fold from which they have wandered so long," he rejoiced.[138] Hobart commended Moore, who would sacrifice personal ease as he exchanged the comforts of home in retirement age for "a land of strangers, and for the difficulties of a depressed and extensive diocese."[139] Looking eagerly ahead, Hobart predicted that if the evangelical service and traditions of the Church should be revived in Virginia, "with what delight shall we all look back to the service of this day!"[140]

Once installed as bishop, Moore was seen daily about the better parts of Richmond, hefting himself up porch steps to pay a call on a sick parishioner or a house of mourning.[141] "It has been my object, since my settlement with this congregation," he wrote to a friend, "to cultivate a friendship with the leading families, in order that I might be able to form an opinion of those features of character and disposition, by which they are distinguished."[142] Although later

Monumental Church efforts would assist the community's poor, the middle and lower classes appear not to have been a priority at all for the new minister after his arrival. Then again, he was simply working with the base membership he had—elites made up the greatest portion of his congregation. They were the group from which he had some hint of encouragement. "From the uniform attendance of our first citizens upon my public labours, I take it for granted that they are disposed to encourage me in the prosecution of that great work in which I am engaged," he wrote a colleague in January 1815.[143]

Richmond's new Presbyterian minister, John Holt Rice, looked on Moore's efforts to win the elites warily. "I have a brother bishop here who attracts notice from the rich and great," Rice wrote to Archibald Alexander, "but I apprehend that he will find it no easy matter to mould them into good churchmen."[144] It was true—the character and disposition Moore encountered in the upper classes surprised him. What New York's Christians considered immoral or excessive was *de rigueur* to Christians in Virginia. A dinner—after church—at a Virginia parishioner's home might include five different kinds of wine and whiskey, and perhaps even a card game.[145] Henry Knight's observations lend an idea of the attitudes and habits that Moore encountered. "As to religion, the Virginians are less zealous, than were our Plymouth sires . . . being brought up without many churches, too few regard the sabbath, except as a holiday; or wherein to begin or end a journey. In some places, toward Norfolk, shops are kept open, only the buyer may walk round to the side door, to evade the law."[146]

Besides recruiting new faces to Monumental, Moore had another serious responsibility: acclimating all the existing professed Episcopalians to the practices of their own church. Breaking the capitol congregation into two separate denominational groups helped with this process, and the opening of Monumental Church, noted a Moore biographer, "enabled the new pastor to segregate his people, and, within its sacred walls, to train them to habits of attachment to the doctrines, discipline, and worship of the Church."[147] The capitol congregation had been syncretistic in practice, and consequently, Moore's Episcopalians were unfamiliar with their own denomination's liturgies and traditions. The antiaristocracy sentiments that throve after the Revolutionary War apparently bred some hostility to high church Episcopal trappings—the cassocks and collars, incense, and ceremony. Perhaps after experiencing some rejection or perhaps snide remarks on account of his surplice and stole, Moore wrote from New York in January 1814, "The prejudices which are entertained by many of the Virginians, against the services of the Church, and the appropriate costume of the clergy afford matter of considerable surprise to a person bred in this part of the union."[148] Wilmer recommended Moore introduce traditions gradually and deal with his congregation "as with babes, with discretion and zeal correct their taste, and strengthen their appetite until they can digest stronger food."[149]

In 1815, after one year in Richmond, Bishop Moore wrote from Richmond to his friend Rt. Rev. William White. While granting that the state of the Episcopal Church in Virginia "would grieve your heart," he added an optimistic note. "Even in those situations, where the Church has been most prostrated, the people are recovering from their torpor: and I hope that Virginia in a few years will assume that appearance, which her friends so warmly desire."[150]

8
REVIVAL

The views and impressions produced by this deplorable occurrence, however painful at the present, may be precious in their effects, and should not be suffered to pass off without originating such resolutions and purposes, as shall become the foundation of a new course of life.

—REV. ARCHIBALD ALEXANDER, 1812

I n a letter to a friend in Williamsburg after the fire, Dr. Philip Barraud of Norfolk noted a turn in Virginia's religious climate and asked, "How does it happen, my Dear Sir, that in all deep and awful afflictions, Man looks to a Divine Author for Succor and for Safety? His appeal in the highest moments of Terror and Dismay is made to the God on High! Nature has planted this in our Bosoms, let Casuists say what they may."[1] Newspaper articles and personal accounts confirm that after the Richmond Theater fire in 1811, Richmonders began attending Christian services in greater numbers with a fervor that ultimately birthed institutions that would last for centuries. Letters from ministers in Virginia eagerly relayed to friends that the people of Richmond were displaying a renewed interest in religion and the church.

Dr. James McCaw, a hero of the fire, was virtually immobilized during the months of his convalescence. The fire at the theater became his spiritual crucible. McCaw's obituary expounded, "His narrow escape on this occasion, and the heavy discipline consequently undergone, induced him to turn his thoughts to his Maker and Preserver. The seed then sown, gradually ripened, and finally matured into a faith, firm and abiding, in the promise of a Saviour." At forty, it seems, Dr. McCaw was reborn. This was not a short-term change, either, a knee-jerk reaction to the fear of death—his experience in the fire and his consequent conversion apparently wrought a permanent change in his life. From that point forward, "in [this] faith," his obituary read, "Dr. McCaw lived and died."[2] Likewise across the city, Richmond's foremost citizens began to warm toward evangelical religion.

For decades, many clerics and historians marked the theater fire as a major spiritual turning point for Richmond. Rev. William Foote, a Presbyterian, described the spiritual aftermath of the fire as a drastic, overnight transformation. "Never perhaps has the sudden destruction of men, women, and children, in one overwhelming ruin, produced a greater moral effect. All classes of community bowed down before the Lord. Christians were moved to efforts of kindness and love, that the gospel might be preached abundantly in Richmond. In the vigorous exertions now made for the spiritual welfare of this busy, pleasure-loving, but now serious city, all Christian denominations took a part."[3] Another nineteenth-century historian, John Little, stated, "From this time a change was wrought in Richmond; the theatre had ceased to exist, and a horror of such exhibitions, based on the memories of the fire, prevented for a long time another from being built. The type and center of gayety and frolic had disappeared, and on its foundation rose the first Episcopal church in the city. Men became more serious, other churches were erected, ministers employed, and the character of the people changed from a love of sport and frolic, to a more serious, sober state of mind."[4]

Even taking into account a degree of exaggeration in Foote and Little's accounts, there is ample evidence that a keen interest in formal religion arose in Richmond following the fire. Warnings of God's judgment may have seemed more believable after the fire. Certainly the dearth of charitable aid organizations and need for sufficient church space for postfire commemorations made Richmonders realize that their community lacked sufficient religious resources for the populace.

In particular, the theater fire was a catalyst for remarkable change in the Presbyterian and Episcopal congregations, which experienced exponential postfire growth and a surge in the creation of charitable outreaches and church societies. This was due in part to the building of permanent church structures for the two separate congregations in accessible areas of the city and the theological shift experienced by the hiring of evangelical, full-time ministers to replace the part-time parsons who had been serving the Presbyterians and Episcopalians.

The Baptist and Methodist congregations—which, unlike the Presbyterians and Episcopalians, already had their own distinct meeting houses—expanded their memberships after the fire, but their growth seems to correspond more with prevailing national denominational trends and local revivals than any direct response to the theater fire. Their theological emphases and activities, already evangelical, and their understanding of appropriate recreational activities for Christians did not change after the fire as did those of Richmond's Presbyterians and Episcopalians. Unlike the joint capitol congregation, which at the time of the fire apparently did not stigmatize theater attendance, the Methodists and Baptists of Richmond did not lose many, if any, parishioners in the Richmond Theater fire; the theater was a forbidden pastime for these denominations and attending the theater carried disciplinary consequences for members.

Presbyterians and Episcopalians tended to attract greater numbers of civic leaders and influential personages, and their newly held post–theater fire religious devotion and identity would have implications for their civic priorities and activities. There would have been a social cost for the gentry who adopted evangelical values and withdrew from the dancing, gambling, drinking, and theatergoing ubiquitous among their peers.[5] Because Richmond wielded considerable religious influence over the rest of the state, the changes this city's re-energized Christians made—creating charitable organizations, taking seats on denominational boards, publishing religious journals—would have statewide, and even nationwide, repercussions.[6]

Early republic Richmond was not known for its religiosity. Richmond historian Mary Newton Stanard wrote in 1923, "For a time in Richmond, now aptly called 'The City of Churches,' atheism was rife, church-going unpopular, especially with the element most warmly attached to Jefferson. Anyone depressed over imagined falling off in church-going since those good old days is borrowing trouble."[7] In January 1810, John Holt Rice, from his parish in Charlotte County, lamented of Richmond (with perhaps a measure of hyperbole), "Presbyterian congregations are decreasing every year, and appear as if they would dwindle to nothing. The Baptists and Methodists are at a stand. A strange apathy has seized the people. . . . As to religion, the very stillness of death reigns amongst us. I can find no resemblance to this part of the country but in Ezekiel's valley of dry bones."[8] The strongest evidence for Richmond's lackadaisical approach to religion seems to be the paucity of congregations in a city of its size. One historian of American religion observes that where congregations form voluntarily, congregation numbers are an excellent gauge of religious commitment.[9] The membership of Richmond's few conventional brick-and-mortar churches in total was less than 10 percent of the city population. Although perhaps deeply felt, religious faith in Richmond did not manifest itself in organized worship on a large scale, partly due to minister shortages, partly due to geography, and partly due to culture.

Although a deeply religious spirit imbued much of the American population in the early nineteenth century, it was not necessarily a churchgoing spirit; nationally, more Americans did not attend church regularly than did.[10]

Several factors contributed to occasional church attendance in Virginia, such as a post-war lack of allegiance to the Church of England and westward relocation.[11] Physical distance from churches also played a role. In 1816 Henry Knight observed, "Richmond is faith without works; Boston works without faith. . . . As they reside so far apart, each [Virginia] plantation has its God's acre, or *corner of graves;* and the funeral service is not infrequently performed a month after the deceased is buried; as they must send, perhaps, a score or two of miles for a clergyman."[12]

Repercussions of the French Revolution and its radical opposition to the established church continued to be felt in America, particularly in Virginia, where many gentry sympathized with a rationalist approach to faith. Brydon painted a dark picture of a Virginia that "was in the grip of a godless form of deism so widespread that not as much as one-tenth of all the people in the commonwealth made any profession at all of belief in the Christian faith."[13] Contemporary clergy viewed deism as an insidious destroyer of religion to which Virginians were particularly susceptible, and historians such as Mark Noll and Nathan O. Hatch attribute Tom Paine's attacks on Christianity for lay disassociation from churches in the mid-1790s.[14] Years after the French Revolution, the works of William Godwin, the father of philosophical anarchism, and Thomas Paine, who released influential publications in the late eighteenth century openly attacking Christianity, were still being read. Privileged young men were prone to adopt the rhetoric of the French revolutionaries, as at William and Mary, where early republic students dated their letters "A.R." (in the year of the Republic) and addressed one another as "Citizen."[15]

Skepticism kept a hold on Virginia's elites, if not the general population, into the nineteenth century and created a lay crisis of faith.[16] As Bishop Meade traveled through Virginia as a young man in the early nineteenth century, whenever he met an educated man in a tavern or on the road, he fully expected to find him "a skeptic, if not an avowed unbeliever."[17]

The extroverted Elizabeth Jaquelin Ambler Carrington, an Episcopalian and sister-in-law to John Marshall, described the Capitol congregation as "a set of modern philosophers, who merely attend because they know not what else to do with themselves. But blessed be God, in spite of the enlightened, as they call themselves, and in spite of Godwin, Paine, and others, we still . . . endeavor to preserve the religion of our fathers."[18] Thomas Coke, an Oxford-educated missionary and convert to Methodism, addressed the capitol congregation in 1791 during one of his nine missionary visits to America. Afterward he wrote, "I preached in *Richmond* . . . to the most dressy congregation I ever saw in America. However, they gave great attention while I spoke for an hour to the *Deists, Socinians,* and *Arians* [all heretical sects]."[19] Historian of Presbyterianism B. R. Wellford believed the "God-defying and man-destroying infidelity of the doctrinaires of the French Revolution" alienated Virginians from a vibrant spiritual life in 1811. He credited the Richmond Theater fire with a change in religious climate. "The startling calamity which shrouded this city in mourning was followed under the blessing of God with beneficent consequences. Under the solemnizing influences of this terrible providence, new life was infused into the churches."[20]

METHODISTS AND THE CALL TO BE SEPARATE

Richmond's Methodists had first held meetings at the Henrico County courthouse, but after neighbors complained loudly about their raucous singing and shouting, permission to congregate at the courthouse was withdrawn.[21] From there, the congregation moved into a stable on Main. (Methodists lived in a well-ordered, disciplined manner and held very lively services—precisely the opposite of Virginia's gentry, who attended well-ordered Episcopal services and enjoyed high-spirited living.)[22] A Methodist church went up on Nineteenth and Franklin in 1798 or 1799, in which morning and evening services were held on Sundays and a night service during the week. Rev. Cowling, the father of a Bank of Virginia bookkeeper, presided.[23] In 1812, the Methodist Richmond Circuit had a membership of 256 whites and 47 "colored members." Churchmen calculated in 1812 that Methodist membership in the state of Virginia grew by 43 blacks, but declined by 188 whites. Bishop Asbury attributed the decline to westward emigration.[24]

Methodists and Baptists actively preached in Richmond after the fire, taking advantage of the now-favorable religious climate. On February 20, 1812, revivalist preachers rode into town—most were men without great educations, faces wearing signs of the itinerant work that kept them on horseback for months out of the year, exposed to the elements as they preached in far-flung parishes. Over sixty Methodist preachers gathered in Richmond for the first meeting of the Virginia Conference of the Methodist Episcopal Church, with the redoubtable Bishop Francis Asbury presiding.[25]

The Methodist church heavily relied on unmarried, male itinerants to travel in defined circuits where there were few or no established ministers, preaching to groups of gathered believers and evangelizing the unchurched. "You have nothing to do but to save souls—Therefore spend and be spent in this work," advised the church's *Doctrines and Discipline*, a guide to Methodist theology and practice that every member was urged to have in his or her home.[26] After adopting a strict lifestyle of regular prayer, study, expository preaching, and fasting, a Methodist preacher had no time for leisure. In 1850, a Methodist writer recalled that Jesse Lee, an itinerant minister, would sally out from the conference on his circuit equipped with his horse, saddlebags, a Bible, and a hymnbook. When arriving in a town, he would attempt to obtain a church in which to speak, although sometimes a schoolhouse or courthouse or private dwelling served instead. If he could find no building, he would proclaim the gospel on the street "and then hasten away to go through the same process in another place, leaving his astonished auditors to reflect upon what they had heard."[27] The preachers were creative; Robert Williams gave his first sermon in Norfolk in 1772 and attracted a confused and "disorderly" crowd by standing at the courthouse door and loudly singing a hymn.[28]

The itinerants did not receive a regular salary. "For his maintenance he literally trusted to Providence," remarked Lee's biographer. Fortunately, he emphasized, Virginians often welcomed in the poor preachers. "Among the scattered population of Virginia, a people proverbial for hospitality, no stranger would be denied a welcome, and the early Methodist preachers experienced the benefit of this rustic hospitality."[29] Thomas Coke visited Williamsburg, Virginia, in the 1790s, and when he asked to be directed to a Methodist in town, his landlady mistakenly sent him to the home of a Presbyterian. Coke recalled, "When I apologized for my mistake, and was retiring, he insisted on my staying at his house, and sent for my horse. He loves God."[30] About a week later he found shelter at a Virginia tavern full of "nothing but dissipation and wickedness," and yet the landlord would accept no payment from the preacher and provided room and board gratis.[31] Due to the dearth of churches in rural parts of Virginia, preachers were enthusiastically welcomed, and the gospel messages fairly well attended. To the townspeople it was a public event—even public entertainment—not only a religious service. The novelty of a Methodist minister's periodical returns stirred excitement, "and the preaching-day, in many cases, became an epoch to be anticipated and remembered with a lively satisfaction," Lee's biographer recalled.[32]

Methodists did not approve of theater attendance and carried the antitheater message to Virginians. Occasionally a Methodist minister would enter a theater, but only for the want of another public place for preaching. Francis Asbury preached in Annapolis in a theater and also in Norfolk to a group of thirty Methodists with no place of worship but an "old, shattered play house."[33] An itinerant by the name of Pilmoor preached in the Charleston Theater in the late eighteenth century. Partway through his sermon, he disappeared; a few "wags, of the baser sort" had arranged for him to stand atop the stage's trap door and unceremoniously dropped him into the cellar. Pilmoor, undaunted, sprang back onto the stage and led his audience into the adjoining yard where he continued his message, adding, "We will, by the grace of God, defeat the devil this time, and not be driven by him from our work."[34]

Despite the abjuration of the theater, it is certain that some Methodists owed the stage a debt for their spellbinding oratorical abilities. Preacher George Whitefield is the most obvious example of this, but others, less well known, profited as ministers from the theatrical discourse they had heard before their conversions.[35] As a teenager in the second decade of the century, according to a biographer, John Summerfield became "excessively fond of the theatre" and adopted shiftless habits. Once unemployed, his love of the stage became even more intense, and he would leave his home for weeks—never telling his parents where he was going—to attend performances and speeches in London. His biographer noted, "He had a perfect passion for listening to eloquent speakers; and it mattered little to him whether he found them in the Pulpit, in the Senate House, at the Bar, or on the Stage."[36] After his conversion, Summerfield's popularity as a Methodist preacher was so great that anywhere it was known that he was to speak would be thronged long before the hour of the service, and on several occasions the avenues to the pulpit were so full that it was necessary to introduce him through a window.[37] Surely some of his oratorical ability was due to the hours he spent rapt in the audience of a London theater.

Attending a play or other popular entertainments was not explicitly forbidden in the Methodist *Doctrines and Discipline* of 1812 but would have been unacceptable according to the church's rules against frivolity and its expectation that believers would not participate in questionable, worldly activities. Some of the first Methodist converts in Yorkshire, England, had, in the words of a critic, "laid aside play-books and poems for Scripture phrases and hymns of [their] own composing."[38] Methodists were to avoid "every useless pleasure of sense [and] imagination," and preachers were exhorted to "never trifle away time."[39] The *Methodist Magazine* contrasted the frivolous woman of the world and the ideal woman of Scripture, saying "the hours of the one are divided between routs and assemblies, and visiting, and theatres, and cards: the other *looketh well to the ways of her household, and eateth not the bread of idleness.*"[40] Idleness was not only inexcusable but, in the Methodist's Arminian theology, put one's salvation at risk. "Do we not loiter away many hours in every week? Each try himself: No idleness is consistent with a growth in grace," warned the Methodist *Doctrines and Discipline.* "Nay, without exactness in redeeming time, you cannot retain the grace you received in justification."[41]

Richmond's Methodists were expected to renounce other entertainments that may have been central to their communities and culturally accepted, such as card playing and folk dancing. Separating oneself not only from disreputable activities but also from one's friends and even one's vocation might be required. A dancing master in Virginia known as "Madcap" attended a few Methodist services dressed in colorful suits of clothing before he became converted. Joining the Methodist society, he renounced the dance, gave up his profitable school, and began to teach writing, reading, and arithmetic.[42]

Joining the church meant, for many, adopting a conspicuously ascetic lifestyle. One of the marks was simple dress. One lively minister from Richmond's First Baptist Church, Jeremiah Jeter, recalled that "for many years the Methodists firmly stood their ground against all changes of fashion," men donning round-breasted coats not fashionable since the days of the Wesleys and the women wearing "simple, neat, convenient" dresses that "contributed much to restrain the extravagances of fashion."[43] One late eighteenth-century convert, an army captain, "got religion" while accompanying Methodist preacher Philip Gatch on his rounds in Virginia one day. Gatch recorded that "immediately he took his knife from his pocket, cut the ruffles from his bosom, and had his hair—which, according to the custom of the time, was long— cut off."[44] Although later in the century Methodists were undistinguishable from other people, in the first few decades of the nineteenth century, it was "quite likely a Methodist would have been expelled from the society if he had appeared publicly in a fashionably-cut coat," Jeter speculated.[45]

* * *

As spring arrived in 1812, grasses poked through the ashes of the theater, the weather warmed, and hope seemed possible for the inhabitants of bereaved Richmond. Irishman Isaac Weld had relished the rejuvenating springtime in Richmond during his travels there. When May arrived, he recorded that the trees were in bloom, and the air in the woods was perfumed with the fragrance of numberless flowers and flowering shrubs. Mockingbirds, doves, jays, and robins darted through blue skies and, as evening fell, thousands of fireflies softly glowed in wooded groves. Weld wrote in charmed wonder, "I have seen the woods sparkling with them in every quarter."[46]

Probably taking advantage of the new openness to religion and excellent attendance on postfire preaching services, in late May 1812 area Methodists conducted a "Camp-Meeting" in New Kent County, just east of Richmond. Camp meetings, or revivals, were proving to be a wildly successful evangelism strategy of the Methodist church. These meetings were not just a church event but a cultural and social phenomenon, and they quickly became a fixture of religious life in the South.

On Wednesday the twenty-eighth, the first day of meetings, only a few rustic pine branch booths and fifteen tents were erected near Boiling Springs—not an encouraging turnout. Nine ministers gathered and prayed for God to bring "strength out of weakness . . . and make known his Almighty Power to the awakening and conversion of many precious souls."[47] A few dozen people arrived on their wagons that Thursday, then more rolled in, until there were several hundred people in attendance, their horses tied to trees in the forest.

Although it was not the case in this instance, Methodist camp meetings were sometimes scheduled to coincide with the arrival of a theatrical troupe, to redirect the attentions of the public toward religion. In the 1820s, theater manager Solomon Smith visited Kentucky and wrote that in Georgetown "the Methodists had raised their banner before us, and had got possession of all the money and all the hearts of the young folk. They fairly conquered us, and drove us from the field!"[48] Camp meetings were held with the most serious of intentions—preaching the gospel in order to save souls for Christ—but crowds arrived with mixed motivations. The usual group of rowdies probably fringed the proceedings near Boiling Springs, sloshing down alcohol and mocking the penitent Christians.

Richmond's Presbyterian minister, John D. Blair, distrusted camp-meeting style religious enthusiasm. In an 1806 Virginia *Argus* article, he described camp meetings as "a common place of rendezvous for all the licentious & lewd."[49] Because camp meetings were open to the public, the audience could and did contain both the pious and the irreverent. Ministers or specially designated burly laymen usually kept the rabble-rousers in line and away from the pulpit during the preaching. Jeremiah Jeter preached at and attended many camp meetings, and he believed that an ordered meeting might be "eminently useful" to win people to faith. Yet he acknowledged the "great danger— certainly in Virginia—that they will be perverted to evil." He warned, "There is a strong tendency to make them occasions of social pleasure, festivity, and even of frivolity, dissipation, and vice. Satan usually attends camp-meetings, and musters and trains his servants for mischief, and much care, discretion, and firmness of purpose are needed to restrain the tendencies to evil."[50]

Although camp meetings featured times of singing and prayer, most of the meeting was spent on gospel messages and preaching. Methodists believed they were called to preach to all unreservedly, as though all were elected for salvation by God.[51] Some Methodist ministers adopted staunchly anti-Calvinist positions and felt it their obligation to combat what they believed was a theological perversion: that God would redeem only those whom he had elected for salvation and all others were doomed. Calvinism seemed to negate the importance of preaching—the central, consuming activity of the Methodists. One Rev. Edward T. Taylor, raised a foster child in Richmond, Virginia, impetuously joined a ship's crew at seven and at seventeen, in 1811, was converted in Boston's Old Bromfield Street Methodist church. Though uneducated, nearly illiterate, and having had only six floundering weeks in seminary, he enthusiastically preached loud, candid, inspired sermons four times a day to immense congregations in Boston. "He was a sturdy Methodist, and, like all the early New England [Methodist] preachers, he felt called to do battle with Calvinism," recorded his biographer. When one Calvinist pastor began to lecture him on the impossibility of saving the nonelect, Taylor responded, "There is no use talking, brother; your God is my devil. Give him my compliments."[52] But many Methodist preachers considered any evangelical preacher a compatriot and believed that engaging in theological arguments was irrelevant and distracting. In the words of one nineteenth-century Methodist, theological disputes over Calvinism were "rubbish . . . thrust into out-of-the-way corners in the libraries of theological seminaries." What was critical was that all believers evangelize, pray, and seek to save souls—that was the central concern.[53]

For five days that May outside Richmond, Methodists preached in the forest morning through night from crude wooden platforms, probably hanging lamps in the branches or pitching huge bonfires once the sun set to provide a dramatic light for the emotional evening services. By the Sabbath, around four thousand from New Kent and neighboring counties had gathered in the clearing, standing for want of seats, pressing close to hear the unamplified preaching, falling to their knees, and weeping in conviction. Because hymnbooks were not widely available, a song leader conducted "lined out" hymns for the congregation, singing a line or two before the crowd repeated the lines back, full-voiced and strong. The din was spectacular, and the haunting folk harmonies of a camp meeting could sometimes be heard a half mile away. At the close of the meeting that Monday, Methodists praised God for seventy converts. Additionally, forty-one Virginians had gone to the front to give their names to the ministers, desiring to be full members of the Methodist Episcopal Church.[54]

The exponential growth of the Methodist Church was one of the stunning features of the nineteenth-century American religious landscape. From sixty-five churches and not quite seven thousand members in 1776, it increased to 13,338 churches and 1.6 million adherents by 1850. The denomination expanded to such an extent that by the 1860s it was the largest religious organization in the nation.[55] The 1850 census shows the Richmond area had nine Methodist congregations, and Virginia, in total, had over a thousand.

BAPTIST GROWTH AND ANTITHEATER INFLUENCE

Late in life, Episcopalian Thomas Drew published his recollections of Richmond's churches in the early nineteenth century. He recalled that under John Courtney's leadership, the Baptists moved out of a shack on Major Dunscombe's property into a new brick structure at Fourteenth and H, constructed in 1802.[56] Baptist historian Robert Baylor Semple noted in 1810 that Baptists were "not the most flourishing sect," although they surpassed other denominations in Richmond with 560 members of the church, both black and white.[57] The presiding elder over First Baptist Church was John Courtney, who in 1812 would have been about seventy years old.[58] He served as pastor from around 1788 through his death in 1824. A veteran of the Revolutionary War, Courtney lived in a small rented Richmond home with his family and worked as a carpenter to earn an income; during his career, Baptist ministers were not paid a salary.[59] Despite his lack of a formal education and slow, plodding speech, Courtney's humble and genuine piety made a deep impression on the townspeople of Richmond. The Baptist Church provided him with great opportunities for social influence. The House of Delegates elected him (rather than Blair or Buchanan) for its chaplain in 1802.[60] During Courtney's tenure, First Baptist held services for both black and white congregants. At this time, most blacks attended churches with whites, and the Methodist and Baptist denominations attracted the lion's share of black believers.[61]

Richmond's Baptist church had been gaining in members and influence; when the Richmond Theater fire struck, the ensuing religious enthusiasm of the community merely added to the momentum that already existed. In the years following the fire, the city's First Baptist Church would increase in numbers but also in social stature by attracting members of higher status.

In October 1810, the Dover Baptist Association, a group of around forty churches of which Richmond was part, had met in the capital city for a four-day conference. "The number of strangers who flocked hither, the respectability of the sect, the simplicity of their principals, and the enthusiasm with which their ministers propagate their tenets, gave a certain *éclat* to their exertions, and a new air to the occupations of the city," reported one Baptist magazine.[62] Eight hundred visitors attended services at the capitol and two local churches; a "singular degree of harmony" prevailed, and Richmond's Methodists actively attended the Baptist messages, making their church available throughout the whole conference. (A Baptist minister recalled that "Baptists did not then—certainly very few ministers among them did—give undue prominence to their distinctive views.")[63]

Richmond-area Baptists evidently experienced a revival in the summer of 1811. By October of that year, the Dover Association had added over eight hundred new members, and by October 1812, they added another 1,500. Other Baptist associations in Virginia reported similarly large expansions.[64] In January 1814, a "considerable reformation" was occurring in First Baptist, with seventy blacks baptized on the morning of the twenty-seventh.[65] Rev. John Bryce, who assisted John Courtney in the pastoral responsibilities at First Baptist from 1810 through 1822, wrote that from April 1813 to April of 1814, they had baptized about two hundred new members, "some of whom are among the first characters in the place."[66] This brought the total membership of Richmond's First Baptist in 1814 to 1,200; they had more than doubled their numbers in four years. "We have additions almost every church-meeting," Bryce added.[67] By the centenary of First Baptist in 1880, Richmond's Baptist presence had grown to the point where the city was home to twenty-one different Baptist congregations.[68]

Virginia's Baptists practiced a congregational style of church leadership in which individual congregations had a great degree of autonomy and functioned in a democratic and independent style, with decisions made by the majority and no ministers holding a higher rank than others.[69] Resolutions were reached by majority rule at monthly or quarterly meetings. There, the congregation addressed church business regarding discipline, appointing deacons and ministers, and providing charity; they did not believe that church government above this congregational level was necessary.[70] Therefore churches exhibited variances in practice and theology, depending on region and leadership. In 1823, Virginia's Baptists formed the Baptist General Association of Virginia, intended to exercise state oversight. However, as Jeremiah Jeter noted, "At that time there was great jealousy in the Associations, and among Baptists generally, of any body that was supposed to be able to encroach on the liberties and prerogatives of the churches."[71] Consequently, the organizers created an association under so many restrictions that it was essentially powerless.

Yet the state's Baptist leaders provided some guidance to their diverse congregations early in the century. In Virginia, the Dover Baptist Association met annually and released a printed version of the minutes as well as a commemorative sermon. The meeting provided a forum for congregations across Virginia to ask questions and receive answers on specific issues in need of clarification, such as the practice of foot washing (decreed by the association as "an act of entertainment"), if music lessons were acceptable for children (the association's answer: "NO!"), or whether they ought to bar those who held Arminian opinions from membership (although Virginia Baptists generally held to Calvinist doctrines, "perfect coincidence of sentiments, in all points is not to be expected").[72] On many issues, such as women voting on the appointment of a new minister, judgment was left to individual congregations.[73] The association also aimed to cultivate acquaintances between churches and their members, advise in complicated matters of discipline, and to supply vacant churches with ministers.[74]

Baptists took to heart the verse "Come out from among them and be ye separate." Believing themselves to be sanctified men and women, they felt an obligation to live in a way that set them apart from their neighbors and bound them closely together as a new set apart community. As one Baptist wrote, they did not want a congregant who "can sing a jovial song at a tavern, and the praises of God in his house. . . . Where the door of a church is wide enough for such gentlemen to walk in, it is generally the case, that purity, simplicity and devotion retreat."[75] Although in many cases less strident or ascetic in issues of dress and behavior than the Methodists, Baptists still abjured that which stank to them of the world, the flesh, and the devil. Baptists believed that Christian congregations ought to portray holiness of life and breaches of conduct brought shame upon the church. A church was a closed community of regenerate members, set apart for the pure and dedicated to their refining—it was not a place for the apathetic or unconverted.

A member who repeatedly engaged in behaviors deemed inappropriate would be excommunicated from the congregation, although congregations extended an opportunity to return upon proof of repentance and a changed life. Of special concern to the Baptists was not only private holiness but public, visible holiness in matters such as sobriety, financial stewardship, and simplicity. Although dress codes were not formally instituted by church leaders, Baptists acquired a reputation for unfashionable appearance, avoiding marks of conspicuous consumption like jewelry and powdered wigs.[76]

An offending member, like "Brother Jenkins" of Richmond's Second Baptist, who in 1825 was found guilty of "too free a use of ardent spirits," would be called to a disciplinary council meeting where he could expect to be admonished by the moderator. Based on the severity of the offense, the display of a repentant or unrepentant spirit, and whether or not this was a repeat offense, the church member might be suspended from church membership for a time or completely excluded from membership. It was not impossible to be reinstated, and upon confession and demonstrated repentance, a person could rejoin the fellowship. In a six-year saga lasting from 1825 through 1831, Ebenezer Jenkins would admit his drunkenness and request to be excluded from membership, be invited to rejoin the church and be restored to the communion of believers, and again (due to intoxication) be formally excluded from fellowship.[77]

Explicit mentions of the theater do not occur in the Dover Baptist Association minutes from 1801 through the 1820s. Based on the minutes from First and Second Baptist's disciplinary meetings, it is clear that Richmond's Baptists forbade theater attendance. However, those who were disciplined for this infraction were guilty of other offenses as well, namely neglect of church meetings. Carelessness toward regular attendance at Baptist meetings probably seemed a more glaring offense when paired with careful attendance at a place of entertainment.

First Baptist Church resolved in February 1826 "that if any member of this church or members, shall visit any place of merriment, amusement or entertainment, contrary to the advice and desire of a respectable number of the members of this church they ought to be and will [be] considered disorderly and dealt with accordingly."[78] Leaders had opportunity to put this in action on December 5, 1829, when the minutes read: "Bros. Myers and Bragg were appointed to wait on Bro Southall and other brethren (if any) who are in the habit of attending the Theatre and cite them to attend the next monthly meeting."[79] In January 1830, Southall's interrogators were not prepared to report, but by February they had apparently been able to reach him and had received an unsatisfactory response.[80] The February 18 minutes read, "The case of *Bro Southall* was then taken up and being heard, he was on motion excluded for attending the theatre, neglect of meetings and contempt of the church."[81]

At the Second Baptist Church, leaders had to deal with a similar infraction. On February 17, 1831, the church took up the case of Brother Staples. "Whereas Mr. Staples has for sometime past habitually failed to attend the regular meetings of this church and has moreover visited the Theatre—and after a conversation with the church has failed to make such explanations or show such signs of penitence as are satisfactory[.] Therefore Resolved that he be excluded from the fellowship of this church."[82] The cases of Southall and Staples were the only instances of theater-related discipline recorded in over a decade at both First and Second Baptist churches, indicating that such transgressions were rare. Situations of intemperance, fighting, foul language, and adultery were far more frequently addressed.

It is difficult to piece together the response of Richmond's Baptist community in the immediate aftermath of the 1811 fire. Most of Richmond's Baptist church records are missing prior to 1820, so no resolutions or mentions of the event can be found there, and Baptists nationally were less likely to print antitheater sermons or editorials than other denominations.[83] Existing expressions seem to range from sympathy to explicit criticism of the theater. Rev. Jacob Gregg, an educated Englishman and a minister at First Baptist Church, participated in Richmond's day of remembrance on January 1, 1812, by preaching a public sermon, and national Baptist religious newspapers and journals published a few pieces of commentary after the fire.[84] Some pieces were little more than neutral reprints of *Enquirer* articles, while a few others contained negative commentary about the theater and its votaries.[85] Baptist minister and sometime Richmond resident Andrew Broaddus wrote a commemorative poem on the burning of the Richmond Theater. The verses were an outpouring of the "warm affections of his heart," as his friend Jeremiah Jeter relayed. Broaddus's poem, published in several newspapers at the time of the catastrophe, seemed to empathize with the mourners.[86]

It is not likely that many Baptists were attending the Richmond Theater the night of the fatal fire. Frequenting a theater was grounds for a member's dismissal, and from the account of Gilbert Hunt, it seems Baptists were hosting a meeting of their own on December 26. Although they did not experience large losses from among their congregants, as was the case for Richmond's Presbyterians and Episcopalians, the fire certainly made a deep and sobering impression on the Baptists, as it did on the whole community. Additionally, the Baptist church's proximity to the theater site made it a triage area for the wounded and dying.

Jeremiah Jeter made reference to this dreadful event in his church's history in a popular antitheater sermon delivered in 1838. That year Jeter joined with other leading ministers in Richmond to condemn the reopening of the Richmond Theater, which had been renamed "The Marshall." In what he later recalled as one of the more powerful moments of his delivery, he declared, "I am standing in a solemn place. The walls of this sanctuary once glittered with the horrid glare of a consuming Theatre. On the very floor, now occupied by this congregation, were laid, in a melancholy group, the dead, and the dying. Within this house were heard the mingled groans, of the expiring, and the shrieks of the bereaved. Then was Richmond clothed in the sable garments of mourning Rachel, weeping for her children, refused to be comforted because they were not."[87] Later in life he wrote of this sermon, "The very floor occupied by the crowded audience had been stained with the blood of the unfortunate devotees of the bewitching amusement. I made such use as I could of these startling facts to dissuade my hearers from attending theaters."[88] The Baptists' own history was entwined with that of the theater fire—Jeter urged that they could not, as a congregation, forget that day which had brought such devastation to their city, and he urged them to boycott the theater. He did, however, refute the "general impression" that the burning of the theater clearly manifested divine condemnation. "The burning of a theatre no more proves that theatrical exhibitions are wrong than the burning of a church proves that the preaching of the gospel is wrong," he wrote in his memoir.[89]

The minister found no evil in writing, reading, or acting out plays, "provided they are of good moral tendency," but he believed that what transpired in theater buildings, "as they are commonly conducted," was demoralizing and that Christians should stay away from such a place.[90] In his sermon, Jeter emphasized, as Quaker Lindley Murray had, that eminent men throughout history (including the First Continental Congress) had opposed the theater. Jeter also echoed the arguments popularized by Witherspoon: patrons of the theater squandered their money on this "sinful waste of the Divine bounty," frequent attendees tended toward moral dissipation, and "time-killing" trifles like plays could not be defended by "serious and conscientious, and especially religious men."[91] He borrowed points from Connecticut Baptist Rev. Robert Turnbull's 1837 book *The Theatre, in its Influence upon Literature, Morals, and Religion* (as reviewed in the Baptist periodical the *Christian Review*), such as the insistence that American patriots should oppose the theater, because indolent and pleasure-seeking citizens undermined civic virtue, national prosperity, and independence.[92] (Because he had never attended a theatrical exhibition, Jeter noted that he was "entirely dependent on the testimony of others for my opinion on this subject.")[93]

Jeter did, on occasion, associate with actors; he had an acquaintance with Anna Cora Mowatt, "an actress of high character and of no mean abilities," in his opinion.[94] After she casually told him that the daughters of William Charles McCready, the British tragedian, were forbidden by their father to attend plays, their friendship only reinforced his opposition to the theater. From her comment Jeter deduced that McCready, a man "under no bias against theatres" whose livelihood and celebrated status relied on their existence, believed the instruction and amusement afforded by the drama could not compensate for the theater's evil influences on his family.[95]

Jeter believed the theater should be avoided not only by Christians but by all citizens. Biblical morality "calls on men to abstain, not only from evil itself, but from the slightest appearance of evil," Jeter maintained. "If a proposed action, after careful and candid examination, appear to be of doubtful propriety, it cannot be performed without incurring the displeasure of God."[96] As another Baptist wrote in the *American Baptist* magazine, although an unconverted man might think that "a ball, or a theatre, or a little gaming, or any other of the common amusements, will not make him any worse than he already is, and he therefore may attend such scenes without danger, whilst a Christian who should be the frequenter of such places would contract a dismal stain. But if the same obligations to duty, and to abstinence lie upon both, then it is no more excusable in one than in the other."[97]

While Richmond's First Baptist Church discouraged theater attendance under the leadership of Courtney, Kerr, and Broaddus, the church solidified its public standing as a leading local adversary of the theater under Jeremiah Jeter nearly two decades later. First Baptist maintained that reputation during and after the Civil War under Rev. John Lansing Burrows, who published a famous sermon opposing theatrical performances after Richmond's theater was enthusiastically rebuilt in 1863.

ESTABLISHING A PRESBYTERIAN PRESENCE IN THE CAPITAL

John Holt Rice, an indefatigable thirty-four-year-old Presbyterian minister, lived in rural Charlotte County, ninety miles southwest of Richmond. Tall and bony with curly brown hair, he was a sensible and likable man, with dignified reserve and quiet passion.[98] He held services in three different Charlotte County locations (the main Cub Creek church, the courthouse, and the Bethesda meeting house), administered pastoral care to parishioners over a 477-square-mile area, and operated a boys' school to supplement his income, thereby supporting his wife, Anne.[99] Additionally, he oversaw the running of his small farm and wrote regularly for the Presbyterian Synod's magazine. Certainly a man with as many responsibilities as this country pastor would have had much to preoccupy him, but in early 1812, when he was not with his parishioners, in his classroom, or in the pulpit, the Richmond Theater fire claimed his imagination.

When Rice entered the county courthouse to preach on Sunday, December 29, a congregant had animatedly relayed news of the Richmond Theater's destruction. Rice had not yet heard. "It made such an impression on my mind," he wrote to longtime friend Judith Randolph.[100] Consumed with concern, he promptly laid aside the text on which he had intended to preach and delivered an extempore discourse about the theater fire and the brevity of life from the book of Isaiah—"Behold all flesh is as the grass."[101]

Friends observed that Rice, although by all accounts a congenial man with a smile that could "break forth into a jocund radiance and benignity, altogether indescribable," most often appeared grave and pensive.[102] During this winter holiday season he became more thoughtful than usual. Rice had long been grieved with the spiritual state of the capital city, aching to see signs of an interest in religion. As a teenager, he rode a market boat down the James River, disembarking in Richmond to accept a tutoring position with the Nelson family of Malvern Hill, just south of town. The vibrant social scene there forced the country boy out of his introverted habits, polishing his manners and transforming the awkward young man into a fine conversationalist. Richmond had a darker pull on Rice as well. Exposed for the first time to luxury and French philosophy, he began to feel alienated from the values of his youth and "a strange coldness towards his God."[103]

Years later, in the summer of 1811, Rice returned to Richmond to evangelize the city that had at one time drawn him into religious doldrums. He preached three times to "considerable congregations of the most attentive people that I ever yet saw," and sadly noted a lack of spiritual knowledge among the masses. "There are very many among them who feel the importance of religion," he wrote to his former colleague and good friend Rev. Archibald Alexander, but "they do not seem, at least the great bulk of them, to know any thing about religious doctrines."[104] He doubted the tiny remnant of Richmond Presbyterians could even afford to support a minister, but he dreamed of a day when his denomination would be well represented in the capital. After the burning of the theater, and the subsequent reports of overpacked churches, Rice could see a door opening—the possibility of spiritual receptivity seemed more likely than ever. For seven years he had faithfully served the country people of western Virginia, but his dark blue eyes glinted as he began to imagine setting out for Richmond City to reap a harvest of souls. There would be many challenges, but it would be a worthwhile mission.

Presbyterian minister Moses Hoge described a "wonderful quickening in the spiritual life of the few scattered Presbyterians in the city" following the fire.[105] He believed the disaster awakened a deep conviction among Presbyterians of the need for an organized church headed by a pastor who could devote himself to the development of a strong organization marked by corporate unity, wisely directed zeal, and systematic efforts toward the extension of Christ's kingdom.[106] Because the tiny flock required a minister with management skills, charisma, and enough vision to launch the effort, the local presbytery, at a meeting at Red Oak Church on March 12, 1812, extended an invitation to John Holt Rice to pastor the fledgling church plant in Richmond. The tall preacher had impressed them during his visits to town in 1811, and his background had instilled the tenacity and organizational ability needed at that moment.

"A wide field is opened there for the labours of a pious and faithful minister of the gospel," Rice believed, but he felt no small degree of trepidation, doubting his own ability to undertake a church planting mission in a city as recalcitrant as Richmond. "The preacher who sets himself against the current there, has need of great strength," he wrote to a friend.[107] He also doubted that the tiny congregation could financially support his family and was afraid that he would again be forced to start a school—a time-consuming undertaking— to scrape by.[108] Yet only one day after the call was communicated, Rice accepted. His pastoral relation to the Cub Creek congregations was dissolved; he delivered his farewell sermon on the last Sunday in April 1812 and bid a tearful good-bye to the hundreds of black and white congregants of his Charlotte County church.[109] Richmond would now be home.

Rice's personality perfectly suited a man who would become the official ambassador and new face of Presbyterianism in the capital. Curly-haired Rice maintained a dignified, ministerial demeanor but had a friendliness and approachability that drew people, especially young people, to him—"He had an agreeable word for every body," one man remembered.[110] He disproved the stereotype of a dour Calvinist—acquaintances called him "quite the life of the company," recalling his entertaining stories and "amusing conversation."[111] On occasions generally dull to all parties concerned, Rice was one to enliven the situation with "timely sallies of humour."[112]

Although a self-defined "thorough Calvinist," Rice spoke positively of other denominations, contending "whether the preachers belong to this or that sect is unimportant" and doing what he could to prosper other "orthodox American Christians who were friendly to liberty."[113] (Rice's approval and cooperative activity, however, did not extend to Roman Catholics, whom he considered enemies of civil liberty.) Anne Rice later wrote that her husband and the Arminian Rev. Buchanan held occasional debates on points of theological disagreement, but such discussions were carried out with an ample helping of good humor and teasing.[114] Regarding issues of social morality, Rice often kept his opinions to himself rather than ruffle feathers. An abstemious teetotaler, he did not object to giving a toast when called on, and he remained quiet about his antislavery viewpoints, believing that a direct movement toward abolition by the church would do harm rather than good.[115] When in Richmond, he did not seem to sermonize against the theater.

John Holt Rice preached his first message to the fourteen founding members of the independent Presbyterian congregation and a substantial number of visitors on the second Sabbath in May 1812. The *Enquirer* announcement read: "The Rev. Mr. John Ht. Rice, being on his way to take up his permanent residence among us, will preach next Sunday morning at the usual hour at the 'Mason's Hall,' introductory to his regular gospel ministry in this city, and it is expected he will continue to occupy said hall regularly thereafter, until the Presbyterian Church, which is in a way of soon being finished for him, shall be ready for occupancy."[116]

The city lacked religious ministers to assist families in recovering from the emotional wounds incurred by the fire, and extra clerics were needed after the "late awful visitation of Providence on that place."[117] Rice was "most anxious that so much distress [from the theater fire] should not be suffered in vain," as he described to a friend, "but one cannot expect that this will be the case unless proper measures are adopted for this purpose. And what more suitable than *evangelical* preaching?"[118] In early 1812, Richmonders clamored into churches. Rice wrote to his friend Rev. Archibald Alexander of Princeton Theological Seminary, after a May visit, "I was surprised to observe the very great numbers who attend church in this place. Every house of worship was crowded; and I was told that not less than five hundred went away from the Mason's Hall (where I preached,) unable to find seats. A spirit of reading, and of inquiry for religious truth, is spreading rapidly among our town folks."[119]

As interest in his preaching and the development of an independent Presbyterian congregation built, Rice searched for lodging. Irish widower John Parkhill, owner of a hardware store, resided in the rooms above his shop. Lonely after the recent death of his wife, he invited Rice, his wife Anne, and their family to live as his guests during their first summer in Richmond. Parkhill had no connection to the Presbyterian Church, or, it seems, to any church. But by the time the Rices moved out of Parkhill's upstairs apartment to lodging on Braddock's Hill in the fall of 1812, they had witnessed the conversion of their host, and Parkhill "became a devoted Christian . . .

and now more zealously, a judicious and efficient helper."[120] In 1815, John Parkhill married Elizabeth Copland, the young woman who escaped the burning theater and ran home to tell her father of the fire that claimed her sister Margaret's life.[121] Elizabeth Copland Parkhill's father, Charles, served as a vestryman in the Episcopal church, but Elizabeth switched allegiances sometime between 1815 and 1817 to the denomination in which her husband was closely involved.[122]

John Holt Rice was officially installed as full-time pastor of the Presbyterian Church in the City of Richmond on October 17, 1812.[123] By April 1813, there were fifty-eight communicants (not including congregants who never officially joined), with more members expected to join that year. Under Rice's twelve-year pastorate, the First Presbyterian Church received 263 new members. While the growing numbers brought joy, these were, however, years of tribulation for the Rice family; Richmond's Presbyterian parishioners could be an exhausting group. Rice wrote to Archibald Alexander, "They expect, and they need much attention from me."[124] During the hours when Rice was not paying visits to those scattered on the fringes of town, his house was usually crowded with their company. But their piety encouraged him: "Some of them I think are the most eminent christians that I know, quite warm and zealous."[125] Although exhausted, he believed that his work had brought forth some good fruit. "I trust that I am not entirely useless here," he wrote friend Judith Randolph. "Several who now rejoice in hope of heaven, were at the time of my coming very thoughtless of their eternal interests, and very ignorant of the way of salvation."[126]

Caroline Homassel Thornton was one who secured a seat at the Mason's Hall that May to hear Rice's first sermon, although she did so secretly. Homassel Thornton, although married, lived with her husband in her parents' home, and they still treated her as a child, expressly prohibiting teenaged Caroline from attending John Holt Rice's meetings. Her parents were afraid that their emotive daughter might become a "fanatic"—an evangelical.[127] The Richard and Homassel family ties had been ever with the Episcopal Church; religious enthusiasm made them suspicious.[128]

Although she had always been a remarkably obedient daughter, she sneaked out of her home and joined a friend to hear Rice preach.[129] In his messages, Rice "uttered no reproaches on Richmond," but spoke on Romans 15:20: "And I am sure that, when I come unto you, I shall come in the fullness of the blessing of the gospel of Christ."[130] His gospel message startled Homassel

Thornton. "He gave me the first insight into my real condition, which was a sinner, in the sight of God, by nature, and showed me where true riches alone could be found. And amid all the splendor (I may truly say) of a gay life and the devotion, indulgence and competency that surrounded me on every side, I longed 'for that living water, which if I drank I should never thirst,' and for that 'peace which passeth all understanding,'" she confessed.[131]

Yet her transition to a strong evangelical faith was not immediate. For the next six years, Homassel Thornton would continue to live with her husband in her parents' well-appointed home, indulged, surrounded by wealth, and feeling "neither the value nor want of money," as she put it.[132] Her days were an easy routine of parties, games, mingling with the best society in the capital, and paying calls to dignitaries like President and Dolley Madison in Washington, D.C. "My heart was not in it," she wrote.[133] Although Thornton's description of her life sounds like nothing more than the respectable, law-abiding doings of a social, close-knit family, it filled her with guilt and left her empty. A whirl of activity masked an internal spiritual barrenness, as she saw it. Rice's words weighed upon her; she could not relish the superficiality any longer. She recalled for her children, "We led a gay and dissipated life, I might term it. Your father was passionately fond of cards, and . . . your father and my uncle and aunt [her adoptive parents] urged my accompanying him, in hopes of seeing me gay again, but the light was shown me, and how could I be happy in darkness[?]"[134] All the glamour, the balls, and her gorgeous wardrobe were nothing more than "an outside show of pleasure," resulting in "no real or substantial enjoyment, I assure you."[135]

While the Episcopalians enjoyed their majestic new Monumental Church, the Presbyterians with whom they had enjoyed fellowship at the capitol congregation struggled to construct a permanent facility. Rather incompetently, perhaps out of thrift, the congregation purchased land at Twenty-eighth and Main, by Rockett's Landing on the James, "out of the way of almost every one," according to a disgusted Rice.[136] At his recommendation, the church sold the lot, but the war wiped out the purchaser's assets, who then defaulted on the payments and relinquished the title. The congregation, bearing the financial burden for property they could not use, then began to default on payments of their minister's salary. Presbyterians strategized that Rice could earn extra support by both operating an academy and collecting pew rentals. But he had neither time nor inclination to launch the former and no church building for the latter.[137] "Not very seldom I was reduced to my last sixpence," Rice wrote of those lean years, "and in fact had not money to go to market."[138] Anne Rice relayed that they were once forced to consider selling their furniture to buy meat for dinner. As she grumbled about the remissness of their congregation, John calmly stated that the Lord would provide and returned to his study. To Anne's surprise, a servant from a country house outside of town knocked on the door with a side of bacon as a gift that very evening.[139] "I was vexed at myself," she candidly reported, "for what had just passed,—half vexed at the lady for granting Mr. Rice such a triumph, and ashamed to go and tell him of a present so opportunely made."[140]

The War of 1812 brought further stresses for Rice when Blair and Bryce, two local ministers, both accepted chaplaincies in the army. By September 1814, the new army chaplains were stationed outside of Richmond, Moore traveled to New York, and Buchanan fell ill. The Episcopalians and Presbyterians were almost completely deprived of preachers, save poor Rice, who was invited to hold services at Monumental Church during that time, as he was essentially the only minister left in town to serve those denominations.[141] During the day, Rice not only visited his own scattered congregation but also paid calls, when requested, to the many sick that belonged to no church or to other denominations.[142] Additionally, the war years were hard ones wherein to raise funds for a new church building—basic articles such as salt, coffee, and brown sugar all sold for prohibitive prices, and other worthy war-related causes called for funds.[143] Yet Rice mustered the determination to see his project through and preserve his denomination's presence in Richmond. "'Don't give up the ship,' was my motto," he later wrote, and he remained in Richmond for another twelve years.[144]

The financial situation of Richmond's Presbyterians between the years of 1812 and 1815 seemed precarious enough to pull them under, causing some Presbyterian churchmen and women to defect and join the Episcopalian worshippers at the securer Monumental Church.[145] If the Presbyterian denomination were to take hold in Richmond, Rice knew he must stay, despite his poverty and despite the constant discouragements. After all, even the main supporters of the Presbyterian cause in Richmond declared that if Rice left, "they should give over" and also join the Episcopalians.[146] To the Richmonders accustomed to ecumenical services at the capitol, the doctrinal differences between the two evangelical churches—Episcopal and Presbyterian—seemed irrelevant, and there was little to bar their transfer from one denomination to another.

"What may be the effect of the bishop's settling here on Presbyterianism, I am not yet able to say. I hope however, that no harm will be done; perhaps just the reverse. I commit the affair to the great Head of the Church," wrote Rice a few months after Richard Channing Moore's arrival at Monumental in 1814.[147] Moore and Rice had become friends, each viewing the other with cordiality. "He is uncommonly friendly with me," said Rice of Moore," and I am resolved that it shall not be my fault if he does not continue so."[148] Rice seems to have had a magnanimous approach to the evangelical Episcopalians and their evangelistic outreaches in Virginia. "I shall always rejoice to hear of Mr. Meade's success," wrote Rice of Episcopal priest William Meade. "I feel towards him as a brother in the gospel of Christ Jesus. Would there were many such as he!"[149]

But tensions occasionally arose. Rice embarked on a long journey in May 1815 and left his congregation under the care of Bishop Moore during the time he was absent. Each Sunday the Presbyterians would enter the side doors of Monumental Church into a setting that was becoming, under Moore's leadership, very different from what they were accustomed to. The genuflecting and weekly celebration of the Eucharist seemed to them "abundant parade and form."[150] Rice's congregation liked Moore's evangelical preaching "and most things in the ministers," they reported to Rice on his return, but they disliked "the keen spirit of proselytism manifested by [the Episcopalians]."[151] In Rice's absence, the Episcopalians apparently had been recruiting from among his flock. "This [proselytism] is ardent and active beyond all doubt. . . . This spirit will produce irritation and offence, which I fear will ripen into controversy," wrote an offended Rice. "May God avert this."[152] Throughout 1815, Rice privately voiced his feeling to correspondents that the Episcopalians were undermining the Presbyterian efforts. "At first I thought that they were setting out on true evangelical principles, and was heartily enough disposed to take them by the hand, and bid them God speed; but it now seems to me, as though they meant to pull down the building of others, in order to erect their own. They aim especially at the Presbyterians, I suppose because they find us more in their way than any other class of people." He prepared himself to defend his congregation as a "Champion of Presbyterianism."[153] That never became necessary as the situation resolved itself, probably aided by the Presbyterians' acquisition of a permanent church building and stronger local identity.

The Presbyterian-owned Rockett's Landing building eventually sold, and the church raised money for a new one near the old Market House and the Mason's Hall on East Franklin Street, where they had been meeting since 1812.[154] By November 16, 1815, Rice could write with relief, "Our new house of worship will, I expect, be covered in within the next fortnight; and there is every reason to hope that it will be finished early next spring. . . . There seems to be but little doubt, but that the pews will be taken up, and there will, very probably, be a call for more than the house will contain. So that, after a long and hard struggle, it seems as though by the favour of a gracious Providence, we should get through all our difficulties."[155] In 1816, the First Presbyterian Church, also known as the "Pineapple Church" for the odd-looking finial on the dome, opened its doors in Richmond. At last the Presbyterians had a home of their own. Although citizens still had to navigate Richmond's dreadful roads to get there, the building of churches in more convenient locations made frequent church attendance possible and attractive for more Episcopalians and Presbyterians. Richmond's leading citizens became more diligent in attending regular church services after this point, according to at least one historian.[156]

Other Christian communities began to work toward obtaining their own ministers and buildings. The small group of Roman Catholics held one of their first services in a classroom at David Doyle's school on March 1, 1812, presided over by a visiting priest.[157] Records also show that Catholics in Richmond petitioned their bishop, Rt. Rev. John Carroll of Baltimore, for a resident priest that year. In September 1812, a missionary, Rev. Dr. Miguel, had been delegated to raise funds for a permanent place of Catholic worship in Richmond.[158] It appears that Miguel did not succeed in his endeavors. Another short-term priest, John McClory, arrived in 1813, and otherwise Catholics must have relied on traveling ministers. Their first permanent church building in Richmond was St. Peter's, built in 1834.[159]

THE NEW EVANGELICAL CLIMATE

How did Richmond's revered ministers Blair and Buchanan fare in the new religious climate? The "Two Parsons" remained active in Richmond but were eclipsed after the fire by the evangelicals who took to their denominations' pulpits. Both clerics befriended the new ministers who arrived in town after the theater fire, particularly John Holt Rice. Buchanan, of the Episcopal church, became a close enough friend to assist the Rice family financially as they had need.[160] Buchanan's nomination for the bishopric failed when Moore was chosen, and he was assigned the rectorship of Henrico Parish.[161] The vestry unanimously called another Yankee Episcopalian south to staff Henrico Parish Church as the assistant minister: a Rev. William Hart who had worked with Moore in New York and married Moore's niece. Hart would eventually assume Buchanan's duties after the minister's death in December 1822.[162]

Despite their kindnesses and likability, Blair and Buchanan represented Virginia's clerical old guard, cronies to the unreformed gentry and participants in their excess. One Episcopal historian wrote that the two "were not remarkable for strictness of doctrine or rigour of discipline."[163] The parsons had considered it no transgression to play a few rounds of nine pins, stuff themselves on Jasper Crouch's rich cooking, and knock back a julep with the upper crust at the monthly Quoit Club parties Buchanan hosted.[164] They probably were not taking an opportunity to evangelize their fellow Quoit Club members either; all participants at Buchanan's barbecues were fined a case of champagne if found discussing business, politics, or religion.[165] In 1923, Mary Newton Stanard, a Richmond author, wrote of the two: "Their religion was sincere and their scholarship genuine, but their black coats made them none the less human and, at proper times, they could play as ardently as they could preach—for they also, were but grown-up boys. . . . Their benevolent acts and their humorous sayings and doings made them idols of the people and rendered their influence immense in their time, and they are among the happiest traditions of the old city today."[166] But the new generation of Presbyterian and Episcopalian fellow clerics did not look with approval on such gambols.

The change in Richmond's religious climate seemed eventually to change one of the "Two Parsons." John D. Blair continued to pastor a church in Richmond—Shockoe Hill Presbyterian, on the corner of Eighth and Franklin—until his death in 1823 and apparently became more conservative in subsequent years.[167] In his Richmond Theater fire commemorative sermon mere days after the catastrophe, Blair had not denounced the theater or theatergoing but instead had demurred, "It is by no means our wish that you should be disqualified for the social duties, or any of the sweet & innocent enjoyments of life: much less to spread over you the gloom of superstitious fear & dread."[168] Ten years later, after John Holt Rice's influence had secured a more evangelical tenor to Richmond Presbyterianism, Blair had assumed a strong stance against the theater.

Blair submitted a piece to Rice's *The Virginia Literary and Evangelical*

Magazine in 1821, at the end of a theater season. "I acknowledge I never was at one of these good peoples' exhibition," Blair first clarified, to distance himself from the stage. He acerbically added that he had been watching the theatergoing citizens of Richmond since the actors and actresses departed to see if their morals had improved, which they should have if the local newspapers were correct in calling the playhouse a "school of morality." He claimed that this assertion surprised him, for he had always considered the theater "a most pernicious nursery of vice."[169] This oppositional position in 1821 seems a departure from Blair's prior opinions. Given the opportunity after the theater fire, he could have warned the populace of its dangers—if he believed there were any—and he did not.

Blair's disapproval, as he outlined in his article, stemmed from a few particularly egregious behaviors on the part of the players: the practice of "interlacing their plays with expressions of their own that were downright smutty & obscene" and, most horrifyingly, cross-dressing. Blair wrote, "Now the word of God does expressly inform us that "they who do these things are an abomination to the Lord." (Deut 22:5) Possibly this may be, in them, a mere sin of ignorance. The Bible is an antiquated Book from which, it may be presumed, these sons & daughters of Thespis have not derived their lessons."[170] What he heard was true—cross-dressing had occurred on a Richmond stage at least once before the fire, but it was hardly scintillating. Between the acts at a performance on November 13, 1811, Thomas C. West groused out the tune "Hard Times or Always Grumbling" while dressed as an old woman.[171]

Blair began his ministry in Richmond when evangelicalism had not yet gripped the populace, and he had lived through Richmond's remarkable decade of religious change, increasingly advocating evangelical stances himself. His funeral in 1823 was used to preach departure from a Presbyterianism that rattled no cages to a more socially engaged faith centered on personal conversion and distancing oneself from the world.[172]

The "rational" ministers John Holt Rice disparaged preached from written sermons, speculated "in a very cool, philosophical manner" on virtue and godliness, and affected superior learning. Evangelicals like himself, on the other hand, while "no enemies to true learning," calculated their preaching to lead their hearers to Jesus Christ as the only hope for lost men.[173] "My mode of preaching, you know, from the small specimen which you have had of it, is evangelical," wrote Rev. Richard Channing Moore to a friend, "exposing to view the awful degeneracy of man, and leading him from every other dependence, to the Lord Jesus Christ for succor and salvation."[174] Methodists and Baptists in Richmond had for years combined the evangelical message with emotive, convicting, dramatic, gospel-centered deliveries. However, with the introduction of evangelical preachers Rice and Moore, this kind of preaching began to spread into Richmond's Presbyterian and Episcopal churches, churches that sometimes held themselves in contrast to the overly enthusiastic, largely lower- and middle-class Methodists and Baptists.

While Rice often spoke for an entire sermon with a hand jammed absentmindedly into his vest, Napoleon-style, he at other times added theatrics for impact. In a New England sermon on the text, "What shall a man give in exchange for his soul?" he illustrated his message with the story of a desperate man hurtling down the Niagara River and tumbling over the mighty falls. As he spun the story of the doomed boater, Rice's face slowly reflected the panic of a man about to meet his end, face flushed, eyebrows arching into his broad, high forehead, his hands raised in horror as he slipped over the imaginary brink of the cascade. "His gesture, his countenance, his whole manner," one man noted, "was such as to give the highest possible effect to the anecdote."[175]

Rev. Richard Channing Moore also believed that people must experience the transforming power of a personal conversion, and thus his sermons centered on a gospel message.[176] The opinion circulated among his fellow clergy that he was "somewhat Methodistical," recalled Bishop William Meade.[177] While biographers were careful to clarify that Moore was "no friend to any religious excitement inconsistent with the decent order and staid character of the Church," they also reported that he "hardly ever preached without moving his whole congregation to tears."[178] Moore, who spoke deliberately and moderately, without agitation, admitted that he encouraged emotive faith, but he denied that he employed any manipulative measures. "I love feeling in religion; nay, I will say that there can be no true religion without it," he wrote to his son. "But then I like to see THAT feeling produced by a faithful disclosure of evangelical truth; by preaching Christ as the power and wisdom of God; by leading men to the Saviour for life, free from everything that looks like management or human contrivance."[179] It should come as no surprise that he incorporated extemporaneous prayer in services, but even when he was reciting the standard, scripted liturgy—the confession, the collect, the prayers of the people—Moore's eyes would glisten and brim over.[180]

Thomas Drew remembered that Moore, when not traveling, "almost always had a lecture on Tuesday evening after tea, at the house of some member of his congregation."[181] Moore's evening talks began with "a short service from the liturgy," according to church reports, and his consequent lectures were often evangelistic in nature. Moore also encouraged parishioners to meet in one another's homes for prayer.[182] His lectures and prayer meetings were not without opposition from the Episcopal hierarchy, who feared that Moore veered into revivalist practices. "[Weekday meetings] are neither inconsistent with the principles, nor prohibited by the canons, of the Church," Moore argued in response. "And, although some condemn them as irregular and methodistical, I cannot, as a minister of Christ, desirous of the salvation of souls, give them up. For I know that God's blessing is upon them."[183] Rice too adopted the practice of weekday lectures, and he held Presbyterian prayer meetings at the home of his neighbors every Wednesday night he was in Richmond.[184]

Prayer meetings, like Moore's evening lectures, garnered some criticism from Episcopalian clerics who believed only the liturgical prayers were appropriate. They also feared that informal meetings would be viewed as a substitute for church, pulling parishioners away from corporate worship and out from under church leadership. In attempting to defend the practice to a fellow minister, Moore wrote, "Should ten, twenty, or fifty of your people choose to meet at a private house, and be disposed to sing a psalm, or hymn, and unite in extempore prayer, there is certainly no canon to forbid it. Is it not better that they should thus pass their time than to waste it in common conversation?"[185] Besides, the participants in Richmond's prayer meetings, he observed, had not radicalized his congregation nor diminished their regard for the Prayer Book, but instead had become "ardently attached to the service of the Church."[186]

There is no record that Richmond's Episcopal laypersons raised an argument against the new meetings—older clerics were the ones who had to be convinced that prayer meetings and weekday lectures weren't going to be "abused to the purposes of fanaticism."[187] From the sheer volume of Moore's gently defensive correspondence, it seems "fanaticism"—or unchecked Christian religious enthusiasm—overtaking Virginia's Episcopalians was a genuine fear. Moore clarified for his critics' benefit: "When we speak of a lecture-room service or a prayer meeting in the Episcopal Church, we mean an orderly assembly in which the service of the Church is treated with due respect, and the exercises are wholly conducted or controlled by the clergy; even so when we speak of a 'revival' in the Episcopal Church, we mean a season of more than usual interest in the subject of religion, produced by the special influence of the Holy Spirit giving efficacy to the ordinary means of grace—such as faithful preaching of the word and fervent prayer."[188]

* * *

The Amicable Society, a men's benevolent society with the object of aiding those "for whom the law made no provision," had been instituted in 1788 and was one of a small handful of Richmond charities predating the theater fire. At the instigation of the new churches, dozens of additional organizations sprung up in the decade after the fire, diverting some of the energies previously spent at balls and the loo table. Moore and Rice heartily encouraged the creation of religious societies and organizations that directed parishioner energies toward charitable activities. Between 1813 and 1818, they were responsible for organizing and supporting nearly ten organizations, including a prayer book and tract distribution society, an education society, a "Female Humane Association" that aided elderly women and orphans, a "Female Cent Society" to help poor youth prepare for the ministry, and multiple missionary societies.[189] One of the first groups to be formed was the Bible Society of Virginia in 1813, which was initially intended to distribute Bibles locally; Rice wrote in 1812 that he had adopted some measures to determine the want of Bibles in Richmond, "which I fear is exceedingly great considering the population."[190] Not exclusive to Richmond, this propensity for establishing benevolent societies arose from the nationally swelling evangelical movement, and the organizations generated maximum energy across America from 1810 to 1830.[191] Powered largely by the middle class, these groups combated the causes of civic disorder—ignorance, vice, poverty, and crime—and supported evangelism.

The Amicable Society went for many years without any additions or with only one or two members added. However, official notes record that revivals in 1811 and 1825 led to a large influx of members.[192] This may indicate that the city of Richmond had been experiencing a revival at the time when the theater fire occurred and that the response to the fire then expanded what had already been occurring. The comment also insinuates that the members who joined during the revivals had been affected by the religious revival and impelled to join for religious reasons.[193] Civic engagement and philanthropy continued to grow in Richmond in subsequent decades.

* * *

Monumental's Sunday school program commenced on November 20, 1817, at Bishop Moore's instigation. In addition to Bible instruction, Richmond's Sunday school teachers taught reading and writing skills to their pupils who lacked basic literacy. Most of the pupils at Monumental hailed from poorer families who could afford no other means of education for their children.[194] "The school was made up almost entirely of poor destitute children," remembered Thomas H. Drew, an instructor. Drew made a point to acquaint himself with the young pupils and assisted in clothing drives for the neediest among them. Knowing full well the threat of disease and danger in impoverished areas of Richmond, he conscientiously visited the homes of every absentee student.[195]

Throughout the 1820s, the pupils met in the balcony galleries of Monumental. With over a hundred students, this arrangement became uncomfortable, and Drew raised eight hundred dollars to erect a school room in the northwest corner of the church yard.[196] Within its first seven years, Monumental's Sunday school educated 365 pupils, and over the next decades, two dozen former pupils would be ordained as ministers.[197]

Free Sunday schools provided an important service in Virginia, which still did not offer primary public education. Few of Virginia's elites held an interest in educating the poor on their dime; Republican Democrats like Thomas Ritchie and Thomas Jefferson were among the more sympathetic. John Randolph, on the other hand, felt that providing public education to poor children would only subsidize and reward educational neglect and spare their families the responsibility of educating them.[198]

By 1818, Richmond's Presbyterians, Methodists, Baptists, and Episcopalians all had active Sunday schools.[199] Beginning around 1815, the Baptist church even hosted a school on weekday evenings just for black students, led by a white teacher. The church discontinued the classes by 1819, however, determining that use of the premises for such a purpose was inappropriate.[200] Other Christian-led literacy-boosting educational efforts inaugurated after the theater fire included a private, apparently ecumenical, subscription Christian library. It was formed around August 1812 to encourage the circulation of religious reading materials and was open six days a week.[201] From 1818 to 1829 John Holt Rice published the *Virginia Evangelical and Literary Magazine,* which was one of the first literary magazines published in Virginia. Including book reviews and covering topics as wide-ranging as Russian poets, French mountaineers, "The Abolition of Christmas," and "Women Not Unequal to Men," the three-dollar-a-subscription, advertisement-free, Whig-leaning publication gained wide readership, even among its ideological enemies.[202]

Reinvigorated churches and religious societies offered previously unavailable opportunities for female education and leadership. The Monumental Church "Bible class" was launched around 1823, and it was "uniformly well attended," according to church convention notes of 1824. The church had 130 communicants, male and female, but attracted nearly that number of enthusiastic females alone for the Bible classes. The class "consisted of from eighty to a hundred ladies, whose religious deportment was highly pleasing, and who, from the readiness with which they answered the questions proposed to them, must have closely studied the subjects under consideration," read the notes.[203]

As religious interest grew in Richmond, so did the need for trained ministers. Virginia lacked sufficient local seminaries and sent their prospective clerics north for divinity school. Both Moore and Rice became convinced of the necessity of training Virginia's ministers in Virginia. After eleven years in Richmond, John Holt Rice received an unexpected letter in the mail stating that the governing board of Princeton University had chosen Rice unanimously as their college president; his reputation for dogged work and his ability to recharge deteriorating institutions had recommended him for the post. Princeton's former president had resigned, and only two of the old faculty remained after a dramatic staff exodus. "We need your services to build up our falling institution; to elevate Nassau hall to that rank among sister colleges which it formerly sustained, and to which I trust it is destined still to attain," beseeched a professor.[204] The board knew it would be hard to dislodge Rice from Virginia but attempted valiantly to do so. Presbyterian Virginians had long had connections with Princeton, beginning with the renowned missionary preacher Samuel Davies, who assumed the presidency of the College of New Jersey—later Princeton University—after the death of Jonathan Edwards in 1759. Rice's close friend Archibald Alexander was a founder and professor at the Princeton Theological Seminary.

Wracked by indecision, Rice postponed the decision for several months. In the end, he turned the Princeton presidency down, expressing a desire instead to stay in Virginia and plant a Presbyterian theological school there, modeled after Princeton's. "I may be more useful here than I could possibly be anywhere else. I do not speak now of the effect of training up men for the South in the North country, nor of the unfitness of most Northern men for our purposes." He added meaningfully, "You know that in general they will not do."[205] The South, Rice believed, needed a southern seminary. And this was his next task. Rice helped to spearhead the foundation of Virginia's Union Theological Seminary at Hampden Sydney College in 1824.

Meanwhile, Richard Channing Moore had been assisting in the founding of an Episcopal theological seminary in Alexandria, Virginia, in 1823.[206] The prospect of locally trained ministers excited him, and he predicted that "mountains of opposition will in a little time become a plain, the Prayer-book will be venerated, [and] our ceremonies approved" if the new ministers trained and serving in Virginia "tread in the steps of their Divine Master!"[207]

* * *

The theater fire and subsequent evangelical influences even tempered popular pastimes in the black community, where dancing had been a ubiquitous and popular diversion. As the nineteenth century progressed, social dancing became grounds for censure or loss of good standing in southern evangelical churches. "In all my life . . . I never saw a Negro dance," noted one Virginian in 1864. "The slaves of the border states are almost invariably members of the Baptist and Methodist societies which are particularly rigid in denying them such amusements. . . . I have rarely known their enthusiasm enlisted in anything except prayer-and-experience meetings and funerals."[208] Blacks found a way around dance prohibitions by incorporating "ring shouts" into their religious meetings, which involved a shuffled walk in a circular pattern and "patting Juba," or keeping a steady rhythm by hitting different parts of the body. Evangelical blacks argued that the ring dances were not truly dancing because participants never crossed their feet.[209]

Blacksmith Gilbert Hunt's life after the theater fire had settled back into its normal rhythm: He rose early and walked downstairs to the blacksmith shop, where his name hung on a small sign over the door. He ignited the flame and pumped the bellows to ready the workshop for the day's tasks. He attended worship services throughout the week at the Baptist church, visited with his wife.

His master had priced Hunt at eight hundred dollars, and it took Hunt until 1829, when he had nearly reached fifty years of age, to collect that sum and purchase his own freedom. He had probably been able to earn a good deal of the money during the war years. Beginning in 1812 and throughout the eighteen-month period when America was at war with Great Britain, business picked up considerably, as Hunt received supply orders from the army. He and his assistants hammered out pickaxes, guns, horseshoes, and grappling hooks for vessels at Norfolk, keeping four forges roaring night and day. Hunt assembled sturdy carriages for transporting cannons and maintained the smithy in the absence of his master, who had retreated with his family into the country to a safer location and left the entire operation to Hunt. Like other urban slaves in Richmond who worked in manufacturing and trades, he was able to negotiate contracts, secure his own lodging, and earn wages. It seems Hunt managed his money well over the years, and that it grew to a significant amount. In 1850, the census listed Hunt as owning fifteen hundred dollars in property.[210] One record indicates that Hunt even bought several slaves. Because he procured them after 1832 legislation that barred free blacks from owning slaves, except for their own family members, his "slaves" probably were his children, purchased in order to protect them from being sold away.[211]

Shortly after purchasing his freedom, Hunt decided to start a new life, and he joined the free blacks emigrating to Liberia. In 1830, he sailed on the schooner *Harriett* from Norfolk in the pitching waves of a violent storm with 160 other émigrés.[212] Once he had arrived on West African shores, along with a few free black friends from the Richmond region, he surveyed the land, pressing five hundred miles into the interior of Liberia. Perhaps he had been looking for greater economic opportunities: a new site to practice his trade or land to purchase for an investment. In a later book, he commented on the rich soil, heavy growth of trees, and natives who were "much more intelligent than I had expected." Savvier too—he mentioned indignantly in his memoirs that a few natives tricked him out of some choice tobacco by fraud.[213]

Hunt did not remain in Liberia, although permanent emigration was probably his original intention. While his journey is sometimes described as a "visit," an African tour would have been uncustomary. It would seem, in any case, that he did not find the economic potential he had hoped for, and within eight months, he returned to Richmond. In 1858 and 1859, writer Philip Barrett collaborated with the *Richmond Whig* newspaper to produce and promote a fifty-cent pamphlet—*Gilbert Hunt, the City Blacksmith*—about Gilbert Hunt's life and accomplishments, as told, purportedly, by Hunt himself.[214] The proceeds of the widely promoted little book went to support the aged blacksmith, who apparently had encountered hard times financially.[215] Based on his own unpleasant experiences in Liberia, Gilbert Hunt actively discouraged his fellow members at First Baptist from emigrating, much to the dismay of the regional auxiliary branch of the American Colonization Society. Hunt was "a complete croaker," one Richmond leader complained all the way to the A.C.S. national headquarters, which may indicate Hunt's strong influence within Richmond's free black community.[216]

Hunt reestablished himself in Richmond and assumed leadership at the Baptist Church as a deacon, although he twice resigned when his church cited him for exhibiting "a most unlovely temper" and "a wholly unchristian spirit" toward other deacons.[217] Yet after each resignation he was reinstated or reappointed. Barrett's model citizen was far more complicated than portrayed in his biography; Hunt also was arrested in the late 1840s for selling liquor without a license.[218] After refusing to show for the trial for nearly two years, Hunt finally appeared and pled "not guilty." Charges were dismissed.

* * *

The fire and ensuing evangelical influence made a pronounced change in the lives of many of Richmond's leading women. Rice's biographer noted, "Many persons (especially ladies) of all churches, *heard him gladly*. Some of those, more particularly, who had lost relatives or friends in the late disaster, *and whose hearts the Lord had thus opened to attend to the things which were spoken of him*, waited upon his ministry with earnest affection, and with a satisfaction which they had never experienced before."[219]

Evangelical feminine ideals of behavior began to color the aristocratic vision of womanhood in Virginia society, and some of Richmond's leading women became agents of religious change after the theater fire. Card playing and gambling among women practically disappeared.[220] Instead of attending to amusements that had become culturally entwined with their social status, greater numbers of society women began engaging in volunteer activities that were profitable to the community.[221]

Certainly Caroline Homassel Thornton was one woman changed by the fire, and her experience led her to make a radical choice for a woman of her station. Rice's gospel message, preached in the Mason's Hall, continued to echo in her conscience, and not long after hearing it "she gave God her *whole* heart," a friend recalled: "[Caroline's] enthusiastic nature made religion her chief joy. . . . She could not admire a sunset or a blade of grass without speaking of the goodness of God."[222] While still living in Richmond, it seems Homassel Thornton began attending the Episcopal Church, the denomination that traditionally had her family's allegiance. However, a fissure developed following the death of her baby when Homassel Thornton invited the minister into her home for what she expected would be a comforting visit. When the minister expressed doubt that her unbaptized child had been saved, this horrified the grieving mother, who developed a strong belief that infant baptism could not possibly be a requirement for salvation.[223] Warming to the idea of adult immersion, she began to visit the local Baptist church, which met with avid opposition from her friends.[224]

Generally speaking, the Baptists had more unpolished, more uneducated, and poorer congregations than the Episcopalians, and Baptist congregations were very popular among free and enslaved blacks. These Baptists, "the principal denomination in her neighborhood," were probably not Caroline's social equals, and perhaps this was the cause of her friends' disapproval. Yet members of the Baptist Church in Virginia could include those from the upper classes. A correspondent to the *Massachusetts Baptist Missionary Magazine* wrote in 1814, "I have heard of a great revival of religion at Richmond; fifty were baptized in one day, and among these were some of the most respectable inhabitants."[225]

John Richard had given her a Bible "without references, as he said, 'I must judge for myself,'" she wrote.[226] So after many years of waiting, she made a decision that surprised friends and family: Caroline Homassel Thornton gave an acceptable testimony of salvation to the church leaders and officially joined the Baptists.[227] Her self-described "warm, enthusiastic, impulsive heart" increasingly resonated with the spontaneous expression of the Baptist faith, and its theology wiped away any doubts that her baby was in heaven.

Homassel Thornton had never lived far from her adoptive parents, the Richards, in Richmond. When, after several years of marriage, she moved out of the Richard home with her husband and daughters Martha and Mary Frances Gallego, her father said, "It would be death to him, the separation, even in the same town, [yet] whatever was conducive to our happiness would be promoted by him."[228] Dr. Thornton, who may indeed have been very happy for some measure of familial independence, took a six-year lease on a residence with a porch and a garden in Court End, and Mr. Richard lavishly furnished the entire home at his own expense. He stopped in for dinner every Sabbath.[229]

A personal crisis occurred when Homassel Thornton relocated to the Thornton ancestral home, Montpelier, near Culpeper, Virginia, ninety miles away. Dr. Thornton inherited the property after his father's death, and "his heart rejoiced" at the prospect of returning to the mountains. But for Caroline and the Richards, this was a devastating turn. "He never cared for life after we left him," wrote Caroline of her father, "and I was severed from all that made life desirable and again the world was a blank to me."[230] The move west tested her loyalties and caused profound distress, but it also deepened her growing devotion. "Had I remained in my earthly Paradise," she wrote of her Court End home in Richmond, "I might have forgotten to *love* and *serve* my Saviour, but trials and troubles of every kind assailed my pathway, and the one thing possessed my heart, *to be a Christian*, a fervent devoted follower of the 'Lord that was slain, but lives again to intercede for me!'"[231]

Though Homassel Thornton lived far from the benevolent societies of her beloved Richmond, she transformed her rural home into a mission field. She swung wide Montpelier's doors to guests of all social stations and made her home a haven where "ministers of all denominations were heartily welcomed."[232] Homassel Thornton took an interest in her slaves as humans with religious and educational potential. She felt a sacred duty to instruct them daily in the Scriptures as well as reading and writing.[233] Therefore Montpelier, though isolated and far from Richmond's swarms of women's benevolent societies, provided another arena for exercising Christian charity in the form of educational outreach and religious tutoring. John Holt Rice's post–theater fire sermons were bearing fruit in unlikely places. The pastimes that had provided her amusement and the expensive goods that granted her social cachet seemed meaningless—the world was changing for Richmond's elites, among whom Caroline had been a star. "One of the most accomplished women of her day," her obituary later noted.[234]

The strengthening evangelical movement in Virginia had its decided detractors, Thomas Jefferson among them. Jefferson found solace believing that its prevalence in the South was likely a craze, that it would fade quickly in the face of more sensible opinions, such as Unitarianism, but he miscalculated. The Unitarians did build a church in Richmond but not until 1830, and the tiny, struggling congregation never obtained the influence they held in New England. Certainly their numbers in Richmond never posed a serious threat to evangelical sects. By 1823, eight houses of worship stood in Richmond, and in 1853, Richmond had over fifteen Christian churches (not including those groups meeting in homes or public spaces), three-quarters of which were evangelical in disposition: three Episcopal, two Presbyterian, three Methodist, three Baptist, one Campbellite (Christian Church or Church of Christ), one Unitarian, one Quaker, and one Roman Catholic.[235] During the second decade of the century, local newspapers, including the *Enquirer*, began to carry religious news along with political news as a matter of course. In the thirty years after the fire, the population of Richmond doubled, but the number of churches quadrupled.[236] The 1860 Census listed twelve actors in the state of Virginia—and 1,437 clergy.

The institutions that Richmond's evangelical Christians created and expanded after the Theater fire provided a structure that preserved their social and cultural influence throughout the century and made them a potent moral force in Richmond. Another assist came from Richmond's small but growing middle class of shopkeepers, merchants, lesser lawyers, and educators, who became core members of local congregations. As critics of many formerly culturally acceptable amusements, they set a moral tone for society, increasingly defining appropriate behavior.

9
RETURN

The Managers of the New-York Theatre deploring in common with their fellow citizens of the United States, the dreadful calamity occasioned by the burning of the Theatre at Richmond, and anxious, as far as human precaution can, to guard against the possibility of a similar accident, have solicited many of the most competent judges to an examination of the Theatre in this city.

—"TO THE PUBLIC," REPRINTED IN *Richmond Enquirer,* JANUARY 18, 1812

The Richmond Theater fire had brought to the public's attention the national problem of unsafe public buildings. Deaths could have been minimized had the building met some very basic safety standards, such as wide hallways and adequate exit doors. "We slept with too fatal security over the evil," the Committee of Investigation lamented. "We trusted and we are ruined. New doors were not opened; the winding stair-case was not straitened; the access to the avenues of the Theatre was not enlarged."[1]

It was not as though Richmond had lacked ample examples of safe theater floor plans. Short and stocky "Billy" Twaits of the Placide & Green Company, had some familiarity with the Drury Lane Theatre, and reported to the Committee of Investigation that Drury Lane had a spacious hall on each side of the building with broad and straight staircases. There were over seven exits from the gallery, pit, and boxes. "Miserable reverse!" he reported, "in the late Richmond Theatre, [there was] but one entrance to the boxes and pit, and that so narrow, that two persons could scarcely pass at the same time—the way then lying through a gloomy passage to a narrow winding stair-case, which terminated in as narrow a lobby."[2] Not surprisingly, Twaits agreed with the committee's verdict that the blame did not lie with his troupe—it was the fault of the building. "It is, therefore, evident, that this ever to be lamented loss, which has at once deprived your city of some of its brightest ornaments, and desolated many families, is wholly attributable to the mal-construction of the late Theatre," Twaits averred.[3]

Actor William Wood described the "dreadful consequences" of the fire in his memoir. "This awful event would alone have arrested for a season the current of the best fortune. It seemed to create a perfect panic, which deterred the largest portion of the audience for a long time from venturing into a crowd, either theatrical or other."[4] Historian of Virginia theater Martin Shockley agreed that the Richmond Theater fire caused "a serious blow to theatrical interests throughout America and inevitably caused bitter prejudice and violent opposition to the theatre in Richmond."[5] The similarities between the Richmond Theater building and other slapped-together playhouses in major cities caused great trepidation in the winter of 1812. A letter from Philadelphia published in the *Enquirer* on January 25, 1812, stated that residents attended Philadelphia's theater in much smaller numbers following the Richmond fire: "The relation of the melancholy loss . . . seems to have thrown a gloom on the countenance of every person here. Nothing [else is] talked of even now; and would you believe . . . the favorite Cooper has been playing here this week for never more than 120 people! And last . . . evening he appeared in LEAR (which . . . has never before failed to draw a crowded house), he played for the amusement of eighty persons only—I hear but little said about the (new) . . . [Olympic] Theatre; it is an elegant building, but like your unfortunate one, has but a single door of Entrance."[6]

Theaters may have been no more or no less structurally sound then other large public buildings, such as courthouses, churches, or schools, but the use of fire in special effects and the likelihood of crowding in order to maximize revenue at popular shows put theaters at special risk for devastation. However, it seems that their function as places of business—at risk of losing money if the public viewed them as dangerous—made theaters more responsive to the public's safety concerns, at least temporarily. When the negative ripple effect of the Richmond Theater fire threatened to affect box office profits, American theater managers snapped into action. The managers of New York's Park Theater recognized that "too much cannot be done to destroy the apprehensions to which a casualty like that we bemoan is too well calculated to give birth." Therefore, after December 26, they and other theater managers along the East Coast felt compelled to advertise safety features in their theaters in order to calm the public and insure that their revenue stream be uninterrupted. They could not afford for patrons and theatergoers to remain home out of fear.

New York's Park Theater managers stated they were "anxious, as far as human precaution can, to guard against the possibility of a similar accident."

The managers compared the shortcomings of Richmond's theater with their own Manhattan facility. Richmond had insufficient exits? The Park Theater had seven exits to the street, including one through the box office, two through "Coffee Rooms," and one freshly bored through a vacant apartment lately occupied by a miniature portrait painter. Richmond housed multitudes of flammable hemp set pieces? The Park Theater used canvas scenes, "painted on both sides, and therefore nearly incombustible." (This of course wasn't true, but paint caught fire less quickly than exposed hemp.) Inattentive staff in Richmond? The Park Theater claimed to have a large number of stagehands constantly engaged in every department where an accident might arise.[7]

As an additional pledge of security, manager Price of the Park Theater invited three separate groups of distinguished citizens to evaluate his facility: engineers, firemen, and eminent political figures. Each group insisted after their inspection that the building was safe.[8]

The first week of January in 1812, the *American Daily Advertiser* published a statement from Warren & Wood, managers of Philadelphia's New Theatre, replying to the "numerous enquiries" received about the structure after "the late most afflicting occurrence in Richmond." The public's attention had been naturally called toward the New Theatre and the means of safety should there be an emergency. Assuring the public that the building was not dangerous, the managers pointed out the New Theatre's fireproof basement, a total of six exterior exits (with boxes, pit, and gallery each having their own separate exit), doors hinged to open both outwardly and inwardly, large Venetian windows which opened to a second-story terrace for an easy leap to the ground, a wide exit corridor, and roomy staircases. Following the Richmond fire, Warren & Wood added additional doors to bring a total of sixteen escape routes from the theater's great hall to the exterior exits. Although the managers doubted that a fire could happen, due to their staff's attentiveness, they advertised that the whole theater could be evacuated "in perfect safety in less than five minutes from the occurrence of any serious alarm."[9]

In Charleston, South Carolina, by late January 1812, the Placide & Green Company was attempting to reestablish themselves in their hometown theater. They were more duty-bound than most to prove theirs was a safe building after watching Richmond's burn down around their ears—and on their watch. Placide & Green (as Placide, Green & Twaits) released a statement assuring the public that their theater in Charleston had undergone "necessary alterations" and would be inspected by guardians of public safety before it opened.[10] The managers were not going to take any gambles that would further disgrace their company. "We trust the [measures] which have been adopted to secure your safety, & at the same time give stability to the establishment, together with every other arrangement calculated to increase your pleasures, by commodiously and safely endeavoring to entertain you, will be rewarded by a return of that liberal patronage which we gratefully acknowledge," the managers optimistically expressed.[11]

In the immediate aftermath of the 1811 debacle, a monthly theater publication in Philadelphia wrote, "We hope this melancholy event will place all managers on their guard."[12] Richmond's Committee of Investigation had also wished for this outcome. Their report concluded with this: "The committee cannot close their melancholy labours without expressing one hope, that irreparable as our own calamities have been, we may not have suffered altogether in vain; that our own misfortunes may serve as beacons to the rest of our countrymen, and that no Theatres should be permitted to be opened in the other cities of the United States, until every facility has been procured for the escape of the audience."[13]

* * *

While some took immediate precautions, American theater managers did not universally act on the lessons learned at the Richmond Theater—although the public expected that they would and continued to attend with a spirit of trust. The fight for building safety would be a long one, and there would be many other high-casualty building fires over the next century—most famously the Brooklyn Theater fire on December 5, 1876, the Iroquois Theater fire in 1903, the Triangle Shirtwaist Factory fire on March 25, 1911, and the Calumet Italian Hall fire in Michigan's Upper Peninsula on December 24, 1913.

The measures that could have prevented the Richmond Theater fire's mass fatalities provided a measuring stick of basic precautions for subsequent decades. During an 1846 conflagration in the Baltimore Theater, the escaping audience realized with horror that the exit doors disallowed their escape. In absolute indignation, the *Spirit of the Times* magazine reported that the doors "with the most gross and unpardonable disregard of life, were so hung as to swing inward, they, of course, were at once closed so that there was no egress. Happily, the fire was at once extinguished, or a most fearful scene would have been witnessed. We did not suppose after the awful accident at Richmond, many years since, that prompting was necessary in the proper hanging of doors in theaters."[14]

Because of their ubiquity, throughout the nineteenth century fire disasters were a topic of public discussion and literary interest. Besides the popular narratives that inevitably followed on the heels of a fatal blaze, some one hundred publications in Europe and America with titles like *Hints for Preventing Damage by Fire in the Construction and Warming of Buildings* and *Fire Protection of Mansions* addressed safety and the prevention of destructive conflagrations.[15] From his vantage point at the close of the century, author and *New York Tribune* journalist Horace Townsend penned an 1883 feature piece in *Frank Leslie's Popular Monthly* concerning fire safety and the three worst theater fires of the century to date. He included Richmond in 1811 (death toll: 72), Brooklyn in 1876 (death toll: 300), and the Ring Theater in Vienna, Austria, in 1881 (death toll: an astounding 794).[16]

Townsend rather drily reported the pattern that resulted after fiery theater disasters:

Quite as curious and worthy of study to the casual observer is the sudden and widespread panic which at some outbreak of fire in a theatre seizes the American nation, and renders them for some space of time keenly alive to the small chance of escape offered to them, should any of the existing places of amusement catch fire when inclosing an audience within their walls. Editorials are written in the newspapers, articles by experts appear in the leading magazines; the receipts of theatres and opera-houses suffer from a temporary diminution; the Fire Department officials bestir themselves and present voluminous reports; everyone comes to the conclusion that each and every place of public entertainment is a death-trap, and that "something ought to be done," and the general result is that matters go on much as they did in the past. Nothing is done to amend those theatres already built; architects and builders continue running up their walls, inclosing a mass of inflammable material insufficiently provided with exits; everyone awaits with equanimity for the next Brooklyn or Park Theatre disaster, and for matters to commence *de novo*.[17]

Fire safety codes for buildings were largely the purview of municipalities, although it seems few ordinances and regulations were actually passed to assure safety, and enforcement was lacking. Many of the first fire-prevention regulations on record in America dealt with private housing, not public structures; in New Amsterdam in 1625, the city ruled on types, locations, and roof coverings on houses, and in 1630, Boston's governor prohibited wooden chimneys and thatched roofs. By the early nineteenth century, most large cities had some preventative fire laws on the books, prescribing construction materials, prohibiting hazardous behavior, and regulating the more dangerous trades.[18] However, this did not mean that detailed building laws or mechanisms for consistent enforcement were in place to protect citizens. In fact, the first building law addressing theater construction would not appear until 1885, when New York City and Boston simultaneously passed a building law calling for the use of sprinklers.[19]

In the absence of regulations regarding public buildings, bottom lines often trumped public safety concerns. Townsend noted, "In America . . . a theatre is a business investment, and the immense cost of [fireproof] construction is sufficient to banish it at once from the consideration of an investor of capital."[20] Additionally, antiregulation sentiment was strong. In 1854, an editorial in the *New York Observer* noted the negligible requirements of building codes with hearty approval. The law did not secure protection for citizens in places which they voluntarily attended, the editorial's writer remarked and then added, "They take the risk . . . if they go and are burned up, it is their own affair. This is what is meant by liberty and free government."[21] Yet evidence mounted that codes for public buildings should be adopted, even if not legally required, due to the apparent inevitability of fire, particularly in places of public entertainment. Townsend wrote: "One rarely hears of a theater succumbing to old age and falling into venerable ruins; it is always either torn down to make room for some more profitable erection, or else its elegy is sung to the accompaniment of the whiz of the fire-hose and the clatter of the engines and reel-carts."[22]

In Townsend's opinion, if business owners would not invest in sturdy, fireproof structures, they should at the very least, provide efficient means of escape and make an investment in some basic equipment as a precaution. "The Theatre, in fact, must be regarded as a lunatic asylum, and as little as possible left to human agency," he maintained. Townsend advised nearly all the sensible measures that have become modern building safety standards: wide corridors and aisles, sufficient exits from the auditorium that let out into an alleyway or the street, escape routes with no twists or turns and no steps, doors capable of opening outward, and ground floors on an inclined plane without steps or breaks. The width of aisles and exit routes, he suggested, ought to correspond with the theater's capacity, and doors and windows ought never be locked when the theater was open. He advised that a recent invention, "patent portable extinguishers," be placed strategically throughout the theater for general use in addition to overhead sprinklers and a complete system of fire hose. A final modern requirement was suggested: regular fire drills for stagehands and other employees.[23]

When civil engineer and theater fire expert William Paul Gerhard compiled his list of "Twelve Prominent Theater Fire Calamities of this Century" in 1896, the Richmond fire was the first he mentioned. Gerhard noted that accidental fires caused by lighting implements coming into contact with scenery, as had been the case in Richmond, instigated nearly all of the twelve fatal fires.[24] While Gerhard encouraged innovations such as a stage fire curtain, ventilating skylights, and "flap seats," he determined that well-distributed exits to decentralize the crowd, along with stage exits and multiple fireproof stairways with handrails, were far more important to protect human life than what was popularly (and misleadingly) called "fireproof construction."[25]

By "fireproof," architects (like Robert Mills, who built a career promoting fireproof construction) usually meant vaulted solid masonry structures that used less wood than was standard at the time. Federal and state governments were the greatest investors in "fireproof construction" throughout the nineteenth century. The phrase often gave the public an unfounded trust that a building was simply not able to burn.[26] While the exterior may have been less vulnerable, the interior contents were still flammable. Lulled into a false sense of imperviousness to fire, owners and patrons could and did become lax about maintaining safety features inside the structure. This susceptibility caused Gerhard to become an early advocate for regular safety inspections by outside authorities who would have the power to revoke a theater's operating license if basic safety measures weren't observed.[27] The first law requiring the inspection of buildings intended for public assembly was not passed until 1867, in New Orleans, and not until 1888 did a Massachusetts law authorize inspectors to deny a building license for safety noncompliance and require the posting of occupancy certificates in large public buildings.[28]

States and municipalities adopted building safety laws and enforcement practices unevenly throughout the nineteenth century. Even up to the First World War, many states lacked egress legislation. Few local building and fire codes were on the books before 1900, and not until fire insurance companies sustained severe losses around that time did the National Board of Fire Underwriters publish their *Recommended National Building Code* in 1905. This publication supplied municipalities with suggestions for reducing fire hazards in and around structures and creating local laws and codes and served as the nation's first and only nationally recognized model building code for decades. Although implementation of this code had the pleasant side effect of saving human lives, it was hoped that its institution would spare fire insurance companies from catastrophic expenses.[29] The National Fire Protection Agency, a nonprofit organization begun in 1896, appointed a Committee on Safety to Life in 1913 to study famous fires and analyze the reasons for fatalities. They produced pamphlets that led to a safety guide published in 1927 titled *Building Exits Code,* which helped the builders of public buildings to incorporate safety features that would protect their structures and patrons from similar future accidents.[30]

FORGETTING THE FIRE

After the Brooklyn Theater fire, a reporter noted that "while the fright lasted, people would not expose themselves to such peril. Gradually that wears away, and thoughtless persons, theatre-going people, will resume their accustomed places, and enjoy the play in spite of the danger which is just as great now as ever."[31]

On the first anniversary of the Richmond Theater fire, a local citizen ran a public notice recommending that all citizens abstain from their usual avocations that Saturday, December 26, suspending slave labor and spending the day "in humiliation and prayer." Ministers were exhorted to "perform Divine service in their respective places of worship," reminding their people to "Be ye ready also, for the Son of man cometh at an hour when ye think not."[32] However, in Richmond, the social season in the winter of 1812 was, although without theatrical entertainment, one of greater festivity than at any time previous, according to local inhabitant Thomas Rutherfoord.[33] The prevailing attitude struck some as patently disrespectful. From Richmond in December 1813, Ellen Mordecai, sister to Samuel, wrote with surprise to her brother as the anniversary of the fire approached. "Today is the twenty-sixth, but it is remembered by few, and observed by only here and there a pious individual. Yesterday there were several dinner parties in town, and today Carriages are continually passing. . . . Louisa also spoke of the Cottillian parties which are every Thursday night. I expressed some surprise when she said there would be one the next evening—Lord she said why *that* happened *two* years ago, and on new years day, *last year* we had a party! The less excusable I replyed—I dare say she thought me affected and I am sure I thought her, unfeeling."[34]

Strikingly, Richmond-area builders did not adopt the simplest of safety measures that would prevent future carnage in the decades after the disaster: Monumental Church even had inward-opening doors installed. On a February night in 1890, strange, potent, smoky fumes fanned through the registers of the Richmond Academy of Music during a performance of *The Rose of Castil*. An unobservant stagehand had tossed oily rags into the furnace, and their pungent chemical odor slowly filtered through the theater. When someone panicked and shouted "Fire!" three-quarters of the audience jumped to their feet and ran for the doors, ready to escape to the street. But on stage, "plucky little Emma Abbott" continued to sing her solo, and her calmness soon reassured the half-panic-stricken crowd, the *Washington Post* reported. Men and women turned and took their seats, the opera concluded, and from the theater rose a storm of applause and bravos for Abbott. The "brave prima donna" was lauded for the way she "averted a Fire Panic in a Richmond Theater," although by encouraging hundreds to stay in a room slowly filling with noxious vapors, she demonstrated disregard for their safety.[35] Considering the audience's unwillingness to evacuate the premises in a dangerous situation, the fact that no second disaster consumed a percentage of the populace was pure luck—or providence.

Lillian Russell visited the Richmond Theater in 1896 and presented *The Little Duke* to a house filled to capacity. During the first act, a small fire began to crackle in the basement. Once detected, the managers quietly sent out a "private fire alarm," summoning a "chemical engine," not unlike a modern portable fire extinguisher, that extinguished the flames. While the engine operated on the fire, managers locked and guarded the theater's exit doors, effectively sealing the audience in the building, fearing someone from outside would frighten the audience with the news.[36] Although a similar decision at Vienna's Ring Theater in 1881 resulted in nearly eight hundred fatalities, the

Washington Post praised the Richmond managers for barricading patrons in and not unnecessarily alarming them by informing them of the blaze. The public approbation Emma Abbott and the Richmond managers received indicates the level to which precautionary safety measures in potential fire situations were not yet appreciated and had not yet become common practice.

Some who had been deeply affected by their experience of the theater fire were forever changed, as journalist Horace Townsend found in the 1880s when he interviewed Richmond natives alive during the 1811 fire. He recounted, "So great was the horror excited by this catastrophe that the writer has been informed by elderly inhabitants of the city, that even after fifty years had passed, many classes still regarded the event as a judgment of heaven, and kept aloof from all theatres, as a matter of principle."[37]

When rumblings about new theater construction in Richmond began only a few years after the original was destroyed, these instigated no small measure of indignation, and people outside of Virginia were not loath to weigh in on the matter. One letter of protest reached the *Religious Remembrancer,* a Presbyterian weekly paper in Pennsylvania: "The newspapers have informed us that the inhabitants of Richmond, in Virginia, propose to build a NEW THEATRE. Thousands who tenderly sympathized with that chastized city, will regret, that mourners should again seek the house of profane mirth. Had I lost a relative by fire in the conflagration of the play-house, surely the recollection of the disaster, if nothing else, would deter me from again frequenting the unhallowed spot. Other amusements, which, to say the least of them, are less prejudicial to the morals of society, might suffice."[38]

To many, building another theater seemed disrespectful of the victims, somehow profaning their memory and diminishing their loss. Richmond stood to be a model city for the rest of America—a permanently chastened, theaterless metropolis, and the construction of another theater would compromise this. But the rumors were true—a proposal for a permanent theater was being actively entertained. British actor Joseph George Holman had purchased a lot five blocks west of Monumental Church on the southeast corner of Seventh and H (now Broad) streets from Christopher Tompkins for a thousand dollars in cash and forty-three shares of stock in the proposed theater.[39] In 1816, the *Richmond Enquirer* openly published a proposal, likely Holman's, to erect another theater in Richmond.

In May 1816, when the *Enquirer* was already covering the possibility of a new theater, lawyer and future U.S. attorney general William Wirt posted a letter to legendary tragedian Thomas Abthorpe Cooper, then in Norfolk, Virginia, cementing plans for Cooper to pay a "surprise" visit to Richmond. Cooper, the "Father of the American Stage" and the man responsible for bringing George Frederick Cooke to America, had a nationwide following and an exhausting touring schedule. The accomplished actor was especially well-loved in the South, where the religious beliefs of the audience had not historically hampered its enjoyment of the entertainment.[40] Fellow English comic actor John Bernard, an associate of Robert Brinsley Sheridan and John Kemble, who toured through and lived in America for twenty-two years, remembered the handsome Cooper's popularity in his *Retrospections*, due largely to his talent, gentlemanly manners, and connections to local notables.[41]

Yet Cooper had to be wary—touring in Virginia's more untamed corners carried no small degree of risk, and even performers in cities sometimes found themselves subject to humiliation, censure, scorn, and even violence. Despite the South's general acceptance of those in the acting profession and captivation with celebrity, performers—including those like Cooper who had a certain stature thanks to their talent and fame—remained socially vulnerable. Contemporary actor and theater manager William Wood wrote, "The young enthusiast views only the bright spots of the picture; he sees the favored actor received with smiles and plaudits; glittering in fine dresses, and talked of with delight. He little dreams of the days and nights of painful toil, the mortifications and insults to which he has been exposed for years, perhaps, before he attained even a moderate estimation."[42] After slanderous allegations were made about Wood's company by a fellow actor, Wood's own wife, when playing Juliet in Philadelphia the summer of 1811, had been hit with a musket ball thrown by a "miscreant" in an upper box, and Wood had been threatened by a dangerous mob of "ruffians."[43] Cooper traveled through Virginia well armed, with a brace of dueling pistols and a gun or rifle in a leather case hung alongside his tandem sulky. His trim English servant George Wilmot followed behind the Cooper carriage and assisted in the repairs whenever the little tandem was "speedily shattered by the roads."[44] The physical discomfort of the voyage was one thing, but greater dangers could rear their heads in actual performances, where unruly crowds could put an actor's life in danger. On one evening in Frederickstown (now Winchester), Virginia, the unflappable Cooper demonstrated that he was more than up to the perils of a Virginia tour. As was his usual practice in a town without a theater, Cooper and comedian John Bernard had engaged the assembly room of a local tavern for their performance. While Cooper powerfully recited a poem by Dryden, a local rowdy hurled a brickbat through the window at his head and the room flew into confusion. After identifying the backwoodsman responsible for interrupting the show, Cooper lunged at his throat and beat the man with his own bat until he begged for mercy. The crowd parted as Cooper reentered the theater, resumed his place next to Bernard, and continued with the program.[45]

Yet Cooper, a handsome actor with drooping eyelids and a dark, brooding brow, quailed at coming to Richmond in 1816. He had no fears for his safety, but rather reservations about the propriety of being one of the first actors to perform in the city of the theater fire. In a letter, Cooper asked Wirt if he should expect a negative response from the public. "As to the temper of the people, never fear it," Wirt replied dismissively. "We have, it is true some hysterical ladies whose nerves may be shaken a little by such an exhibition— This is very natural. . . . But I am much mistaking if you will not find torrents eager to catch at the offer." In case Cooper doubted the support of the local leadership, Wirt enclosed a personal note from Governor Wilson Cary Nicholas, bearing Cooper "good will."[46]

Not billing his performance as a play, but rather as a dramatic speech or presentation, which is what Wirt apparently did, would ensure a smoother reception, although Wirt advised Cooper that people would "lik[e] it more the nearer it approaches to theatrical representation."[47] Key to the plan though, was Cooper's covert arrival and a complete lack of prior publicity. Any advance notice of the performance would in all probability give Richmond's newly invigorated religious community time to rally and suppress it. Instead of advertising Cooper's coming, Wirt "thought it better for you to take us by surprize and give us no time to start and circulate false notions of sentimental delicacy." A visit by one of the nation's foremost actors would be the first step of Wirt's plan, a way to whet the public's appetite for a permanent home for dramatic shows in Richmond. "It will be a fine entering wedge to a theater which Mr. Holman, who is here, promises us," Wirt wrote to Cooper.[48]

Richmonders had put up with substandard entertainment for years in the absence of the theater, and many were starved for something superior to the current amateur fare. Samuel Mordecai indicated to his sister how dismal the situation had become after he watched a handful of touring equestrians and entertainers present a traveling show at the Eagle Tavern in early 1818. "The people of Richmond are desperately in want of public amusements," he wrote to Rachel Mordecai in North Carolina, describing the performers. "Such discord, such awkwardness and such ugliness I never saw combined in any other set—Ulysses would have required no wax to stop his ears had the syrens sung thus—The Shawl Dance was a jig by a ponderous lady holding a scarf before her—The wreath dance was jumping an ornamental rope and the mathematical experiments were the old slight of hand tricks with cards, cups and balls." Sloppy routines should have rallied no great turnout, but in fact "at least 400 persons were present at this exquisite entertainment," Mordecai sarcastically recorded, "and were so charitable as to applaud ten times where they hissed once."[49] Efforts had been made—unsuccessfully—to raise the quality of Richmond entertainment. A private museum intending to educate and simultaneously amuse opened in 1817, exhibiting fossils and paintings, but stumbled along with sporadic attendance until it was forced to close some years later.[50]

Some citizens, like the *Enquirer* editorialist "Talma" (whose moniker was the name of a French actor), and Thomas Ritchie, expressed concern that the lack of a theater had actually encouraged more lascivious pastimes in Richmond, which presented greater social dangers. "It is with much satisfaction we look forward to this elegant amusement," wrote Ritchie of an upcoming stage production in 1817, "when we trust those gross and dangerous sensualities, which have taken its place, and occupied the leisure moments of the young and the gay, will vanish in a great degree."[51] "Talma" supported the theater as an agent capable of raising the moral tone of Richmond, even if the productions weren't all spotless morality plays. ""If you have no places of public amusement, where the pleasures of taste and intellect may chasten and correct the grosser passions, you encourage the lowest sensuality and fill the gambling houses, the taverns, and the brothels. The town therefore, who wishes well to morality and to religion, should . . . deeply consider the consequences of driving a large portion of his fellow beings, to the haunts of hopeless infamy, who might, by being lured to, I will not shy *comparatively* innocent amusements [the theater], be insensibly reclaimed to respectability."[52]

Yet in the years between 1811 and 1819, when Richmond lacked a theater, the city experienced a decline in crime rates, which would have corroborated theater critics' belief that stage plays contributed to a city's corruption.[53] The absence of a theater was certainly not the sole cause; the beginning of the decline trajectory also coincided with a January 27, 1812, resolution by the Common Hall to appoint a permanent, salaried master of police.[54]

* * *

Concerned about the influence a new theater might have on parishioners, Episcopalians debated theatergoing in their annual convention in May 1816. Unwilling to expressly forbid theater attendance or adopt compulsory measures, church leaders decided not to bar communion or full membership to Episcopalians who frequented the theater.[55] "[The return of the theater] is exciting considerable discussion in all the variety of circles of which our society is composed, and does at length become the subject of *pulpit denunciation*," the editorialist and theater aficionado "Talma" noted on May 25, 1816. Local Christian feeling against the theater was such that "Talma" feared the convention might reach a different conclusion and decide to excommunicate members on the grounds of theater attendance. "Persuade, advise, exhort and reason—but leave denunciation [i.e. excommunication] to the Lord, Peter, and his followers. He may damn us for ever, yet fail to convince us, that a brown leaf is good mutton . . . or that Theatrical Representations are the inventing of the Devil."[56]

Rev. Richard Channing Moore's convictions would be tested as momentum grew for building a new theater. How could his congregation's affection for drama, balls, and gaming be reconciled with the Episcopal baptismal vow to "renounce the pomps and vanities of the wicked world," wondered Moore, convinced that Christians should fundamentally look and live differently from those who did not claim to be among the faithful. "It was a work of great difficulty for those who preached . . . to illy instructed congregations, to induce them to adopt the rigid discipline of a godly life," noted Moore's biographer. "Many of the communicants had been accustomed freely to mingle with others in the ordinary gayeties and pleasure of fashionable life."[57]

Changing long-seated predilections for the theater proved no easy task. The South had an extensive history of theatergoing and in fact was home to the nation's first play performed in English, the first college dramatic performance, the first professional actor, and the first theater.[58] Moore had a difficult time pulling Richmond Episcopalians on board with his evangelical views against the theater. To a sympathetic parishioner, Moore wrote, "I cordially concur with you in your views . . . that we may with equal propriety attempt to serve God and mammon as to reconcile an indulgence in fashionable amusements, with the divine life, but the remedy, the remedy—how is it to be applied? In this city, much as I wish to check the evil, I confess myself at a loss how to proceed."[59]

Actor William Wood spent his childhood in post-Revolutionary New York, where his father was the master of Trinity Church School, an Episcopal institution. Wood occasionally attended plays with his friends, the sons of Episcopal clergymen and the bishop. He mentioned this in his 1855 memoir to show "the estimation which the drama held in those days," when highly respected citizens made up the audience.[60] Although Episcopalians had demonstrated more acceptance of the theater than other denominations, even among Episcopal congregations sentiments about the theater had undergone a change since those last two decades of the eighteenth century. As an example of this, Moore had not been at loggerheads about "worldly amusements" with his congregation in New York. There, "the relinquishment of balls, the theatre and card table, formed the 'sine qua non' of admission to the communion in my Church," he explained from Richmond to a friend, "but whether the temper of my present flock would submit to the same rule of conduct, God only knows. I am apprehensive it would produce a commotion overwhelming in its effects and desolating to our interests."[61] He feared that forcing his congregation to choose between the theater and the church would drive members from Monumental permanently—the attachment was simply too strong to their social life and too weak to the fledgling church. Using "austerity" instead of "persuasion," Moore worried, would perhaps "give rise to a reaction dreadful in its tendency, and expose his offspring to evils incalculably great," should the members consequently decide to never again cross a church threshold. The chief problem was that in Richmond, he had no parish buy-in—not even from the leadership. "Were there a few laymen of distinction in this place who would sanction the attempt, and enforce it with their influence, perhaps it might succeed," he reflected, "but in all my conversations upon the subject, with some truly excellent men belonging to my Church, they express the greatest apprehension, and I do not know at present of any who would uphold me in the conflict."[62]

THE OPENING AND THE UNCERTAIN FUTURE OF THE NEW THEATER

Although some believed that there could never be theaters in Richmond after such a devastating blaze, Jeremiah Jeter recalled that the terrors of the burning theater faded by degrees from the public memory.[63] The theater's grand reopening eight years after the greatest disaster in the history of early American theater was a long wait for some, for others entirely premature. An April 1817 editorial in Richmond's *Christian Monitor* surmised disapprovingly that another theater indubitably would go up. "Deep as the impressions of grief no doubt are on the minds of the people of Richmond, it is probable that before these impressions are effaced by the lenient hand of time, before the sable ensigns of mourning are laid aside, another theatre will be erected, crowded with an audience as gay and as numerous as the former." However, the editorialist proposed a means of keeping the tragedy in memory and improving the morals of the audience: To begin, patrons should be able to buy tickets only at the Monumental Church's portico, where they would be required to read over the names of the dead before making their purchase. The first play launched at the new theater should be the story of the 1811 theater fire, with the performers dramatically reenacting the shrieks and groans of the dying and the frantic distress of those who had escaped. Repeat performances of the production should be held every December 26.[64]

The *Enquirer* reported on September 30, 1817, that plans for theater construction were coming along at a swift clip, despite the death of the project's backer, Joseph Holman. His son-in-law, Mr. Gilfert, was appointed in his place and an architect from New York called in to suggest improvements to the building plans. The first story's walls had already been erected, and the opening was anticipated for the summer of 1818.[65]

As in the construction of Monumental Church, backers organized a committee, which sold two-hundred-dollar shares to the theater to provide capital funding. Some of the city's most influential citizens, including William Wirt, Thomas Ritchie, John Wickham, Francis Gilmer, William Hay, Jr., Edward Mayo, and several Foushees subscribed the forty thousand dollars necessary to finance the endeavor. In total, 104 townspeople became stockholders.[66] Not surprisingly, a leading item of business at one of the first shareholder meetings was arranging for fire insurance.[67]

The theater garnered financial support from several people deeply affected by the first fire: John Wickham, whose daughter Julia and two sons had narrowly escaped death; Carter Page, who badly broke his leg during his escape with his wife; survivor Gurden H. Bacchus; and John Marshall.[68] In 1813, John Marshall's only daughter, Mary, wed twenty-five-year-old Jacquelin Burwell Harvie, the brother of burn victims Edwin and Juliana Harvie. The Marshalls did not lose any immediate family to the fire, but they married into a family of multiple victims and certainly were aware of the concerns of victims' families.

"*The erection of a Theatre in this city* is a subject still of infinite delicacy," wrote "Talma" in 1816. "No persons, I believe in the world, can have more respect for the feelings of those who have so much cause to regret [what occurred] here, than many who are anxious to see the erection of another." The editorialist believed it was high time that Richmonders move past the disaster. "Four years have however now elapsed, since the disastrous event, which called forth all our sympathies—The population of Richmond has greatly changed, and is ever changing—Few persons are left in it, who were the *immediate* sufferers in that ever-to-be-lamented calamity. With them, I am persuaded, the question is safely one of right or wrong, and if they are convinced of [the theater's] general good tendency . . . they will generously sacrifice their feelings to the public interest."[69]

The haste at which this particular project was progressing, however, was something of an embarrassment. As the *Enquirer* pointed out in September 1817, the public overlooked two other vital projects in favor of building the theater. "Will it not be some reflection on our city if the Theatre should be open before the Monument [to the victims] is completed. Why does it sleep? Let us amuse the living—but let us also think of the ashes of the dead. Another reflection never fails to press upon us, while we think of Richmond. The Theatre may open next year . . . but where is our *Academy*? Why does that first of buildings yet sleep in the dust? Never—oh! Let us never say, that we have done our duty to our children or to ourselves, and we raise that edifice almost from the sleep of the grave. What! Shall the Capital of Virginia remain without one public Academy?"[70]

This same argument would resurface in 1838, with the opening of the Marshall Theater. Jeremiah Jeter of Richmond's First Baptist Church appealed to the city's men of influence to "arrest the growing evils of Dramatic Amusements" and redirect their attentions from funding the theater to other worthy claims on their attention. Jeter chided leaders for supporting an institution "whose influence on the morals and happiness of the country is, to say the very least, equivocal" while the city went without a public library, while the Young Men's Lyceum was unendowed, and while many females needed employment.[71]

Moore brought the issue of Christians and the theater back to the 1818 Virginia Episcopal convention, perhaps hoping for a more strident statement forbidding church members from attending. At the convention in 1815, when a few ministers attempted to establish a code of discipline banning "only the grosser vices of drunkenness, gaming, extortion, &c." the effort met with great opposition. Critics brayed that antitheater Episcopalians were "establishing a Methodist Church" and "the clergy only wanted the power."[72] However, the disposition of Episcopal clergy had changed by 1818. After a "warm and animated" discussion, all clerics and a majority of the laity agreed on another Episcopal resolution stating formal disapproval (but not a direct prohibition) of theater attendance and other "reproach[es] on the Church," although members would not be excommunicated for attending.

> Whereas, differences of opinion prevail as to certain fashionable amusements, and it appears desirable to many that the sense of the Convention should be expressed concerning them; the Convention does hereby declare its opinion, that gaming, attending on theatres, public balls, and horse-racing, should be relinquished by all communicants of this Church, as having the bad effects of staining the purity of the Christian character, of giving offence to their pious brethren, and of endangering their own salvation, by their rushing voluntarily into those temptations against which they implore the protection of their Heavenly Father; and this Convention cherishes the hope, that this expression of its opinion will be sufficient to produce conformity of conduct, and unanimity of opinion among all the members of our communion.[73]

Southern culture in the first two decades of the nineteenth century tended to be confrontational, violent, and driven less by personal religion than by personal honor. Evangelicalism offered an alternative way of life amid an often hostile cultural climate, a way of life that eventually was more widely adopted.[74] Although Moore's brand of evangelical Christianity was increasingly gaining a foothold in Richmond, it could not completely displace the traditional views on entertainment. This proved to be the case even after Richmond's great losses in the theater fire, when many Virginians, particularly in the upper classes, dismissed vitriolic sermons and condemnatory editorials that circulated after the fire as "Yankee cant."[75] If an amusement failed to meet religious standards, one could always rename the amusement to make it acceptable. In a nineteenth-century short story about antebellum Richmond life, the protagonist attends the circus with the blessing of her guardian after creatively referring to it as a "menagerie," where she could examine wild animals. "The good Episcopalian [guardian] would have been horrified by the mention of ring and clown, and ground-and-lofty tumbling, but saw no earthly harm in allowing her sons, her young step-daughter and her guests to make up a party under the escort of the Major . . . 'to study natural history.'"[76]

* * *

Animosity in the church toward the theater created uncomfortable dilemmas for Christian actors. William Wood's wife, Juliana Westray Wood, an actress and regular church attendee, sat in a Baltimore pew one Sunday around 1816 as her minister preached against the drama *Bertram* then being performed. Despite the fact that the piece was written by a clergyman and "every doubtful line or allusion had been carefully struck out by the licenser," according to Wood, the minister lambasted the actress "capable of representing the heroine of this shameful production." That actress was none other than Juliana Wood, sitting only a few pews from the speaker, "in full view of every person present."[77]

Samuel Mordecai's anecdotal tale about Frances Willems Green implies that a similarly uncomfortable situation was created in Richmond. John Maddux, the local bill collector and a towering, rawboned Quaker, daily strode through Richmond with a distinctive, purposeful gait. Going door to door in his plain gray garb, the imposing man collected on delinquent accounts. Sometime after 1814, he had occasion to call on Frances Green, the by-then faded English actress of the Placide & Green Company, still living alone and in poverty in a Richmond tenement, still unable to pay her bills. Mordecai reported her husband "had become dissipated and left her destitute," perhaps turning to alcohol and rakish behavior.[78] Maddux felt compassion for Green and asked the distraught woman if she attended church. When she replied that she had no one with which to go, he offered to attend an Episcopal

Church—in which she had been raised—with her. The Quaker and the actress in mourning garb entered through a side door of Monumental Church and took seats in an available pew, much to the astonishment of the congregation. With a strengthening antitheater sentiment now in play, Episcopalians whose daughters had befriended Nancy Green now doubted the propriety of her mother's appearance in church—the church beneath which her daughter was buried. One Episcopalian afterward disparaged Maddux's guest, and in response, Maddux replied, "I carried a poor, desolate sinner to hear the word of God, but I do assure thee I saw many there who stared at her, that required the word as much as that poor soul did."[79]

A new theater in Richmond opened its doors on June 11, 1819. In deference to sensitive local opinion, soon after the opening of the theater, the managers purchased and razed an adjacent building widely considered a fire hazard. Another rickety nearby building, called the "Circus," was also torn down and the lumber auctioned off in July.[80] The Enquirer, as might be expected, since editor Ritchie was a shareholder in the controversial new theater, evenly noted the coming of new shows and wished for the theater's prosperity. In a May 28 article, he commended the new theater's manager, the cosmopolitan Charles Gilfert of Charleston, South Carolina, for being "extremely liberal in providing both novelty and talent to gratify the theatrical taste of our town. . . . It is to be hoped that his success will equal his liberality."[81]

The theater resumed its place as an appealing spot to socialize. Young Frances Taliaferro visited Richmond with her mother in 1820, after the theater had been open for a year. During her visit, she attended both the church and the theater, and her letter implies that the latter stop was not controversial. She wrote, "Yesterday we went to the Monumental Church and heard Mr. Lowe deliver an excellent sermon, he took his text from the sixteenth chapter of Matthew 24th verse[,] he explained it admirably well, and is I think the most persuasive speaker I ever heard. . . . Lucy Ann and myself intend to Richmond this Evening to go to the Theatre, I have not heard what Play is to be performed but I will tell you in my next."[82]

In the ten years after its construction, however, shares to the theater sold cheaply, inferior acting companies ambled through, and the theater sunk into a dilapidated condition. Also, while Richmond maintained some enthusiasm for theatrical spectacle, it was significantly tempered, despite support of the theater by prominent families and encouragement from the Enquirer.[83] Speculating that it was because of the "deep impressions which [the fire] produced," the *Southern Literary Messenger* of February 1835 noted, "The taste for theatrical exhibitions [in Richmond] has not kept pace with the increase of wealth and population." Despite the new theater's safe construction and accessible location, it was only occasionally patronized, when the appearance of some attractive star, or celebrated performer, was announced.[84] Besides the extant prejudices that contributed to the theater's financial troubles, greater economic factors also played a role; the theater construction coincided with the Panic of 1819 and the bursting of a real estate bubble. The new theater became not only financially precarious but also a fire trap. In 1836, the *Richmond Whig* drew the attention of shareholders to their theater, remarking that it was necessary to take "some measures to secure it from the designs of incendiaries. It contains large quantities of combus[t]ible matter, and its taking fire would prove disastrous to adjacent property. It is believed to be marked for conflagration by incendiaries."[85]

In 1837 and 1838, shareholders invested in renovations, and the upgraded theater was dubbed "The Marshall," after Chief Justice John Marshall, long an advocate of local cultural centers and supporter of civic projects. This renovation was apparently successful, and the theater regained popularity, but the new institution was not without controversy. Rev. Jeremiah Jeter of First Baptist Church recalled, "In the winter of 1837–'38 theatrical exhibitions were not only re-established, but largely patronized in the city. Many of the plays were believed to be of demoralizing influence, and some of the scenes offensive to a refined and virtuous taste."[86] This galvanized local ministers, who met together and agreed to preach on the subject from their respective pulpits in a Christian "war on the theatre." Richmond's churches were unanimous in their denunciation of the institution. Presbyterians, Episcopalians, Methodists, and Baptists had not organized to openly condemn the local theater in 1811 or 1812 following the disastrous blaze, yet their joint disapproval emerged with clarity only a few decades later. Now united by common evangelical views on sin, time, and entertainment, each church (save the Quakers) that had been present in Richmond in 1811 publicly decried the theater and its influence.

The ministers chose different texts on which to preach and chose subtly different emphases. Rev. Dr. William S. Plumer of First Presbyterian led the assault with a sermon on the text: "Lead us not into temptation," portraying the theater as a minefield of dangers for the Christian believer. Plumer apparently emphasized the duty all Christians had to avoid evils from which they prayed for deliverance.[87] Rev. Dr. W. A. Smith of Trinity Methodist cautioned that opportunities to indulge in sin abounded where playhouses were present, and this caused social problems for Christians as well as for those who did not believe. Smith preached that theatrical amusements originated in human depravity and were sinful on their own, but they also intensified degeneracy in a community. He argued that where there were theaters, "grog shops, houses of licentiousness, and other places of dissipation and vice were sure to flourish."[88]

Dr. George Woodbridge of Monumental Church and Jeter also preached vigorous attacks on theater attendance (the contents of Woodbridge's sermon were not recorded). Jeter's sermon made such an impression that members of the Commonwealth's legislature requested its publication and distribution.[89] Jeter spoke with assurance and conviction that the horror felt in the aftermath of the fire ought to be remembered and felt anew at the presence of a theater in Richmond. After describing the tragic scene on December 26, 1811, with the dead and dying lying on their very church floor, Jeter asked his congregation at First Baptist, "Who would then have visited such a scene of merriment and trifling, not to say of dissipation and vice? No; until the impression of that awful visitation was effaced, the population of this Metropolis, had no relish for Theatrical Entertainments. And why not? If they are *right* now, they were right then. If they were *wrong* then, they are wrong now."[90]

The Marshall's managers retaliated by writing a burlesque based on the sermons and creating characters based on puns of the parsons' names (e.g., Plumer became a plumber). Advertisements in large capital letters were posted all over the city "to the amusements of many," noted Jeter, who had escaped parody by his unconventional surname.[91]

* * *

Resistance to the presence of a theater in Richmond lessened over the decades of the nineteenth century. By the mid-1850s, Richmond was considered the entertainment capital of the upper South, with the theater a central attraction.[92] The most famous American actors again made Richmond a regular stop, and the city became a trial ground for plays before they went on stage in New York.[93] During the 1858–59 season, a young dark-haired actor of distinguished thespian lineage named John Wilkes Booth performed in Richmond as a member of the Marshall's stock company.[94]

In 1862, the Marshall Theater that Booth knew burned to the ground. This time, no one was inside. Richmonders soon reconstructed it with materials smuggled in through the blockade. "With surprising energy, and regardless of cost, in these pinching times of war, a splendid building, with most costly decorations, has been reared from the ashes of the old. Builders, artists, workmen, have devoted themselves with an enterprise and industry that would be praiseworthy, if, in any sense, their work were useful in these pressing times of war," chided John Lansing Burrows in a February 1863 sermon.[95] Pastor of Richmond's First Baptist Church from 1854 to 1874, Burrows was appalled that men of military age were performing instead of fighting on behalf of the Confederacy. "Shall we all go and laugh and clap to the music and the dance, while the grasp of relentless foes is tightening upon the throats of our sons, and the armed heels of trampling hosts are bruising the bosom of our beloved mother land?" he asked. He was not disposed, he insisted, to make "any captious or churlish denunciation of the theatre, merely because it is a place of amusement" but believed the rebuilt establishment would become a gathering place for the "vile, the unprincipled, and the mere pleasure loving" who flocked to the bustling wartime capital. He anticipated that the new theater would include a third tier, that scandalous and lucrative fixture of the early to mid-nineteenth-century theater wherein prostitutes found regular seating and a place to meet prospective customers.[96]

The theater manager, John Hill Hewitt, confirmed the poor character of his staff and wrote regretfully that during the war "money flowed into the treasury but often had I cause to upbraid myself for having fallen so low in my own estimation, for, I had always considered myself a gentleman, and I found that, in taking the control of this theatre and its vagabond company I had forfeited my claim to a respectable stand in the ranks of Society—with one or two exceptions, the company I had engaged was composed of harlots and 'artful dodgers.'"[97]

However disreputable the cast and audience, a theater that had once reminded the city of nothing but grief now offered a reprieve from despondency. At the lavish new theater's opening performance in 1863, an actor recited:

> A fairy ring
> Drawn in the crimson of a battle plain,

From whose weird circle every loathsome thing
And sign and sound of pain
Are banished . . .
Amid the terrors of the wildest fray,
Let us among the charms of Art while
Fleet the deep gloom away.[98]

In 1895, the theater, a monument to Confederate resourcefulness, was renovated to become a furniture store, and with that, the direct lineage of the 1811 Richmond Theater came to an end.[99] By this time, Richmond had other theaters that had taken its place.

* * *

German engineer August Foelsch determined that from 1750 through 1877, there had been five hundred fires in Europe and America that had ruined theaters, an average of about twenty-five leveled theaters a year.[100] Despite the frequency of such disasters, the Richmond tragedy loomed large in American memory throughout the nineteenth century. In the 1840s, after a fire at the "Boz Ball" burned through a floor of the Park Theater in New York City, a writer warned of the destruction that might have occurred had the fire not been brought under control. "Such a scene occurred in a Theatre in Richmond, not very many years ago, and the tale of that night of horrors still makes the ears tingle and the hearts bleed, of those that hear it."[101]

"A more heart-rending and melancholy event than that of the burning of the Theatre on Shockoe Hill, Richmond, Va., has never, perhaps, taken place in this country," wrote the author of *The Fireman's Own Book* in 1860, before the carnage of the Civil War eclipsed that of Richmond's disastrous blaze. "It is a matter which caused general mourning at the time, throughout the United States, and is often mentioned at the present day," added the writer.[102] In his 1868 autobiography, theater manager Solomon Smith reported, "The cry of "FIRE!" in a theatre is a most alarming sound. It is alarming anywhere, but *in a theater* particularly so. Ever since the burning of the Richmond Theatre, whereby a great number of persons perished, the least alarm of any kind amongst a large assemblage is attributed to *fire,* and a rush is sure to be made for the doors—the "Richmond fire" being uppermost in the minds of all."[103]

An elderly Caroline Homassel Thornton wrote at the end of her life that the impressions and scenes from that terrible night in December were still so vivid, so clear, that the passing decades had not managed to erase them. "Each year I feel suspended from that window, & see the figure of death lying beneath it. . . . All seems written on my heart in letters of blood."[104]

EPILOGUE

With her grown children communicants of the Episcopal Church and the denomination becoming increasingly evangelical, Homassel Thornton began to strongly consider leaving the Baptists and rejoining the church of her youth. She eventually returned to its fold and died an Episcopalian. A friend noted after her death that this denominational transfer did nothing to dampen her zeal. "Her love of God and her Saviour was so great that she took all denominations in her embrace and was as enthusiastic in her religion as she had ever been in all things else."[1]

"See me here at seventy-five, solitary and alone . . . with only half my house and nothing to call mine but my noble trees, grass and flowers and the lonely scenery, and the bright rising and setting sun to illumine my pathway to the grave, and lead me on to glory," Thornton wrote to her grandchildren from her mountain home. "Oh! I feel like one who treads alone some banquet hall deserted, whose lights are fled, whose garlands dead, and all but me departed! But memory is triumphant still and I am happy in the reminiscences of days past and gone." She looked about her room. There stood her long-departed mother's mirror and work stand, her mantel clock just opposite Caroline's bed. Despite the ghosts that surrounded her in her old age, "here I do feel my Saviour so near me," she wrote.

Through Caroline's narrative, the Thornton grandchildren would learn of Richmond's leading families, their homes, their habits, and their experiences in the Richmond Theater fire. But Thornton longed for her life story to be more than any history lesson or genealogical exercise, to convey a message of redemption—of the possibility of joy in the midst of loss, the ability to see God's work in the fires of life. And so she penned the story of her life. "Although it can be but a simple narrative and a recital of the goodness and mercy of God towards your mother, who each day feels a deeper sense of her own unworthiness and a more entire dependence on her blessed, adorable and loving Saviour, but if it should only lead you, my children, to a firmer trust and belief in the great truths of the Gospel, when you see our entire inability to reap the smallest degree of permanent happiness from the things of time and sense, Oh! how truly shall I be compensated for this labor of love."[2]

* * *

An "immense crowd" in Richmond celebrated the eightieth birthday of Monumental Church on Sunday, December 30, 1894 (which was not the exact anniversary, but gave extra time for the interior to be renovated). Ministers from two denominations commemorated the event, and a vested choir sang at both services. Fenner S. Stickney, the Episcopalian rector of Monumental, gave an address in the morning, and eminent Southern divine Moses D. Hoge, a Presbyterian, supplied the afternoon address. Hoge "dwelt at some length upon the brotherhood which should exist between all the denominations," noted the *Washington Post,* and he made reference to the days when Monumental's congregation mixed with the Presbyterians in the capitol church.[3]

The very next year, in 1895, Monumental suffered a fire of its own. The *New York Evangelist Magazine* noted that although the fire threatened the entire building, it was "happily soon extinguished." Further reading of the article reveals that the reputation of Theater Square had changed. Where the theater had ushered many from life to death in 1811, the magazine observed, the site had become a place "where now for all the years since the words of Grace have been preached, and many brought from death to life."[4]

AFTERWORD, 2022

Louisiana State University Press published *The Richmond Theater Fire* in 2012, a few months after the fire's two-hundredth anniversary on December 26, 2011. Since then, I have watched the story stir interest in a lesser-known chapter of Virginia's history, and even reshape Richmond's spaces.

The preface begins with a scene: Monumental Church, the memorial to the 1811 Richmond Theater fire victims, in a state of disrepair. A decade later, the Historic Richmond Foundation (HRF) has renovated and revived the white building on Broad Street thanks to donors and generous foundations. Monumental Church now has a stabilized roof, HVAC, and balcony floorboards that won't snap beneath your feet. The formerly all-white sanctuary looks as it did in 1814, and frankly, it's a bit of a shocker. Paint analysis determined the walls were originally a pale salmon pink, and the altar a bright Prussian blue. Artisans used turkey feathers and other tools to recreate the altar's faux marble finish and to brush faux wood-grain patterns on the inner sanctuary doors. The effect is quirky, bold, and historically accurate.

Conover Hunt, former director of the HRF, oversaw the production of an exact replica of Monumental's marble urn monument after the original began to dissolve. From the portico where the replica is now installed, visitors look over a beautifully landscaped lawn and terrace, once a gravel lot. The Dr. Waverly M. Cole and Dr. John R. Cook Memorial Terrace features an in-ground granite time line of the site, educating pedestrians and visitors. A restored iron fence rings the property. There's always another expensive project on the docket, as anyone with an old home understands, but these renovations transformed the church in a remarkable way. Monumental, as in past centuries, is again a popular wedding spot, with brides posing on the staircases. And the changes aren't only physical: Executive Director Cyane Crump is also taking a fresh interpretive look at the space and exploring creative ways to use this architectural treasure.

Over the past decade, it's been an honor to share my research not only at Monumental (usually during the festive Christmas at Court End celebration), but with the HRF, the Wilton House, the Library of Virginia, the Virginia Museum of History and Culture, the Virginia Forum, and the Anesthesia History Association Conference, among others. My lectures have often doubled as a delightful show-and-tell time, with readers bringing found treasures to share, including the likes of photocopied family letters and newspaper articles. I owe thanks for two special finds to Mary Hunton, a tireless advocate for Monumental Church with a family connection to Caroline Hommasel Thornton. She let me know there was a much better image than the grainy photocopy of a mimeograph of a photograph of an elderly Caroline I had plunked into my slide show. In fact, she told me there were two oil portraits held by descendants that family lore claimed were of young Caroline and Philip Thornton. The years and descriptions matched up, so I reached out. The owners of the originals (who wish to remain anonymous) generously allowed me to use the Thornton portraits from their private family collection in this newest edition, and I couldn't be more thrilled to include these beautiful images of the couple bookending my tale.

One gentleman toted an original letter from December 27, 1811, in a wooden frame to a book talk at the Virginia Museum of History and Culture. The author? Future president John Tyler, who witnessed the fire as a first-term state legislator from Charles City County. In the note to his sister, Maria Henry Seawell, he claimed he'd been "prevented from going to the theatre myself" thanks to a "providential interference." While sleeping in his lodgings, he was woken by the sound of bells around eleven o'clock, and he "hastened to the scene of misery as soon as possible." Whether from smoke inhalation or shock, once there he struggled to breathe and felt a "deadly dizziness" so powerful he had to "retire from the scene" for a moment to collect himself. Tyler described "the haggard forms of females with looks of madness their hair in wild disorder streaming to the wind, flying they knew not whither and imploring assistance in voices of agony and despair." He melodramatically imagined his five sisters as those women, mingled in the chaos of that night. What if *they* had been inside? We understand Tyler's questions because we ask them now in the wake of disaster: What if he took the later flight? What if I hadn't been delayed in traffic? What if that had been my family?

The past is a foreign country where they do things differently, as L.P.

Hartley famously noted. Attempting to understand early republic Richmond and the actions of the people who lived there requires a certain amount of historical empathy. Mass casualty disasters lose their impact unless we stop to notice the individuals affected. That's why the delivery of Mary Love Scott's arresting portrait by Cephas Thompson was such a gift to Richmond. After Dr. David Nelson purchased the painting for his Tuscaloosa, Alabama, home, he learned that the subject was a victim of the theater fire. Moved, he felt Scott belonged back in Richmond. In a serendipitous turn, the Valentine, Richmond's marvelous history museum, was on the lookout for a piece that would represent a victim or survivor of the fire. The opportunity to acquire this portrait came at the perfect time, and the Valentine now features Scott's portrait in its permanent *This Is Richmond, Virginia* exhibit.

On January 20, 2015, I joined more than a hundred others for a historical play reading hosted by the Henley Street Theatre and Richmond Shakespeare (now combined as the Quill Theatre) at Monumental Church. Afterward, I had the honor of being on a panel with Greg Kimball of the Library of Virginia, Olivier Delers of the University of Richmond, Emily Davis of the HRF, and play director Melissa Rayford. The evening's performance? Scenes from *The Father, or Family Feuds and Raymond and Agnes, or The Bleeding Nun*. In a historic first, actors performed the 1811 playbill from Richmond's most tragic night of theater on the very site it debuted. At the point in *Raymond and Agnes* where Hopkins Robinson discovered sparks floating down from above, the actor portraying him stopped, turned to the audience, and said, "The house is on fire!" The footlights glowed red, and all went dark. We departed the theater deeply moved, remembering that the crypt below our feet contained the remains of patrons who would never leave, people whose last memories were the scenes we'd just witnessed.

With the new edition, I have included an appendix containing a victim list, an overdue inclusion. Although I'd hoped to include a map, the minute detail in Richard Young's *Plan of the City of Richmond* from 1809 prevents easy transfer to a standard-sized book page. I refer the curious reader to the digitized version in the Library of Virginia's collection. In the name of consistency, I retained the American spelling of "theater" throughout. If you are on Team Theatre, I apologize and will have to live with your displeasure. As is always the lamentable case, new research and helpful resources come to the author's notice after submission of the final draft. F. Claiborne Johnston's "A More Complete Record of Those Who Perished in the Richmond Theater

Fire, December 26, 1811," completed in 2011, is one such treasure. Johnston put years into archival sleuthing, and readers desiring to learn more about the genealogies of the victims should avail themselves of this compendium, held at the Library of Virginia and the Virginia Museum of History and Culture.

Due to formatting limitations, there are some observations I will have to make here instead of in the original text. My discussions of Richmond life in the first chapter ought to have noted the outsized economic role of the slave trade. In 1800 Virginia claimed 40 percent of America's total enslaved population, and from 1800 to 1860, Richmond was, except for New Orleans, the largest center of human trafficking in America. The commonwealth has long attempted to conceal evidence of the slave trade's ubiquity, but paving over sites has not erased them. The physical landscape bears witness to the scars of slavery, from the Manchester docks to the now-empty plinths on Monument Avenue. In 2011, the Slave Trail Commission began recognizing these important locations and unveiled the first markers for the Richmond Slave Trail, revealing another look at Virginia's trade in enslaved Africans.

Through my book I had the privilege of meeting Richmond civil rights leader and author of *Richmond's Unhealed History*, Rev. Benjamin Campbell. An Episcopal priest, Campbell's knowledge of Richmond's religious and racial history is encyclopedic, and he was instrumental in creating the Richmond Slave Trail. He always encourages me to consider questions about the intersection of religion, history, and racism. One question worthy of more examination in *The Richmond Theater Fire* is this: How did post-fire religious revivals affect slavery and racism in Richmond? The answer is not much. In the immediate aftermath of the fire, preachers railed against immorality in Virginia, but few included slavery as one of the city's besetting sins. It seems astonishing in retrospect. Moralists beheld a society trafficking in coffles of abused, handcuffed children, but decided Richmond earned its fire-smiting for fancy lace gowns and theatergoing. In short, the theater fire reoriented Virginia's religious life and moral values while leaving its commitment to human trafficking essentially unchanged. These are historical facts with lingering repercussions.

In 2010, Lauren F. Winner wrote *A Cheerful and Comfortable Faith: Anglican Religious Practice in the Elite Households of Eighteenth-Century Virginia*. There she notes that Virginia's Episcopal Church was "almost dead" in 1811, but that it revived in a "turnaround . . . so dramatic" that historians likened the transformation to a phoenix bursting from the ashes. The Richmond Theater fire, I believe, explains at least in part that 1811 turning point. Chapter eight of this

book centers on the subsequent religious enthusiasm Episcopalians brought
to the commonwealth. Sadly, this revival failed to address the sin of racism.
In fact, while the Episcopal Church established thriving missionary societies,
prayer meetings, and seminaries, it simultaneously promoted theological jus-
tifications for slavery. In 1847, when Virginia's Bishop William Meade argued
that brutalizing enslaved people was necessary and Biblical "correction," he
deservedly found himself in Frederick Douglass's rhetorical crosshairs. Enthusiastically defending this "peculiar institution" became an unholy obsession
for the Virginia diocese.

One might also ask if the post-fire boom in church construction included
majority black churches. Although white Richmond residents erected a spate
of church buildings in the 1820s and '30s, the General Assembly flatly denied
Richmond's black Christians when they petitioned for a "House of public
worship" in 1822. Systemic racism and a desire to stifle opportunities for autonomy and leadership are to blame for a paucity of black church construction
after the fire, not a lack of interest on the part of black believers. While evangelical denominations in the South like the Baptists and Presbyterians had, in
the late eighteenth century, taken stands against slavery, by 1812 they largely
supported Virginia's inhumane, caste-system status quo. Presbyterian John
Holt Rice's view was an outlier, but a complicated one. He declared slavery evil
but emancipation "impractical," and supported deportation to Africa through
the American Colonization Society. For this, Southern critics decried his
"liberalism." Rice eventually decided churches should not take public stands
against slavery as this would "injure religion." For the next century, as slavery
and Jim Crow reigned, Richmond's white churches remained conspicuously
silent and commonly complicit.

In recognition of the deep damage done, Rice's and Meade's denominations are now addressing racism and taking steps to collectively repent. After
the tragedy at Mother Emmanuel Church in Charleston and the election of
Bishop Michael Curry—the Episcopal Church in America's first black presiding bishop—in 2015, Episcopalians issued a resolution to work for racial
justice and address systemic racism and launched programs like "Becoming
Beloved Community." An audit followed in 2020, identifying internal systems
and structures that diminished the voices of people of color. Virginia Theological Seminary, founded by slaveholders, began distributing reparations in 2021.
As for the Presbyterians, Richmond's Union Theological Seminary published
a history of the seminary in 2016 "in an effort of reflection, repentance, and

renewal." Author William B. Sweetser Jr. acknowledged that Rice's successor in leadership at the seminary, George Baxter, led the charge in opposing the Presbyterian General Assembly's condemnation of slavery, and seminary leadership went on to support the Confederate cause. However, in 2020 Union released a statement proclaiming the seminary would "acknowledge and actively resist the systemic racism that is so toxic and destructive in our society, and in the history of our own institution" and would "work together to enact change." Frederick Law Olmsted described Virginians in 1860 as "people who have been dragged along in the grand march of the rest of the world, but who have had, for a long time and yet have, a disposition within themselves only to step backward." Maybe Olmsted is wrong; it looks as though the religious communities born out of the embers of the theater fire are taking steps forward.

Much gratitude to my editor Rand Dotson and the team at Louisiana State University Press for shepherding so many good books into the world and for seeing this paperback edition through. I'm also grateful to have a supportive writing community. Authors Sarah Hand, Angele McQuade, and Anne Blankman provided friendship and a sounding board over soup at the Virginia Museum of Fine Arts cafe. Collaborating with acclaimed novelist Rachel Beanland is a joy, as is having someone to gossip with about the long-forgotten personalities of Poe-era Richmond. I'm thrilled that her newest book is set during the Richmond Theater fire. Her unique ability to bring entire cities to life with scrupulous attention to detail will make her forthcoming novel on the Richmond Theater fire one to snatch up. I'm also grateful for groups like the Mid-Atlantic SCBWI chapter and the James River Writers who make writing a less solitary task.

Speaking of solitude, or the lack of it, ten years ago I completed this book with two diapered children underfoot (the reason why I thank nearly as many babysitters as archivists in my acknowledgments). One becomes efficient under those circumstances, but writing and research-related travel with young children remain challenging—a situation only exacerbated by the pandemic. It is my hope that the academy, the historical field, and the writing community will reimagine fellowships, funding, and conferences, developing creative ways to accommodate and support the work of women writers, no matter their life stage. We have so much to say.

APPENDIX

1811 RICHMOND THEATER FIRE VICTIM LIST

1. Alcock (*son of John Alcock*)
2. Anderson, Margaret* (*Margaretta*)
3. Bausman, Adeline* ("granddaughter of Joseph Jacobs")
4. Bosher, Mary (*Polly, Mrs. John,* "expired Sat. night")
5. Botts, Benjamin*
6. Botts, Jane Tyler* (*Jenny*)
7. Braxton, Anna F.* (*Mrs. Tayloe/Taylor Braxton*)
8. Brown, William* ("overwhelmed by the crowd")
9. Clay (*Claw, Clary*), Mary*
10. Convert, child*
11. Convert, Josephine*
12. Conyers, Sarah C.* (*Sally*)
13. Cook, Rebecca* ("wife of William Cook")
14. Cook, child* (*possibly also named Rebecca*)
15. Copland, Margaret*
16. Coutts (*Coutes*), Elvira* (*Elvin/a*)
17. Craig, Ann* ("daughter of Mrs. Adam Craig")
18. Davis (*David*), Mary*
19. Dixon, George* ("a youth")
20. Edmundson, James ("a free mulatto boy who expired afterwards")
21. Elliott, Judith*
22. Ferrill (*Ferril*), Robert* ("a mulatto boy")
23. Frazier (*Frayser*), Thomas* ("a youth")
24. Gallego, Mary*
25. Gatewood, Sally*
26. Gibbon, James* (*Lt.*)
27. Gibson, Eleanor Sanderson*
28. Girardin, child* (male)
29. Girardin (*Geradine*), Polly Cole* (*Mary*)

30. Graff (*Goff*), Fanny* ("a woman of colour")
31. Green, Ann Morton* (Nancy)
32. Greenhow, Mary Ann* (*Ann*)
33. Griffin, Patsy* (*Patsey*)
34. Gwathney (*Gwathmey*), Lucy*
35. Harvie, Edwin James* ("Esq. expired Sun. night")
36. Harvie, Julianna* (*Julia*)
37. Heron (*Herron*), Sarah*
38. Hunter, Arianna* (*Marian, Anania, Mariana*)
39. Jacobs, Eliza* (*Elizabeth*, "dau. of Joseph")
40. Jacobs, Joseph*
41. Jerrod (*Gerard*), Mrs.*
42. Johnson, Betsy* (*Betsey*, "a woman of colour, free")
43. Judah, Judith* ("Barack Judah's child")
44. Laforest (*La Forest*), Jane Cole Lipscombe*
45. Lecroix (*Lacroix*), Thomas*
46. Lesslie (*Leslie*), Ann* (*Mrs. John*)
47. Lipscombe, Margaret Booth ("niece of Mrs. LaForest")
48. Littlepage, Miss*
49. Marks (*Marx*), Zipporah* (*Cyprian, Zepparah*, "wife of Mordecai")
50. Marshall, Almarine*
51. Mayo, Louisa*
52. Moss, Mrs.*
53. Nelson, Maria*
54. Nuttal* (*Thomas*, "a carpenter")
55. Page, Elizabeth*
56. Page, Mary*
57. Patterson, Elizabeth* ("overwhelmed by crowd")
58. Patterson, Nancy* ("woman of colour supposed to have perished")
59. Philadelphia, (*Philadelphian*, "missing")
60. Pickett (*Pickit, Picket*), Mrs.*
61. Pleasant* ("a mulatto woman belonging to Mrs. William Rose")
62. Raphael (*Raphiel*), Charlotte* ("daughter of Soloman Raphael")
63. Rozier (*Rizi*), Jean Baptiste* (*John B.*)
64. Schaub (*Shaub, Schrub*), John*

65. Scott, Mary Love*
66. Smith, George William*
67. Southgate, William* ("son of Wright")
68. Stevenson, Elizabeth* (*Eliza*)
69. Trouin (*Tronin*), Cecilia*
70. Trouin (*Tronin*), Sophia*
71. Venable, Abraham (*Abram*) B.*
72. Wade, Jane* ("a young woman")
73. Waldon (*Walden*), James*
74. Wanton, Edward* ("a youth")
75. Welch, John* ("a stranger, nephew to Sir A. Pigott, late from England")
76. Whitlock (*Whitelocke*), Mary Gabriella* (*Mary, May*)
77. Wilson, Lucinda C.* (*Mrs. Thomas*)

Note: Over a dozen sources were examined to create this list, and spellings differed. The italicized variations provided here were found in less authoritative sources, and the notes in quotations were taken from the *Richmond Enquirer* (December 28 and 31, 1811; January 2 and 4, 1812) and the *Petersburg Intelligencer* (December 31, 1811). Names followed by an asterisk are those inscribed on the sides of the sarcophagus monument in the portico of Monumental Church. For more genealogical detail on the victims, see F. Claiborne Johnston, Jr.'s "A More Complete Record of Those Who Perished in the Richmond Theater Fire," available from the Library of Virginia. Considering the number of persons present in Richmond for the winter social season, it is likely that the fire claimed more than seventy-seven victims on the night of December 26, 1811. Many who do not appear in "official" death lists died of their fire-related injuries at later dates. The names listed here are those that have been captured in the historical record.

NOTES

PREFACE

1. William Smart to Ann Nixon, January 16, 1812, William Smart Papers, Library of Virginia.

PROLOGUE

1. All details in prologue are taken from Caroline Homassel Thornton, "Autobiography of Mrs. Caroline Homassel Thornton (1795–1875)," Albemarle County Historical Society Papers, 1945–46: 22–40.

CHAPTER ONE

1. F. Arant Maginnes, *Thomas Abthorpe Cooper: Father of the American Stage, 1775–1849* (Jefferson, NC: McFarland, 2004), 147.

2. "Baltimore, May 31," *Richmond Enquirer*, June 11, 1811.

3. Maginnes, *Thomas Abthorpe Cooper*, 150–51.

4. Geddeth Smith, *Thomas Abthorpe Cooper: America's Premier Tragedian* (Cranbury, NJ: Associated University Presses, 1996), 153.

5. William Dunlap, *Memoirs of the Life of George Frederick Cooke, Esquire, Late of the Theatre Royal, Covent Garden*, vol. 1 (New York: D. Longworth, 1813), 66. Also see Christopher M. S. Johns, "Theater and Theory: Thomas Sully's "George Frederick Cooke as Richard III," *Winterthur Portfolio* 18, no. 1 (Spring 1983): 27–38.

6. "The Southern Stage, Actors and Authors, Dramatic Literature: Part Three," the *Dramatic Mirror, and Literary Companion*, (May 7, 1842), 90.

7. William Dunlap, *History of the American Theatre*, vol. 2 (London: Richard Bentley, New Burlington Street, 1833), 297.

8. Susanne K. Sherman, "Thomas Wade West, Theatrical Impressario, 1790–1799," *William and Mary Quarterly* 9, no. 1 (January 1952): 23; Jeffrey Richard, "A British or an American Tar? Play, Player, and Spectator in Norfolk, 1797–1800," in *Drama, Theatre, and Identity in the American New Republic*, Cambridge Studies in American Theatre and Drama, No. 22 (New York: Cambridge University Press, 2005), 262–63.

9. Ibid.

10. Ibid., 10, 27. Obituary in *Virginia Argus*, August 2, 1799.

11. Susanne K. Sherman, *Comedies Useful: Southern Theatre History 1775–1812*, ed. Lucy B. Pilkington (Williamsburg, VA: Celest Press, 1998), 136.

12. Martin Staples Shockley, *The Richmond Stage, 1784–1812* (Charlottesville, VA: University Press of Virginia, 1977), 329–35.

13. Ibid., 337–38. Cast list can be found in Bryan Akers, ed., *Graphic Description of the Burning of the Richmond Theatre, December 26, 1811. Compiled from the Lips of Eye-witnesses* (Lynchburg, VA: News Book and Job Office Print, 1879), 11–12.

14. *Richmond Enquirer,* September 21, 1810; Agnes M. Bondurant, *Poe's Richmond,* reprinted by the Edgar Allan Poe Museum, September 1999 (Richmond, VA: Garrett & Massie, 1942), 128.

15. Shockley, *Richmond Stage,* 351. Also the *Richmond Enquirer,* December 21, 1811.

16. Susan Archer Weiss, "Reminiscences of Edgar Allan Poe," *The Independent* 57 (August 25, 1904): 443–48.

17. John P. Little, *History of Richmond* (Richmond, VA: Dietz, 1933), 118.

18. "First Theater Fire, Conflagration at Richmond, Va., in December, 1811," *Washington Post,* January 3, 1904.

19. Ibid.

20. Common Council Minutes regarding Theater Fire, December 28, 1811, vol. 3, 171; James Drinard Papers, Manuscripts, Virginia Historical Society, Richmond, VA; Agnes Evans Gish, *Virginia Taverns, Ordinaries and Coffee Houses* (Westminster, MD: Willow Bend Books, 2005), 193.

21. Catherine Allgor, *Parlor Politics: In Which the Ladies of Washington Help Build a City and a Government* (Charlottesville, VA: University Press of Virginia, 2002), 112.

22. Recollections of Mary Gibbon Carter in "Richmond Romance," *Richmond Dispatch,* April 16, 1899.

23. "Communication Describing the Fire at Richmond," *Mirror of Taste and Dramatic Censor* 4 (December 1811): 427.

24. Dolley Madison to Sally Coles Stevenson, December 15, 1812, UVA Rotunda, Dolley Madison Papers Digital Edition.

25. Arthur Singleton (Henry Knight, pseud.), *Letters from the South and West* (Boston: Richardson & Lord, J. H. A. Frost, printer, 1824), 59.

26. John Melish, *Travels through the United States of America, in the years 1806 & 1807, and 1809, 1810, & 1811; including an account of passages betwixt America and Britain, and travels through various parts of Britain, Ireland, & Canada. With corrections and improvements till 1815* (Philadelphia: Printed for the Author, 1818), 171.

27. Ibid., 160.

28. U.S. Census Bureau, 1800 and 1810 National Census for Richmond (City), Virginia. In 1810, the free population stood at 5,997 and the slave population at 3,738.

29. Samuel Mordecai, *Richmond in By-Gone Days,* republished from the second edition of 1860 (Richmond, VA: Dietz, 1946), 275–76.

30. Susan Dunn, *Dominion of Memories: Jefferson, Madison and the Decline of Virginia* (New York: Basic Books, 2007), 89.

31. Robert Hunter, Jr., from an uncited passage in Virginius Dabney, *Richmond: The Story of a City* (New York: Doubleday, 1976), 34.

32. Dabney, *Richmond,* 32.

33. *Richmond Enquirer,* December 28, 1812.

34. Dabney, *Richmond,* 31.

35. "Main Street, Richmond, Virginia," *Gleason's Pictorial Drawing-Room Companion,* April 23, 1853, 264.

36. Marie Tyler-McGraw and Gregg D. Kimball, *In Bondage and Freedom: Antebellum Black Life in Richmond, Virginia* (Chapel Hill: University of North Carolina Press, for the Valentine Museum of the Life & History of Richmond, 1988), 12.

37. Merrill D. Peterson, *Thomas Jefferson and the New Nation: A Biography* (New York: Oxford University Press, 1970), 981–83. There is a record of John & Joseph Boyce, bookbinders and stationers in Richmond at this time in the *Richmond Enquirer,* January 11, 1812.

38. Melish, *Travels,* 175.

39. Dunn, *Dominion of Memories,* 72.

40. Ibid., and Singleton, *Letters from the South,* 67.

41. Blair in Philip B. Price, *The Life of the Reverend John Holt Rice, D.D.,* Historical Transcripts, No. 1 (Richmond: Library of Union Theological Seminary in Virginia, 1963), 56, and Bondurant, *Poe's Richmond,* 81.

42. Cynthia A. Kierner, "'The Dark and Dense Cloud Perpetually Lowering over Us': Gender and the Decline of the Gentry in Postrevolutionary Virginia," *Journal of the Early Republic* 20, no. 2 (Summer 2000): 213; Bondurant, *Poe's Richmond,* 86.

43. Dabney, *Richmond,* 78.

44. Thornton, "Autobiography," 31.

45. Fillmore Norfleet, *Saint-Memin in Virginia: Portraits and Biographies* (Richmond: Dietz, 1942), 166.

46. *Calamity at Richmond: Being a Narrative of the Affecting Circumstances Attending the Awful Conflagration of the Theatre, in the City of Richmond, on the Night of Thursday, the 26th of December, 1811* (Philadelphia: John F. Watson, 1812), 28; Norfleet, *Saint-Memin,* 166.

47. Marie Tyler-McGraw. *At the Falls: Richmond, Virginia, and Its People* (Chapel Hill: University of North Carolina Press, for the Valentine Museum of the Life & History of Richmond, 1994), 84.

48. Bernard J. Henley, "Schooldays in Richmond, 1810–1811: A Student's Memoir," *Richmond Literature and History Quarterly,* Fall 1978, 42–43; Thornton, "Autobiography," 31.

49. *Richmond Enquirer,* August 28, 1810.

50. Thornton, "Autobiography," 31.

51. Ibid., 28–29. Company members regularly found extra projects like teaching or writing to fill their time and increase their income (Sherman, *Comedies Useful,* 161).

52. Marie Tyler-McGraw, *An African Republic: Black and White Virginians in the making of Liberia* (Chapel Hill: University of North Carolina Press, 2007), 67–68.

53. Weld, *Travels,* 1:190.

54. Singleton, *Letters from the South,* 65.

55. Weld, *Travels,* 1:191.

56. Mordecai, *Richmond,* 265–66.

57. Richmond made 1,073 swords out of the state total of 1,081. Out of the 5,188 guns manufactured in Virginia, Richmond City made 3,468 ("A Series of Tables of Several Branches of American Manufacturers of Every County in the Union so far as they are returned in the reports of the Marshals, and of the secretaries and of their respective assistants, in the autumn of the year 1810: Together with returns of certain doubtful Goods, Productions of the Soil and agricultural stock, so far as they have been received," U.S. Census Bureau, Census of Population and Housing, 1810, Richmond, Virginia, 89–114).

58. Jeremiah Jeter, *The Recollections of a Long Life* (Richmond, VA: Religious Herald Co., 1891), 15.

59. Weld, *Travels*, 1:192–93.

60. Ibid.

61. Jeter, *Recollections*, 14.

62. Singleton, *Letters from the South*, 71.

63. William A. R. Goodwin, "The Right Reverend Richard Channing Moore, D.D. Second Bishop of Virginia and The Beginnings of the Theological Seminary in Virginia: An Address Delivered at the Alumni Meeting of the Virginia Theological Seminary on June 4th, 1914" (Published by Order of the Alumni Association, 1914), 12.

64. Norfleet, *Saint-Memin*, 46; Dabney, *Richmond*, 85–87.

65. Philip Vickers Fithian, *Journal and Letters, 1767–1774*, ed. John Rogers Williams (Princeton, NJ: University Library, 1900), 235.

66. Sherman, "Thomas Wade West," 13.

67. James Drinard Papers, Manuscripts, Virginia Historical Society.

68. Margaret Pearson Mickler, "The Monumental Church," MA Thesis, University of Virginia, 1980, 8.

69. Sherman, "Thomas Wade West," 14.

70. Ibid., 26.

71. Mickler, "Monumental," 9.

72. 1816 map (copied from an 1804 map), James Drinard Papers, Manuscripts, Virginia Historical Society. Margaretta West , then the proprietress of the Norfolk Theatre, had died on June 6, 1810, in Norfolk.

73. "Report of the Committee of Investigation," *Richmond Enquirer*, December 31, 1811.

74. Ibid.

75. Ibid.

76. Dunlap, *A History of the American Theater*, 2:298–99; Akers, *Graphic Description of the Burning of the Richmond Theatre*, 3.

77. Edward A. Wyatt, "Three Petersburg Theatres," *William and Mary College Quarterly Historical Magazine*, 2nd ser., vol. 21, no. 2 (April 1941): 91.

78. Samuel Hughes to Capt. John Hughes, December 29, 1811, Personal Papers Collection, Archives and Manuscripts, Library of Virginia.

79. *Inventory of the Church Archives of Virginia: Negro Baptist Churches in Richmond*. Historical Records Survey, Work Projects Administration (Richmond, VA: Historical Records Survey of Virginia, June 1940), iv; Tyler-McGraw and Kimball, *In Bondage and Freedom*, 37; Jeter, *Recollections*, 209–11.

80. Philip Barrett, *Gilbert Hunt, the City Blacksmith* (Richmond: James Woodhouse, 1859), 7.

81. *Richmond Enquirer*, October 9, 1810.

82. "Extract of a Letter from a sufferer in the late dreadful calamity at Richmond," *Petersburg Intelligencer*, January 3, 1812.

83. Patricia C. Click, *The Spirit of the Times: Amusements in Nineteenth-Century Baltimore, Norfolk, and Richmond* (Charlottesville, VA: University Press of Virginia, 1989), 40.

84. Kathryn Fuller-Seeley, *Celebrate Richmond Theater* (Richmond: Dietz, 2002), prologue.

85. Monroe served as governor of Virginia from 1799 to1802 and as an interim acting governor from January 19, 1811, through April 3, 1811.

86. William Henry Foote, *Sketches of Virginia, Historical and Biographical,* 2nd series (Philadelphia: J. B. Lippincott, 1855), 321.

87. Little, *History of Richmond,* 122.

88. Click, *Spirit of the Times,* 35. First names in Bondurant, *Poe's Richmond,* 4.

89. *Calamity at Richmond,* preface, ii.

90. George Wythe Munford, "The Two Parsons," from *The Two Parsons; Cupid's Sports; The Dream; and The Jewels of Virginia* (Richmond: J. D. K. Sleight, 1884), 445.

91. "For the Enquirer," *Richmond Enquirer,* January 21, 1812.

92. Norfleet, *Saint-Memin,* 45.

93. Ibid., 157.

94. "Extract of a Letter from a sufferer in the late dreadful calamity at Richmond," *Petersburg Intelligencer,* January 3, 1812.

95. James K. Sanford, ed., *Richmond, Her Triumphs, Tragedies & Growth* (RichmondVA: Produced and distributed by Metropolitan Richmond Chamber of Commerce, 1975), 73. In 1810, the free population stood at 5,997 and the slave population at 3,738 (U.S. Census Bureau, 1800 and 1810 National Census for Richmond [City], Virginia).

96. "Report of the Committee of Investigation," *Richmond Enquirer,* December 31, 1811.

97. *Calamity at Richmond,* 23.

98. Library of Congress records have correspondence between Gibbon and all of the presidents named here.

99. Gibbon's presence on the *Philadelphia* and trials in Tripoli are noted in the *Enquirer* on December 31, 1811. However, U.S. Navy records from this period are incomplete, and a crew muster roll for the *Philadelphia* in 1803 is not extant in the U.S. Naval History and Heritage records nor in National Archives records.

100. Sanford, *Richmond Triumphs,* 75.

101. Richmond Theater Fire File, Valentine Richmond History Center, Richmond, VA; see also "Richmond Romance," *Richmond Dispatch,* April 16, 1899.

102. Dabney, *Richmond,* 135.

103. Click, *Spirit of the Times,* 35.

104. Singleton, *Letters from the South,* 71–72; Maginnes, *Thomas Abthorpe Cooper,* 75.

105. Margaretta West, the theater manager who at one time ran the Richmond Theater, advised patrons to surround themselves with their friends in order to keep their distance from thieves and prostitutes in attendance (Sherman, *Comedies Useful,* 163).

106. Foote, *Sketches of Virginia,* 321.

107. Singleton, *Letters from the South,* 71–72.

108. Robert Gamble, Jr., to James Breckinridge, December 27, 1811, Manuscripts, Breckinridge family papers, 1740-1902, Virginia Historical Society, Richmond, VA.

109. *Richmond Times-Dispatch,* January 4, 1938.

110. Smith, *Definer of a Nation,* 7, 255.

111. "He Looked Like This: John Marshall," *Richmond Literature and History Quarterly* 2, no.

1 (Fall 1979): 45; C.M.S. "The Home Life of Chief Justice Marshall." *William and Mary Quarterly*, 2nd ser., vol. 12 (January 1932): 68.

112. C.M.S., "Home Life," 68.

113. Smith, *Definer of a Nation*, 98.

114. Sedgwick to Rufus King, May 11, 1800, in Charles R. King, ed., *Life and Correspondence of Rufus King*, 236–38, vol. 3 (New York: G. P. Putnam's Sons, 1896).

115. C.M.S., "Home Life," 68.

116. Frances Norton Mason, *My Dearest Polly: Letters of Chief Justice John Marshall to His Wife, with Their Background, Political and Domestic, 1779–1831* (Richmond, VA: Garrett & Massie, 1961), 209; see also Smith, *Definer of a Nation*, 395.

117. For more about Copland, see Mordecai, *Richmond*, 123; E. Lee Shepard, "Sketches of the Old Richmond Bar: Charles Copland," *Richmond Literature and History Quarterly* 3, no. 4 (n.d.): 32.

118. Shepard, "Sketches: Copland," 30.

119. Charles Copland, *Diary of Charles Copland*, December 26, 1811, Archives and Manuscripts. Library of Virginia.

120. Mary Dudley Chappelmann, "History of the Fire and Police Departments of Richmond, Virginia" (Richmond, Virginia: Firemans' Mutual Aid Association and Police Benevolent Association, 1952), 4.

121. "Extract of a Letter from a sufferer in the late dreadful calamity at Richmond," *Petersburg Intelligencer*, January 3, 1812.

122. Shockley, *Richmond Stage*, 391, appendix II; Pilkinton, *Theater in Norfolk, Virginia, 1788–1812*, PhD diss., 1993 (Ann Arbor, MI: UMI Dissertation Services, University of Michigan), 432, 557. Sherman, *Comedies Useful*, 223–26.

123. Names in Norfleet, *Saint-Memin*, 167.

124. "Extract of a Letter from a sufferer in the late dreadful calamity at Richmond," *Petersburg Intelligencer*, January 3, 1812.

125. Ibid. Girardin's relationship to Doyle mentioned in Munford, "The Two Parsons," 444.

126. Usually nameless, the stagehand is identified in one source the as "Yohe," a carpenter (Akers, *Graphic Description of the Burning of the Richmond Theatre*, 10–11).

127. Shockley, *Richmond Stage*, 407.

128. Norfleet, *Saint-Memin*, 168–69. Mary Ann's sister Fanny Chisman Wills was married to James Cole, Robert Greenhow's business partner. Cole was also the brother of Mrs. Polly Girardin, Louis Girardin's wife. Store location from advertisement in the *Richmond Enquirer*, February 22, 1811, and Norfleet, *Saint-Memin*, 39.

129. "The St. Memin Collection of Portraits," *William and Mary College Quarterly Historical Magazine* 9, no. 3 (January 1901): 145.

130. All descriptions from Robert Greenhow to John T. Mason, February 7, 1812, quoted in Norfleet, *Saint-Memin*, 168–69.

131. *Richmond American Standard*, Special Issue, Friday, December 27, 1811.

132. "Report of the Committee of Investigation," *Richmond Enquirer*, December 31, 1811.

133. Ibid.

134. Ibid.

135. Facts are drawn from the accounts of Thomson F. Mason, G. Huntington Bacchus, and Jedediah Allen ("Statements," *Richmond Enquirer*, January 2, 1812).

136. Dabney, *Richmond*, 119.

CHAPTER TWO

1. Thornton, "Autobiography," 35.

2. John Lynch, "Statements," *Richmond Enquirer*, January 2, 1812; Norfleet, *Saint-Memin*, 157.

3. Mason, *My Dearest Polly*, 209.

4. G. Huntington Bacchus, "Statements," *Richmond Enquirer*, January 2, 1812.

5. Ibid.

6. "Report of the Committee of Investigation," *Richmond Enquirer*, December 31, 1811.

7. Samuel Hughes to Capt. John Hughes, December 29, 1811, Personal Papers Collection, Archives and Manuscripts, Library of Virginia.

8. Notes on Hughes from the Library of Virginia's Richmond Theater fire research reference page.

9. Jedediah Allen, "Statements," *Richmond Enquirer*, January 2, 1812.

10. Thomson F. Mason, "Statements," *Richmond Enquirer*, January 2, 1812.

11. "Domestic," *Richmond Enquirer*, January 11, 1812.

12. Edmund Pendleton, Jr., "Statements," *Richmond Enquirer*, January 2, 1812.

13. William Maxwell, *A Memoir of the Rev. John H. Rice, D.D.* (Richmond, VA: R. I. Smith, 1835), 72–73.

14. "Terrible Recollections," *Baltimorean*, November 16, 1872.

15. Ibid.

16. G. Huntington Bacchus, "Statements," *Richmond Enquirer*, January 2, 1812.

17. Description of smoke found in "Extract of a Letter from a sufferer in the late dreadful calamity at Richmond," *Petersburg Intelligencer*, January 3, 1812.

18. M. W. Hancock, "Statements," *Richmond Enquirer*, January 2, 1812; Akers, *Graphic Description of the Burning of the Richmond Theatre*, 4.

19. John Lynch, "Statements," *Richmond Enquirer*, January 2, 1812.

20. Thomson F. Mason, "Statements," *Richmond Enquirer*, January 2, 1812.

21. J. G. Jackson and M.W. Hancock, "Statements," *Richmond Enquirer*, January 2, 1812.

22. "Narrative," *Richmond Enquirer*, December 31, 1811.

23. *Narrative & Report of the Causes and Circumstances of the Deplorable Conflagration at Richmond, Virginia, from Letters and Authentic Documents* (Richmond: Shaw & Shoemaker, 1812), 23.

24. M. W. Hancock, "Statements," *Richmond Enquirer*, January 2, 1812.

25. Thomson F. Mason, "Statements," *Richmond Enquirer*, January 2, 1812.

26. Robert Greenhow, Sr., to John T. Mason, February 7, 1812, in Norfleet, *Saint Memin*, 168–69.

27. Ibid.

28. John Hastings Marks to Reuben Lewis, January 22, 1812, Small Special Collections Library, University of Virginia. Dabney's obituary in *Richmond Enquirer*, November 25, 1825.

29. Robert Greenhow, Sr., to John T. Mason, February 7, 1812, in Norfleet, *Saint Memin*, 168–69.

30. Jedediah Allen, "Statements," *Richmond Enquirer*, January 2, 1812.

31. "Extract of a Letter from a sufferer in the late dreadful calamity at Richmond," *Petersburg Intelligencer*, January 3, 1812.

32. Ibid.

33. Ibid., and Joseph Wheelan, *Jefferson's Vendetta: The Pursuit of Aaron Burr and the Judiciary* (New York: Carroll & Graf, 2005), 103.

34. "Overwhelming Calamity," *Richmond Enquirer*, December 28, 1811.

35. Extract of a Letter to the Editors of the Mercantile Advertiser, dated Richmond, December 27, 1811, quoted in *Narrative & Report*, 45.

36. Ibid., 5.

37. Thomson F. Mason, "Statements," *Richmond Enquirer*, January 2, 1812.

38. "Report of the Committee of Investigation," *Richmond Enquirer*, December 31, 1811.

39. M. W. Hancock, "Statements," *Richmond Enquirer*, January 2, 1812.

40. Ibid.

41. John Lynch, "Statements," *Richmond Enquirer*, January 2, 1812.

42. Street width of 120 feet on H and 69 on Twelfth recorded on 1816 map (copied from an 1804 map), James Drinard Papers, Manuscripts, Virginia Historical Society.

43. *Richmond American Standard*, Special Issue, Friday, December 27, 1811.

44. Ibid.

45. Edmund Pendleton, Jr. "Statements," *Richmond Enquirer*, January 2, 1812.

46. John Coalter to St. George Tucker and John Prentis, December 29, 1811, Tucker Coleman Papers, Manuscripts and Rare Books Department, Swem Library, College of William and Mary.

47. Thornton, "Autobiography," 35.

48. Barrett, *City Blacksmith*, 29.

49. Dabney, *Richmond*, 98; Mordecai, *Richmond*, 356.

50. "Terrible Recollections," *Baltimorean*, November 16, 1872.

51. Barrett, *City Blacksmith*, 49.

52. Mordecai, *Richmond*, 216.

53. "Obituary," *Albion, A Journal of News, Politics, and Literature*, January 17, 1846, 33.

54. "Extract of a Letter from a sufferer in the late dreadful calamity at Richmond," *Petersburg Intelligencer*, January 3, 1812.

55. Quoted in Hugh A. Garland, *The Life of John Randolph of Roanoke*, 9th ed. (New York: D. Appleton, 1854), 295.

56. "Disturbances in Virginia," *Hagers-Town (PA) Gazette*, July 10, 1810.

57. Lawyer Charles Copland, who lost his daughter in the theater fire, defended Gabriel in a 1799 trial over a fight with a former white overseer named Absalom Johnson. Gabriel reportedly bit off "a considerable part" of Johnson's left ear (Philip Schwartz, *Twice Condemned: Slaves and the Criminal Laws of Virginia, 1705–1865* [Union, NJ: Lawbook Exchange, Ltd., 1998], 257, 266–67 footnote).

58. Quoted in Dabney, *Richmond*, 57.

59. Chappelmann, *History of Fire and Police*, 4.

60. Dabney, *Richmond*, 59.

61. "Disturbances in Virginia," *Hagers-Town (PA) Gazette*, July 10, 1810.

62. Thomas R. Joynes, to Levin S. Joynes, December 27, 1811, *Virginia Magazine of History and Biography* 51, no. 3 (July 1943): 298.

63. "It was determined by two magistrates that she 'was not advised to do it by any person,' and was not participating in a greater conspiracy as they may have feared [Domestic Occurrences, Richmond, December 23]," *Federal Gazette and Philadelphia Evening Post*, December 31, 1790.

64. Schwartz, *Twice Condemned*, 266.

65. Joynes to Joynes, December 27, 1811, *Virginia Magazine of History and Biography*.

66. "Overwhelming Calamity," *Richmond Enquirer*, December 28, 1811.

67. Munford, "The Two Parsons," 445.

68. J. G. Jackson, "Statements," *Richmond Enquirer*, January 2, 1812.

69. G. Tucker, "Statements," *Richmond Enquirer*, January 2, 1812.

70. Chappelmann, *History of Fire and Police*, 6.

71. Robert Alonzo Brock, "*Historical Sketch: The Richmond, Virginia fire department, its organization and equipment: with an account of its precursors form the initial organization "effective friendship" in 1816* (Richmond: Published under the auspices of the Firemen's Relief Assn., 1894), 23.

72. Mark Tebeau, *Eating Smoke: Fire* in Urban America, *1800–1950* (Baltimore: Johns Hopkins University Press, 2003), 28

73. Akers, *Graphic Description of the Burning of the Richmond Theatre*, 10.

74. Copland lost his first wife, Becky Nicholson of Williamsburg, in 1800 when she was only thirty-three; she left him with nine children (*Virginia Argus*, August 5, 1800). He married his second wife, Heningham Carrington Bernard in 1808.

75. Charles Copland, *Diary of Charles Copland*, December 26, 1811, Archives and Manuscripts. Library of Virginia.

76. Ibid.

77. Ibid.

78. D. Doyle, "Statements," *Richmond Enquirer*, January 2, 1812.

79. "Extract of a Letter from a sufferer in the late dreadful calamity at Richmond," *Petersburg Intelligencer*, January 3, 1812. Henry Heth's first name in Norfleet, *Saint-Memin*, 46.

80. "Extract of a Letter from a sufferer in the late dreadful calamity at Richmond," *Petersburg Intelligencer*, January 3, 1812; Norfleet, *Saint-Memin*, 166–67.

81. "Report of the Committee of Investigation," *Richmond Enquirer*, December 31, 1811.

82. "Extract of a Letter from a sufferer in the late dreadful calamity at Richmond," *Petersburg Intelligencer*, January 3, 1812.

83. *Narrative & Report*, 7.

84. Maxwell, *Memoir of Rice*, 72.

85. Coalter to Tucker and Prentis, December 29, 1811, Tucker-Coleman Papers, Manuscripts and Rare Books Department, Swem Library, College of William and Mary.

86. Ibid.

87. *Narrative & Report*, 50.

88. Quoted from Thomas Rutherfoord's autobiography in Munford, "The Two Parsons," 448–49. Thomas Wilson served four terms as mayor of Richmond, 1812–13, 1814–15, 1816–17, and 1818. A typical term of service during those years was only a year in duration.

89. *Narrative & Report*, 13. Description of spectators at urban fires in George P. Little, *The Fireman's Own Book: Containing Accounts of Fires throughout the United States, as Well as other Countries* (Boston: 1860), 16.

90. December 29, 1811, John Durbarrow Blair Sermons in the John Durbarrow Blair Papers, 1781–1823, 2nd ser. From the Robert Alonzo Brock Collection at the Huntington Library, San Marino, California. Copy in Manuscripts, Library of Virginia.

91. Placide escaped without his own watch, boots, and great coat, according to one source, which also reported that his daughter Eliza was briefly feared dead, but he later discovered her at home in their apartment (*Richmond Enquirer*, January 11, 1812, and "Supplementary Particulars of the Fire at Richmond," *Mirror of Taste and Dramatic Censor* 4 [December 1811]: 494; see also Akers, *Graphic Description of the Burning of the Richmond Theatre*, 5, 8).

92. Akers, *Graphic Description of the Burning of the Richmond Theatre*, 6. The orchestra this season included Mr. Gallagher, clarinet; John La Taste, flute, violin, dancer; Lewis Boucherie on piano; Mr. Ribes on violin; as well as Misters Adde and Grain (Pilkinton, *Theatre in Norfolk, Virginia*, 436).

93. Quoted from Thomas Rutherfoord's autobiography in Munford, "The Two Parsons," 448–49. Once taken to neighboring homes, some of the injured stayed for long periods of time ("Terrible Recollections," *Baltimorean*, November 16, 1872; see also Akers, *Graphic Description of the Burning of the Richmond Theatre*, 4).

94. "Extract of a Letter from a sufferer in the late dreadful calamity at Richmond," *Petersburg Intelligencer*, January 3, 1812.

95. *Narrative & Report*, 45.

96. "Communication Describing the Fire at Richmond," *Mirror of Taste and Dramatic Censor* 4 (December 1811): 430.

97. Thomas Wilson's wife died when she remained in her seat and refused to join the crowds ("Conclusion," *Richmond Enquirer*, January 2, 1812).

98. Mordecai, *Richmond*, 214–15.

99. Ibid., 215.

100. Barrett, *City Blacksmith*, 29.

101. A John Holt Rice biographer suggests it was only six or seven minutes before the fire had entirely consumed the building (Maxwell, *Memoir of Rice*, 73).

102. Thornton, "Autobiography," 36.

103. Ann Tuke Alexander, *Remarks on the Theatre, and on the Late Fire at Richmond, in Virginia* (York, Eng.: T. Wilson & Son, 1812), "Casualties," 38.

104. Mordecai, *Richmond*, 59.

105. Tuke Alexander, *Remarks on the Theatre*, "Casualties," 38.

106. "Terrible Recollections," *Baltimorean*, November 16, 1872.

107. Ibid.

108. Ibid.

109. Dunlap, *History of the American Theatre*, 2:301.

110. Quoted in *Calamity at Richmond*, 29.

111. Dunlap, *History of the American Theatre*, 2:300.

112. Akers, *Graphic Description of the Burning of the Richmond Theatre*, 8.

113. Marion Harland, "Judith: A Chronicle of Old Virginia." *The Continent; an Illustrated Weekly Magazine*, September 5, 1883, 299.

114. Tuke Alexander, *Remarks on the Theater*, "Casualties," 38.

115. "Extract of a Letter from a sufferer in the late dreadful calamity at Richmond," *Petersburg Intelligencer*, January 3, 1812.

116. Robert Greenhow to John T. Mason, February 7, 1812, quoted in Norfleet, *Saint-Memin*, 168–69.

117. Munford, "The Two Parsons," 449.

118. Charles Copland, *Diary*.

119. Jeter, *Recollections*, 214.

CHAPTER THREE

1. Thomas R. Joynes to Levin S. Joynes, December 27, 1811, in *Virginia Magazine of History and Biography* 51, no.3 (July 1943): 298.

2. Munford, "The Two Parsons," 447.

3. John Coalter to St. George Tucker and John Prentis, December 19, 1811, Tucker-Coleman Papers.

4. Little, *History of Richmond*, 126.

5. *Narrative & Report*, 4.

6. Akers, *Graphic Description of the Burning of the Richmond Theatre*, 7.

7. "Common Council of the City of Richmond Ordinance, passed at 11 o'clock, December 27th, 1811," *Richmond Enquirer*, December 28, 1811.

8. "Domestic," *Richmond Enquirer*, January 11, 1812.

9. Ibid.

10. "Extract of a Letter from a Gentleman in Richmond to a Friend in Boston," *Rhode-Island American, and General Advertiser*, January 7, 1812.

11. Chater & Livermore charred brass watch face in the collections of the Virginia Historical Society.

12. *Richmond Enquirer*, January 9, 1812; Akers, *Graphic Description of the Burning of the Richmond Theatre*, 7.

13. Little, *History of Richmond*, 124.

14. Barrett, *City Blacksmith*, 31.

15. Ibid. Louisa Mayo obituary in *Richmond Enquirer*, January 2, 1812.

16. Barrett, *City Blacksmith*, 29.

17. Janet Duitsman Cornelius, *"When I Can Read My Title Clear": Literacy, Slavery, and Religion in the Antebellum South* (Columbia: University of South Carolina Press, 1991), 77; Singleton, *Letters from the South*, 69.

18. Cornelius, *"When I Can Read My Title,"* 2.

19. Virginia's state anti-literacy statutes found in the appendix of Heather Andrea Williams, *Self-taught: African American Education in Slavery and Freedom* (Chapel Hill: University of North Carolina Press, 2005), 208–11. Janet Cornelius notes that few were ever prosecuted for violating these laws, and that slave owners were not expressly prohibited from teaching their own slaves to read (*"When I Can Read My Title Clear,"* 33–34).

20. *Richmond Enquirer*, December 30, 1811.

21. Rev. John Blair, Sermon, December 29, 1811 (John Durbarrow Blair Papers, Archives and Manuscripts, Library of Virginia).

22. *Calamity at Richmond,* 46–47.

23. Little, *History of Richmond,* 125.

24. Benjamin Rush, *The Autobiography of Benjamin Rush,* ed. George W. Corner (Princeton, NJ: Pub. for the American Philosophical Society by Princeton University Press, 1948), 298.

25. Jeter, *Recollections,* 214.

26. "Narrative," *Richmond Enquirer,* December 31, 1811.

27. Norfleet, *Saint-Memin,* 165.

28. Coalter to Tucker and Prentis, December 29, 1811, Tucker-Coleman Papers.

29. Henry St. George Tucker to St. George Tucker, January 20, 1812, Manuscripts and Archives, Library of Virginia.

30. Robert Gamble, Jr., to James Breckinridge, December 27, 1811 ("Friday night 2 o clock"), Breckinridge Family Papers, Manuscripts and Archives, Library of Virginia.

31. Robert Gamble, Jr. to James Breckinridge, 27 December 1811 [time not given], Breckenridge Family Papers, Manuscripts and Archives, Library of Virginia.

32. Philip Barraud to St. George Tucker, December 31, 1811, Barraud Family Papers, 1779–1904, Manuscripts and Rare Books Department, Swem Library, College of William and Mary.

33. "Historical and Genealogical Notes," *William and Mary Quarterly* 23, no. 1 (July 1914): 70.

34. Leroy Anderson's occupation listed in Sarah C. Watts Papers, Manuscripts and Rare Books Department, Swem Library, College of William and Mary.

35. "Domestic," *Richmond Enquirer,* January 11, 1812.

36. Ibid.

37. "To the Editor of the Lynchburg Star," *Richmond Enquirer,* January 30, 1812.

38. Postscript in Coalter to Tucker and Prentis, December 2, 1811, Tucker-Coleman Papers.

39. William Black to James Brown, January 16, 1812, James Brown Letters, Archives and Manuscripts, Library of Virginia.

40. William Smart, Gloucester, Virginia, to Ann Nixon, London, England, January 16, 1812, William Smart Papers, Archives and Manuscripts, Library of Virginia, Richmond, Virginia. Biographical details from William Smart's unpublished "The Life of William Smart Written and Dictated by Himself," William Smart Papers.

41. Robert Gamble, Jr., to James Breckinridge, December 27, 1811, Breckinridge Family Papers.

42. *Narrative & Report,* 4.

43. "A List of Dead and Missing," *Richmond Enquirer,* December 28, 1811.

44. *Calamity at Richmond,* 26; "Extract of a letter from Richmond to a gentleman in Boston," Springfield, MA *Hampshire Federalist,* January 9, 1812.

45. William Brown to James Brown, July 28, 1809, James Brown Letters, Archives and Manuscripts, Library of Virginia.

46. "Communication," *Richmond Enquirer,* January 18, 1812.

47. Found in Tuke Alexander, *Remarks on the Theatre,* "Narrative," 10.

48. Susan Bowdoin to Robert Wash, Esq., May 11, 1812, Special Collections, Colonial Williamsburg Rockefeller Library.

49. Published January 12, 1812. An original 3x5-inch book with wooden cover and leather on the spine can be found at the Valentine Richmond History Center, Richmond, VA.

50. (No title), *The Cynick*, December 12, 1811 (original copy backdated two weeks prior to the fire), 202.

51. *Richmond Enquirer*, January 14, 1812.

52. Little, *History of Richmond*, 124.

53. "Richmond Theatre," *Massachusetts Baptist Missionary Magazine*, March 1812, 147.

54. The letterpress reads: "The Burning of the Theatre in Richmond, Virginia on the night of 26th December 1811, / By which awful Calamity upwards of ONE HUNDRED of its most valuable Citizens suddenly lost their lives, and many others, were much injured. Published Feb. 25th 1812 by B. Tanner No. 74 South 8th St. Philadelphia."

55. M. W. Hancock, "Statements," *Richmond Enquirer*, January 2, 1812.

56. G. Huntington Bacchus, "Statements," *Richmond Enquirer*, January 2, 1812.

57. Tuke Alexander, *Remarks on the Theatre*, "Casualties," 38.

58. Ibid.

59. "Statements," *Richmond Enquirer*, January 2, 1812.

60. "Memorable Disasters," *Richmond Enquirer*, January 11, 1812.

61. Ibid.

62. The two exceptions were accounts by men who were outside the theater when the fire began.

63. "Statements," *Richmond Enquirer*, January 2, 1812.

64. Taken from "A letter from a friend of the Editor of the *Petersburg Intelligencer*, who had lost his venerable mother in the conflagration at Richmond" (*Calamity at Richmond, 28–29*).

65. "Narrative," *Richmond Enquirer*, December, 31 1811.

66. Charles Copland, *Diary of Charles Copland*, December 26, 1811, Archives and Manuscripts. Library of Virginia.

67. "Statements," *Richmond Enquirer*, January 2, 1812.

68. Barrett, *City Blacksmith*, 23.

69. Copland, *Diary*, December 26, 1811.

70. "Statements," *Richmond Enquirer*, January 2, 1812.

71. *Richmond Enquirer*, July 12, 1811.

72. *Richmond Enquirer*, February 8, 1812.

73. "Overwhelming Calamity," *Richmond Enquirer*, December 28, 1811.

74. Anonymous, "Richmond and Its Fire Department(s)," *Richmond Literature and History Quarterly* 2, no. 2 (Fall 1979), 38.

75. Others on the list specify "free" after "woman of colour" so it can be assumed Nancy was enslaved.

76. "Anniversary of a Holocaust," *Washington Post*, December 26, 1894.

77. Robert Gamble, Jr., to James Breckinridge, December 27, 1811 ("Friday night 2 o clock"), Breckinridge Family Papers.

78. "Great Fire Disasters of the Past," *Washington Post*, March 5, 1908.

79. Margaret Hindle Hazen and Robert M. Hazen, *Keepers of the Flame: The Role of Fire in American Culture 1775–1925* (Princeton, NJ: Princeton University Press, 1992), 66.

80. "Burning of Theatres," *New York Observer and Chronicle,* September 14, 1854, 1.

81. "For the Enquirer," *Richmond Enquirer,* January 25, 1812.

82. *Richmond Enquirer,* December 27, 1811; John Coalter to St. George Tucker, December 29, 1811, Tucker-Coleman Papers.

83. Both the Executive Council Report and the Legislative Report are found in the *Richmond Enquirer,* January 4, 1812.

84. Dunn, *Dominion of Memories,* 151.

85. "For the Enquirer," *Richmond Enquirer,* January 25, 1811.

86. George William Smith, Executive Papers, December 27, 1811, Archives and Manuscripts, Library of Virginia.

87. W. A. Christian, *Richmond: Her Past and Present* (Richmond, VA: L. H. Jenkins, 1912), 76.

88. *Virginia Argus,* January 6, 1812; Shockley, *Richmond Stage,* 374. See also *Richmond Enquirer,* January 4, 1812.

89. *Richmond Enquirer,* January 4, 1812.

90. Fisher, *History of the Monumental Church,* 9–10.

91. "Report of the Committee of Investigation," *Richmond Enquirer,* December 31, 1811.

92. *Richmond Enquirer,* January 11, 1812.

93. "Richmond, October 2. FIRE," *Federal Republican & Commercial Gazette,* (Baltimore, MD) October 6, 1810.

94. "Richmond, May 22," *Poulson's American Daily Advertiser,* (Philadelphia, PA)May 28, 1810.

95. "Report of the Committee of Investigation," *Richmond Enquirer,* December 31, 1811.

96. Ibid.

97. Little, *History of Richmond,* 121.

98. "To the Citizens of Richmond," *Richmond Enquirer,* December 31, 1811.

99. Maginnes, *Thomas Abthorpe Cooper,* 75; Bruce McConachie, "American Theatre in Context, from the Beginnings to 1870," in *Cambridge History of American Theatre: Beginnings to 1870,* volume 1, ed. Don B. Wilmeth and Christopher Bigsby (New York: Cambridge University Press, 1998), 128. Philadelphia repealed the First Continental Congress's ban in 1789 and many other cities followed after.

100. Shockley, *Richmond Stage,* 376.

101. William Wirt to St. George Tucker, January 29, 1812. Tucker-Coleman Papers.

102. Ibid.

103. *Richmond Enquirer,* January 11, 1812.

104. Historian Suzanne Sherman improbably describes the journey thus: "It was a gay and congenial group that sailed down the James River that day, enjoying the weather, the scenery and each other's company" (*Comedies Useful,* 242). It seems unlikely that this was the mood, considering they had just lost a favorite cast member, young Nancy Green, in the disastrous theater fire, had had a profitable season truncated, and had been effectively driven out of town.

105. *Richmond Virginia Patriot,* January 24, 1812, quoted in Shockley, *Richmond Stage,* 376.

106. Pilkinton, *Theatre in Norfolk, Virginia,* 436.

107. Mordecai, *Richmond,* 181. It seems John William Green retired permanently from the Charleston Company after 1812 (Pilkinton, *Theatre in Norfolk, Virginia,* 487).

CHAPTER FOUR

1. Dabney, *Richmond*, 99.

2. Charles Shively, *A History of the Conception of Death in America, 1650–1860* (New York: Garland, 1988), 172 and 155.

3. "Common Council of the City of Richmond Ordinance, passed at 11 o'clock, December 27th, 1811," *Richmond Enquirer*, December 28, 1811.

4. Common Hall Commissioners meeting resolutions, December 27, 1811, *Richmond Enquirer*, December 28, 1811.

5. Tuke Alexander, *Remarks on the Theatre*, "Interment of the Dead," 33. Dabney reports that the cemetery attached to the Henrico Parish Church was the burial place of early citizens, and it contains the bodies of over 1,300 people (*Richmond*, 17–18).

6. *Narrative & Report*, 41. Also Shockley, *Richmond Stage*, 364.

7. Amended ordinance quoted in Fisher, *History of the Monumental Church*, 11–12. Also published as "An Ordinance," *Richmond Enquirer*, December 31, 1811.

8. Ibid.

9. Ibid., also Common Council Minutes regarding Theater Fire, December 28, 1811, vol. 3, 171, James Drinard Papers, Manuscripts, Virginia Historical Society.

10. "Resolutions of the Richmond citizens' meeting," *Richmond Enquirer*, December 28, 1811.

11. "Common Council of the City of Richmond Ordinance, passed at 11 o'clock, December 27th, 1811," *Richmond Enquirer*, December 28, 1811.

12. "Interment of the Dead." *Richmond Enquirer*, December 31, 1811.

13. *Calamity at Richmond*, 24.

14. "Interment of the Dead." *Richmond Enquirer*, December 31, 1811. It seems the bodies of those who died after the fire were not interred in separate coffins. Modern imaging of the crypt has revealed the presence of the two large boxes, but no smaller ones or other coffins. The Patterson and Harvie remains may have been in shrouds or transferred to the mahogany boxes (Conover Hunt, executive director of the Historic Richmond Foundation, interview by author, October 15, 2006).

15. Anne S. Rice to William Sprague, May 1, 1854, quoted in William Sprague, *Annals of the American Pulpit: Or, Commemorative Notices of Distinguished American Clergymen of Various Denominations, From the Early Settlement of the Country to the Close of the Year Eighteen Hundred and Fifty Five*, Episcopalian (New York: R. Carter, 1859), 5:327.

16. *Richmond Enquirer*, December 31, 1811; Fisher, *History of the Monumental Church*, 13–14; Munford, "The Two Parsons," 448.

17. Tuke Alexander, *Remarks on the Theatre*, "Interment of the Dead," 34.

18. *Richmond Enquirer*, January 4, 1812.

19. "Domestic," *Richmond Enquirer*, January 11, 1812.

20. Ibid.

21. "Funeral Procession," January 9, 1812, *Richmond Enquirer*.

22. "Invitation," January 14, 1812, *Richmond Enquirer*.

23. Tuke Alexander, *Remarks on the Theatre*, 36; *Richmond Enquirer*, January 2, 1812. See also Christian, *Richmond: Past and Present*, 79–80; J. L. Burrows, "History of the Church," pp. 43–105

in *The First Century of The First Baptist Church of Richmond Virginia, 1780–1880* (Richmond, VA: Carlton McCarthy, 1880), 118.

24. Sermon, December 29, 1811, John Durbarrow Blair Sermons in the John Durbarrow Blair Papers, Archives and Manuscripts, Library of Virginia.

25. William Hill, *A sermon, delivered in the Presbyterian meeting-house in Winchester, on Thursday the 23d Jan. 1812; being a day of fasting and humiliation, appointed by the citizens of Winchester on account of the late calamitous fire at the Richmond theatre* (Winchester, VA: Printed at the office of the Winchester Gazette, 1812), 15.

26. Ibid.

27. Mordecai Family Papers 1649–1947, Subseries 3.2, Folder 112, Southern Historical Collection, Louis Round Wilson Special Collections Library, University of North Carolina.

28. "Common Council of the City of Richmond Ordinance, passed at 11 o'clock, December 27th, 1811." *Richmond Enquirer*, December 28, 1811.

29. "Awful Conflagration," *Panoplist, and Missionary Magazine*, January 1812, 382.

30. *A Concise Statement of the Awful Conflagration of the Theatre, in the City of Richmond; which happened on the Night of Thursday the 26th of December last* (published in Philadelphia: n.p., January 11, 1812), preface (Rare Books, Virginia Historical Society).

31. Archibald Alexander, *A Discourse Occasioned by the Burning of the Theatre in the City of Richmond, Virginia, on the Twenty-Sixth of December, 1811, by which Awful Calamity a Large Number of Valuable Lives were Lost. Delivered . . . at the Request of the Virginia Students Attached to the Medical Class, in the University of Pennsylvania* (Philadelphia: Printed by John Weldwood Scott for Daniel Wilson, 1812), 19–20.

32. *Richmond Enquirer*, January 4, 1812.

33. "Awful Conflagration," *Panoplist, and Missionary Magazine*, January 1812, 382.

34. "Resolution of Twelfth Congress, Senate, 31 December, 1811," *Wilmington (DE) American Watchman*, January 8, 1812.

35. "For the Enquirer," *Richmond Enquirer*, January 14, 1812.

36. Common Council Proclamation of December 27, 1811, in Fisher, *History of the Monumental Church*, 5. See also Campbell to Campbell, care of Barraud, February 7, 1812, Tucker-Coleman Papers.

37. "To the Members of the Virginia Legislature," *Richmond Enquirer*, February 6, 1812.

38. "Communication Describing the Fire at Richmond," *Mirror of Taste and Dramatic Censor* 4 (December 1811), 431.

39. *Richmond Enquirer*, January 9, 1812.

40. Ibid., February 4, 1812.

41. Ibid., December 24, 1812.

42. Thornton, "Autobiography," 36.

43. Ruth Baldwin Barlow to Dolley Madison, March 4, 1812, in Holly C. Shulman, ed. Dolley Madison Digital Edition, (Charlottesville: University of Virginia Press, 2009), Documents, 1812.

44. Fisher, *History of the Monumental Church*, 15–16; *Richmond Enquirer*, February 8, 1812.

45. "(SMITHFIELD,) Isle of Wight County, January 14th, 1812," *Richmond Enquirer*, January 9, 1812.

46. Samuel Miller, *A Sermon, Delivered January 19, 1812, at the Request of a Number of Young Gentlemen of the City of New York: Who had Assembled to Express their Condolence with the Inhabitants of Richmond, on the late Mournful Dispensation of Providence in that City* (New York: Whiting & Watson, 1812), frontispiece (Rare Books, Virginia Historical Society, Richmond). See also report in *Richmond Enquirer*, January 25, 1812.

47. "Communication," *Richmond Enquirer*, February 6, 1812.

48. Drs. Hare, Chapman, Rogers, and Horner, to name four (Joseph Carson, *A History of the Medical Department of the University of Pennsylvania: From Its Foundation in 1765 with Sketches of the Lives of Deceased Professors* [Philadelphia: Lindsay & Blakiston, 1869], 90–182).

49. O.P.Q., "The Alexander Family," *Christian Observer*, February 9, 1860, 22.

50. Alexander, *A Discourse Occasioned by the Burning*, 11.

51. O.P.Q. "The Alexander Family," 22.

52. "University of Pennsylvania, January 1st, 1812." *Richmond Enquirer*, January 9, 1812.

53. "Philadelphia, Jan. 7, 1812," *Richmond Enquirer*, January 14, 1812.

54. *An Account of the great fire, which destroyed about 250 buildings in Newburyport, on the night of the 31st of May, 1811. Taken principally from the statements which have appeared in the public newspapers* (Newburyport, MA): W. & J. Gilman, 1811), 4–6.

55. *At a meeting of the Governor and Council of the State of Connecticut, at Middletown, on the 3d day of July A. D. 1811. Hartford, Connecticut, 1811*, portfolio 5, folder 3 (Washington, D.C.: Library of Congress Printed Ephemera Collection).

56. Sanford, *Richmond Triumphs*, 111.

57. "Fire at Newburyport," *Panoplist, and Missionary Magazine*, March 1812, 475.

58. "Conclusion," *Richmond Enquirer*, January 2, 1812.

59. "For the Enquirer. Benjamin Botts," *Richmond Enquirer*, January 4, 1812.

60. Ibid.

61. Ibid.

62. Munford, "The Two Parsons," 446–47.

63. Notice, *Richmond Enquirer*, January 7, 1812.

64. Ibid.

65. "Narrative," *Richmond Enquirer*, December 31, 1811.

66. "Edwin James Harvie," *Richmond Enquirer*, January 4, 1812.

67. "Communication to the Editor of the Enquirer," *Richmond Enquirer*, April 21, 1807.

68. Advertisement, *Richmond Enquirer*, July 12, 1811.

69. Also *Richmond Enquirer*, October 30, 1812. Edwin's widow, Martha Harvie, had "infant children" (*Richmond Enquirer*, December 28, 1811).

70. "Public Notice," *Richmond Enquirer*, February 6, 1812.

71. Smith, *Definer of a Nation*, 423.

72. Notice, *Richmond Enquirer*, January 28, 1812. Mordecai reported that Smith lived in a "neat wooden building in between Franklin, Main, 27th and 28th, nearer Church Hill" (*Richmond*, 139; Christian, *Richmond: Past and Present*, 75).

73. *Acts Passed at a General Assembly of the Commonwealth of Virginia, Begun and Held at the Capitol in the City of Richmond, On Monday the Second Day of December, in the Year of Our Lord, One*

Thousand Eight Hundred and Eleven, and of the Commonwealth the Thirty-Sixth (Richmond: Printed by Samuel Pleasants, Printer to the Commonwealth, 1812), 128–29.

74. Ibid. Although many sources list Smith's second wife as "Jane Read Jones Smith," William Hamilton Bryson, ed., in *Virginia Law Books: Essays and Bibliographies* (Philadelphia: American Philosophical Society, 2000), mentions the 1808 marriage of Lucy Jones, widow of Meriwether Jones, to George William Smith. Additionally, the act allocating funds for the family of the deceased Governor Smith in the *Acts Passed at the General Assembly*, 1812 (chap. CVI, pp. 128–29) lists his wife as "Lucy F. Smith." This last being the most authoritative document, Smith's wife is called Lucy in this text.

75. "Communication," *Richmond Enquirer*, January 14, 1812.

76. "Notice," *Richmond Enquirer*, January 14, 1812.

77. "What an affecting Picture is the follow-lowing [*sic*]! COMMUNICATION," *Richmond Enquirer*, January 4, 1812.

78. Mrs. Marks's first name is given sometimes as Zipporah and sometimes as Cyprian. Marks is also sometimes spelled Marx. She is named as the wife of Mordecai, and Charlotte's father is Solomon Raphael (*Richmond Enquirer*, January 4, 1812).

79. Robert Gamble, Jr., to James Breckinridge, December 27, 1811, Breckinridge Family Papers; *Richmond Enquirer*, February 8, 1812.

80. Notice, "Cornelia Academy," *Richmond Enquirer*, January 2, 1812.

81. "Communication." *Richmond Enquirer*, January 14, 1812.

82. Ibid.

83. Ibid.; see also *Southern Literary Messenger* 2, no. 12 (August 1835): 667.

84. *Richmond Enquirer*, September 1, 1812.

85. "To the Members of the Virginia Legislature," *Richmond Enquirer*, February 6, 1812.

86. Samuel Hughes to Capt. John Hughes, December 29, 1811, Personal Papers Collection, Archives and Manuscripts, Library of Virginia.

87. "To the Members of the Virginia Legislature," *Richmond Enquirer*, February 6, 1812.

88. *Acts Passed at a General Assembly*, 5, 6, 18. Full list of appropriations found in "Part I."

89. Also see Bondurant, *Poe's Richmond*, 138; Samuel Mordecai to Rachel Mordecai, February 12, 1812, Mordecai Family Papers 1649–1947.

90. Anonymous, "Fire Departments," 37.

91. 1797 Union Fire Company Rules, Broadside 1797:2, Virginia Historical Society, Richmond.

92. Ibid.

93. Brock, "Historical Sketch," 19.

94. Gish, *Virginia Taverns*, 155; and Union Fire Company Rules Broadside, 1787, Virginia Historical Society, Richmond.

95. "Fire at Richmond (Extract of a Letter), Richmond, November 23," *Portsmouth (N.H.) Federal Observer*, December 13, 1798.

96. "Richmond, Jan. 4," *Pennsylvania Herald, and General Advertiser*. January 16, 1788.

97. Union Fire Company Broadside, 1787, Virginia Historical Society.

98. Chappelmann, *History of Fire and Police*, 3.

99. "Fire!!! Richmond, Oct. 30," *Portland (ME) Eastern Argus*, November 15, 1810.

100. Tebeau, *Eating Smoke*, 19.

101. "More Conflagrations," *Richmond Enquirer,* January 18, 1812.

102. "Extinction of Fires" and "Another Correspondent," *Richmond Enquirer,* January 23, 1812.

103. "Another Correspondent," *Richmond Enquirer,* January 23, 1812.

104. "Extinction of Fires," *Richmond Enquirer,* January 23, 1812.

105. "To the Editor of the Enquirer. January 18, 1812." *Richmond Enquirer,* January 23, 1812.

106. "Notice," *Richmond Enquirer,* January 23, 1812.

107. Tebeau, *Eating Smoke*, 30–31.

108. Notice, *Richmond Enquirer,* January 30, 1812.

109. Anonymous, *Fire Departments*, 38.

110. Brock, "Historical Sketch," 14–16.

111. Ibid., 25. The society would later suffer with the fall of the Confederacy and the extensive war-related damage in Richmond; however its legally required reserve fund enabled it to recover swiftly.

112. An example of slave firefighting: Sewell Osgood, hero of the January 1812 fire saw "no impropriety" in crediting "3 people of color, whose assistance, in preserving the house I was on, was very material." Two appear to be free blacks and the third enslaved ("To the Editor of the Enquirer," *Richmond Enquirer,* January 23, 1812).

113. Barrett, *City Blacksmith*, 9.

114. Ibid.

115. Ibid., 10.

116. Mordecai, *Richmond,* 146; Dabney, *Richmond,* 156.

117. Mordecai, *Richmond,* 147.

CHAPTER FIVE

1. Thornton, "Autobiography," 36.

2. Ibid.

3. Thornton, "Autobiography," 37.

4. Ibid.

5. Ibid.

6. Advertisement dated December 7, *Richmond Enquirer,* December 31, 1811.

7. Mordecai, *Richmond,* 226–27.

8. Ibid., 228.

9. Benjamin Bates *The Virginia almanack, for the year of our Lord 1812 . . . Adapted to the latitude and meridian of Richmond. Calculated by Benjamin Bates, of Hanover County, Virginia* (Richmond, VA: Printed and sold by Samuel Pleasants, for Robert Gray, Alexandria, 1811), 37.

10. Singleton, *Letters from the South,* 75.

11. Tuke Alexander, *Remarks on the Theatre,* "Casualties," 37.

12. "Obituary," *Albion, A Journal of News, Politics, and Literature,* January 17, 1846, 33.

13. Tuke Alexander, *Remarks on the Theatre,* "Casualties," 37.

14. "Obituary," *Albion, A Journal of News, Politics, and Literature,* January 17, 1846, 33.

15. Mordecai, *Richmond,* 216–17.

16. Albert Howard Carter III and Jane Arbuckle Petro, *Rising from the Flames: The Experience of the Severely Burned* (Philadelphia: University of Pennsylvania Press, 1998), 137.

17. "Best Remedy for Burns," *Richmond Enquirer,* January 4, 1812. In the *Enquirer,* he is referred to as Dr. Lyon. However, Dr. James *Lyons* was educated in Scotland, London, and Paris and had a large, successful practice in Richmond beginning in 1809; he has the correct background and timing to be the author of this article. Additionally, the names Lyon and Lyons are often used interchangeably in archives at that time. See the Dr. James Lyons (1762–1830) entry in the Samuel Bassett French Biographical Sketches, Archives and Manuscripts, Library of Virginia.

18. "Best Remedy for Burns," *Richmond Enquirer,* January 4, 1812.

19. Ibid.

20. Bates, *Virginia Almanack,* 1812, 34.

21. Hazen and Hazen, *Keepers of the Flame,* 92, 108.

22. "Best Remedy for Burns," *Richmond Enquirer,* January 4, 1812.

23. Ibid.

24. Hazen and Hazen, *Keepers of the Flame,* 86. Daniel Drake, "History of Two Cases of Burn, Producing Serious Constitutional Irritation," *Western Journal of the Medical and Physical Sciences* 4, no. 1 (1830–31): 48–60.

25. "Best Remedy for Burns," *Richmond Enquirer,* January 4, 1812.

26. Ibid.

27. Thornton, "Autobiography," 38.

28. "Terrible Recollections," *Baltimorean,* November 16, 1872.

29. "Cures &c.," Bates, *Virginia Almanack,* 1812, 32.

30. Caroline Homassel Thornton, her handwritten notes on the Theater Fire, Greene Family Papers, Manuscripts, Virginia Historical Society, Richmond.

31. Barraud to Tucker, December 31, 1811, Barraud Family Papers.

32. Monroe to Bentalou, January 1, 1812, Library of Virginia.

33. Ibid.

34. Wirt to Tucker, January 29, 1812, Tucker-Coleman Papers.

35. "Extract of a Letter from a sufferer in the late dreadful calamity at Richmond," *Petersburg Intelligencer,* January 3, 1812.

36. Little, *History of Richmond,* 125.

37. "The Burning of the Richmond Theatre," from the *American Messenger,* quoted in the *New York Observer and Chronicle,* September 14, 1854, 1.

38. Ibid.

39. Copland, *Diary.*

40. Susan Bowdoin to Robert Wash, Esq., May 11, 1812, Special Collections, Colonial Williamsburg Rockefeller Library.

41. Thornton, "Autobiography," 38.

42. John Randolph to Thomas Abthorpe Cooper, January 16, 1812, Archives and Manuscripts, Library of Virginia.

43. Coalter to Tucker, December 29, 1812, Tucker-Coleman Papers.

44. Copland, *Diary.*

45. Ibid.

46. Ellen Mordecai to Solomon Mordecai, December 26, 1813, Mordecai Family Papers 1649–1947.

47. Thornton, "Autobiography," 30.

48. "Extract of a Letter from a sufferer in the late dreadful calamity at Richmond," *Petersburg Intelligencer*, January 3, 1812.

49. "To Sympathizing Friends and Patrons," *Richmond Enquirer*, January 9, 1812.

50. *Richmond Enquirer*, August 28, 1810.

51. Norfleet, *Saint-Memin*, 167.

52. Notice, *Richmond Enquirer*, January 30 and February 1, 1812.

53. "Circular," *Richmond Enquirer*, February 4, 1812. His later activities detailed in Bondurant, *Poe's Richmond*, 82, and the *American Beacon and Commercial Diary*, September 24, 1817.

54. "Circular," *Richmond Enquirer*, February 4, 1812.

55. Henley, "Schooldays in Richmond," 43.

56. Ibid.

57. Andrew Rolle, "Exploring an Explorer: Psychohistory and John Charles Frémont," *Pacific Historical Review* 51, no. 2 (May 1982): 136.

58. "Virginia Legislature, House of Delegates," *Richmond Enquirer*, December 21, 1811.

59. *Richmond Enquirer*, August 28, 1810.

60. Henley, "Schooldays in Richmond," 43.

61. *Richmond Enquirer*, January 14, 1812.

62. Shively, *Conception of Death*, 185–87.

63. Thomas Bomar, hand-copied from the book *The Miscellaneous Writings of the Rev. Thomas Bomar* (Philadelphia: Rackliff & Jones, 1837), Manuscripts, Virginia Historical Society, Richmond.

64. Manuscript signed "Robert Meanwell," sent to Thomas Ritchie under conditions of anonymity, written January 6, 1812, Tucker-Coleman Papers.

65. St. George Tucker to Robert Greenhow, January 3, 1812, Tucker-Coleman Papers.

66. Ibid.

67. William Meade, *Old Churches, Ministers and Families of Virginia*, vol. 2 (Philadelphia: J. B. Lippincott, 1891), 223.

68. Richard M. Scott to St. George Tucker, May 15, 1812, Tucker-Coleman Papers.

69. Poetry manuscript draft, AmsS, May, 1812, Tucker-Coleman Papers.

70. *Richmond Enquirer*, January 25, 1812.

71. "Another Earthquake," *Richmond Enquirer*, January 25, 1812.

72. Ibid.

CHAPTER SIX

1. "Theatre on Fire. AWFUL CALAMITY! A Letter from Richmond Dated December 27," 1811:1, Broadsides, Virginia Historical Society.

2. Increase Mather, D.D., *Burnings bewailed: in a sermon, occasioned by the lamentable fire which was in Boston, Octob. 2. 1711. In which the sins which provoke the Lord to kindle fires, are enquired into. B.* (Boston: Sold by Timothy Green, 1711), 33.

3. Ibid., preface.

4. George Richards, *Repent! Repent! Or Likewise Perish! The Spirit of an Evening Lecture, February 16, 1812; on the Late Calamity at Richmond, Virginia* (Philadelphia: Lydia R. Bailey, 1812), 24–25. Located in Rare Books, Virginia Historical Society, Richmond.

5. Ibid., 25.

6. "Virginia Legislature: Extracts from the Journal of the House of Delegates," *Richmond Enquirer,* December 24, 1812.

7. Mordecai, *Richmond,* 90. George Wythe Munford also addresses this incident in his book *The Two Parsons,* "Duel between Parson Buchanan and Colonel Tateham." Munford adds that Tatham (the author of books on inland navigation and tobacco cultivation) was mentally unstable and probably drunk at the time. Tatham died on February 22, 1819, and his obituary may be found in the *Virginia Patriot and Richmond Daily Mercantile Advertiser* of February 23, 1819.

8. Tuke Alexander, *Remarks on the Theatre,* "The Theatre &c.,"10. A short biographical sketch of Ann Tuke Alexander is available in "An Irishman at London Yearly Meeting in 1794," *Journal of the Friends Historical Society* 15 (1918): 15, n. 35. She wrote the abolitionist tract "An Address to the Inhabitants of Charleston, South Carolina" in 1805.

9. Robert Sutcliff, *Travels in Some Parts of North America, in the Years 1804, 1805, & 1806,* 2nd ed., improved (York, Eng.: W. Alexander, 1815), 109.

10. M. A. DeWolfe Howe, ed., "Journal of Josiah Quincy, Jr., 1773," *Proceedings of the Massachusetts Historical Society* 49 (June 1916): 463.

11. Sutcliff, *Travels,* 109.

12. Ibid., 109–10.

13. Dunn, *Dominion of Memories,* 40–41.

14. January 25, 1804, in Everett S. Brown, "The Senate Debate on the Breckinridge Bill for the Government of Louisiana 1804," *American Historical Review* 22 (1917): 361–63. Quoted in Linda K. Kerber, *Federalists in Dissent: Imagery and Ideology in Jeffersonian America* (Ithaca, NY: Cornell University Press, 1970), 25, note.

15. Sutcliff, *Travels,* 108.

16. Tuke Alexander, *Remarks on the Theatre,* "The Theatre &c.," 9–10.

17. Jeter, *Recollections,* 214–16.

18. Miller, *A Sermon,* 15–16.

19. "The Theatre," *Zion's Herald,* December 28, 1825, 2. This journal was published by Methodist laymen and was not an official church magazine, so its statements cannot be taken as authoritative stances of the Methodist Church.

20. Rees Lloyd, *The Richmond Alarm: A Plain and Familiar Discourse in the Form of a Dialogue Between a Father and His Son: in Three Parts: Written at the Request of a Number of Pious Persons by an Independent Minister* (Philadelphia: J. Bioren, Printer, 1814), 77–79.

21. David Grimsted, *Melodrama Unveiled: American Theater and Culture, 1800–1850* (Chicago: University of Chicago Press, 1968; reprint, Berkeley: University of California Press, 1987), 28, 33.

22. Ibid., 31.

23. Ibid., 27, 31.

24. It was taken for granted that a republic would best succeed if her people were governed

by the kind of internal restraint that religion provided. See Alexis de Tocqueville, *Democracy in America,* trans. Henry Reeve (London: Saunders & Otley, 1835), 211.

25. James H. Hutson, *Religion and the Founding of the American Republic* (Washington, D.C.: Library of Congress, 1998), 62.

26. Lloyd, *The Richmond Alarm,* 117.

27. Ibid., 118.

28. Grimsted, *Melodrama Unveiled,* 25.

29. Jeter, *Recollections,* 216–17.

30. Grimsted, *Melodrama Unveiled,* 25.

31. Witherspoon's lengthy polemic was recommended by name to Richmond readers in an editorial in the *Richmond Enquirer* on January 16, 1812. Rev. Samuel Miller, a New York City Presbyterian, reissued Witherspoon's tract in 1812, adding his sermon about the Richmond Theater fire and a condemnation of the theater signed by ten other ministers. See also Grimsted, *Melodrama Unveiled,* 25.

32. *A Serious Inquiry into the Nature and Effects of the Stage and a Letter respecting Play Actors by John Witherspoon also, a Sermon on the burning of the Theatre at Richmond, &c., by Samuel Miller D.D. pastor of the First Presbyterian Church of New-York together with an introductory address, by Several Ministers in New-York, &c.* (New York: Whiting & Watson, printed by D. & G. Bruce), 1812), 33.

33. Ibid., "Foul, polluted" quote, 108; "never having exchanged a word" quote, 127; thrift quote, 60; soul endangerment, 179.

34. Ibid., 57.

35. Hill, *A Sermon,* 7.

36. Ibid.

37. Dunlap, *History of American Theatre,* 1:407.

38. *Particular accou[nt] of the dreadful [fire] at Richmond, Virginia, December 26, 1811. Which destroyed the theatre and the house adjoining, and in which more than sixty persons were either burnt to death, or destroyed in attempting to make their escape.* Printed for and sold by J. Kingston, and all the Booksellers in the United States (Baltimore: B. W. Sower & Co., Printers, 1812). Rare Books, Virginia Historical Society, Richmond, 34–35

39. Click, *Spirit of the Times,* 35. Claudia Durst Johnson notes that by the 1830s and 1840s, "the relinquishing of the third tier to prostitutes had become an established national tradition, not only in New York, but in most large cities, including Boston, Chicago, Philadelphia, St. Louis, Cincinnati, Mobile, and New Orleans, among others" (*Church and Stage: The Theatre as Target of Religious Condemnation in Nineteenth-Century America* [Jefferson, NC: McFarland, 2008], 123).

40. Durst Johnson, *Church and Stage,* 124.

41. Ibid., 121, 126

42. *Particular Account,* 34–35.

43. Robert May, *Voice from Richmond, and Other Addresses to Children and Youth* (Philadelphia: American Sunday-School Union), 1842, 3–5.

44. May, *Voice from Richmond,* 11–12.

45. Ibid., 274.

46. Ibid., 280–82.

47. Ibid., 31.

48. Ibid, 14–15.

49. Ibid, 16–18.

50. Lloyd, *The Richmond Alarm*, 77.

51. Alexander, *A Discourse Occasioned by the Burning*, 18.

52. "Correspondence," *Mirror of Taste and Dramatic Censor* 1, no.1 (January 1810); collected in *The Mirror of Taste and Dramatic Censor*, vol. 1 (Philadelphia: Bradford & Inskeep, Smith & McKenzie, printers, 1810), 104.

53. Ibid., 105.

54. Ibid., 103–4.

55. Lloyd, *The Richmond Alarm*, 77.

56. (Witherspoon), *A Serious Inquiry*, 108–9, 127.

57. Durst Johnson, *Church and Stage*, 72.

58. Anna Cora Mowatt, *Autobiography of an Actress; or Eight Years on the Stage* (Boston: Ticknor, Reed, & Fields, 1854), 37–38.

59. Ibid., 218.

60. Ibid., 214.

61. Ibid., 312–13.

62. Samuel Mordecai to Rachel Mordecai, November 2, 1811, quoted in Bondurant, *Poe's Richmond*, 129.

63. "I had promised to give it, when finished, to Green's daughter, who, poor girl, perished in the theatre" (William Wirt to Judge Dabney Carr, March 31 1813; quoted in Kennedy, *Life of William Wirt*, 307).

64. *Richmond Enquirer*, October 15, 1811.

65. "Recollections of the Park Theatre; No. IV. Mr. Wallack—Mr. Cooper," *New York Times*, September 15, 1872.

66. Maginnes, *Thomas Abthorpe Cooper*, 157.

67. Ibid., 197. Mary Fairlie Cooper and Priscilla Tyler's correspondence is held by the University of Alabama.

68. Ibid.

69. Ibid., 199.

70. Marion Harland, *Marion Harland's Autobiography: The Story of a Long Life* (New York: Harper & Brothers, 1910), 289.

71. Ibid., 291.

72. James D. Knowles, Review of *The Theatre, in its Influence upon Literature, Morals and Religion*, by Robert Turnbull, in *Christian Review*, vol. 2 (Boston: Gould, Kendall & Lincoln, 1837), 399.

73. "Communication," *Richmond Enquirer*, January 16, 1810.

74. "Introductory address, by Several Ministers in New-York" ([Witherspoon], *A Serious Inquiry*, 16).

75. Tuke Alexander, *Remarks on the Theatre*, "The Theatre &c.," 19.

76. *Calamity at Richmond*, ii.

77. (Witherspoon), *A Serious Inquiry*, 60–61.

78. Lloyd, *The Richmond Alarm* 74–75.

79. He gives no examples of what might constitute justifiable recreation ([Witherspoon], *A Serious Inquiry* [sermon by Samuel Miller], 169). See also David H. Fischer, *Albion's Seed: Four British Folkways in America*, vol. 1 (New York: Oxford University Press, 1989), 368–73.

80. (Witherspoon), *A Serious Inquiry,* 48, 58.

81. Stewardship included not only money, but time and talents (Tuke Alexander, *Remarks on the Theatre,* "The Theatre &c.," 24).

82. Peter R. Henriques, *He Died as He Lived: The Death of George Washington* (Mt. Vernon, VA: For the Mount Vernon Ladies' Association, 2000), 57–58.

83. James Muir, *Repentance, or Richmond in Tears,* (Alexandria, VA: n.p., 1812), 58.

84. Miller, "Sermon," in (Witherspoon), *A Serious Inquiry,* 169.

85. Fischer, *Albion's Seed,* 373.

86. Ibid., 359.

87. Miller, "Sermon," in (Witherspoon), *A Serious Inquiry,* 187.

88. Munford, *The Two Parsons,* "Sermon by Parson Buchanan: The House of Mourning to be Preferred to the House of Feasting," 192.

89. Moore to his son (unnamed), August 11, 1824 (John Prentiss Kewley Henshaw, *Memoir of the Life of the Rt. Rev. Richard Channing Moore, D.D., Bishop of the Protestant Episcopal Church in the Diocese of Virginia* [Philadelphia: W. Stavely & Co., 1843], 54).

90. Jeter, *Recollections,* 205–6.

91. Emphasis mine. "Obituary: Dea. Daniel Trabue," *American Baptist Magazine and Missionary Intelligencer,* January 1, 1820, 270.

92. May, *Voice from Richmond,* 30.

93. (Witherspoon), *A Serious Inquiry,* 179.

94. "Awful Conflagration," *Panoplist, and Missionary Magazine,* January 1812, 382.

95. Knowles, Review of Robert Turnbull's *The Theatre, in its Influence upon Literature, Morals and Religion* (1837), 404. Although anachronistic, this work is cited due to its influence on Richmond minister Jeremiah Jeter, of First Baptist Church, who preached an influential sermon against the reopening of the Richmond Theater in 1838.

96. Emphasis mine. Alexander, *A Discourse Occasioned by the Burning,* 24.

97. "Gregory Gravity" annotations dated January 24, 1812, on flyleaf and margins of Alexander's *A Discourse Occasioned by the Burning of the Theatre in the City of Richmond, Virginia, on the Twenty-Sixth of December, 1811, by which Awful Calamity a Large Number of Valuable Lives were Lost. Delivered . . . at the Request of the Virginia Students Attached to the Medical Class, in the University of Pennsylvania* (Philadelphia: Farrand, Hopkins, Zantzinger & Co., 1812). Located in Miscellaneous Pamphlets, Special Collections, Library of Virginia.

98. *Calamity at Richmond,* iii.

99. (No title), *The Cynick,* December 12, 1811 (original copy backdated two weeks prior to the fire), 204.

100. Munford, "The Two Parsons," 448.

101. Sermon, December 29, 1811, John Durbarrow Blair, Papers, 1781–1823, Series II. From the Robert Alonzo Brock Collection at the Huntington Library, San Marino, CA. Copy in Manuscripts, Library of Virginia.

102. "Richmond, Jan. 29, 1812," *Richmond Enquirer,* February 4, 1812.

103. The account comes from the works of Josephus and the fifth chapter of Acts.

104. Luke 13:2–5, King James Version (KJV).

105. Muir, "Richmond in Tears," 41.

106. Ibid., 41–42.

107. Hill, *A Sermon,* 10.

108. Samuel Gilman, *Monody on the Victims and Sufferers by the Late Conflagration in the City of Richmond, Virginia* (Boston: Charles Williams, T. B. Wait & Co. Printers, 1812), 19-20. Located in Manuscripts and Rare Books Department, Swem Library, College of William and Mary. Samuel Gilman's professions found in Samuel A. Eliot, ed., *Heralds of a Liberal Faith,* vol. 2: "The Pioneers" (Boston: American Unitarian Association: 1910), 274–80.

109. A Theocrate, *Five important questions : on the subject of the divine government of the world, occasioned by serious reflections on the alarming and awfully severe visitation of the theatre in Richmond, December 1811, stated and answered, in a letter to an honourable young gentleman in office.* (No publisher given, 1812), 11. Rare Books, Virginia Historical Society, Richmond.

110. Joseph Dana, *Tribute of Sympathy: A Sermon, Delivered at Ipswich (Mass.) January 12, 1812, on the Late Overwhelming Calamity at Richmond in Virginia* (Newburyport, MA: Printed by E.W. Allen, 1812), 11.

111. Munford, *The Two Parsons,* "Sermon by Parson Buchanan: The House of Mourning to be Preferred to the House of Feasting," 201.

112. Hill, *A Sermon,* 8.

113. Romans 6:23, KJV.

114. Hill, *A Sermon,* 11.

115. Miller, *A Serious Inquiry,* 163.

116. (No title), *The Cynick,* December 12, 1811 (original copy backdated two weeks prior to the fire), 199, 204.

117. Ibid., 201.

118. P.Q., "The Young Men of Boston, and the Rev. Mr. Sabin's Discourse," *The Polyanthos,* February 1, 1812, 24. Sabin was the chaplain of the Massachusetts House of Representatives the winter of 1811–12 when he delivered the sermon. His health failing, he died soon after ([No title], *Zion's Herald,* May 10, 1877, 148).

119. "Gregory Gravity" annotations dated January 24, 1812, on flyleaf and margins of Archibald Alexander's *A Discourse Occasioned by the Burning of the Theatre,* Miscellaneous Pamphlets, Special Collections, Library of Virginia.

120. Ibid.

121. Ibid.

122. Ibid. Gregory Gravity's writing uses words and phrases similar to those of the anonymous author of the Watson critique in *The Cynick,* leading me to speculate that perhaps they were one and the same.

123. Fisher, *History of the Monumental Church,* 192.

124. He was a backer of the new theater built in Richmond in 1819 (Martin Staples Shockley, "The Proprietors of Richmond's New Theatre of 1819," *William and Mary College Quarterly Historical Magazine* 19, no. 3 [July 1939]: 303).

125. Harland, *Autobiography*, 288. Date sometimes given as 1852 (Fuller-Seeley, *Celebrate Richmond Theater*, 4). They separated after seven years of marriage.

126. "Another Earthquake," *Richmond Enquirer*, January 25, 1812. Also *Richmond Enquirer*, February 8, 1812.

127. Mary Andrews to Eliza Whiting, January 20, 1812, Manuscripts and Rare Books Department, Swem Library, College of William and Mary.

128. "Another Earthquake," *Richmond Enquirer*, January 25, 1812.

129. "Memorable Disasters," *Richmond Enquirer*, January 11, 1812.

130. Jack Larkin, *The Reshaping of Everyday Life 1790–1840* (New York: Harper & Row, 1988), 18.

131. "For the Enquirer: Amor Patrie," *Richmond Enquirer*, February 6, 1812.

132. Ritchie quote in "For the Enquirer: Amor Patrie," *Richmond Enquirer*, February 6, 1812.

133. "Another Earthquake," *Richmond Enquirer*, February 8, 1812.

134. "Memorable Disasters," *Richmond Enquirer*, January 11, 1812.

135. Ibid.

136. Ibid.

137. Ibid.

138. "A Word to the Wise!" *Richmond Enquirer*, January 23, 1812. See also Shockley, *Richmond Stage*, 378. Later in the century, theater critic William Winter catalogued and published indiscretions and crimes committed by clergymen as a counterattack to ministerial assaults on the character of performers (Durst Johnson, *Church and Stage*, 173).

139. *Virginia Patriot*, January 31, 1812, in Shockley, *Richmond Stage*, 379.

140. *Virginia Argus*, February 13, 1812, in Shockley, *Richmond Stage*, 379.

141. "Communication," *Virginia Patriot*, February 25, 1812, in Shockley, *Richmond Stage*, 380.

142. "Counter Communication," *Virginia Patriot*, March 3, 1812, in Shockley, *Richmond Stage*, 380.

143. Knowles, Review, 393.

144. Durst Johnson, *Church and Stage*, 53.

145. Ibid., 161.

CHAPTER SEVEN

1. St. John's was built in 1741 (Troubetzkoy, *City of Churches*, 1, 5, 7, 10).

2. Ibid., 2.

3. Fisher, *History of the Monumental Church*, 174.

4. Burrows, "History of the Church," *First Baptist*, 51.

5. Foote, *Sketches of Virginia*, 320.

6. Thomas H. Drew to Col. Thomas H. Ellis, June 8, 1868, in Fisher, *History of the Monumental Church*, 176. Mary Newton Stanard refers to "Lynch's soul-inspiring flute" (*Richmond: Its People and Its Story* [Philadelphia: J. B. Lippincott, 1923], 73).

7. Thomas H. Drew to Col. Thomas H. Ellis, June 8, 1868, in Fisher, *History of the Monumental Church*, 174–76.

8. George MacLaren Brydon, "*Historic Parishes: Saint Paul's Church, Richmond*," reprinted from the *Historical Magazine of the Protestant Episcopal Church*, (n.p., September 1954), 3; Price, *Life of Rice*, 56.

9. Fisher, *History of the Monumental Church*, 83.

10. Description of Buchanan in Anne S. Rice to William Sprague, May 1, 1854, quoted in Sprague, *Annals of the American Pulpit*, Episcopalian, 5:326.

11. Fisher, *History of the Monumental Church*, 84.

12. Ibid., 182.

13. Ibid., 85. At his death, Buchanan generously left money to the Ambler daughters, all of whom were conspicuous members of the Monumental Church congregation (Fisher, *History of the Monumental Church*, 79, 184).

14. Anne Rice to Sprague, May 1, 1854, quoted in Sprague, *Annals of the American Pulpit*, Episcopalian, 5:327.

15. Henshaw, *Memoir of Richard Channing Moore*, 148.

16. Christian, *Richmond: Past and Present*, 75; Price, *Life of Rice*, 77.

17. William Sweet, *Virginia Methodism, a History* (Richmond, VA: Whittet & Shepperson, 1955), 149; "The Cause of Religious Toleration, Richmond, VA, October 6, 1810," *Massachusetts Baptist Missionary Magazine* quoted in *Vermont Baptist Missionary Magazine*, January 1, 1812, 150.

18. Troubetzkoy, *City of Churches*, 2.

19. Price, *Life of Rice*, 57.

20. The church was rendered weak not only because of lost membership but also from new laws. In 1802, a law was passed that forced parishes to give up their glebe lands upon the death or departure of their rector. Additionally, ministerial salaries were made voluntary and the church's incorporated status was rescinded (John Frank Waukechon, *The Forgotten Evangelicals: Virginia Episcopalians, 1790–1876*, Ph.D. diss., 2000 [Ann Arbor, MI: UMI Dissertation, University of Texas at Austin, 2000], 164).

21. "Protestant Episcopal Church," *Richmond Enquirer*, May 31, 1805.

22. John N. Norton, *The Life of the Right Rev. Richard Channing Moore, D.D., Bishop of Virginia*, 2d ed. enl. (New York: General Protestant Episcopal S. School Union & Church Book Society, 1860), 38.

23. Footnote in Henshaw, *Memoir of Richard Channing Moore*, 113.

24. One hundred and seven churches existed, but only the forty mentioned were staffed (Waukechon, *The Forgotten Evangelicals*, 164).

25. Henshaw, *Memoir of Richard Channing Moore*, 138.

26. Sprague, *Annals of the American Pulpit*, Episcopalian, 5:320. Also John Tyler to William Sprague, December 14, 1848, in ibid., 321.

27. Susan H. Godson, Ludwell H. Johnson, Richard B. Sherman, Thad W. Tate, Helen C. Walker, *The College of William & Mary: A History*, vol. I: "1693–1888" (Williamsburg, VA: King & Queen Press, 1993), 197; David Holmes, ed., "Introduction," in *A Nation Mourns: Bishop James Madison's Memorial Eulogy on the Death of George Washington* (Mount Vernon, VA: Mount Vernon Ladies' Association, 1999), 17.

28. Holmes, "Introduction," *A Nation Mourns*, 16.

29. Godson et al., *William and Mary*, 1:195–97. Madison sought (at various points) a position as a Norfolk custom's collector, to be reassigned to another academic institution, and, as his health failed, to retire completely from the school.

30. Ibid., 182.

31. Ibid., 182–83.

32. Ibid., 183.

33. Sprague, *Annals of the American Pulpit*, Episcopalian, 5:321.

34. Benjamin S. Ewell to the Rev. William Brown, September 12, 1873, quoted in Godson et al., *William and Mary*, 1:183.

35. Meade, *Old Churches*, 1:28–29.

36. Ibid., 29. Also in David Holmes, *A Brief History of the Episcopal Church* (Harrisburg, PA: Trinity Press International, 1993), 19.

37. Meade, *Old Churches*, V 1:29.

38. Ibid., 27.

39. Bishop James Madison to C. S. Todd, 1811, quoted in C. S. Todd to William Sprague, October 9, 1849, in Sprague, *Annals of the American Pulpit*, Episcopalian, 5:324.

40. John Tyler to William Sprague, December 14, 1848, in Sprague, *Annals of the American Pulpit*, Episcopalian, 5:323.

41. Holmes, *Episcopal Church*, 27.

42. Holmes, "Introduction," *A Nation Mourns*, 16.

43. Godson et al., *William and Mary*, 1:197.

44. George MacLaren Brydon, "A List of Clergy of the Protestant Episcopal Church Ordained after the American Revolution, Who Served in Virginia between 1785 and 1814, and a List of Virginia Parishes and Their Rectors for the Same Period," *William and Mary College Quarterly Historical Magazine*, 2nd ser., vol. 19, no. 4 (October 1939): 398.

45. Ibid.

46. Holmes, *Episcopal Church*, 22; see also S. Charles Bolton, "Colonial Period," *Encyclopedia of Religion in the South*. 2nd ed., ed. Samuel S. Hill, Charles H. Lippy, and Charles Reagan Wilson (Macon, GA: Mercer University Press, 2005), 3.

47. Ministers listed are found in Brydon, "A List of Clergy," 398–423.

48. Ibid., and Meade, *Old Churches*, 2:71.

49. Sermon quoted in Sprague, *Annals of the American Pulpit*, Episcopalian, 5:320.

50. Ibid., 319.

51. Meade, *Old Churches*, 1:30–31.

52. Ibid., 451.

53. Brydon. *A List of Clergy*, 397–98.

54. Henshaw, *Memoir of Richard Channing Moore*, 112.

55. John Tyler to William Sprague, December 14, 1848, in Sprague, *Annals of the American Pulpit*, Episcopalian, 5:321 and 5:323; C. S. Todd to William Sprague, October 9, 1849, in ibid., 5:324.

56. Holmes, *Episcopal Church*, 27.

57. Rice to Archibald Alexander, September 9, 1811, in Maxwell, *A Memoir of Rice*, 68.

58. "City of Richmond in Common Council Report," *Richmond Enquirer*, December 28, 1812. Other members included Joseph Marx, Ben. Hatcher, Wm. Fenwick, Thomas Taylor.

59. "The Monument," *Richmond Enquirer*, February 8, 1812.

60. Fisher, *History of the Monumental Church*, 20–23.

61. Shockley, *Richmond Stage*, 381.

62. Ibid.

63. Fisher, *History of the Monumental Church*, 21–22.

64. One-third of the expense to purchase the ground went to the Common Hall committee, and the church association covered the other two-thirds. From the "City of Richmond in Common Council Reports," *Richmond Enquirer*, February 17, 1812, and March 7, 1812. This can also be found in Fisher, *History of the Monumental Church*, 21–23.

65. James Drinard Papers, Manuscripts, Virginia Historical Society, Richmond; *Norfolk and Portsmouth Herald*, January 3, 1812.

66. James Drinard Papers; Suzanne Sherman, "Thomas Wade West, Theatrical Impressario, 1790–1799," *William and Mary Quarterly* 9, no. 1 (January 1952): 12.

67. James Drinard Papers.

68. Fisher, *History of the Monumental Church*, 178; Christian, *Richmond Past and Present*, 81.

69. Quoted in Christian, *Richmond Past and Present*, 82.

70. Shepard, "Sketches: Copland," 31.

71. Interestingly, the records in the City Council minutes already refer to it as an "Episcopal Church" (Common Council Minutes regarding Theater Fire, January 20, 1812, 3:172; James Drinard Papers.

72. Fisher, *History of the Monumental Church*, 22.

73. Shockley, *Richmond Stage*, 386.

74. Ibid., 382.

75. Sherman, "Thomas Wade West," 26.

76. Benjamin Henry Latrobe's architectural drawings for a Richmond "Theatre, Assembly Rooms and an hotel" (1797–98) in the Prints and Photographs Division, Library of Congress; Margaret Pearson Mickler, "The Monumental Church" (Master's in Architectural History thesis, University of Virginia, 1980, 8–9); "An Architect Looks at Richmond," *Virginia Cavalcade* 16, no. 3 (1967): 22.

77. Shockley, *Richmond Stage*, 389.

78. Korene Greta O. Wilbanks, "Robert Mills and the Brockenbrough House, Richmond Virginia, 1817–1822" (MA thesis, Virginia Commonwealth University, 1999), 15.

79. John Morrill Bryan, *America's First Architect: Robert Mills* (New York: Princeton Architectural Press, 2001), 73.

80. Mickler, "The Monumental Church," 15.

81. Bryan, *America's First Architect*, 22.

82. Mickler, "The Monumental Church," 16.

83. Benjamin Henry Latrobe to John Brockenbrough, March 22, 1812, in Bryan, *America's First Architect*, 100.

84. Benjamin Henry Latrobe to Robert Mills, May 26, 1812, in ibid., 102.

85. Benjamin Henry Latrobe to Robert Mills, July 22, 1812, in ibid., 103.

86. Benjamin Henry Latrobe to John Brockenbrough, March 22, 1812, in ibid., 101.

87. Benjamin Henry Latrobe to Robert Mills, May 26, 1812, in ibid., 102.

88. Shockley, *Richmond Stage*, 382.

89. Common Council Minutes regarding Theater Fire, March 15, 1813, 3:263; James Drinard Papers.

90. Rhodri Windsor Liscombe, *Altogether American: Robert Mills, Architect and Engineer, 1781–1855* (New York: Oxford University Press, 1994), 54.

91. Ibid.

92. Ibid. Letter dated May 20, 1813.

93. The monument was $7,800 according to Mills's 1816 memorandum book in ibid., 54.

94. Monumental quickly lost value when reappraised in the next decade; in 1822 it was reevaluated at twenty thousand dollars, in 1829 it was worth only $17,500, although it maintained that value for the next three decades (Mutual Assurance Society of Virginia, Declarations, vol. 55, reel no. 6, Record number 1051 for Monumental Church, January 14, 1818, Library of Virginia).

95. Robert Mills to Sarah Zane, December 13, 1812, Manuscripts, Virginia Historical Society, Richmond.

96. Quoted in Wilbanks, *Robert Mills*, 35.

97. George MacLaren Brydon, in *Historic Parishes: Saint Paul's Church*, 6.

98. Fisher, *History of the Monumental Church*, 179.

99. Shively, *Conception of Death*, 192.

100. Liscombe, *Altogether American*, 54.

101. Robert Alexander, "The Young Professional in Philadelphia and Baltimore, 1808–20," in *Robert Mills: Architect*, ed. John Morrill Bryan (Washington, D.C.: American Institute of Architects Press, 1989), 47.

102. Fisher, *History of the Monumental Church*, 179.

103. Joseph said the following to his brothers after they sold him into slavery in Egypt, "But as for you, ye thought evil against me; but God meant it unto good . . . to save much people alive." (Genesis 50:20, KJV).

104. Liscombe, *Altogether American*, 57.

105. Mills to Zane, December 13, 1812, Virginia Historical Society, Richmond.

106. Ibid.

107. Foote, *Sketches of Virginia*, 327.

108. Ibid.

109. Price, *Life of Rice*, 70.

110. "Communication: Monumental Church," *Virginia Patriot*, May 7, 1814. Quoted in Fisher, *History of the Monumental Church*, 34.

111. Fisher, *History of the Monumental Church*, 65.

112. Singleton, *Letters from the South*, 57–58.

113. For more about Benjamin Latrobe's contributions to Richmond, see "An Architect Looks at Richmond," 28.

114. John Morrill Bryan, "Robert Mills: Education and Early Drawings." Pp. 1–35 in *Robert Mills: Architect*, ed. John Morrill Bryan (Washington, D.C.: American Institute of Architects Press, 1989), 17.

115. "The Monumental Church," *Poulson's American Daily Advertiser*, April 21, 1814.

116. Ibid.

117. Fisher, *History of the Monumental Church*, 179. Macmurdo's daughter Martha Ann Elizabeth married theater fire widower Patrick Gibson in 1813.

118. Hustings Court records found in Fisher, *History of the Monumental Church*, 35–38. For more of Greenhow's civic and religious involvement after the fire, see Norfleet, *Saint-Memin*, 168–69.

119. Meade, *Old Churches*, 2:221–22.

120. Ibid., 224; Fisher, *History of the Monumental Church*, 188–89.

121. Meade, *Old Churches*, 1:30. Theological seminary planning information on pp. 40–42.

122. Meade, *Old Churches*, 2:221.

123. Appeal from John Bracken and James Henderson (reporting on the proceedings in New Haven); they were surviving members of the Standing Committee, Williamsburg, April 14, 1812, in Fisher, *History of the Monumental Church*, 51–52.

124. J. H. Hobart (to Edmund I. Lee?), December 18, 1813, New York, in Henshaw, *Memoir of Richard Channing Moore*, 133.

125. From Board of Visitors minutes, July 22, 1870, in Godson et al., *William and Mary*, 1:201.

126. Ibid.

127. Meade, *Old Churches*, 1:38. See also Fisher, *History of Monumental Church*, 53–62.

128. Goodwin, "Moore: An Address," 17.

129. W. H. Wilmer to Moore, January 27, 1813, in Henshaw, *Memoir of Richard Channing Moore*, 121.

130. Moore to W. H. Wilmer, undated, in ibid., 123.

131. Henshaw, *Memoir of Richard Channing Moore*, 139 and 73.

132. Goodwin, "Moore: An Address," 17; Henshaw, *Memoir of Richard Channing Moore*, 106.

133. Henshaw, *Memoir of Richard Channing Moore*, 71.

134. Ibid.

135. Waukechon, *Forgotten Evangelicals*, 53–54. "The religious atmosphere had changed tremendously under the powerful Evangelical preaching of Bishops Moore and Meade, and the great number of strong Evangelical preachers who gathered in Virginia under their leadership" (Brydon, *Historic Parishes*, 6).

136. Singleton, *Letters from the South*, 61.

137. John Henry Hobart, *The origin, the general character, and the present situation of the Protestant Episcopal Church in the United States of America a sermon preached in St. James's Church in the city of Philadelphia on Wednesday, May 18th, A.D. 1814, on the occasion of the opening of the General Convention of the said Church, and of the consecration of the Right Rev. Bishop Moore of Virginia* (Philadelphia: Printed for Bradford & Inskeep by J. Maxwell, 1814), 36.

138. Quoted in Fisher, *History of the Monumental Church*, 60.

139. Hobart, *Sermon Preached in St. James's Church*, 37.

140. Ibid., 38.

141. Henshaw, *Memoir of Richard Channing Moore*, 152, 154.

142. Moore to Edmund I. Lee, Esq., January 24, 1815, in Henshaw, *Memoir of Richard Channing Moore*, 144, 150.

143. Ibid., 144. Church records from those formational days indicate that some personally affected by the theater fire became deeply involved in Monumental Church. In 1817 Robert

Greenhow married Elizabeth, an officer of the Sunday school. Heningham Copland, Charles's wife, became a director of the school; Julia Wickham taught there (Norfleet, *Saint-Memin*,168–69); "History of the Sunday School," in *The First Century of the First Baptist Church of Richmond, Virginia 1780–1880* (Richmond, VA: Carlton McCarthy, 1880), 175–76.

144. Rice to Archibald Alexander, December 13, 1814, in Maxwell, *A Memoir of Rice*, 180.

145. Goodwin, *Moore: An Address*, 12.

146. Singleton, *Letters from the South*, 68–69.

147. Henshaw, *Memoir of Richard Channing Moore*, 149.

148. Moore to W. H. Wilmer, January 8, 1814, in Henshaw, *Memoir of Richard Channing Moore*, 131.

149. W. H. Wilmer to Moore, December 28, 1813, in ibid., 130.

150. Moore to Rt. Rev. William White, Richmond, November 14, 1815, "Monumental Church Correspondence between Rectors and Communicants," Manuscripts, Virginia Historical Society, Richmond.

CHAPTER EIGHT

1. Phillip Barraud to St. George Tucker, December 31, 1811, Tucker-Coleman Papers, Manuscripts and Rare Books Department, Swem Library, College of William and Mary.

2. "Obituary," *Albion, A Journal of News, Politics, and Literature*, January 17, 1846, 33.

3. Foote, *Sketches of Virginia*, 322.

4. Little, *History of Richmond*, 127.

5. Jewel Spangler, *Virginians Reborn: Anglican Monopoly, Evangelical Dissent, and the Rise of the Baptists in the Late Eighteenth Century* (Charlottesville: University of Virginia Press, 2008), 142. This was the case for gentry converts to the Baptist Church or to any evangelical denomination that encouraged nonconformity to the world.

6. Jeter, *Recollections*, 294.

7. Stanard, *Richmond: Its People*, 71.

8. Rice to Archibald Alexander, January 28, 1810, in Maxwell, *A Memoir of Rice*, 50–51.

9. Patricia U. Bonomi, *Under the Cope of Heaven: Religion, Society, and Politics in Colonial America*, updated ed. (1986; New York: Oxford University Press, 2003), 220.

10. This statistic matches national 1780s statistics, indicating that Richmond had not experienced a great change in church attendance, despite scattered revivals throughout the state of Virginia in the interim years (Mark Noll, *A History of Christianity in the United States and Canada* [Grand Rapids, MI: William B. Eerdmans, 1992, reprinted 1999], 166, 228).

11. Noll, *History of Christianity*, 166.

12. Singleton, *Letters from the South*, 68–69.

13. Brydon, *Historic Parishes: Saint Paul's Church*, 5–6.

14. Noll, *History of Christianity*, 166; Nathan O. Hatch, *The Democratization of American Christianity* (New Haven, CT: Yale University Press, 1989), 225.

15. Godson et al., *William and Mary*, 1:180.

16. Anne C. Loveland, *Southern Evangelicals and the Social Order, 1800–1860* (Baton Rouge: Louisiana State University Press, 1980), 46; Brydon, *Historic Parishes: Saint Paul's Church*, 6.

17. Meade, *Old Churches*, 1:29.

18. Quoted in Burrows, "History of the Church," 51.

19. Thomas Coke, *Extracts of the Journals of the Late Rev. Thomas Coke, L.L.D.; Comprising Several Visits to North-American and the West Indies; His Tour Through a part of Ireland, and His Nearly Finished Voyage to Bombay in the East-Indies: to which is Prefixed, A Life of the Doctor* (Dublin: Methodist Book Room, 1816), 176. About four years prior Coke had spoken in Richmond and found them to be a "very respectable and very attentive congregation" (97); Stanard, *Richmond: Its People*, 73.

20. B. R. Wellford, "History of the First Presbyterian Church," Pp. 43–61 in *First Presbyterian, Richmond, Virginia: Proceedings of the Celebration of the Eightieth Anniversary of Its Organization, May 1, 1892* (Richmond, VA: Whittet & Shepperson, General Printers, 1892), 45–46.

21. Dabney, *Richmond*, 67.

22. Rhys Isaac, *The Transformation of Virginia, 1740–1790* (Chapel Hill: University of North Carolina Press for the Omohundro Institute of Early American History and Culture, 1982), 269.

23. Thomas H. Drew to Col. Thomas H. Ellis, June 8, 1868, in Fisher, *History of the Monumental Church*, 175.

24. Sweet, *Virginia Methodism*, 150. See also Stanard, *Richmond: Its People*, 71–72. Emigration was sometimes prompted by conscience; many Methodist and Quaker emigrants were abolitionists who moved west to Ohio or Kentucky so as not to live any longer amid slavery (Charles F. Irons, "Antebellum Period," *Encyclopedia of Religion in the South*, 11).

25. *Richmond Enquirer*, February 6, 1812; Christian, *Richmond: Past and Present*, 82. The conference minutes, held at the Randolph-Macon College McGraw-Page Library Special Collections, are a straightforward record of preaching appointments and financial concerns without mention of the fire or any other current event.

26. *The Doctrines and Discipline of the Methodist Episcopal Church*, 15th ed. (New York: Published by Daniel Hitt and Thomas Ware, for the Methodist Connection in the United States, J. C. Totten, Printer, 1812), 39.

27. "Rev. Jesse Lee," *Methodist Quarterly Review*, vol. 32: 4th series, vol. 2, Ed. J. McClintock (New York: Lane & Scott, Joseph Longking, Printer: 1850), 62.

28. McTyeire, *A History of Methodism*, 266.

29. "Rev. Jesse Lee," *Methodist Quarterly Review*, vol. 2 (January, 1850), 62.

30. Thomas Coke, *Extracts of the Journals of the Late Rev. Thomas Coke, L.L.D.*, 8.

31. Ibid., 60.

32. "Rev. Jesse Lee," *Methodist Quarterly Review*, vol. 2 (January, 1850), 62.

33. Abel Stevens, *History of the Methodist Episcopal Church in the United States of America*, vol. 4 (New York: Phillips & Hunt, 1884), 305; and McTyeire, *A History of Methodism*, 305.

34. Stevens, *History of the Methodist Episcopal Church*, 108.

35. See Harry S. Stout, *The Divine Dramatist: George Whitefield and the Rise of Modern Evangelism* (Grand Rapids, MI: William B. Eerdmans, 1991).

36. William Sprague, *Annals of the American Pulpit: Or, Commemorative Notices of Distinguished American Clergymen of Various Denominations, From the Early Settlement of the Country to the Close of the Year Eighteen Hundred and Fifty-Five. Methodist*, vol. 7 (New York: R. Carter & Brothers, 1859), 640.

37. Ibid., 643.

38. W. H. Daniels, *Illustrated History of Methodism in Great Britain and America, from the Days of the Wesleys to the Present Time* (New York: Phillips & Hunt, 1879), 175.

39. *Doctrines and Discipline* (1812), 55, 37.

40. "Woman.—The Contrast. An Extract." *Methodist Magazine*, January 1, 1820, 26. Emphasis in original.

41. *Doctrines and Discipline* (1812), 64.

42. "Memoir of Mr. George Shadford," *Methodist Magazine*, April 1, 1818, 137.

43. Jeter, *Recollections,* 306.

44. John M'Lean, *Sketch of Rev. Philip Gatch* (Cincinnati: Swormstedt & Poe, R. P. Thompson, Printer, 1854), 86.

45. Jeter, *Recollections,* 82, 305. Jeter notes that dress rules were enforced more rigorously than intemperance rules, which amounted to a double standard that was stricter for women.

46. Weld, *Travels,* 1:198.

47. Stith Mead, "Camp Meeting," quoting the *Richmond Enquirer,* June 9, 1812, *William & Mary Quarterly Historical Magazine,* July 1924, 210.

48. Solomon Smith, *Theatrical Management in the West and South for Thirty Years* (New York: Harper & Brothers, 1868), 48, 60.

49. John Durbarrow Blair Papers, Archives and Manuscripts, Library of Virginia.

50. Jeter, *Recollections,* 162.

51. Daniels, *Illustrated History of Methodism,* 192–93. George Whitefield, an eighteenth-century Methodist minister, diverged from his friend John Wesley in this and became a Calvinist. He had a following of Methodists (a party called the "Lady Huntingdon Connection" after Whitefield's patroness), but they remained a small minority.

52. Ibid., 563–67.

53. Ibid., 194.

54. Mead, "Camp Meeting," 210.

55. William M. Newman and Peter L. Halvorson, *Atlas of American Religion: The Denominational Era, 1776–1990* (Walnut Creek, CA: AltaMira Press, 2000), 18, 76, 77. The 13,338 churches represented over one-third of the church total in America in 1850. The 1.6 million adherents figure includes members of all three Methodist branches extant at the time.

56. Thomas H. Drew to Col. Thomas H. Ellis, June 8, 1868, in Fisher, *History of the Monumental Church,* 174–75. More on the early years of this church in W. H. Gwathmey, "The House of One Franklin," in *The First Century of The First Baptist Church,* 143. See also C. Walthall, "Houses of Worship," in *The First Century of the First Baptist Church,* 149.

57. J. L. Burrows, "History of the Church," in *The First Century of the First Baptist Church,* 68; W. D. Thomas, "Deceased Pastors," in ibid., 119; Robert Baylor Semple, *A History of the Rise and Progress of the Baptists in Virginia,* rev. and exp. by G. W. Beale (Richmond, VA: Pitt & Dickinson, 1894), 118, 143.

58. Semple, *Rise and Progress of the Baptists,* 143.

59. Jeter, *Recollections,* 311.

60. Sarah B. Bearss, ed., "John Courtney," *Dictionary of Virginia Biography,* vol. 3: Caperton–Daniels (Richmond: Library of Virginia, 2006), 487. Speaking style in Burrows, "History of the Church," 74.

61. So there would always be white oversight, slaves could not maintain their own

churches nor could they assemble for worship except under a white minister. Until 1848, no law prohibited free blacks or mulattoes from assembling together, but the meeting became an unlawful assembly with the presence of a single slave (*Inventory of the Church Archives of Virginia,* Work Projects Administration, p. v).

62. "The Cause of Religious Toleration," *Vermont Baptist Missionary Magazine,* January 1, 1812, 152.

63. Jeter, *Recollections,* 21.

64. "Religious Intelligence: Extract of a Letter from a very pious *Itinerant Preacher* in Virginia [William Brame], to a Ministering Brother in Boston, dated Richmond, Nov. 18, 1812," *Massachusetts Baptist Missionary Magazine,* March 1813, 276. Mention of the 1811 revival in Rev. Noell, Essex Co., Virginia, to Dr. Rogers, Philadelphia, "Religious Intelligence," *Massachusetts Baptist Missionary Magazine,* March 1812, 146.

65. "Revivals of Religion: Richmond," *Massachusetts Baptist Missionary Magazine,* March 1814, 27.

66. John Bryce to the Editor, "Revival of Religion in Richmond, Virginia," April 16, 1814, *Massachusetts Baptist Missionary Magazine,* June 1814, 45.

67. Ibid.

68. Burrows, "History of the Church," 104.

69. "Cause of Religious Toleration," *Vermont Baptist Missionary Magazine,* January 1, 1812, 151.

70. Spangler, *Virginians Reborn,* 146.

71. Jeter, *Recollections,* 108.

72. Foot washing, Minutes of the Dover Baptist Association (hereafter DBA), October 1813 in Hanover, 12; music lessons, Minutes of the DBA, October 1806 in York, 4; Arminianism, Minutes of the DBA, October 1811 in Westmoreland, 7–8. Historian of Virginia Baptists Robert Baylor Semple described two men at variance regarding the doctrines of free will and grace, one a strident Calvinist and another a decided Arminian. They agreed on adult believer baptism and were "therefore both Baptists," as Semple records (Semple, *Rise and Progress of the Baptists,* 108). It seems the Baptist Church provided a big tent when it came to shades of Calvinism (Jeter, *Recollections,* 281, 285).

73. Minutes of the DBA, October 1824 in Middlesex, 8.

74. "Cause of Religious Toleration," *Vermont Baptist Missionary Magazine,* January 1, 1812, 151.

75. "Objections against Joining a Baptist Church Answered," *American Baptist Magazine and Missionary Intelligencer,* November 1, 1820, 431.

76. Spangler, *Virginians Reborn,* 138.

77. Meetings related to Ebenezer Jenkins held on June 13, 1825, March 23, 1826, November 19, 1829, January 21, 1830, February 18, 1830, and April 21, 1831 (*Minutes of the Second Baptist Church of Richmond, Virginia,* Virginia Baptist Historical Society, Richmond).

78. February 11, 1826, First Baptist Church Book, bk. 1, "Minutes, First Baptist Church (Richmond), 1825–1830" (photostat), Virginia Baptist Historical Society, Richmond.

79. December 5, 1829, Minutes, 1825–1830, First Baptist Church Book.

80. January 2, 1830, and February 18, 1830, in ibid.

81. February 18, 1830, in ibid.

82. *Minutes of the Second Baptist Church of Richmond, Virginia,* Virginia Baptist Historical Society, Richmond.

83. This may be due to the extemporaneous and spontaneous nature of many Baptist sermons—such sermons would have been difficult to reproduce in writing after the fact.

84. Thomas H. Drew to Col. Thomas H. Ellis, June 8, 1868, in Fisher, *History of the Monumental Church,* 174–75.

85. "Richmond Theatre," *Massachusetts Baptist Missionary Magazine,* March 1812, 147.

86. "Soon shall my dreary journey end / My bosom cease to sigh . . . / Adieu all earthly hopes and fears / I soon shall rise / Above the skies / And wipe away my briny tears" (Jeter, *Recollections,* 282); James B. Taylor, *Virginia Baptist Ministers,* series 2 of 2 (New York: Sheldon & Company, 1860), 248.

87. Jeremiah B. Jeter, *A Discourse on the Immoral Tendency of Theatrical Amusements* (Richmond, VA: William MacFarlane, 1838), 16.

88. Jeter, *Recollections,* 216.

89. Ibid., 214–15.

90. Ibid., 217.

91. Jeter, *A Discourse,* 7–8.

92. Ibid., 12. He cited ancient Greece as an example; Knowles, Review of *The Theatre,* 404.

93. Jeter, *Recollections,* 217.

94. Ibid., 217–18.

95. Ibid., 218.

96. Jeter, *A Discourse,* 3.

97. "Theophilos," "On the Duties to be Enforced on the Unconverted," *American Baptist Magazine and Missionary Intelligencer,* September 1, 1822, 410.

98. William Buell Sprague, *Annals of the American Pulpit: Or, Commemorative Notices of Distinguished American Clergymen of Various Denominations, From the Early Settlement of the Country to the Close of the Year Eighteen Hundred and Fifty-Five,* Presbyterian, vol. 4 (New York: R. Carter & Brothers, 1859), 330.

99. Maxwell, *A Memoir of Rice,* 31–34.

100. Rice to Judith Randolph , January 1 1812, in Maxwell, *A Memoir of Rice,* 74.

101. Ibid.

102. Sprague, *Annals of the American Pulpit,* Presbyterian, 4:332.

103. Foote, *Sketches of Virginia,* 245.

104. Letter dated September 9, 1811, in Maxwell, *A Memoir of Rice,* 68.

105. Moses D. Hoge, "Portraitures of Four Pastors," in *First Presbyterian, Richmond, Virginia: Proceedings of the Celebration of the Eightieth Anniversary of Its Organization, May 1, 1892* (Richmond, VA: Whittet & Shepperson, General Printers, 1892), 18–19.

106. Ibid.

107. Rice to Judith Randolph, March 6, 1812, in Maxwell, *A Memoir of Rice,* 77.

108. Rice to Archibald Alexander, October 19, 1811, in ibid., 69.

109. Foote, *Sketches of Virginia,* 323.

110. Sprague, *Annals of the American Pulpit,* Presbyterian, 4:332.

111. Ibid.

112. Ibid., 4:340.

113. Rice to Theodoric T. Randolph, September 23, 1812, in Maxwell, *A Memoir of Rice,* 87; Sprague, *Annals of the American Pulpit,* Presbyterian, 4:333.

290 NOTES TO PAGES 196–200

114. Anne S. Rice to Sprague, *Annals of the American Pulpit,* Episcopalian, 5:326.

115. Sprague, *Annals of the American Pulpit,* Presbyterian, 4:340; and Loveland, *Southern Evangelicals,* 193.

116. Thomas H. Drew to Col. Thomas H. Ellis, June 8, 1868, in Fisher, *History of the Monumental Church,* 176. A May 8, 1812, *Richmond Enquirer* announcement is quoted.

117. Rice to Judith Randolph, January 17, 1812, in Maxwell, *A Memoir of Rice,* 75.

118. Ibid. Emphasis is Rice's.

119. Rice to Archibald Alexander, May 14, 1812, in Maxwell, *A Memoir of Rice,* 79–80.

120. Price, *Life of Rice,* 66.

121. *Manual for Members of the First Presbyterian Church in Richmond, Va: compiled by order of session, Oct. 1833* (Richmond: Printed by T. W. White, 1833), Rare Books, Virginia Historical Society, Richmond; *Virginia Patriot,* February 4, 1815.

122. *Henrico Parish Vestry Book,* April 8, 1807, and May 12, 1812–December 16, 1817, Manuscripts, Virginia Historical Society, Richmond.

123. *Manual for Members of the First Presbyterian.*

124. Rice to Archibald Alexander, February 25, 1813, in Maxwell, *A Memoir of Rice,* 89.

125. Ibid., 90.

126. Rice to Judith Randolph, March 9, 1813, in Maxwell, *A Memoir of Rice,* 90.

127. Thornton, "Autobiography," 38.

128. Ibid., 39. Her birth father, Charles Marcel Homassel, a French immigrant, had Catholic family in France but "was a Protestant by faith" himself. His wedding to Caroline Richard Homassel in 1787 was celebrated in St. Peter's of Philadelphia and in a Catholic church, out of respect for Charles's family (ibid., 25).

129. Meetings advertised in *Richmond Enquirer,* January 30, 1812, and February 1, 1812; Thornton, "Autobiography," 38.

130. Foote, *Sketches of Virginia,* 324; Price, *Life of Rice,* 62.

131. Thornton, "Autobiography," 38.

132. Ibid.

133. Ibid., 37.

134. Ibid.

135. Ibid.

136. Rice to Archibald Alexander, undated, in Maxwell, *A Memoir of Rice,* 100.

137. Price, *Life of Rice,* 58.

138. Ibid., 100–101.

139. Foote, *Sketches of Virginia,* 326.

140. Ibid.

141. Rice to Judith Randolph, September 16, 1814, in ibid., 104.

142. Rice to Archibald Alexander, November 16, 1815, in ibid., 120.

143. Mordecai, *Richmond,* 326.

144. Rice to Archibald Alexander, undated, in Maxwell, *A Memoir of Rice,* 101.

145. Maxwell, *A Memoir of Rice,* 104.

146. Rice to Archibald Alexander, undated, in Maxwell, *A Memoir of Rice,* 101.

147. Rice to Archibald Alexander, December 15, 1814, in ibid., 109.

148. Price, *Life of Rice,* 71.

149. Rice to Judith Randolph, March 6, 1812, in Maxwell, *A Memoir of Rice,* 77.

150. Rice to William Maxwell, Esq, June 2, 1815, in ibid., 113.

151. Ibid. Rice to William Maxwell, Esq, June 2, 1815, in Maxwell, *A Memoir of Rice, 113.*

152. Price, *Life of Rice,* 76.

153. Rice to Archibald Alexander, November 16, 1815, in Maxwell, *A Memoir of Rice,* 120–121.

154. Location in Chappelmann, *History of Fire and Police,* 3.

155. Rice to Archibald Alexander, November 16, 1815, in Maxwell, *A Memoir of Rice,* 120.

156. Dabney, *Richmond,* 99.

157. Christian, *Richmond: Past and Present,* 82.

158. Thomas H. Drew to Col. Thomas H. Ellis, June 8, 1868, in Fisher, *History of the Monumental Church,* 177.

159. Troubetzkoy, *City of Churches,* 3, 25.

160. Foote, *Sketches of Virginia,* 328–29.

161. Fisher, *History of the Monumental Church,* 63. Buchanan donated $333 to the building of Monumental Church.

162. Meade, *Old Churches,* 1:143.

163. Henshaw, *Memoir of Richard Channing Moore,* 148.

164. Mordecai, *Richmond,* 261–62.

165. Smith, *Definer of a Nation,* 160–61.

166. Stanard, *Richmond: Its People,* 73.

167. Price, *Life of Rice,* 56.

168. Sermon, December 29, 1811 (John Durbarrow Blair Sermons in the John Durbarrow Blair Papers, Archives and Manuscripts, Library of Virginia).

169. Article draft submitted to John Holt Rice's *Literary and Evangelical Magazine,* November 30, 1821 (John Durbarrow Blair, Papers, 1781–1823, Series II, From the Robert Alonzo Brock Collection at the Huntington Library, San Marino, California, copy in Manuscripts, Library of Virginia).

170. Ibid.

171. Shockley, *Richmond Stage,* 345.

172. Funeral sermon by Jesse H. Turner on January 10, 1823 (John Durbarrow Blair, Papers, 1781–1823, Series II; copy in Manuscripts, Library of Virginia.

173. Rice to Theodoric T. Randolph, 23 September, 1812, in Maxwell, *A Memoir of Rice,* 86.

174. Moore to Edmund I. Lee, Esq., January 24, 1815, in Henshaw, *Memoir of Richard Channing Moore,* 144.

175. Rev. Benjamin M. Smith to William Buell Sprague (?), March 11, 1857, in Sprague, *Annals of the American Pulpit,* Presbyterian, 4:331.

176. Norton, *Life of Moore,* 120, 92.

177. Meade, *Old Churches,* 1:38; Norton, *Life of Moore,* 118.

178. Fisher, *History of the Monumental Church,* xiv; Norton, *Life of Moore,* 53; Henshaw, *Memoir of Richard Channing Moore,* 95.

179. Moore to his son "C," February 23, 1832, in Henshaw, *Memoir of Richard Channing Moore,* 279.

180. Henshaw, *Memoir of Richard Channing Moore,* 155.

181. Fisher, *History and Reminiscences*, 181; Norfleet, *Saint-Memin*, 168–69.

182. Fisher, 99.

183. Henshaw, *Memoir of Richard Channing Moore*, 81.

184. Price, *Life of Rice*, 66.

185. Moore to Rev. Mr.——, January 13, 1823, in Henshaw, *Memoir of Richard Channing Moore*, 83.

186. Ibid., 84, 92.

187. Henshaw, *Memoir of Richard Channing Moore*, 93.

188. Ibid., 94.

189. Norton, *Life of Moore*, 56, 57 (see also *Richmond Enquirer*, May 6, 1815, quoted in Fisher, *History of the Monumental Church*, 67); Price, *Life of Rice*, 91, 101.

190. Price, *Life of Rice*, 65, 91; Rice to Alexander, May 14, 1812, quoted in Maxwell, *Memoir of Rice*, 80.

191. Hutson, *Religion and the Founding*, 111; Mark Noll, *The Work We Have to Do: A History of Protestants in America* (New York: Oxford University Press, 2002), 61.

192. Records of the Amicable Society quoted in Mordecai, *Richmond*, 257–58.

193. Ibid., 257. Members who joined during the revivals (and whose families were deeply affected by the theater fire) included: (1811) Robert Gamble, John G. Gamble, John Adams, John Brockenbrough, Charles J. Macmurdo, Samuel Myers, Joseph Marx, James Gibbon, James McClurg, John Wickham, Carter B. Page; (1825) S(amuel?) Jacobs, Gurden Huntington Backus (Bacchus), Richard and Temple Gwathmey, William Munford, John Ambler, and John Parkhill. Dr. James McCaw joined in 1812, and Samuel Pleasants and Robert Greenhow in 1813.

194. Bondurant, *Poe's Richmond*, 75.

195. Fisher, *History of the Monumental Church*, 162, 186.

196. Ibid., 161.

197. Ibid., 162, 170–73.

198. Dunn, *Dominion of Memories*, 73.

199. J. D. K. Sleight, "The Sabbath School," in *First Presbyterian*, 36. See also Price, *Life of Rice*, 90. Presbyterians may have had the first; some records indicate it began in 1816.

200. Blanche S. White, *Richmond Baptists Working Together* (Richmond, VA: Richmond Baptist Association, 1961), 12, quoted in Marie Tyler-McGraw and Gregg D. Kimball, *In Bondage and Freedom: Antebellum Black Life in Richmond, Virginia* (Chapel Hill: University of North Carolina Press, for the Valentine Museum of the Life & History of Richmond, 1988), 63.

201. Bondurant, *Poe's Richmond*, 115.

202. Alfred J. Morrison, "The Virginia Literary and Evangelical Magazine, Richmond, 1818–1828," *William and Mary Quarterly* 19, no. 4 (April 1911): 266, 269.

203. Quoted in Fisher, *History of the Monumental Church*, 89.

204. Ph[ilip] Lindsley to Rice, September 28, 1822, in Foote, *Sketches of Virginia*, 376–78.

205. Ibid., 384.

206. Brydon, *Historic Parishes: Saint Paul's Church*, 6.

207. Moore to W. H. Wilmer, January 8, 1814, in Henshaw, *Memoir of Richard Channing Moore*, 131–32.

208. Moncure Conway, 1864, quoted in Dena Epstein, *Sinful Tunes and Spirituals: Black Folk Music to the Civil War* (Urbana: University of Illinois Press, 1977), 211.

209. Tyler-McGraw and Kimball, *Bondage and Freedom*. 44.

210. U.S. Census, Richmond City, 1830–60, quoted in Tyler-McGraw and Kimball, *Bondage and Freedom*, 58.

211. Tyler-McGraw and Kimball, *Bondage and Freedom* , 57.

212. Barrett, *City Blacksmith*, 12.

213. Ibid., 13.

214. Dabney, *Richmond*, 156.

215. Barrett, *City Blacksmith*, 4.

216. Tyler-McGraw and Kimball, *Bondage and Freedom*, 56.

217. John O'Brien, "From Bondage to Citizenship: The Richmond Black Community, 1865–67" (Ph.D. diss., University of Rochester, 1975), 58–60, 62, quoted in Tyler-McGraw and Kimball, *Bondage and Freedom*, 57.

218. *Commonwealth vs. Hunt*, Richmond City Hustings Court Minute Book 17, 1847–48, pp. 44, 50, 62, 88, 172, 253, 266, 494, Library of Virginia, quoted in Tyler-McGraw and Kimball, *Bondage and Freedom*, 57.

219. Maxwell, *A Memoir of Rice*, 79, quoted in Price, *Life of Rice*, 64.

220. He suspected that after the fire gambling was mostly confined to "a portion of those who enact laws against it, and themselves test the futility of their own enactments" (Mordecai, *Richmond*, 197).

221. Marie Tyler-McGraw, *At the Falls: Richmond, Virginia, and Its People* (Chapel Hill: University of North Carolina Press, for the Valentine Museum of the Life & History of Richmond, 1994), 86. During the years 1810–30, benevolent societies "generated their maximum energy" (Hutson, *Religion and the Founding*, 111;. see also Donald G. Mathews, *Religion in the Old South* [Chicago: University of Chicago Press, 1977], 88).

222. Obituary of Caroline Homassel Thornton, signed JST, Greene Family Papers, Manuscripts, Virginia Historical Society, Richmond.

223. "G.W.M." Biographical Sketch of Homassel Thornton, Greene Family Papers.

224. Ibid.

225. "Revivals of Religion: Richmond," letter dated January 29, 1814, *Massachusetts Baptist Missionary Magazine*, March 1814, 26.

226. Thornton, "Autobiography," 39.

227. "G.W.M." Biographical Sketch of Caroline Homassel Thornton, undated, Greene Family Papers.

228. Thornton, "Autobiography," 39.

229. Ibid.

230. Ibid., 40.

231. Caroline Homassel Thornton, Diary, 1841–1872, Greene Family Papers.

232. "G.W.M." Biographical Sketch of Homassel Thornton, undated, Greene Family Papers.

233. Ibid.

234. Obituary of Caroline Homassel Thornton, signed JST, Greene Family Papers.

235. "Main Street, Richmond, Virginia," *Gleason's Pictorial Drawing-Room Companion*, April 23, 1853, 264.

236. Richmond's population was 20,153 in 1840, including slave and free, according to the 1840 U.S. census. There were 23 churches by 1840, "4 Baptist, 1 Campbellite, 4 Episcopal,

1 Friends, 2 Jews' Synagogues, 1 Lutheran, 4 Methodist, 3 Presbyterian, 1 Roman Catholic, 1 Universalist, and 1 African" (Daniel Haskel and J. Calvin Smith, *Complete Descriptive and Statistical Gazetteer of the United States with an Abstract of the Census and Statistics for 1840* (New York: Sherman & Smith, 1848), 568.

CHAPTER NINE

1. "Report of the Committee of Investigation," *Richmond Enquirer*, December 31, 1811.

2. Ibid.

3. Ibid.

4. William Wood, *Personal Recollections of the Stage, Embracing Notices of Actors, Authors, and Auditors, During a Period of Forty Years* (Philadelphia: Henry Carey Baird, 1855), 142–43.

5. Shockley, *Richmond Stage*, 302.

6. One hundred and twenty was still too many for one preacher in Pennsylvania, who wrote, "To the shame of this populous city and to the astonishment of every reflecting mind, whilst the burning ashes of our brethren at Richmond are presented to our view . . . the citizens of Philadelphia are rioting in mirth and dissipation, and the Theatre groaning under the weight of its attending votaries" (*A Concise Statement of the Awful Conflagration*, preface).

7. "To the Public," *Richmond Enquirer*, January 18, 1812.

8. Ibid. The New York theater community continued to remember the Richmond Theater fire for years, as evidenced in a script held in the University of Virginia Special Collections. Entitled "The Knights; a farce, in two acts," this copy, published in New York City in 1813, had an elegy in remembrance of the Richmond Theater fire victims at the end of the booklet.

9. "For the *American Daily Advertiser*, Philadelphia, Jan. 6, 1812," *Richmond Enquirer*, January 14, 1812.

10. "Charleston Theatre, *to the Public*," *Richmond Enquirer*, January 30, 1812.

11. Ibid.

12. "Communication Describing the Fire at Richmond," *Mirror of Taste and Dramatic Censor* 4 (December 1811): 430.

13. "Report of the Committee of Investigation," *Richmond Enquirer*, December 31, 1811.

14. "Things Theatrical," *Spirit of the Times*, September 26, 1846, 372.

15. Terence Russell, "Fire Prevention and Fire Protection in Buildings and Habitable Environments: Works Published in the 19th Century," and "Fires and the Work of the Fire Services: Works Published in the 19th Century" (*The Built Environment: A Subject Index 1800–1960* [Surrey, Eng.: Gregg, 1989], 880–85, 899–903).

16. Horace Townsend, "Fires in Theatres, and Their Prevention," *Frank Leslie's Popular Monthly* 15, no. 3. (March 1883): 312.

17. Ibid.

18. Sara Wermiel, *The Fireproof Building: Technology and Safety in the Nineteenth-Century American City* (Baltimore: Johns Hopkins Press, 2000), 11.

19. Ibid., 132. That same year Boston passed a law attempting to scale the means of egress to occupancy in public buildings. Theaters had minimum stairway and corridor widths prescribed (ibid., 196).

20. Townsend, "Fires in Theatres, and Their Prevention," 316.

21. "Burning of Theatres," *New York Observer and Chronicle,* September 14, 1854, 1.

22. Townsend, "Fires in Theatres, and Their Prevention," 316–18.

23. Ibid.

24. William Paul Gerhard, *Theatre Fires and Panics: Their Causes and Prevention* (New York: John Wiley & Sons, 1896), 18.

25. Ibid. 30–35. Flap seat reference in William Paul Gerhard, *Safety of Theatre Audiences and of the Stage Personnel against Danger from Fire and Panic* (London: British Fire Prevention Committee, 1899), 18.

26. Wermiel, *Fireproof Building,* 8, 12, 17.

27. Gerhard, *Theatre Fires and Panics,* 40.

28. Wermiel, *Fireproof Building,* 197.

29. "Fire safety—Life safety," in *Encyclopedia of Architecture, Design, Engineering and Construction,* ed. Joseph A. Wilkes (New York: John Wiley & Sons, 1988).

30. Ibid.

31. "Burning of Theatres," *New York Observer and Chronicle,* December 14, 1876.

32. *Richmond Enquirer,* December 19, 1812, quoted in Fisher, *History of the Monumental Church,* 29.

33. Dabney, *Richmond,* 92.

34. Ellen Mordecai to Solomon Mordecai. December 26, 1813, Mordecai Family Papers, 1649–1947. Quoted in Bondurant, *Poe's Richmond,* 138–39.

35. "Music Quieted Their Fears," *Washington Post,* February 13, 1890.

36. "Cool Heads Prevented a Panic," *Washington Post,* January 5, 1896.

37. Townsend, "Fires in Theatres, and Their Prevention," 312.

38. "To the Editor of the Religious Remembrancer," *Religious Remembrancer,* August 12, 1815, 198.

39. Shockley, "Proprietors," 302.

40. Sherman, "Thomas Wade West," 13

41. John Bernard, *Retrospections of America, 1797–1811* (New York: Harper & Brothers, 1887), 164–65.

42. Wood, *Personal Recollections,* xvii.

43. Ibid., 147–50.

44. Maginnes, *Thomas Abthorpe Cooper,* 131.

45. Bernard, *Retrospections of America,* 165–67.

46. William Wirt to Thomas Abthorpe Cooper, May 19, 1816, University of Virginia Small Special Collections.

47. Ibid.

48. Ibid.

49. Samuel Mordecai to Rachel Mordecai, February 8, 1818, quoted in Bondurant, *Poe's Richmond,* 140–41.

50. It was up for sale in 1833 by Thomas Ritchie, the last remaining member of the board (Bondurant, *Poe's Richmond,* 140).

51. "Richmond, September 30," *Richmond Enquirer,* September 30, 1817.

52. "The Theatre," *Richmond Enquirer,* May 25, 1816.

53. Joshua D. Rothman, *Notorious in the Neighborhood: Sex and Families across the Color Line in Virginia, 1787–1861* (Chapel Hill: University of North Carolina Press, 2003), 98.

54. *Richmond Enquirer*, January 30, 1812.

55. "The Theatre," *Richmond Enquirer*, May 25, 1816.

56. Ibid.

57. Henshaw, *Memoir of Richard Channing Moore*, 172.

58. See n. 6 in Sherman, "Thomas Wade West," 13.

59. Moore to unnamed parishioner, October 23, 1817, in Henshaw, *Memoir of Richard Channing Moore*, 173.

60. Wood, *Personal Recollections*, 24–25.

61. Moore to unidentified parishioner, October 23, 1817, in Henshaw, *Memoir of Richard Channing Moore*, 174.

62. Ibid.

63. Jeter, *Recollections*, 215.

64. "To the Editor of the Christian Monitor," *Christian Monitor*, April 26, 1817.

65. "Richmond, September 30," *Richmond Enquirer*, September 30, 1817.

66. Shockley, "Proprietors," 303.

67. Ibid., Also, Mordecai, *Richmond*, 57. Existing Mutual Assurance Society records do not indicate that the Richmond Theater that burned in 1811 was insured.

68. Page and Marshall have the interesting distinction of being backers of both Monumental Church's construction and the building of the new theater (Records of Deeds of the Hustings Court of Richmond, XVIII, 333–36, June 20, 1820; quoted in Shockley, "Proprietors," 303).

69. "The Theatre," *Richmond Enquirer*, May 25, 1816.

70. "Richmond, September 30," *Richmond Enquirer*, September 30, 1817.

71. Jeter, *A Discourse*, 15–16.

72. Meade, *Old Churches*, 1:39.

73. Quoted in Henshaw, *Memoir of Richard Channing Moore*, 175.

74. Waukechon, *Forgotten Evangelicals*, 36; Noll, *History of Christianity*, 226.

75. William H. Gaines, Jr., "The Fatal Lamp, or Panic at the Play," *Virginia Cavalcade* 2, no. 1 (1952): 8.

76. Harland, "Judith: A Chronicle of Old Virginia," 304.

77. Wood, *Personal Recollections*, 208–9.

78. Mordecai, *Richmond*, 181. Maiden name and country of origin for Mrs. Green found in Dunlap's *History of American Theater*, 1:234.

79. Mordecai, *Richmond*, 182.

80. Shockley, "Proprietors," 304–5.

81. "The Theatre," *Richmond Enquirer*, May 28, 1819. For more about Gilfert's salon of celebrities and artists, see Maginnes, *Thomas Abthorpe Cooper*, 172.

82. Frances Amanda (Booth) Taliaferro to Hester Eliza (Van Bibber) Tabb, August 28, 1820, Manuscripts, Virginia Historical Society, Richmond.

83. This "New Theatre," sometimes called the "Marshall Theatre," was not referred to as such until 1838, when it was rebuilt after significant deterioration (Shockley, "Proprietors," 302).

84. "Virginia Gazetteer," *Southern Literary Messenger* 1, no. 6 (February 1835): 259.

85. *Richmond Whig,* April 1, 1836, in Shockley, "Proprietors," 306.

86. Jeter, *Recollections,* 215.

87. Ibid., 216.

88. Ibid., 215.

89. Ibid.

90. Jeter, *A Discourse,* 16.

91. Jeter, *Recollections,* 217.

92. Fuller-Seeley, *Celebrate Richmond Theater,* 1, 3.

93. Sanford, *Richmond Triumphs,* 110.

94. Asia Booth Clarke, *John Wilkes Booth: A Sister's Memoir,* ed. Terry Alford (Jackson: University Press of Mississippi, 1996), xv.

95. John Lansing Burrows, "The New Richmond Theatre: A Discourse, Delivered on Sunday, February 8, 1863" (Richmond: Smith, Bailey & Co., 1863). Original held in the Virginia Baptist Historical Society Library Archives, Richmond.

96. Ibid.

97. "The New Richmond Theatre," *The Confederate Reader: How the South Saw the War,* ed. Richard Barksdale Harwell (Mineola, NY: Dover, 1989; first published in 1957 by Longmans, Green), 156.

98. *Southern Illustrated News,* February 21, 1863.

99. "Richmond Theater to be Closed: Many Histrionic Geniuses Have Trod Its Boards in Days Gone By," *Washington Post,* March 9, 1895.

100. Gerhard, *Theatre Fires and Panics,* 4–6. Gerhard stated that the average was about nineteen fires a year from around 1850 through the time of his writing in 1896 (p. 7).

101. "A Ball Room on Fire!" From the *N.Y. Observer,* quoted in the *Christian Reflector,* March 23, 1842.

102. Little, *The Fireman's Own Book,* 18.

103. Solomon Smith, *Theatrical Management,* 60. Also in Solomon Smith, "Fire in a Theatre," *Spirit of the Times,* April 15, 1848, 87.

104. Caroline Homassel Thornton, Diary, 1841–1872, Greene Family Papers.

EPILOGUE

1. Biographical Sketch of Caroline Homassel Thornton, signed GWM, undated, Greene Family Papers.

2. Thornton, "Autobiography," 24.

3. "A Historic Edifice" *Washington Post,* December 31, 1894.

4. "Ministers and Churches," *New York Evangelist,* January 1895, 31.

BIBLIOGRAPHY

Primary Sources

Acts Passed at a General Assembly of the Commonwealth of Virginia, Begun and Held at the Capitol in the City of Richmond, On Monday the Second Day of December, in the Year of Our Lord, One Thousand Eight Hundred and Eleven, and of the Commonwealth the Thirty-Sixth. Richmond, VA: Printed by Samuel Pleasants, Printer to the Commonwealth, 1812.

Akers, Bryan, ed. *Graphic Description of the Burning of the Richmond Theatre, December 26, 1811. Compiled from the Lips of Eye-witnesses.* Lynchburg, VA: News Book & Job Office Print, 1879.

Alexander, Archibald. *A Discourse Occasioned by the Burning of the Theatre in the City of Richmond, Virginia, on the Twenty-Sixth of December, 1811, by which Awful Calamity a Large Number of Valuable Lives were Lost. Delivered . . . at the Request of the Virginia Students Attached to the Medical Class, in the University of Pennsylvania.* Philadelphia: Printed by John Weldwood Scott for Daniel Wilson, 1812.

An Account of the great fire, which destroyed about 250 buildings in Newburyport, on the night of the 31st of May, 1811. Taken principally from the statements which have appeared in the public newspapers. Newburyport, MA: W. & J. Gilman, 1811.

Barraud Family Papers, 1779–1904. Manuscripts and Rare Books Department, Swem Library, College of William and Mary.

Barrett, Philip. "Gilbert Hunt." *Friends' Intelligencer,* March 27, 1858, 20–22.

———. *Gilbert Hunt: The City Blacksmith.* Richmond, VA: James Woodhouse & Co., 1859.

Bates, Benjamin. *The Virginia almanack, for the year of our Lord 1812 . . . Adapted to the latitude and meridian of Richmond. Calculated by Benjamin Bates, of Hanover County, Virginia.* Richmond, VA: Printed and sold by Samuel Pleasants, for Robert Gray, Alexandria, 1811.

Bernard, John. *Retrospections of America, 1797–1811.* New York: Harper & Brothers, 1887.

Blair, John Durbarrow. Papers, 1781–1823, 2nd ser. From the Robert Alonzo Brock Collection at the Huntington Library, San Marino, California. Copy in Manuscripts, Library of Virginia.

Breckinridge Family Papers, 1740–1902. Manuscripts, Virginia Historical Society, Richmond.

Brock, Sallie A. "A Glimpse at Richmond." *Riverside Magazine for Young People. An Illustrated Monthly* (December 1870): 543–47.

Brown, James. Letters. Archives and Manuscripts, Library of Virginia.

Bryson, William Hamilton, ed. *Virginia Law Books: Essays and Bibliographies.* Philadelphia: American Philosophical Society, 2000.

"Burning of the Richmond Theatre." *Ladies' Garland and Family Wreath,* May 1838, 299–301.

"The Burning of the Richmond Theatre." From the *American Messenger. New York Observer and Chronicle,* September 14, 1854, 1.

Burrows, John Lansing. "The New Richmond Theatre: A Discourse, Delivered on Sunday, February 8, 1863." Richmond: Smith, Bailey & Co., 1863. Original held in the Virginia Baptist Historical Society Library Archives, Richmond.

Burton, Lewis W. *Annals of Henrico Parish, Diocese of Virginia, and Especially of St. John's Church, the Present Mother Church of the Parish, From 1611 to 1884.* Richmond, VA: Williams Printing Company, 1904. Reprinted as *The Annals and History of Henrico Parish Diocese of Virginia and St. John's P.E. Church,* with added index by Thomas L. Hollowak. Ed. J. Staunton Moore. Baltimore: Genealogical Publishing, 1979.

Clark, Martha. *Victims of Amusements.* Philadelphia: T. B. Peterson, 1819[?].

Clarke, Asia Booth. *John Wilkes Booth: A Sister's Memoir,* ed. Terry Alford. Jackson: University Press of Mississippi, 1996.

Coalter-Tucker Family Letters, 1802–19. Personal Papers Collection, Library of Virginia, Richmond.

Coke, Thomas. *Extracts of the Journals of the Late Rev. Thomas Coke, L.L.D.* Dublin: Printed by R. Napper for the Methodist Book-Room, 1816.

"Communication Describing the Fire at Richmond," *Mirror of Taste and Dramatic Censor* 4 (December 1811): 427.

A Concise Statement of the Awful Conflagration of the Theatre, in the City of Richmond; which happened on the Night of Thursday the 26th of December last. Published in Philadelphia, January 11, 1812. Rare Books, Virginia Historical Society, Richmond.

"Correspondence," *Mirror of Taste and Dramatic Censor* 1, no.1 (January 1810); collected in *The Mirror of Taste and Dramatic Censor,* vol. 1. Philadelphia: Bradford & Inskeep, Smith & McKenzie, printers, 1810.

Copland, Charles. *Diary of Charles Copland.* Archives and Manuscripts, Library of Virginia.

Cornelius, Janet. "We Slipped and Learned to Read: Slave Accounts of the Literacy Process, 1830–1865." *Phylon (1960–)* 44, no. 3. (3rd Qtr., 1983).

D., L. "The Theatre." *Boston Recorder,* January 22, 1820, 14.

Dana, Joseph. *Tribute of Sympathy: A Sermon, Delivered at Ipswich (Mass.), January 12, 1812, on the Late Overwhelming Calamity at Richmond in Virginia.* Newburyport, MA: Printed by E.W. Allen, 1812.

Dashiell, George. *A Sermon Occasioned by the Burning of the Theatre in the City of*

Richmond, Virginia on the Twenty-sixth of December, 1811: by which Disastrous Event More than One Hundred Lives Were Lost. Baltimore: J. Kingston, 1812.

De Selding, Charles. *Documents, Official and Unofficial, Relating to the Case of the Capture and Destruction of the Frigate PHILADELPHIA, at Tripoli, on the 16th February, 1804*. Washington: John T. Towers, 1850.

The Doctrines and Discipline of the Methodist Episcopal Church. 15th ed. New York: Published by Daniel Hitt and Thomas Ware, for the Methodist Connection in the United States, J. C. Totten, printer, 1812.

Drake, Daniel. "History of Two Cases of Burn, Producing Serious Constitutional Irritation." *Western Journal of the Medical and Physical Sciences* 4, no. 1 (1830–31): 48–60.

Drinard, James. Papers. Virginia Historical Society. Richmond, Virginia.

Dunlap, William, *A History of the American Theater*. Vol. 1. London: Richard Bentley, New Burlington Street, 1833.

———. *A History of the American Theater*. Vol. 2. London: Richard Bentley, New Burlington Street, 1833.

———. *Memoirs of the Life of George Frederick Cooke, Esquire, Late of the Theatre Royal, Covent Garden*, vol. 1. New York: D. Longworth, 1813.

First Baptist Church Book. Book One: "Minutes, First Baptist Church (Richmond), 1825–1830." Photostat. Virginia Baptist Historical Society, Richmond.

Fithian, Philip Vickers. *Journal and Letters, 1767–1774*. Ed. John Rogers Williams. Princeton, NJ: University Library, 1900.

Foote, William Henry. *Sketches of Virginia, Historical and Biographical*. 2nd ser. Philadelphia: J. B. Lippincott, 1855.

Gerhard, William Paul. *Safety of Theatre Audiences and of the Stage Personnel against Danger from Fire and Panic*. London: British Fire Prevention Committee, 1899.

Gilman, Samuel. *Monody on the Victims and Sufferers by the Late Conflagration in the City of Richmond, Virginia*. Boston: Charles Williams, T. B. Wait & Co. Printers, 1812. Manuscripts and Rare Books Department, Swem Library, College of William and Mary.

The Good old Virginia almanack, for the year of our Lord, 1808. Richmond, VA: Printed by Thos. Nicolson, near the Bank of Virginia, 1807.

Goode, James E. *Full Account of the Burning of the Richmond Theatre, on the Night of December 26, 1811*. Richmond, VA: J. E. Goode, 1858. Manuscripts and Rare Books Department, Swem Library, College of William and Mary.

"Gravity, Gregory." Annotations dated January 24, 1812, on flyleaf and margins of Archibald Alexander's *A Discourse Occasioned by the Burning of the Theatre in the City of Richmond, Virginia, on the Twenty-Sixth of December, 1811, by which Awful Calamity a Large Number of Valuable Lives were Lost. Delivered . . . at the Request of the Virginia*

Students Attached to the Medical Class, in the University of Pennsylvania. Philadelphia: Farrand, Hopkins, Zantzinger, & Co., 1812. Located in Miscellaneous Pamphlets, Special Collections, Library of Virginia.

Greene Family Papers, 1795–1947. Manuscripts, Virginia Historical Society.

Harland, Marion. *Marion Harland's Autobiography: The Story of a Long Life.* New York: Harper & Brothers, 1910.

———. "Judith: A Chronicle of Old Virginia." *The Continent; an Illustrated Weekly Magazine,* September 5, 1883, 298–306.

Haskel, Daniel, and J. Calvin Smith. *Complete Descriptive and Statistical Gazetteer of the United States with an Abstract of the Census and Statistics for 1840.* New York: Sherman & Smith, 1848.

Henrico County Census Information, 1810. Richmond: University of Virginia, Geostat Center: Historical Census Browser. From historical volumes of the U.S. Census of Population and Housing, 1810.

Henrico Parish Vestry Book, April 8, 1807; May 12, 1812–December 16, 1817. Manuscripts, Virginia Historical Society. Richmond, Virginia.

Henshaw, John Prentiss Kewley. *Memoir of the Life of the Rt. Rev. Richard Channing Moore, D.D., Bishop of the Protestant Episcopal Church in the Diocese of Virginia.* Philadelphia: W. Stavely & Co., 1843.

Hill, William. *A sermon, delivered in the Presbyterian meeting-house in Winchester, on Thursday the 23d Jan. 1812; being a day of fasting and humiliation, appointed by the citizens of Winchester on account of the late calamitous fire at the Richmond theatre.* Winchester, VA: Printed at the office of the *Winchester Gazette,* 1812.

Hobart, John Henry. *The origin, the general character, and the present situation of the Protestant Episcopal Church in the United States of America [microform] a sermon preached in St. James's Church in the city of Philadelphia on Wednesday, May 18th, A.D. 1814, on the occasion of the opening of the General Convention of the said Church, and of the consecration of the Right Rev. Bishop Moore of Virginia.* Philadelphia: Printed for Bradford & Inskeep by J. Maxwell, 1814.

Holmes, David, *A Brief History of the Episcopal Church.* Harrisburg, PA: Trinity Press International, 1993.

———. ed. *A Nation Mourns: Bishop James Madison's Memorial Eulogy on the Death of George Washington.* Mount Vernon, VA: Mount Vernon Ladies' Association, 1999.

Ingersoll, Robert G. "The Gods." Pp. 7–90 in *The Gods and Other Lectures,* by Robert G. Ingersoll. Washington, D.C.: C. P. Farrell, 1879.

Jefferson, Thomas. Papers. 1st ser.: General Correspondence. 1651–1827. Library of Congress.

Jeter, Jeremiah B. *A Discourse on the Immoral Tendency of Theatrical Amusements.* Richmond, VA: William MacFarlane, 1838.

————. *The Recollections of a Long Life*. Richmond, VA: Religious Herald Co., 1891.

Joynes, Thomas R., to Levin S. Joynes, December 27, 1811. In *Virginia Magazine of History and Biography* 51, no. 3 (July 1943): 297–99.

Knowles, James D. Review of *The Theatre, in its Influence upon Literature, Morals and Religion*, by Robert Turnbull. Pp. 393–405 in *Christian Review*, vol. 2. Boston: Gould, Kendall & Lincoln, 1837.

Lloyd, Rees. *The Richmond Alarm: A Plain and Familiar Discourse in the Form of a Dialogue Between a Father and His Son: in Three Parts: Written at the Request of a Number of Pious Persons by an Independent Minister*. Philadelphia: J. Bioren, Printer, 1814.

Madison, Dolley. Papers. Holly C. Shulman, ed., The Dolley Madison Digital Edition. Charlottesville: University of Virginia Press, 2009.

"Main Street, Richmond, Virginia." *Gleason's Pictorial Drawing-Room Companion*, April 23, 1853, 264.

Manual for Members of the First Presbyterian Church in Richmond, Va: compiled by order of session, Oct. 1833. Richmond: Printed by T. W. White, 1833. Rare Books, Virginia Historical Society. Richmond.

Mather, Increase, D. D., *Burnings bewailed: in a sermon, occasioned by the lamentable fire which was in Boston, Octob. 2. 1711. In which the sins which provoke the Lord to kindle fires, are enquired into*. Boston: Sold by Timothy Green, 1711.

May, Robert. *Voice from Richmond, and Other Addresses to Children and Youth*. Philadelphia: American Sunday-School Union, 1842.

Meade, William. *Old Churches, Ministers and Families of Virginia*. Vol. 1. Philadelphia: J. B. Lippincott, 1891.

————. *Old Churches, Ministers and Families of Virginia*. Vol. 2. Philadelphia: J. B. Lippincott, 1891.

Melish, John. *Travels through the United States of America, in the years 1806 & 1807, and 1809, 1810, & 1811; including an account of passages betwixt America and Britain, and travels through various parts of Britain, Ireland, & Canada. With corrections and improvements till 1815*. Philadelphia: Printed for the Author, 1818. Library of Congress.

Miller, Samuel. *A Sermon, Delivered January 19, 1812, at the Request of a Number of Young Gentlemen of the City of New York: Who had Assembled to Express their Condolence with the Inhabitants of Richmond, on the late Mournful Dispensation of Providence in that City*. New York: Whiting & Watson, 1812. Rare Books, Virginia Historical Society, Richmond.

Mills, Robert, Richmond, to Miss Sarah Zane, Philadelphia, December 13, 1812. Manuscripts, Virginia Historical Society. Richmond.

Minutes of the Dover Baptist Association, 1801–40. Virginia Baptist Historical Society, Richmond.

Minutes of the Second Baptist Church of Richmond, Virginia. Virginia Baptist Historical Society, Richmond.

M'Lean, John. *Sketch of Rev. Philip Gatch*. Cincinnati, OH: Swormstedt & Poe, R. P. Thompson, Printer, 1854.

Moore, Richard Channing. *Christ Crucified, the Foundation of the Christian's Hope. A Sermon, preached in the Monumental Church in the City of Richmond, on Tuesday, May 23, 1815. On the Occasion of the Meeting of the Convention of the Diocese of Virginia, and of the ordination of the Revd. William Hawley. By the Right Reverend, Richard Channing Moore, D.D. Bishop of the Prot. Epis. Church, Virginia*. Richmond: Printed by Ritchie & Trueheart, 1815. Rare Books, Virginia Historical Society, Richmond.

———, Richmond, to Rt. Rev. William White, November 14, 1815. "Monumental Church Correspondence between Rectors and Communicants." Manuscripts, Virginia Historical Society. Richmond.

Mordecai Family Papers, 1649–1947. Southern Historical Collection. Louis Round Wilson Special Collections Library, University of North Carolina.

Mordecai, Samuel. *Richmond in By-Gone Days*. Republished from the Second Edition of 1860. Richmond, VA: Dietz, 1946.

Mowatt, Anna Cora. *Autobiography of an Actress; or, Eight Years on the Stage*. Boston: Ticknor, Reed, & Fields, 1854.

Muir, James. *Repentance, or Richmond in Tears*. Alexandria, Virginia: 1812.

Narrative & Report of the Causes and Circumstances of the Deplorable Conflagration at Richmond, Virginia, from Letters and Authentic Documents. Richmond, VA: Printed for the Public: January, 12th, 1812.

Olmstead, Frederick Law. *Journey in the Seaboard Slave States*. New York: Dix & Edwards, 1856.

Particular accou[nt] of the dreadful [fire] at Richmond, Virginia, December 26, 1811. Which destroyed the theatre and the house adjoining, and in which more than sixty persons were either burnt to death, or destroyed in attempting to make their escape. To which is added, some observations on theatrical performances; and, an essay from the Virginia Argus, proving profaneness inconsistent with politeness. Printed for and sold by J. Kingston, and all the Booksellers in the United States. Baltimore: B. W. Sower & Co., Printers, 1812. Rare Books, Virginia Historical Society, Richmond.

Richards, George. *Repent! Repent! Or Likewise Perish! The Spirit of an Evening Lecture, February 16, 1812; on the Late Calamity at Richmond, Virginia*. Philadelphia: Lydia R. Bailey, 1812. Rare Books, Virginia Historical Society, Richmond.

Richmond City Hustings Court Minute Book 17, 1847–48. Library of Virginia.

Richmond Theater Fire File, Valentine Richmond History Center, Richmond, VA

Rush, Benjamin. *The Autobiography of Benjamin Rush*. Ed. George W. Corner. Princeton, NJ: Princeton University Press for the American Philosophical Society, 1948.

Sabin, Elijah Robinson. *A Discourse Preached on Tuesday, February 1812 in Presence of the Supreme Executive of Massachusetts, by Request of the Young Men of Boston, Commemorative of the Late Calamitous Fire at Richmond.* Boston, James Scott, 1812.

Scharf, John Thomas, and Thompson Westcott. *History of Philadelphia, 1609–1884.* 3 vols. Vol. 2. Philadelphia: L. H. Everts & Co., 1884.

"*A Series of Tables of Several Branches of American Manufacturers of Every County in the Union so far as they are returned in the reports of the Marshals, and of the secretaries and of their respective assistants, in the autumn of the year 1810: Together with returns of certain doubtful Goods, Productions of the Soil and agricultural stock, so far as they have been received.*" U.S. Census Bureau, Census of Population and Housing, 1810 Census. Richmond, Virginia: 89–114.

A Serious Inquiry into the Nature and Effects of the Stage and a Letter respecting Play Actors by John Witherspoon also, a Sermon on the burning of the Theatre at Richmond, &c., by Samuel Miller D.D. pastor of the First Presbyterian Church of New-York together with an introductory address, by Several Ministers in New-York, &c. New York: Whiting & Watson, D. & G. Bruce, Printers, 1812.

Sharp, Joshua. *Johnson and Warner's Virginia almanac, for the year of our Lord 1812 . . . Calculated for the latitude and meridian of Richmond (Virginia).* Richmond, VA: Published at Johnson & Warner's bookstore, 1811.

Shenandoah. [psued.] "A Tale—But No Fiction." *Album and Ladies' Weekly Gazette*, May 23, 1827, 4–5.

Singleton, Arthur (Henry Knight, pseud.). *Letters from the South and West.* Boston: Richardson & Lord, J. H. A. Frost, Printer, 1824.

William Smart Papers, Archives and Manuscripts, Library of Virginia, Richmond, VA

George William Smith Executive Papers. Archives and Manuscripts, Library of Virginia, Richmond, VA.

Smith, Solomon. *Theatrical Management in the West and South for Thirty Years.* New York: Harper & Brothers, 1868.

"The Southern Stage, Actors and Authors, Dramatic Literature: In Three Parts. Part Three. Notes of the Drama in the South and West. From Dunlap's History of the American Stage. H. G. Pearson," the *Dramatic Mirror, and Literary Companion. Devoted to the Stage and Fine Arts* (May 7, 1842): 90.

Sutcliff, Robert. *Travels in Some Parts of North America, in the Years 1804, 1805, & 1806.* 2nd ed., improved. York, Eng.: W. Alexander, 1815.

Taylor, James B. *Virginia Baptist Ministers.* In two series. 2nd ser.. New York: Sheldon & Company, 1860.

"Terrible Recollections," *Baltimorean*, November 16, 1872.

"A Theocrate." *Five important questions: on the subject of the divine government of the world, occasioned by serious reflections on the alarming and awfully severe visitation of the theatre in Richmond, December 1811, stated and answered, in a letter to an honourable young gentleman in office.* 1812. Rare Books, Virginia Historical Society, Richmond.

Thompson, D. P. "Presentiments." *Home Magazine,* March 1853, 411–12.

Thornton, Caroline Homassel. "Autobiography of Mrs. Caroline Homassel Thornton (1795–1875)." Albemarle County Historical Society Papers, Charlottesville, Virginia. Volume 6. 1945–46, 22–40.

———. Diary, 1841–72. Manuscripts, Virginia Historical Society, Richmond.

Townsend, Horace. "Fires in Theatres, and Their Prevention." *Frank Leslie's Popular Monthly* 15, no. 3 (March 1883). APS Online.

Tucker-Coleman Papers, 1664–1945, 1770–1907. Manuscripts and Rare Books Department, Swem Library, College of William and Mary, Williamsburg, VA.

Tuke Alexander, Ann. *Remarks on the Theatre, and on the Late Fire at Richmond, in Virginia.* York, Eng.: T. Wilson & Son, 1812.

Watson, John F. *Calamity at Richmond: Being a Narrative of the Affecting Circumstances Attending the Awful Conflagration of the Theatre, in the City of Richmond, on the Night of Thursday, the 26th of December, 1811.* Philadelphia: John F. Watson, 1812.

Sarah C. Watts Papers, Manuscripts and Rare Books Department, Swem Library, College of William and Mary, Williamsburg, VA.

Weiss, Susan Archer. "Reminiscences of Edgar Allan Poe." *The Independent . . . Devoted to the Consideration of Politics, Social and Economics,* August 25, 1904, 57.

Weld, Isaac, Jr. *Travels through the states of North America : and the provinces of Upper and Lower Canada during the years 1795, 1796, and 1797.* 4th ed. 2 vols., Piccadilly, London: Printed for J. Stockdale, 1807.

Wirt, William. *The Letters of the British Spy.* 10th ed., revised and corrected. New York: J. & J. Harper, 1832.

Wood, William. *Personal Recollections of the Stage, Embracing Notices of Actors, Authors, and Auditors, During a Period of Forty Years.* Philadelphia: Henry Carey Baird, 1855.

Wyatt, Edward A. "Three Petersburg Theatres." *William and Mary College Quarterly Historical Magazine,* 2nd ser., vol. 21, no. 2 (April 1941): 83–110.

Secondary Sources

Alexander, Robert. "The Young Professional in Philadelphia and Baltimore, 1808–20." Pp. 25–74 in *Robert Mills: Architect.* Ed. John Morrill Bryan. Washington, D.C.: American Institute of Architects Press, 1989.

Allgor, Catherine. *Parlor Politics: In Which the Ladies of Washington Help Build a City and a Government.* Charlottesville: University Press of Virginia, 2002.

Anonymous. "Richmond and Its Fire Department(s)." *Richmond Literature and History Quarterly* 2, no. 2 (Fall 1979): 37–38.

"An Architect Looks at Richmond." *Virginia Cavalcade* 16, no. 3 (1967): 22–29.

Bearss, Sarah B., ed. *Dictionary of Virginia Biography.* Vol. 3: Caperton-Daniels. Richmond: Library of Virginia, 2006.

Boles, John B. *The Great Revival: Beginnings of the Bible Belt.* Religion in the South. John B. Boles, series ed. Lexington: University Press of Kentucky, 1996. Originally published as *The Great Revival, 1787–1805: The Origins of the Southern Evangelical Mind.* Lexington: University Press of Kentucky, 1972.

Bondurant, Agnes M. *Poe's Richmond.* Reprinted by the Edgar Allan Poe Museum, September 1999. Richmond, VA: Garrett & Massie, 1942.

Bonomi, Patricia U. *Under the Cope of Heaven: Religion, Society, and Politics in Colonial America.* Updated ed., originally published 1986. New York: Oxford University Press, 2003.

Booty, J. E. *William Meade: Evangelical Churchman.* Paper delivered on the occasion of the observance of the Centennial of the Right Reverend William Meade, 1789–1862. Unknown publisher, 1962.

Brock, Robert Alonzo. "Historical Sketch": Pp. 12–28 in *The Richmond, Virginia fire department, its organization and equipment: with an account of its precursors from the initial organization "effective friendship" in 1816.* Richmond: Published under the auspices of the Firemen's Relief Assn., 1894.

Bryan, John Morrill. *America's First Architect: Robert Mills.* New York: Princeton Architectural Press, 2001.

———. "Robert Mills: Education and Early Drawings." Pp. 1–35 in *Robert Mills: Architect.* Ed. John Morrill Bryan. Washington, D.C.: American Institute of Architects Press, 1989.

Brydon, George MacLaren. *Historic Parishes: Saint Paul's Church, Richmond.* Reprinted from the *Historical Magazine of the Protestant Episcopal Church,* New Brunswick, NJ. Volume 23 (September 1954).

———. "A List of Clergy of the Protestant Episcopal Church Ordained after the American Revolution, Who Served in Virginia between 1785 and 1814, and a List of Virginia Parishes and Their Rectors for the Same Period." *William and Mary College Quarterly Historical Magazine.* 2nd ser., vol. 19, no. 4 (October 1939): 397–434.

Burrows, J. L. "History of the Church." Pp. 43–105 in *The First Century of The First Baptist Church of Richmond Virginia, 1780–1880.* Richmond, VA: Carlton McCarthy, 1880.

Butler, Jon. *Awash in a Sea of Faith: Christianizing the American People.* Cambridge, MA: Harvard University Press, 1990.

Calhoon, Robert M. *Evangelicals and Conservatives in the Early South, 1740–1861.* Columbia: University of South Carolina Press, 1988.

Caroli, Betty Boyd. *First Ladies.* Expanded edition. New York: Oxford University Press, 1995.

Carson, Joseph. *A History of the Medical Department of the University of Pennsylvania: From its Foundation in 1765 with Sketches of the Lives of Deceased Professors.* Philadelphia: Lindsay & Blakiston, 1869.

Carter, Albert Howard III, and Jane Arbuckle Petro. *Rising from the Flames: The Experience of the Severely Burned.* Philadelphia: University of Pennsylvania Press, 1998.

Chappelmann, Mary Dudley. "History of the Fire and Police Departments of Richmond, Virginia." Richmond: Firemans' Mutual Aid Association and Police Benevolent Association, 1952.

Christian, W. A. *Richmond: Her Past and Present.* Richmond, VA: L. H. Jenkins, 1912.

Click, Patricia C. *The Spirit of the Times: Amusements in Nineteenth-Century Baltimore, Norfolk, and Richmond.* Charlottesville: University Press of Virginia, 1989.

C.M.S. "The Home Life of Chief Justice Marshall." *William and Mary Quarterly,* 2nd ser., vol. 12 (January 1932): 67–69. Originally published in the *Richmond Dispatch* of April 18, 1879.

Cornelius, Janet Duitsman. *"When I Can Read My Title Clear": Literacy, Slavery, and Religion in the Antebellum South.* Columbia: University of South Carolina Press, 1991.

Dabney, Virginius. *Richmond: The Story of a City.* New York: Doubleday, 1976.

Daniels, W. H. *Illustrated History of Methodism in Great Britain and America, from the Days of the Wesleys to the Present Time.* New York: Phillips & Hunt, 1879.

Dunn, Susan. *Dominion of Memories: Jefferson, Madison and the Decline of Virginia.* New York: Basic Books, 2007.

Egerton, Douglas R. "Gabriel's Conspiracy and the Election of 1800." *Journal of Southern History* 56, no. 2 (May 1990): 191–214.

Eliot, Samuel A. ed. *Heralds of a Liberal Faith,* Vol. 2, "The Pioneers." Boston: American Unitarian Association, 1910.

Epstein, Dena. *Sinful Tunes and Spirituals: Black Folk Music to the Civil War.* Urbana: University of Illinois Press, 1977.

Evelyn, Douglas Everett. *A Public Building for a New Democracy: The Patent Office Building in the Nineteenth Century.* Ph.D. diss., George Washington University, Washington, D.C., 1997.

"Fatal Lamp, or Panic at the Play, The." *Virginia Cavalcade* 2, no. 1 (1952): 4–8.

Fischer, David H. *Albion's Seed: Four British Folkways in America.* Volume I. New York: Oxford University Press, 1989.

Fisher, George D. *History and Reminiscences of the Monumental Church, Richmond, Virginia, from 1814 to 1878.* Richmond: Whittet & Shepperson, 1880.

Foote, William Henry. *Sketches of Virginia, Historical and Biographical.* 2nd ser. Philadelphia: J. B. Lippincott, 1855.

Fuller-Seeley, Kathryn. *Celebrate Richmond Theater.* Richmond, VA: Dietz, 2002.

Garland, Hugh A. *The Life of John Randolph of Roanoke.* 9th ed. New York: D. Appleton, 1854.

Gerhard, William Paul. *Theatre Fires and Panics: Their Causes and Prevention.* New York: John Wiley & Sons, 1896.

Gish, Agnes Evans. *Virginia Taverns, Ordinaries and Coffee Houses.* Westminster, MD: Willow Bend Books, 2005.

Godson, Susan H., Ludwell H. Johnson, Richard B. Sherman, Thad W. Tate, and Helen C. Walker. *The College of William & Mary: A History.* Vol. 1, 1693–1888. Williamsburg, VA: King & Queen Press, 1993.

Goodwin, William A. R. *The Right Reverend Richard Channing Moore, D.D. Second Bishop of Virginia and The Beginnings of the Theological Seminary in Virginia: An Address Delivered at the Alumni Meeting of the Virginia Theological Seminary on June 4th, 1914.* Published by Order of the Alumni Association, 1914.

Grimsted, David. *Melodrama Unveiled: American Theater and Culture, 1800–1850.* Chicago: University of Chicago Press, 1968. Reprint, Berkeley: University of California Press, 1987.

Gwathmey, W. H. "The House of One Franklin." Pp. 143–47 in *The First Century of The First Baptist Church of Richmond Virginia, 1780–1880.* Richmond, VA: Carlton McCarthy, 1880.

Hammond, John. *The American Puritan Elegy: A Literary and Cultural Study.* Cambridge: Cambridge University Press, 2000.

Harwell, Richard Barksdale, ed. *The Confederate Reader: How the South Saw the War.* Mineola, NY: Dover, 1989; first published in 1957 by Longmans, Green.

Hatch, Nathan O. *The Democratization of American Christianity.* New Haven, CT: Yale University Press, 1989.

Hazen, Margaret Hindle, and Robert M. Hazen. *Keepers of the Flame: The Role of Fire in American Culture 1775–1925.* Princeton, NJ: Princeton University Press, 1992.

Henley, Bernard J. "A Richmond Clerk Invented the Post Office Box." *Richmond Literature and History Quarterly* 2, no. 3 (Winter 1979): 38–39.

———. "Schooldays in Richmond, 1810–1811: A Student's Memoir." *Richmond Literature and History Quarterly,* 1, no. 2 (Fall 1978): 42–43.

———. "He Looked Like This: John Marshall." *Richmond Literature and History Quarterly* 2, no. 1 (Fall 1979): 45.

Henriques, Peter R. *He Died as He Lived: The Death of George Washington.* Mount Vernon, Virginia: For the Mount Vernon Ladies' Association, 2000.

Hill, Samuel S., Charles H. Lippy, and Charles Reagan Wilson, eds. *Encyclopedia of Religion in the South.* 2nd ed. Macon, GA: Mercer University Press, 2005.

"Historical and Genealogical Notes." *William and Mary Quarterly* 23, no. 1 (July 1914): 70.

Hoge, Moses D. "Portraitures of Four Pastors." Pp. 15–28 in *First Presbyterian, Richmond, Virginia. Proceedings of the Celebration of the Eightieth Anniversary of Its Organization, May 1, 1892.* Richmond: Whittet & Shepperson, General Printers, 1892.

Holland, Barbara. *Gentlemen's Blood: A History of Dueling from Swords at Dawn to Pistols at Dusk.* Bloomsbury, NY: Bloomsbury, 2003.

Hubbell, Jay B. "Poe's Mother: With a Note on John Allan." *William and Mary College Quarterly Historical Magazine,* 2nd Ser., vol. 21, no. 3 (July 1941), 250–54.

Hume, Janice Rose. *Private Lives, Public Virtues: Historic Newspaper Obituaries in a Changing American Culture.* Ph.D. diss., University of Missouri, Columbia, 1997.

Hunt, Conover. Executive Director of the Historic Richmond Foundation. Interview by author, October 15, 2006.

Hutson, James H. *Religion and the Founding of the American Republic.* Washington, D.C.: Library of Congress, 1998.

Inventory of the Church Archives of Virginia: Negro Baptist Churches in Richmond. Historical Records Survey, Work Projects Administration. Richmond: Historical Records Survey of Virginia, June 1940.

Isaac, Rhys. *The Transformation of Virginia, 1740–1790.* Chapel Hill: University of North Carolina Press for the Omohundro Institute of Early American History and Culture, 1982.

Isenberg, Nancy. *Fallen Founder: The Life of Aaron Burr.* New York: Viking, 2007.

Jackson, Luther P. "Free Negroes of Petersburg, Virginia." *Journal of Negro History* 12, no. 3 (July 1927): 365–88.

Johns, Christopher M. S. "Theater and Theory: Thomas Sully's "George Frederick Cooke as Richard III," *Winterthur Portfolio* 18, no. 1 (Spring 1983): 27-38.

Johnson, Claudia Durst. *Church and Stage: The Theatre as Target of Religious Condemnation in Nineteenth-Century America.* Jefferson, NC: McFarland, 2008.

Kennedy, John Pendleton. *Memoirs of the Life of William Wirt, Attorney-general of the United States.* Vol. 1. New York: Blanchard & Lea, 1854.

Kerber, Linda K. *Federalists in Disssent: Imagery and Ideology in Jeffersonian America.* Ithaca, NY: Cornell University Press, 1970.

———. *Women of the Republic: Intellect and Ideology in Revolutionary America.* Chapel Hill: University of North Carolina Press, 1980.

Kierner, Cynthia A. "'The Dark and Dense Cloud Perpetually Lowering over Us': Gender and the Decline of the Gentry in Postrevolutionary Virginia." *Journal of the Early Republic* 20, no. 2 (Summer 2000): 185–217.

Kimball, Gregg D. *American City, Southern Place: A Cultural History of Antebellum Richmond.* Athens: University of Georgia Press, 2000.

King, Charles, ed. *Life and Correspondence of Rufus King.* New York: G. P. Putnam's Sons, 1896.

Lafferty, John J. *Sketches and Portraits of the Virginia Conference, Methodist Episcopal Church, South.* Richmond, VA: Christian Advocate Office, 1890.

Larkin, Jack. *The Reshaping of Everyday Life 1790–1840.* New York: Harper & Row, 1988.

Lewis, Jan. *The Pursuit of Happiness: Family and Values in Jefferson's Virginia.* New York: Cambridge University Press, 1983.

Liscombe, Rhodri Windsor. *Altogether American: Robert Mills, Architect and Engineer, 1781–1855.* New York: Oxford University Press, 1994.

Little, George P. *The Fireman's Own Book: Containing Accounts of Fires throughout the United States, as Well as other Countries.* Boston: 1860.

Little, John P. *History of Richmond.* Richmond, VA: Dietz, 1933.

Loveland, Anne C. *Southern Evangelicals and the Social Order, 1800–1860.* Baton Rouge: Louisiana State University Press, 1980.

Lovett, Richard. *The History of the London Missionary Society, 1795–1895.* 2 vols. Vol. 1. London: Oxford University Press.

Maginnes, F. Arant. *Thomas Abthorpe Cooper: Father of the American Stage, 1775–1849.* Jefferson, NC: McFarland, 2004.

Marsden, George, *Understanding Fundamentalism and Evangelicalism.* Grand Rapids, MI: Wm. B. Eerdmans, 1991. Reprinted 2000.

Mason, Frances Norton. *My Dearest Polly: Letters of Chief Justice John Marshall to His Wife, with Their Background, Political and Domestic, 1779–1831.* Richmond, VA: Garrett & Massie, 1961.

Mathews, Donald G. *Religion in the Old South.* Chicago: University of Chicago Press, 1977.

Maxwell, William. *A Memoir of the Rev. John H. Rice, D.D.* Richmond, VA: R. I. Smith, 1835.

McConachie, Bruce. "American Theatre in Context, from the Beginnings to 1870." In *The Cambridge History of American Theatre: Beginnings to 1870.* Vol. 1. Ed. Don B. Wilmeth and Christopher Bigsby. New York: Cambridge University Press, 1998.

McKay, John. "1811 Theater Fire Changed History in Richmond." *Richmond Times-Dispatch,* December 26, 1988.

McTyeire, Holland N. *A History of Methodism.* London: Richard D. Dickenson, 1885.

Mead, Stith. "Camp Meeting." *William and Mary College Quarterly Historical Magazine,* 2nd ser., vol. 4 (July 1924): 210.

Meade, Robert Douthat. "John Randolph of Roanoke: Some New Information." *William and Mary College Quarterly Historical Magazine,* 2nd ser., vol. 13, no. 4 (October 1933): 256–64.

Meade, William. *Old Churches, Ministers and Families of Virginia.* Vols. 1 and 2. Originally published in 1857. Reprint, Philadelphia: J. B. Lippincott, 1891.

Mickler, Margaret Pearson. "The Monumental Church." Master's in Architectural History thesis, University of Virginia, Charlottesville, VA. 1980.

Morrison, Alfred J. "The Virginia Literary and Evangelical Magazine, Richmond, 1818–1828." *William and Mary Quarterly* 19, no. 4 (April 1911): 266–72.

Munford, George Wythe. "The Two Parsons." In *The Two Parsons; Cupid's Sports; The Dream; and The Jewels of Virginia.* Richmond: J. D. K. Sleight, 1884.

Murrell, Amy E. "Calamity at Richmond! Fire and Faith in a Young Virginia City." Unpublished seminar paper, University of Virginia, December 1995.

Najar, Monica. *Evangelizing the South: Gender, Race, and Politics in the Early Evangelical South, 1765–1850.* Ph.D. diss., University of Wisconsin, Madison, 2000.

Newman, William M., and Peter L. Halvorson. *Atlas of American Religion: The Denominational Era, 1776–1990.* Walnut Creek, CA: AltaMira Press, 2000.

Noll, Mark. *America's God: From Jonathan Edwards to Abraham Lincoln.* New York: Oxford University Press, 2002.

———. *A History of Christianity in the United States and Canada.* Grand Rapids, MI: William B. Eerdmans, 1992. Reprinted 1999.

———. *The Work We Have to Do: A History of Protestants in America.* New York: Oxford University Press, 2002.

Norfleet, Fillmore. *Saint-Memin in Virginia: Portraits and Biographies.* Richmond: Dietz, 1942.

Norton, John N. *The Life of the Right Reverend Richard Channing Moore, D.D., Bishop of Virginia.* 2nd ed., enl. New York: General Protestant Episcopal S. School Union & Church Book Society, 1860.

Peterson, Merrill D. *Thomas Jefferson and the New Nation: A Biography.* New York: Oxford University Press, 1970.

Phoebus, George A. *Beams of Light on Early Methodism in America.* New York: Phillips & Hunt, 1887.

Pilkinton, Lucy Blandford. *Theater in Norfolk, Virginia, 1788–1812.* Ph.D. diss., University of Michigan, Ann Arbor, 1993.

Price, Philip B. *The Life of the Reverend John Holt Rice, D.D.* Historical Transcripts no. 1. Richmond: Library of Union Theological Seminary in Virginia, 1963.

Rankin, Richard. *Ambivalent Churchmen and Evangelical Churchwomen: The Religion of the Episcopal Elite in North Carolina, 1800–1860.* Columbia: University of South Carolina Press, 1993.

Resendes, Karen. "A Beacon That Cannot Be Hid: The Religious Impact of the Richmond Theater Fire of 1811." College of William and Mary term paper. Shared with permission of author. 1995.

"Reverend Jesse Lee," *Methodist Quarterly Review.* Vol. 32, 4th ser., Volume II. Ed. J. McClintock. New York: Lane & Scott, Joseph Longking, Printer, 1850.

Richard, Jeffrey. "A British or an American Tar? Play, Player, and Spectator in Norfolk, 1797–1800." *Drama, Theatre, and Identity in the American New Republic.* Cambridge Studies in American Theatre and Drama, no. 22. New York: Cambridge University Press, 2005.

Rolle, Andrew "Exploring an Explorer: Psychohistory and John Charles Frémont," *Pacific Historical Review* 51, no. 2 (May 1982): 135–63.

Rothman, Joshua D. *Notorious in the Neighborhood: Sex and Families across the Color Line in Virginia, 1787–1861.* Chapel Hill: University of North Carolina Press, 2003.

Russell, Terence. "Fire Prevention and Fire Protection in Buildings and Habitable Environments: Works Published in the 19th Century," and "Fires and the Work of the Fire Services: Works Published in the 19th Century" Pp. 880–85 and 899–903 in *The Built Environment: A Subject Index 1800–1960.* Surrey, Eng.: Gregg, 1989.

Sanford, James K., ed. *Richmond, Her Triumphs, Tragedies and Growth.* Richmond, VA: Produced and distributed by Metropolitan Richmond Chamber of Commerce, 1975.

Scharf, John Thomas, and Thompson Westcott. *History of Philadelphia, 1609–1884.* 3 vols. Vol. 2. Philadelphia: L. H. Everts & Co., 1884.

Schwartz, Philip. *Twice Condemned: Slaves and the Criminal Laws of Virginia, 1705–1865.* Union, NJ: Lawbook Exchange, 1998.

Semple, Robert Baylor. *A History of the Rise and Progress of the Baptists in Virginia.* Rev. and ex. by G. W. Beale. Richmond, VA: Pitt & Dickinson, 1894.

Shepard, E. Lee. "Sketches of the Old Richmond Bar: Charles Copland." *Richmond Literature and History Quarterly* 3, no. 4: 30–33.

Sherman, Susanne K. *Comedies Useful: Southern Theatre History 1775–1812.* Ed. Lucy B. Pilkinton. Williamsburg, VA: Celest Press, 1998.

———. "Thomas Wade West, Theatrical Impresario, 1790–1799." *William and Mary Quarterly* 9, no. 1 (January 1952): 10–28.

Shively, Charles. *A History of the Conception of Death in America, 1650–1860.* New York: Garland, 1988.

Shockley, Martin Staples. "The Proprietors of Richmond's New Theatre of 1819." *William and Mary College Quarterly Historical Magazine,* 2nd ser., vol. 19, no.3 (July 1939): 302–8.

———. *The Richmond Stage, 1784–1812.* Charlottesville: University Press of Virginia, 1977.

Sleight, J. D. K. "The Sabbath School." Pp. 36–42 in *First Presbyterian, Richmond, VA. Proceedings of the Celebration of the Eightieth Anniversary of Its Organization, May 1, 1892.* Richmond, VA: Whittet & Shepperson, General Printers, 1892.

Smith, Geddeth. *Thomas Abthorpe Cooper: America's Premier Tragedian.* Cranbury, NJ: Associated University Presses, 1996.

Smith, Jean Edward. *John Marshall: Definer of a Nation.* New York: Henry Holt, 1996.

Spangler, Jewel. *Virginians Reborn: Anglican Monopoly, Evangelical Dissent, and the Rise of the Baptists in the Late Eighteenth Century.* Charlottesville: University of Virginia Press, 2008.

Sprague, William Buell. *Annals of the American Pulpit: Or, Commemorative Notices of Distinguished American Clergymen of Various Denominations, From the Early Settlement of the Country to the Close of the Year Eighteen Hundred and Fifty-Five.* Episcopalian. Vol. 5. New York: R. Carter & Brothers, 1861.

_____. *Annals of the American Pulpit: Or, Commemorative Notices of Distinguished American Clergymen of Various Denominations, From the Early Settlement of the Country to the Close of the Year Eighteen Hundred and Fifty-Five.* Presbyterian. Vol. 4. New York: R. Carter & Brothers, 1859.

——. *Annals of the American Pulpit: Or, Commemorative Notices of Distinguished American Clergymen of Various Denominations, From the Early Settlement of the Country to the Close of the Year Eighteen Hundred and Fifty-Five.* Methodist, Vol. 7. New York: R. Carter & Brothers, 1859.

Stanard, Mary Newton. *Richmond: Its People and Its Story.* Philadelphia: J. B. Lippincott, 1923.

Stevens, Abel. *History of the Methodist Episcopal Church in the United States of America.* Vol. 4. New York: Phillips & Hunt, 1884.

"The St. Memin Collection of Portraits." *William and Mary College Quarterly Historical Magazine* 9, no. 3 (January 1901): 145–51.

Stout, Harry S. *The Divine Dramatist: George Whitefield and the Rise of Modern Evangelism.* Grand Rapids, MI: William B. Eerdmans, 1991.

Sweet, William. *Virginia Methodism, a History.* Richmond, VA: Whittet & Shepperson, 1955.

Tebeau, Mark. *Eating Smoke: Fire in Urban America, 1800–1950.* Baltimore: Johns Hopkins University Press, 2003.

Thomas, W. D. "Deceased Pastors." In *The First Century of The First Baptist Church of Richmond Virginia, 1780–1880.* Richmond, VA: Carlton McCarthy, 1880.

Tocqueville, Alexis de. *Democracy in America.* Trans. Henry Reeve. London: Saunders & Otley, 1835.

Troubetzkoy, Ulrich. *Richmond, City of Churches: A Short History of Richmond's Denominations and Faiths, Issued Incident to America's 350th Birthday, 1607–1957.* Richmond, VA: Southern Bank & Trust, 1957.

Tyler, Lyon Gardiner, ed. *Encyclopedia of Virginia Biography.* Volume II. New York: Lewis Historical Publishing Company, 1915.

Tyler-McGraw, Marie. *An African Republic: Black and White Virginians in the Making of Liberia.* Chapel Hill: University of North Carolina Press, 2007.

_____. *The American Colonization Society in Virginia, 1816–1832: A Case Study in Southern Liberalism.* Ph.D. diss., George Washington University, Washington, D.C., 1980.

——. *At the Falls: Richmond, Virginia, and Its People.* Chapel Hill: University of North

Carolina Press, for the Valentine Museum of the Life & History of Richmond, 1994.

Tyler-McGraw, Marie, and Gregg D. Kimball. *In Bondage and Freedom: Antebellum Black Life in Richmond, Virginia*. Chapel Hill: University of North Carolina Press, for the Valentine Museum of the Life & History of Richmond, 1988.

Walthall, C. "Houses of Worship." Pp. 148–52 in *The First Century of The First Baptist Church of Richmond Virginia, 1780–1880*. Richmond, VA: Carlton McCarthy, 1880.

Waukechon, John Frank. *The Forgotten Evangelicals: Virginia Episcopalians, 1790–1876*. Ph.D. diss., University of Texas at Austin, 2000.

Wellford, B. R. "History of the First Presbyterian Church." Pp. 43–61 in *First Presbyterian, Richmond, VA. Proceedings of the Celebration of the Eightieth Anniversary of Its Organization, May 1, 1892*. Richmond, VA: Whittet & Shepperson, General Printers, 1892.

Wermiel, Sara. *The Fireproof Building: Technology and Safety in the Nineteenth-Century American City*. Baltimore: Johns Hopkins Press, 2000.

Wharton, Anne Hollingsworth. *Social Life in the Early Republic*. Philadelphia: J. B. Lippincott, 1903.

Wheelan, Joseph. *Jefferson's Vendetta: The Pursuit of Aaron Burr and the Judiciary*. New York: Carroll & Graf, 2005.

Whipple, A. B. C. *To the Shores of Tripoli: The Birth of the U.S. Navy and Marines*. New York: William Morrow, 1991.

Wilbanks, Korene Greta O. *Robert Mills and the Brockenbrough House, Richmond Virginia, 1817–1822*. Master's thesis, Virginia Commonwealth University, Richmond, VA. 1999.

Wilkes, Joseph A., ed. *Encyclopedia of Architecture, Design, Engineering and Construction*. New York: John Wiley & Sons, 1988.

Williams, Heather Andrea. *Self-taught: African American Education in Slavery and Freedom*. Chapel Hill: University of North Carolina Press, 2005.

Wyatt, Edward A. "Three Petersburg Theatres." *William and Mary College Quarterly Historical Magazine*, 2nd ser., vol. 21, no. 2 (April 1941): 83–110.

Newspapers and Periodicals

Albion, A Journal of News, Politics, and Literature
American Baptist Magazine and Missionary Intelligencer
American Beacon and Commercial Diary
American Messenger
American Standard (Richmond)
The Baltimorean
Christian Monitor

Christian Review

The Continent; an Illustrated Weekly Magazine

The Cynick

Dramatic Mirror, and Literary Companion

Federal Gazette and Philadelphia Evening Post

Federal Republican & Commercial Gazette (Baltimore, MD)

Frank Leslie's Popular Monthly

Gleason's Pictorial Drawing-Room Companion

Hagers-Town Gazette (PA)

Hampshire Federalist (Springfield, MA)

The Independent

Massachusetts Baptist Missionary Magazine

Methodist Magazine

Methodist Quarterly Review

Mirror of Taste and Dramatic Censor

New York Evangelist

New York Observer and Chronicle

Panoplist, and Missionary Magazine

Pennsylvania Herald, and General Advertiser

Petersburg Intelligencer

Portsmouth (N.H.) Federal Observer

Poulson's American Daily Advertiser (Philadelphia, PA)

Religious Remembrancer

Rhode-Island American, and General Advertiser

Richmond Dispatch

Richmond Enquirer

Richmond Literature and History Quarterly

Richmond Virginia Patriot

Richmond Whig

Southern Illustrated News

Southern Literary Messenger

Spirit of the Times

Vermont Baptist Missionary Magazine

Virginia Argus

Virginia Cavalcade

Washington Post

Western Journal of the Medical and Physical Sciences

Zion's Herald

ACKNOWLEDGMENTS

This book has been written over the course of six years, and the assistance and unflagging support of many people made it possible. The text is based on my graduate thesis, and I wish to express my appreciation to Carol Sheriff and the late Rhys Isaac, both of whom offered helpful guidance and criticism in the early stages of my research, and also to my thesis committee at the College of William and Mary: Christopher Grasso, LuAnn Homza, and especially James Whittenburg, for their insight. I was honored to be part of such a special and collegial academic community during my time in Williamsburg.

It meant a great deal to have encouragement in the early stages from Doug Welsh, Clay McLeod Chapman, and Andrew Carroll. Their excitement about this project gave me the confidence to move forward with the manuscript. At Louisiana State University Press, I thank Rand Dotson for patiently walking me through the publication process, from my initial proposal to print, and Neal Novak and the other staff members who lent their time and talents to the making of this book. This is a far better document than it might have been thanks to Brent Tarter's scrupulous attention to detail. Thanks to Jonathan DenHartog for his suggestions and Jo Ann Kiser for her careful editing. I owe a debt of gratitude to Conover Hunt (formerly of the Historic Richmond Foundation); Lara Otis at the University of Maryland Architecture Library; Susan Riggs at the Swem Library archives; Meg Musselwhite, David Holmes, and Scott Nelson (who connected me with Karen Resendes) at William and Mary; James Windsor at Celest Press; Prudence Doherty at the University of Vermont; and Judee Showalter of the Methodist archives at Randolph Macon College. For their help in acquiring images, I thank Katherine Wilkins and Jamison Davis at the Virginia Historical Society, Howell Perkins at the Virginia Museum of Fine Arts, and, at the Library of Virginia, Bill Bynum and especially Dale Neighbors. Bob Oller artfully reimagined the theater based on primary documents. To the Poe Museum in Richmond, the Valentine Richmond Historical Center, the John Marshall Foundation, the Historic Richmond Foundation, and the University of Virginia's Small Special Collections Library: thank you all for your assistance along the way and for being such careful caretakers of the state's amazing archives, records, and stories. Responsibility for any oversights or errors in this volume is, of course, entirely mine. Louise Wood, Skyla Freeman, Susan and Jack Baker, Stephen Baker, Kiersten Anderson, Rebecca Good, Marika Klein, my graduate school colleagues, and friends at St. Christopher's and Church of the Resurrection blessed me greatly with their encouragement, advice, and occasional babysitting. My husband Mark and I spent one of our first dates viewing Chapman's play "Volumes of Smoke" and wandering through historic Richmond. Since then he has unselfishly shared me with this project, and its completion is due in no small part to him and his support.

I dedicate this book to my remarkable parents: Douglas Henne, who planned family vacations around historical sites, and Gaylee Henne, who let me check out as many books from the library as I wanted, in multiples of five. Thank you for welcoming me back for those months when I polished the manuscript and unexpectedly met the man who'd sweep me off my feet, for watching the ensuing grandchildren so I had a few undistracted moments to work, and for kindling a love of American history that has lasted my whole life. This book exists because of the two of you. I hope you'll sit still long enough to read it.

Meredith Henne Baker, 2011

INDEX

CPSIA information can be obtained
at www.ICGtesting.com
Printed in the USA
LVHW090931220723
753082LV00001B/94